Contents

SPIRES OF EXCELSIOR MIX FOXGLOVES and dainty pink columbines flank a stream in this Oregon garden. For more information, see page 302.

Cycles

The year 2002 was one of those once-in-a-century happenings: an occasion for two numerals in bookend arrangement. But though a calendar rarity, bookends are a perfect metaphor for each year in the garden: it starts in the dead of winter, waxes to summer's apex, then wanes to the point from which it began.

This annual cycle is, of course, old stuff to *Sunset Magazine*—long revered as the font of *new stuff* by Western gardeners of all ages and levels of experience. The West, with its varied topography, diverse climates, melting-pot populace, and overall gung-ho spirit, is a gardening world unto itself—an idiosyncratic mix of traditions and futuristic expression, assimilating plants and ideas from cultures worldwide. Capturing this vibrancy and reporting on it has been *Sunset*'s mission for more than a century.

The merry mélange that was 2002 offered up the diverse gardening information that *Sunset* readers have come to expect. Intrepid reporters revealed events and gardens to visit for inspiration, nurseries to explore for temptation, new books to read, and innovative products to check out. But—reflecting the population explosion occurring in Western nurseries—it was plants that crowded toward center stage in the year's cast of topical players. And among plants there was indeed something for all tastes.

In-depth reporting on widely adapted favorites focused on dahlias, daylilies, and tall bearded irises. Also in the "favorites" category, two articles explored the latest offerings among those cool-season mainstays, pansies and chrysanthemums; December highlighted camellias. Penstemons, our flashy-flowered Western natives, received thorough coverage in June, and the previous month featured equally vivid garden workhorses . . . the verbenas.

Each Western climate claims its unique complement of gardening advantages and drawbacks. In the "yes, you *can* do it" category came information on clematis and peonies that thrive in mild-winter climates, cold-tolerant ice plants, drought-tolerant perennials for the high desert, Mediterranean plants to grow in mountain and intermountain zones, and yellow roses that resist their traditional foliage nemesis, blackspot.

For garden planners, varied resources were on offer. February profiled the easiest flowers to grow for cutting, with tips on planting and display as well. April listed long-blooming perennials; October inventoried plants to use for a fall-color garden. In the "special effects" realm were the best plants for hedges, classic "statuesque" perennials, and some highly successful candidates for hanging baskets. And—in what might have been titled "Who needs flowers?"—August enumerated a host of plants that provide vibrant and varied garden color from foliage alone.

Gardeners who favor edible crops were not disappointed. The new 'Julia Child' tomato was unveiled in January—and with a name like that, it must be good! Blueberries (even for mild-winter California), dwarf cherries, and the hardiest fruit trees satisfied those who like their edibles sweet. March outlined the culture, harvest, and uses of the nine essential culinary herbs; April featured vegetable gardens designed for appearance as well as productivity.

Running a close second to articles on plants were features on their deployment in the landscape. January opened with an arresting piece on planning and planting a year-round garden; snow-country gardeners saw the possibilities for winter beauty using ornamental grasses and colored-stem dogwoods. Garden renovations and makeovers were tackled in spring issues; weekend gardeners learned to construct and adorn an "instant" patio for three seasons. November's section demonstrated how to create a garden that can become a habitat for all sorts of wildlife. Other garden design articles included Mediterranean style, water features, and even cactus-dominated arrangements for the desert garden.

Although the *Sunset* gardening year has the earmarks of a world tour, it is simply a survey of all the West has to offer its lucky residents. In the West, those annual "bookends" encompass an entire library.

THIS SUNNY GARDEN ROOM is just the right spot for ordering plants and seeds and planning the year's outdoor garden. You'll find ideas for bringing the pleasures of a garden into your home on pages 18–23.

January

Sunset's favorite
All-Americas for 2002

■ Each year, All-America Selections honors the top new plants based on their performance around the United States. We tried out the 2002 winners in *Sunset's* display garden in Menlo Park, California, and these are our four favorite ornamentals. Look for seedlings in nurseries this spring or order seeds now from the sources listed below.

OUR FOUR FAVORITES

'Chilly Chili' ornamental pepper (below right). For such a compact plant—8 to 12 inches tall and 6 to 10 inches wide—it produces a prodigious amount of fruit: We counted more than 150 pods on a single plant. The 2-inch-long pods turn from yellow to orange to red as they mature. However, despite their fiery color, these peppers have no heat—and not much flavor either.

'Magical Michael' basil. Though it smells delicious (rather spicy, like cloves), this basil's sparse foliage limits its use as a culinary herb. Still, it's worth growing as an ornamental. Quite compact (15 inches tall and 12 inches wide), the plant carries heads of tiny purple-and-white blossoms that fade to bronze as they age. Fresh or dried, the blooms add an aromatic surprise to bouquets.

Rudbeckia hirta **'Cherokee Sunset'** (below left). Handsome double and semidouble flowers 3 to 4½ inches across come in rich autumnal shades, including bronze, gold, mahogany, and orange. The plants top out at about 30 inches, with foot-long flower stems.

'Sparkler Blush' cleome. This hybrid is supposed to grow only 3 feet tall by 3 feet wide, but in our garden it grew taller (up to 5 feet). We admired its multibranched form and fluffy, 5-inch pink blossoms.

SOURCES

Park Seed Company (800/845-3369 or www.parkseed.com) sells these four varieties. Stokes Seeds (800/263-7233 or www.stokeseeds.com) sells all the listed varieties except 'Chilly Chili'. — *Sharon Cohoon*

E. SPENCER TOY (2)

snowscaping in Colorado

■ Ornamental grasses can be an attractive element of the winter landscape. For example, flame grass (*Miscanthus sinensis* 'Purpurascens') glows in the snowbound side yard pictured above in Littleton, Colorado. This long-lived perennial grass forms a showy fountain 3 to 4 feet tall and 2 to 3 feet wide, with silvery flower plumes rising above the foliage in late summer. The leaves turn orange red in fall, then fade to reddish brown. Flame grass is hardy in *Sunset* climate zones 2B–3B (Denver, Salt Lake City). Plants are available from Shady Oaks Nursery (800/504-8006 or www.shadyoaks.com).

In the front yard (left), newly fallen snow flocks the boughs of dwarf spruce and clings to the bare branches of deciduous trees and shrubs. When the snow melts, the evergreen spruce will stand out in verdant contrast to the twiggy tracery of the leafless trees and shrubs. Year-round interest is one reason why many professional designers use evergreens to compose about one-third of any landscape. — *Marcia Tatroe*

DAVID WINGER (2)

tomato named for a culinary legend

■ It took an exceptional tomato to earn the distinction of being named after Julia Child, one of America's most celebrated chefs. But after several years of searching, testing, and tasting, Gary Ibsen, founder of TomatoFest in Carmel, California, found a worthy candidate.

The 'Julia Child' tomato is an heirloom variety that bears large reddish pink fruits averaging 10 to 14 ounces each, with intense, rich tomato flavor, a near-perfect balance of acidity and sweetness, and firm, meaty flesh that contains plenty of juice. The fruits are admirably suited for salads, sandwiches, fresh salsa, and pasta dishes.

A vigorous, indeterminate plant, with potato leaf–like foliage, it needs to be staked, trellised, or grown in tall cages. Fruits are ready to harvest 78 days after transplanting.

Initially, seeds of 'Julia Child' are available only from Ibsen at TomatoFest ($4.50 per packet; 888/989-8171 or www.tomatofest.com). Part of the proceeds will be donated to Child's appointed charity, the American Institute of Wine & Food programs for children's education.

— *Kris Wetherbee*

RICK WETHERBEE

CLIPPING

• **Victory gardens.** Gardening is exactly what America needs in troubling times, says Stanley Tinkle, secretary of the California Organic Gardening Club, in one of the club's recent newsletters. "When a worldview based on optimism and progress must do battle with a worldview based on repression and xenophobia, I have no doubt where a beautiful and productive garden will weigh in," he states. Whether your garden consists of a few pots, a small square, or an entire yard, Tinkle says, it gives you a sense of security, peace, and centering—not to mention bounty to share with neighbors and friends. "If you visit it daily and come away feeling rested and renewed, that's a peaceful victory, and it's a victory garden." — *S.C.*

Perfect 'Peace'

NEW ROSE 'Peace' is good, says Ping Lim, rose hybridizer for Bailey Nurseries, but 'Love & Peace' is even better. The first is, of course, one of the most famous roses in modern history. A beloved hybrid tea smuggled out of France just before Nazi occupation, it was introduced to the world at the war's end and planted by the millions as a symbol of peace in the decade that followed. The latter, hybridized by Lim and Jerry Twomey, is one of its offspring—an All-America Rose Selections winner for 2002.

'Love & Peace' has the high-centered exhibition form of its paternal parent, 'Peace.' (Its maternal parent is an un-

THOMAS J. STORY

named seedling with species rose ancestry.) Its coloring is similar but richer—deeper yellow, edges blushed a darker pink. Foliage is dark green, glossy, and abundant. It even has fragrance—a light, fruity scent. 'Love & Peace' develops the best color in cooler climates. ('Peace' is also notably paler in hot climates.) Near the coast, powdery mildew may be a problem.

If you can't find 'Love & Peace' in your local nursery, order from Edmunds' Roses (888/481-7673 or www.edmundsroses.com). — *S.C.*

ELEVATED POOL
a grade above

■ Opting for a swimming pool aboveground rather than below set the whole tone for this backyard in Palm Springs. There were practical and environmental as well as aesthetic motives for this decision, says the garden's designer, landscape architect Michael Buccino. This part of the property sloped upward away from the house. Leveling the land was one option. However, Buccino suggested building a raised pool that would double as a retaining wall—and minimize earthmoving and native habitat disturbance. This arrangement also gave the owners an elevated deck that felt as if it were perched right on the edge of the desert.

The selected plants—all native, including creosote bush, encelia, ocotillo, and prickly pear cactus—contributed to this close-to-nature feeling. So did planting in casual groupings almost up to the edge of the pool. "We wanted the desert to look like it was rushing in," says Buccino. The carefully considered pool material played a part too; flagstone, tile facing, and the pool's smooth pebble surface are all a neutral desert tan. "When you're up on the deck, you feel almost enveloped by the desert," he adds.

Conversely, the raised pool makes the lawn area near the house feel more like an oasis. "It's like a barrier holding back the desert and makes the grassy area feel more enclosed and intimate." — *S.C.*

STEVEN GUNTHER

'Polka' rose canes trained along a three-wire fence bloom in spring. Outward-growing canes are pruned off to keep plants narrow; remaining canes are attached with ties.

rose wall

■ Climbing roses are remarkably versatile. They can clamber up a trellis, sprawl over an arbor, twine up a pillar, and climb along a wall. Rose expert Robert Cowden also discovered they make wonderful living fences.

While searching for a way to complete the circle of David Austin roses planted at the Gardens at Heather Farm in Walnut Creek, California, Cowden stumbled across a reference in the library there that mentioned three-wire fence systems for training roses.

Nice idea, but there were no instructions. So Cowden developed his own

design, creating a 60-foot-long curving fence of 6-foot-tall, 6-by-6 redwood posts (you could substitute 4-by-4s) spaced 6 feet apart. The posts are capped; bases are set in concrete footings. Three evenly spaced wires attached to turnbuckles support 'Polka' roses.

"The system is very adaptable," says Cowden. "By decreasing or increasing the number of posts, it can be designed to fit any size garden."

Other great roses for a fence: 'Alister Stella Gray' (light yellow), 'Altissimo' (red), 'Climbing Iceberg' (white), 'Lavender Lassie' (lavender pink), 'Westerland' (apricot, sold as shrub rose), 'Zéphirine Drouhin' (pink).

— *Lauren Bonar Swezey*

CLIPPING

• **New white-fleshed peach.** Gardeners in inland valleys, from Redding and Santa Rosa to Fresno and Bakersfield, will find a new freestone peach in nurseries this winter. Developed by Mack Edwards of Springville, California, 'Ambrosia' has supersweet, low-acid white flesh; the plant is resistant to peach leaf curl. Shop for 'Ambrosia' at your nursery or call (877) 318-9198 to find a source near you.

NORM PLATE

the **trellis** as garden art

■ Most gardeners use trellises to support plants. But on the wall of Elisa and Tim Corcoran's garden on Bainbridge Island, Washington, trellises serve as decorative art. When artist Sue Skelly first saw the bare cedar-shake wall, she told the Corcorans, "You really have to let me do something with this." They assented, so Skelly made a number of trellises ranging from 3 to 9 feet long and arrayed them on the wall. The Corcorans like the shapes, which resemble giant sword fern fronds.

Skelly formed the trellises by weaving flexible branches of Western red cedar. To prevent wood-to-wood contact, she used copper tubing to create a small space between the trellises and the shake wall.

Skelly makes both wattle trellises and fences at her studio in Poulsbo, Washington (360/598-5447). — *Jim McCausland*

Bright twigs chase the winter blues

■ Fiery stems of certain dogwoods can brighten the darkest winter days. In addition to displaying richly colored twigs, the plants we describe below have foliage and form that makes them garden-worthy all year. Use any one of them as the focal point of a garden bed or place a plant in front of a white wall or fence to create a striking contrast. Look for these varieties in nurseries now, either as bare-root or container plants.

Cornus alba 'Argenteomarginata' ('Elegantissima') displays magenta branches in winter. In spring, it puts out pale green leaves with silver margins. It grows vigorously into a 10-foot-tall thicket.

C. sanguinea 'Midwinter Fire', one of the bloodtwig dogwoods, has branches in colors that leap like flames from red at the bottom to orange and yellow at the tips. Its leaves turn vivid yellow in fall. The plant grows slowly to 10 by 10 feet.

C. stolonifera 'Isanti' (shown below) is one of the redtwig dogwoods. Its crimson stems in winter are followed by dark green leaves and white flowers in summer. It forms a compact 5- by 5-foot shrub.

With dogwoods, the brightest color appears on the newest branches. To stimulate this new growth, cut one-third of the stems to the ground in early spring. — *Mary-Kate Mackey*

BACK TO BASICS

LINDA HOLT AYRISS

Protect tender plants. Bananas and other tropicals are popular landscape plants. To keep them alive through winter in milder climates (lows in the mid-20s to low 30s), drape burlap or a blanket over plants (support on stakes so covers don't touch leaves). For added protection, set a lighted bulb or string of lights inside. In colder climates, transplant specimens into containers to move indoors. — *Lauren Bonar Swezey*

JANET LOUGHREY

pacific northwest • checklist

PLANTING

☐ **BARE-ROOT STOCK.** Zones 4–7: Shop nurseries this month for bare-root berries, grapes, fruit and shade trees, perennial vegetables (asparagus, horseradish, and rhubarb), and ornamental shrubs and roses. Plant immediately. Zones 1–3: Plant as soon as bare-root stock arrives in nurseries and the soil can be worked.

☐ **HARDY PERENNIALS.** Start seeds of aster, delphinium, hellebore, Shasta daisy, veronica, and viola in a coldframe or greenhouse. About a month before the last spring frost, transplant seedlings into the garden.

☐ **WINTER COLOR.** Zones 4–7: Set out English daisies, pansies, and primroses whenever the soil is dry enough to work.

☐ **WINTER-FLOWERING SHRUBS.** Zones 4–7: Shop nurseries for blooming specimens of coast silk-tassel *(Garrya elliptica)*, cornelian cherry *(Cornus mas)*, ornamental hazelnuts, pussy willows, sasanqua camellia, *Viburnum* x *bodnantense*, wintersweet *(Chimonanthus praecox)*, and a wide array of witch hazels. Buy what you like and plant right away.

MAINTENANCE

☐ **FEED ASPARAGUS AND RHUBARB.** Spread a 1- to 2-inch layer of composted manure over the root zones of established plants of asparagus and rhubarb.

☐ **INSPECT STORED BULBS.** Check summer-blooming bulbs in storage. If any are shriveled, sprinkle water on them to rehydrate them. Throw out any with signs of rot, except dahlia tubers: Cut the bad spots out of those, dust with sulfur, and store separately.

☐ **APPLY DORMANT OIL.** On a mild, dry day, spray leafless fruit trees and roses with horticultural oil to kill overwintering insects.

☐ **CARE FOR HOUSEPLANTS.** First snip off dead or yellow leaves, then rinse dust off plants by setting them under lukewarm shower water. Fertilize only those plants that are flowering or setting fruit now; wait until spring to feed others.

☐ **PROTECT YOUNG TREES FROM SUNSCALD.** Trees with trunks less than 4 inches in diameter are vulnerable to sunscald, a damaging form of sunburn caused when the low winter sun shines on the tender bark. Paint the trunks with white latex or protect them with a commercial tree wrap.

☐ **PRUNE FRUIT TREES.** Zones 4–7: First, cut out dead and diseased branches. Then remove closely parallel or crossing branches. Finally, prune for shape. Zones 1–3: Hold off on pruning until spring.

☐ **PRUNE ROSES.** Zones: 4–7: Cut back hybrid tea roses to a vase shape made from the strongest three to five canes. Prune landscape roses to shape. Zones 1–3: Wait until spring. ◆

WHAT TO DO IN YOUR GARDEN IN JANUARY

PLANTING

☐ **ANTIQUE APPLES.** Zones 7–9, 14–17: Following are a few favorite apple varieties of Carolyn Harrison, owner of Sonoma Antique Apple Nursery; all offer great flavor (use them for cider, cooking, or eating out of hand): 'Ashmead's Kernel' (a russet with sweet, dense flesh), 'Belle de Boskoop' (crisp, tangy), 'Northern Spy' (classic old-fashioned apple taste), 'Sierra Beauty' (sweet-tart, good keeper), and 'Spitzenburg' (spicy, sweet-tart). To order, call (707) 433-6420 or go to www.applenursery.com.

☐ **BARE-ROOT.** Zones 7–9, 14–17: This is the prime month to buy and plant dormant roses, shrubs, fruit and shade trees, and vines. Bare-root plants cost less and adapt more quickly than container plants.

☐ **BERRIES.** Zones 7–9, 14–17: Blackberries, raspberries, and strawberries are all available bare-root this month. For a treat, try 'Olallie' blackberry. The huge 1½-inch-long berries are sweet and succulent, and the plant is well adapted to Northern California. Or plant a row of flavorful 'Sequoia' strawberries.

☐ **ORNAMENTAL VEGETABLES.** Zones 7–9, 14–17: Ornamental vegetables add a colorful new dimension to flower beds. Some cool-season choices include cabbage, kale, red and green lettuces, and Swiss chard. Mix them with calendulas, Iceland poppies, pansies, stock, and violas.

Sunset CLIMATE ZONES
☐ Mountain (1-2)
☐ Valley (7-9)
☐ Inland (14)
☐ Coastal (15-17)

DEBRA LAMBERT

☐ **SUMMER-BLOOMING BULBS.** Now's the time to order special varieties of begonias, dahlias, gladiolus, lilies, and other summer-blooming bulbs by mail. Try Dutch Gardens (800/818-3861 or www.dutchgardens.com) or McClure & Zimmerman (800/883-6998 or www.mzbulb.com).

☐ **VEGETABLE SEEDS.** Zones 7–9, 14–17: Sow seeds of cool-season vegetables for planting out in February. Try rainbow chard (All-America Selections winner 'Bright Lights' is a tasty one from Renee's Garden; www.reneesgarden.com) or lettuce ('Alan Chadwick's Rodan' and 'Bronze Arrow' are two favorites available from Bountiful Gardens; 707/459-6410 or www.bountifulgardens.org).

MAINTENANCE

☐ **FEED PLANTS.** Zones 7–9, 14–17: Apply fertilizer to annuals, vegetables, and cool-season lawns (bluegrass, fescue).

☐ **PRUNE.** Zones 7–9, 14–17: Dormant deciduous plants, such as flowering vines, fruit and shade trees, grapes, and roses should be pruned now. Use pruning shears for small cuts up to ¾ inch in diameter and loppers for cuts ¾ to 1 inch in diameter. A pruning saw is best for branches larger than 1 inch in diameter. Wait to prune spring-flowering plants such as lilacs and Japanese snowball until after they bloom.

☐ **TUNE UP HOUSEPLANTS.** Wash the leaves periodically to help prevent spider mite and other insect infestations. If plants are movable, transport them to the shower and give them a thorough rinse. Remove yellowing or dead leaves. Using sharp pruning shears or scissors, trim brown edges from leaf tips (follow the leaf shape as you cut). Apply fertilizer at half strength. ◆

southern california · checklist

PLANTING

☐ **BARE-ROOT.** Nurseries still have plenty of roses, and stone fruit tree supplies are at their peak. (To find the best varieties for your area, especially if you live in a minimal-chill area, consult the *Sunset Western Garden Book* or the California Rare Fruit Growers website, www. crfg.org.) Other options include cane berries, grape and kiwi vines, and perennial vegetables like artichokes, asparagus, horseradish, and rhubarb.

☐ **SEASONAL COLOR.** There's still time to plant winter annuals, Iceland poppies, and pansies, especially along the coast. And low-desert gardeners (zone 13) can plant petunias. Winter-flowering vines are another way to get color into the garden. Or pot up some winter-blooming succulents such as flowering aloe, echeveria, and kalanchoe.

☐ **SEEDS.** Place orders for warm-season flowers and vegetables. To have seedlings ready to transplant to the garden in early spring, start seeds indoors as soon as they arrive.

☐ **WINTER VEGETABLES.** It's still possible to start cool-season crops from seed, especially lettuces and other greens. Onions, peas, and radishes are other possibilities. You can also set out broccoli, brussels sprouts, and cabbage seedlings.

Sunset
CLIMATE ZONES

1-3 7-9 11 13 14-24

DEBRA LAMBERT

MAINTENANCE

☐ **CARE FOR CAMELLIAS.** If camellia petal blight is a problem (petals turn brown and rot in the center of the flower), keep ground beneath the plants clean by removing fallen flowers and leaves promptly. Pick off and discard infected flowers. If there are pine trees in your neighborhood, collect fallen needles to use as mulch under your camellias; they add needed acidity to the soil when they break down.

☐ **PRUNE DECIDUOUS FRUIT TREES.** To encourage the new growth that will bear the next crop, all stone fruit trees need some pruning. But the amount of pruning needed differs for each type. Consult a good reference book on pruning before proceeding or check out the California Rare Fruit Growers website, www.crfg.org.

☐ **PRUNE ROSES.** The traditional way to prune roses is to take out dead, damaged, or crossing branches, and then prune back all the remaining canes by one-third to one-half, making cuts just above an outward-facing bud. A much faster method is to use hedge clippers to cut back all canes the same amount, then go back and prune dead and diseased branches. This works best with smaller-caned roses like floribundas, miniatures, and polyanthas.

☐ **TUNE UP YOUR TOOLS.** Sharpen the blades on shovels and hoes, then rub down wood handles with boiled linseed oil. Replace or hone dull blades on pruning shears.

PEST AND WEED CONTROL

☐ **APPLY DORMANT SPRAY.** After pruning, spray roses with horticultural oil to smother overwintering insects like mites and scale.

☐ **MANAGE WEEDS.** Mulch flower and vegetable beds to keep down weeds encouraged by winter rains. Check areas seeded with annuals, vegetables, or wildflowers; as plants come up, so will weeds. Hand-pull or hoe them carefully. ◆

mountain · checklist

PLANNING AND PLANTING

☐ **ORDER VEGETABLE SEEDS.** These regional firms offer seeds of vegetables that have proved themselves in the intermountain West. Call for catalogs or check out the websites: D.V. Burrell Seed Growers Co. (719/254-3318 or www.watermelon.com/burrell/), Irish Eyes & Garden City Seeds (877/733-3001 or www.irish-eyes.com), Plants of the Southwest (800/788-7333 or www.plantsofthesouthwest.com), Rocky Mountain Seed Co. (303/623-6223), and Seeds Trust/High Altitude Gardens (208/788-4363 or www.seedsave.org).

☐ **PLANT AN INDOOR HERB GARDEN.** A sunny kitchen window is the perfect spot to grow culinary herbs in winter. Start basil and parsley from seed. Plant pots of chives, oregano, rosemary, sage, and other favorites purchased from a garden center in an attractive container.

☐ **SOW HARDY PERENNIALS.** Seeds of most hardy perennials, including butterfly weed, columbine, liatris, and penstemon, require a period of chilling to germinate. Start seeds now in soil-filled pots and place them outdoors out of direct sun. Keep the soil moist, and whenever snow is available, pile it on the pots. After six weeks of chilling, bring pots into a greenhouse or set them on a sunny windowsill to sprout. When seedlings have two sets of true leaves, transplant them into individual containers. Continue growing them indoors until spring, then set them out in the garden.

Sunset
CLIMATE ZONES

☐ 1-3   ☐ 10-11

DEBRA LAMBERT

☐ **WINTER INTEREST.** Even without leaves, many deciduous shrubs and trees display brightly colored fruits or bark that can enhance the winter landscape. For red or orange berries or fruits, consider cotoneaster, crabapple, hawthorn, pyracantha, rose, silver buffaloberry, and sumac. For colored bark or twigs, try beauty bush, corkscrew willow, mountain mahogany, Mormon tea, and redtwig and yellowtwig dogwood.

MAINTENANCE

☐ **MULCH FLOWER BEDS.** Overlap old Christmas tree boughs and evergreen prunings on top of beds to protect tender and recently planted perennials and bulbs. Hay, straw, and pine needles also work.

☐ **PRUNE TREES, SHRUBS.** Winter is the ideal time to prune—you can easily see the branch structure of leafless deciduous trees and shrubs. Cut out dead, diseased, crossing, and closely parallel branches. Don't prune lilacs and other early-spring bloomers because you could be cutting off this year's flowers.

☐ **WATCH FOR FROST-HEAVED PLANTS.** When soil freezes and thaws in recurrent cycles, it can heave fall-planted perennials and small shrubs out of the ground. If this happens, add soil around the base of the plant to cover any exposed roots.

☐ **WATER.** Dry winter conditions can seriously dehydrate plants. When snow or rain has not fallen for several weeks and the ground is dry 3 to 4 inches beneath the surface (use a trowel to check), set out a sprinkler to soak all plantings thoroughly. Irrigate when the temperature is above freezing. Water at midday when the surface of the soil is not frozen solid. — *M.T.* ◆

WHAT TO DO IN YOUR GARDEN IN JANUARY

PLANTING AND PLANNING

☐ **ORDER PLANTS, SEEDS.** These mail-order firms offer ornamental plants and vegetables that have proved themselves in the Southwest. ***Ornamentals:*** High Country Gardens (800/925-9387 or www. highcountrygardens.com), Plants of the Southwest (800/788-7333 or www.plantsofthesouthwest.com), and Wild Seed (602/276-3536). ***Vegetables:*** Native Seeds/SEARCH (520/622-5561 or www.nativeseeds. org), Roswell Seed Company (505/622-7701), and Seeds of Change (888/762-7333 or www. seedsofchange.com).

☐ **PLANT BARE-ROOT FRUIT TREES.** Zones 12–13 (Tucson, Phoenix): Choose low-chill varieties of apples ('Anna' or 'Dorsett Golden'), apricots ('Gold Kist' or 'Katy'), peaches ('Babcock' or 'Flordaprince'), and plums ('Santa Rosa').

☐ **PLANT BARE-ROOT ROSES.** Zones 11 (Las Vegas) and 12–13: Dig a planting hole about 2 feet wide and 1 foot deep. Mix 1 cubic foot of compost into the backfill soil. Form a 10-inch-tall cone of soil in the middle of the hole and spread the rose's roots over the cone. Replace the backfill soil, firming it gently. Water the soil thoroughly and rock the rose back and forth to settle it in. When you're done, the graft or bud union, if the rose has one, should be well above the soil surface.

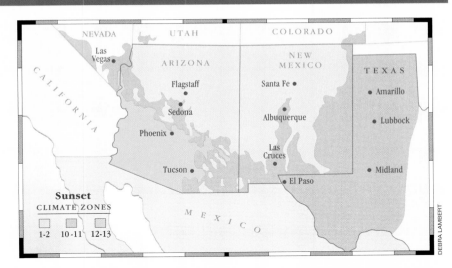

☐ **SOW COOL-SEASON COLOR.** Zones 12–13: Plant seeds of larkspurs, nasturtiums, and stock. Set out transplants of bachelor's buttons, calendulas, pansies, petunias, snapdragons, sweet alyssum, and wallflowers.

☐ **START VEGETABLES.** Zone 10 (Albuquerque): Set out bare-root crowns of asparagus. Begin seeds of peppers and tomatoes indoors in containers; seedlings will be ready to transplant outside in about eight weeks. Zones 11–13: Set out transplants of artichoke and asparagus root crowns. Sow seeds of beets, bok choy, carrots, lettuces, radishes, spinach, and Swiss chard directly in the ground.

MAINTENANCE

☐ **FERTILIZE BEARDED IRIS.** Zones 11–13: Late in the month, spread fertilizer around plants and scratch it into the soil; then water thoroughly.

☐ **PRUNE HYBRID TEA ROSES.** Zones 12–13: Remove all dead canes and cut remaining canes back by a third.

☐ **WATER.** Zone 10: Give evergreens a deep soaking once a month if weather remains dry. Zones 11–13: If there has been no rain, irrigate trees and shrubs deeply every three weeks; water succulents, including cactus, every four to five weeks. — *Mary Irish* ◆

I go to nature to be soothed and healed, and
to have my senses put in order.

— John Burroughs

rooms in bloom

A full-fledged greenhouse room or just a few pots
on a windowsill can bring the outdoors in

By Kathleen N. Brenzel

Convert a deck or porch

A deck, veranda, or porch off the back of the house makes a perfect garden room if you give it walls of greenery and a vine-covered ceiling.

To add a sense of enclosure to the 12- by 40-foot deck pictured at left, owners Claudia Schmutzler and Jeanie Werner of Huntington Beach, California, created a "floating wall" along one side: They hung framed windows from galvanized steel chains anchored to overhead beams with eye bolts. 'Concord' grape vines and morning glory ramble over the trellis roof, shading the deck in summer, dangling clusters of ripe fruits in August, then—when leafless in winter—allowing sunlight through.

Cozy furnishings add to the roomlike feel. Indoor lamps add softly glowing light in the evening.

Nineteenth-century naturalist Burroughs's secret for finding tranquility in a stressful world is familiar to anyone who loves gardens—places where flowers bloom, water trickles softly in a fountain, and the scent of jasmine or roses wafts in the air. • But how can you enjoy a garden in this month of cold weather, rain, or snow? Bring it indoors. You can add a sunroom or conservatory to your house to create a warm, sunny place for plants and people, or turn a family room or a sunny nook off the kitchen into a garden room with a few carefully chosen plants, furnishings, and accessories. A bay window or porch can be converted into a bit of Eden, too, with a scattering of bright floral-patterned pillows and a few blooming plants or a tabletop fountain and a collection of birdhouses. • Even in coastal Southern California, where mild winters make it possible to garden outdoors nearly year-round, it's nice to have a room where orchids and other frost-tender plants are always happy and where you can relax and putter on rainy days. • Here and on the following pages, we look at ways to bring the pleasures of a garden indoors.

Quick Idea #1

Wheatgrass, embellished with Johnny-jump-up blooms in water-filled vials, makes a simple, pretty arrangement for a table. You can easily start your own grass from seed; many markets also sell it in 4-inch pots.

Transform an existing room

Artist Maria del Carmen Calvo found the perfect place for her orchids in a space that housed a whirlpool bath. Before the remodel, the 9- by 11-foot "room" off her bedroom was surrounded by four existing walls and a door, but no ceiling.

To create the very romantic room pictured above, Calvo took out the whirlpool bath, added a ceiling with plenty of skylights, and removed the windows between the bedroom and the new orchid room to open up the two rooms to each other. She brought in some favorite furnishings, including a comfortable couch covered with snowy white fabric. A foot-wide bench under the windows holds a collection of orchids.

What garden rooms need

The best environments for keeping plants happy indoors—and avoiding damage to a home's interior—have the following elements.

■ Light. To thrive, most indoor plants need at least some natural light. Blooming plants such as orchids and kalanchoe need more light than palms. Some indoor gardeners add windows to brighten a room; an alternative is a prefab greenhouse window over the kitchen sink.

■ Good orientation to the sun. South-facing windows provide the best light for most plants. East-facing windows make the most of morning light, provided that it's not shaded by trees. A western exposure gives enough light for most plants, but hot afternoon sun can burn foliage. North-facing windows are good only for plants that take low light.

■ Screening. To protect plants from intense sunlight, especially from west-facing windows, put up bamboo blinds or translucent curtains.

■ Comfortable temperatures. Like people, most houseplants thrive with average indoor temperatures—about 68° to 72° during the day and no lower than 55° at night. Some plants—notably dwarf citrus, cyclamen, cymbidium, and miniature roses—like it cooler, as low as 60° during the day and 50° to 55° at night. Display all plants out of drafts and away from fireplaces and heater vents.

■ Humidity. Dry heat, common in most houses during the winter, is fine for cactus and succulents, but it's tough on tropicals such as African violets,

bromeliads, and orchids. To raise humidity levels around these plants, fill wide saucers with pebbles or decorative glass, add water, then set the pots atop the pebbles. Mist plants every other day with a fine spray of tepid water.

■ Waterproof flooring or other moisture protectors. Brick, tile, and linoleum best withstand water spills and moisture. Hardwood flooring is fine for garden rooms as long as pots and saucers (which can transfer moisture to the wood) do not contact the floor directly. Put cork pads underneath saucers or slip terra-cotta or iron feet beneath pots and saucers to lift them off the floor.

Add a sunroom or conservatory

The conservatory pictured above, custom-built in England by Amdega Conservatories (800/449-7348), opens to the back of John and Christine Davis's Tudor-style brick house in the heart of Silicon Valley. "It is the most used room in the house," says Christine. "We eat there, play there, entertain there. Sit, sip wine, and enjoy the backyard from there. My son even does his homework there."

Interior designer Marie Peterson of Chelsea Court Designs in Los Gatos, California, suggested the conservatory instead of a standard room addition. She worked with architect Monty Lucas and contractor Larry Smith to pull together the look and install the structure.

Quick Idea #2

This indoor planting in a glazed green pot (15 inches in diameter and 13 inches tall) celebrates the shades and textures of green. In the center is a strappy-leafed dracaena, with leaves striped chartreuse and white, planted from an 8-inch nursery pot. 'Cascade' ivy, from a 6-inch pot, tumbles out around it; two small yellow-spotted crotons from 4-inch nursery pots are tucked in near the front. The container sits on a wrought-iron plant stand.

Quick Idea #3

A roll-around window box, painted off-white and fitted with casters for easy moving, contains potted kalanchoe, bromeliad, and croton. Plastic boxes inside contain drips. Directions for making a window box like the one pictured above, designed by Peter O. Whiteley, appear on www.sunset.com/garden/planter.html. Dining chair from the Far Company, San Francisco (415/553-7774).

One room, two looks

A visit to antiques warehouses, import stores, home and garden centers, and nurseries can inspire your garden room's decor. Here, we show two different looks—one rustic country and the other softly romantic—for the same space. Gather furnishings and collectibles whose colors and styles blend together well.

Rustic workroom

Weathered country furnishings fill this garden room—just the right spot for ordering plants and seeds and planning the year's outdoor garden. An antique wood cabinet holds garden books and colorful glazed pottery. Other elements that add to the room's garden appeal include:

■ Potted plants. Maidenhair ferns, crotons, and ivy spilling from an antique metal wall fountain thrive in the room's soft natural light. For details about the grass pot behind the table and the large mixed planting near the window, see pages 19 and 21, respectively.

■ Colorful seat cushion. The cushion cover pictured is made from two bright sunflower-motif napkins stitched together.

■ Garden art. Citrus box labels in green frames brighten the wall behind the birch-bark birdhouse.

SOURCES: Furnishings from J Hill Country, San Francisco (415/522-1190); sunflower napkins from Les Alpilles de Provence, Balboa Island, CA (949/673-0719 or www. lesalpilles-provence.com).

Tips from pros

"I'd put a piece of wrought iron against a wall to create the illusion of a Victorian fence and a fabulous green antique water pump in the corner with a plant on top."

— John Fornachon
J Hill Country (rustic European antiques), San Francisco

"I'd use fabrics featuring big cabbage roses or bold stripes. I'd bring in framed botanical prints or pressed flowers—10 or so in beautiful frames—and perhaps a floral-print screen. I'd stack hatboxes covered in floral-print paper in a corner. And, on a table, I'd fill a weathered basket or wooden trough with garden-fresh vegetables."

— Ann Bertelsen
Senior Editor, Style, *Sunset*

"Paint a couple of wooden Adirondack chairs a pretty color, like French blue, bring them indoors, then add cushions covered with striped or floral fabric. Put a tiny cafe table between them. Don't forget some garden statuary, a lantern or wrought-iron candleholders, and a small fountain for the sound of water. The more romance you can bring indoors, the better."

— Sharron Saffert
On the Veranda (garden accessories and furnishings), Phoenix

"My garden room has many old leaded-glass windows that open onto the garden and an antique dictionary stand that holds a mammoth plant encyclopedia. The cork wall covering allows me to tack up my tear-outs from magazines. I put cutting starts on a 1950s brass-and-glass tea cart so I can move them into just the perfect spot for light. A huge glass vase is filled with dried blossoms from my garden. Dried hydrangeas hang everywhere."

— Gail Chapman
A Garden of Distinction (garden accessories and furnishings), Seattle

Romantic retreat

This cozy corner has a light, breezy style that brings to mind lazy days on a rose-covered veranda. Natural wicker furnishings and soft pastel colors set the tone. A bird cage holds a small potted fern. Other easy-to-find accessories pictured above:

■ A steel trellis. Spray-painted blue and mounted to the wall, it recalls the shape of a garden gate.

■ Floral-patterned covers. To decorate the chair cushions, the covers were cut and hemmed from standard pillowcases.

■ Clustered pots. They hold pink cyclamen, maidenhair fern, pink polka-dot plant, and fragrant pink stock. A French flower bucket—painted the same blue as the pots and embellished with an antique rose label—contains a potted miniature rose.

SOURCES: "Torbay" armchair from Pier 1 Imports (800/447-4371); wall trellis from Kinsman Company (800/733-4146); "Petticoat Floral" pillowcases from Ralph Lauren Home; bird cage from Cost Plus World Market (800/267- 8758). ◆

24

Seed pioneers

It's a brave new world of flower and vegetable varieties, thanks to these seed specialists

By Lauren Bonar Swezey and Jim McCausland

■ Twenty years ago, most gardeners didn't know the difference between an 'Anaheim' and a habanero pepper. An haricot vert? To the uninformed, it sounded more like a foreign hairstyle than a green bean. And mesclun? These colorful mixes of baby lettuces and greens are standard fare now in grocery stores, home gardens, and restaurants.

Thanks to a group of individuals who are passionate about finding great new varieties and making them available, such delicacies are commonly available. Five Western pioneers—Mary Ballon of West Coast Seeds, Tom and Julie Johns of Territorial Seed Company, Rose Marie Nichols McGee of Nichols Garden Nursery, Renee Shepherd of

CLOCKWISE FROM TOP LEFT: Cut-and-come-again zinnia at Renee's Garden and Renee Shepherd; Howard-Yana Shapiro and seed-drying tables at Seeds of Change; Mary Ballon in a field of corn at West Coast Seeds and 'Siletz' tomatoes; tomato trials at Territorial Seed Company, 'Charmant' cabbage, and owners Tom and Julie Johns.

25

Renee's Garden, and Howard-Yana Shapiro of Seeds of Change—have brought an international flavor to our kitchen gardens.

Looking for alpine strawberry seeds? You can order French 'Mignonette' from Renee's Garden. Tasty greens? Nichols Garden Nursery sells seeds of Asian, French, Italian, and American salad and cooking greens. Need to spice up your cooking? You'll find seeds of 'Bolivian Rainbow' and Mexican 'Hidalgo' chilies at Seeds of Change.

"This is an ecumenical business," explains Shepherd. "We bring in seeds from all over the world, and every seed has a story."

Each of the five seed companies described here offers a wide selection of flower, herb, and vegetable seeds, many of which are unique. Each company has grown and evaluated the seeds in its own trial gardens here in the West.

Pantry Trio globe onions from Renee's Garden

THOMAS J. STORY

RENEE'S GARDEN
Felton, California

Renee Shepherd never intended to own a seed packet business. She was teaching in the Environmental Studies Department at the University of California at Santa Cruz when a manager of a Dutch seed company (the husband of a graduate student) challenged her to try growing gourmet vegetable varieties at her home garden in Felton.

Shepherd quickly realized the possibilities of bringing these and many other varieties into American gardens. She traveled through Europe and contacted seed growers around the world to learn the seed trade. "At the time, gardeners here didn't have access to the richness and diversity that was available elsewhere in the world," says Shepherd. "I wanted to share what I found."

PROUDEST ACHIEVEMENT

Her packets contain an amazing amount of information about the specific seeds contained inside thanks, in part, to an added flap on the back.

CURRENT FOCUS

"Getting gardeners to try perennials from seed"—an inexpensive way to expand your perennial collection. Also fragrant sweet peas, lettuce mixes, and vegetable trios, which are three different kinds packaged together (the seeds are stained so you know what you're planting).

GROWER'S FAVORITES

Vegetables and herbs: 'Blush Batavians' French crisp lettuce; 'Cinderella's Carriage' pumpkin; Garden Candy orange, red, and yellow cherry tomatoes; 'Profuma di Genova' basil; and Rainbow Sherbet orange, red, and yellow icebox watermelons. **Flowers:** 'Angel Wings' miniature rose, 'April in Paris' sweet pea, 'Belle Blanche' datura, 'Persian Carpet' zinnias, and 'Stained Glass' salpiglossis. *Seeds are available at nurseries. (888) 880-7228 or www.reneesgarden.com.*

SEEDS OF CHANGE
Santa Fe, New Mexico

Howard-Yana Shapiro has lived two lives: cultural anthropologist in Mesoamerica, South America, and Asia, and, for the past 10 years, one of the driving forces behind Seeds of Change. His company's catalog sells open-pollinated seeds (whose offspring set seeds that gardeners can save and replant), organically grown seeds (some of which are heirloom varieties), as well as others developed by the company—'Martian Giant' tomato, for instance. "Our goal is to push for organic, sustainable agricultural systems and biodiversity," says Shapiro.

As vice president of agriculture, Shapiro oversees the seed business and spends much of his time seeking new varieties, while researching sustainable chocolate production for the company's owner, M&M/Mars. He works and lives at his farm just north of Santa Fe.

PROUDEST ACHIEVEMENT

"We hold the largest collection of organic seed in the world," says Shapiro. About 600 varieties fill this catalog, and hundreds more are offered online.

CURRENT FOCUS

New and unusual vegetables like red corn and yacon (an edible tuber from Bolivia), flowers (yellow cosmos), and herbs (lime basil).

GROWER'S FAVORITES

Vegetables and herbs: All legumes ("they're the soldiers of agriculture that fix nitrogen and provide mulch," says Shapiro), 'Dinosaur Gourd', potatoes (they sell 11 kinds), 'Purple Wave' mustard greens, 'Rainbow Inca' corn, and slow-bolt cilantro. **Flowers:** 'Bright Lights' cosmos, 'Cempoalxochitl' and 'Pesche's Gold' marigold, 'Double Gold' gloriosa daisy, and 'Endurance' sunflower *(Helianthus argophyllus x annuus). (888) 762-7333 or www. seedsofchange.com.*

NICHOLS GARDEN NURSERY
Albany, Oregon

Rose Marie Nichols McGee began working at this nursery, which she runs with her husband, Keane, with her founder-parents in 1978. "I like my father's statement of purpose," says Rose Marie, "which is to bring people closer to nature through gardening. That still fits us."

Nichols was the first nursery to introduce elephant garlic. Since taking over, Rose Marie and Keane have let their own passions filter into the catalog: supplies for making wine and beer, for example, and seeds for lots of flowers.

Rose Marie's

CURRENT FOCUS

The heart of the business is vegetable seeds, plus easy-to-grow flowers and herbs, especially new varieties of lavender and rosemary.

GROWER'S FAVORITES

'Golden Honey Bunch' tomatoes, 'Ring of Fire' sunflower, 'Indian Summer' rudbeckia. Also, cardoon. What do you do with it? "Scrub the bloom off the stems (that's the bitter part), slice into 3-inch lengths, and boil it for 20 minutes in water. Then layer it two deep in a baking dish, top with parmesan, and bake at 350° until the cheese is brown." *(800) 422-3985 or www.nicholsgardennursery.com.*

TOP LEFT: Keane and Rose Marie Nichols McGee with cardoon. ABOVE: Lettuce and Swiss chard bed (with bean towers) at Nichols Garden Nursery.

WEST COAST SEEDS
Vancouver, British Columbia

Raised in a farm family that grew nearly all the food it consumed, Mary Ballon opened Territorial Seeds's Canadian franchise in 1983, then her own company in 1998. "My goal is to supply the best seed for organic growers in our region," Mary told us, referring to coastal British Columbia, Washington, and Oregon (shipping seed across the Canadian border isn't a problem). She's found that the best-scoring varieties grown on her farm, which you're welcome to visit, tend to be hybrids.

Mary's

CURRENT FOCUS

More than half of her 600 varieties are vegetables (including Asian vegetables), a third are flowers—especially those that attract beneficial insects—and the rest are culinary herbs.

GROWER'S FAVORITES

'Sweet Tooth' corn, a supersweet bicolor that starts in cooler soil, produces big cobs. Also 'Vancouver' brussels sprouts, sweet basil, 'Sonata' cosmos, and Old Spice mix sweet peas. *(604) 952-8820 or www.westcoastseeds.com.*

TERRITORIAL SEED COMPANY, Cottage Grove, Oregon

Committed to the notion that Pacific Northwest gardeners should be able to grow Territorial's vegetables every day of the year, Tom and Julie Johns offer both summer and winter catalogs. Each contains a mix of hybrid and open-pollinated varieties, all tested at the farm.

The Johns favor open-pollinated seeds. "That way, people can select seed for their own climate," Tom says. "Saving seed is getting to be a lost art." ◆

Tom and Julie's

PROUDEST ACHIEVEMENT

To keep open-pollinated varieties from disappearing, Territorial grows many of its own. "We have 12 acres of certified organic tomatoes grown for seed," says Tom, "plus lots of cucumbers and squash. We even do our own seed cleaning."

CURRENT FOCUS

Mostly vegetables (including lots of garlic), plus flowers and culinary herbs.

GROWERS' FAVORITES

Heirlooms like the 1885 European lettuce, Cracoviensis, a large butterhead with red-and-green leaves. Also 'Delicata' squash, 'Erfurter Zwerg' aster, and 'Sundance Kid' sunflower. *(541) 942-9547, (541) 942-9881 (fax), or www.territorialseed.com.*

LEFT: Spring show pairs pink and red tulips with dogwood. CENTER: Rudbeckia is a summer star with ornamental grasses. RIGHT: Million Bells pair with red coleus.

Head-start gardening

Having a colorful garden in all seasons takes planning.
Now is the time to start

By Jim McCausland and Sharon Cohoon

In January, color catalogs flood your mailbox, their glossy photographs of frothy pink-flowering trees, plump lilac and peony blooms, and dewy roses tempting you to buy, buy, buy. But hold on. Instead of ordering one of this or that—whatever captures your fancy—add some method to the madness. By determining which plants bloom at the same time and which ones complement the colors on the trees, shrubs, and bulbs already growing in your garden, you can combine them in striking vignettes.

To get you started, the seasonal charts on pages 29–34 list some of the West's most stellar color makers, along with their flower colors, bloom times, and a few of our favorite ways to use them. Try the combinations as listed or let them serve as guidelines for pairing plants of your own choice.

Before you buy, spend some time at the nursery mixing and matching flower and foliage colors. Begin with a favorite plant—one that you want to anchor the garden's palette. Then use a cart to move it next to other kinds to find the best pairings. (Make sure companion plants have the same water and sunlight requirements.)

Don't forget to factor white and blue into your planting scheme; both do a great job of cooling off and separating drifts of hot-colored plants, as do gray-foliaged plants such as santolina, artemisia, and dusty miller.

Note: The time when plants will actually bloom depends upon the weather, how early or late you plant them, and where you live. Plants near the coast generally bloom earlier in the spring and, in most cases, for a longer time than those in inland climates. ◆

Winter and spring planting in California

January is the prime month to put in plants sold bare-root (including roses and deciduous trees such as flowering cherries); along the coast, you can set out winter-flowering annuals and perennials as well. If soil isn't too soggy, natives and plants from Mediterranean climates (lavender and pride of Madeira, for instance) can go into the ground too.

In February, start shopping for summer-blooming bulbs, such as canna, tuberous begonia, and gladiolus, to tuck into beds between established landscape plants.

In March, nurseries will be well stocked with spring-flowering trees, shrubs, annuals, and perennials. By then temperatures warm up enough to let you plant nearly anything.

As early as April, start shopping for summer perennials to fill in gaps. In May, weather is mild enough to begin planting tropicals (hibiscus, mandevilla).

When you choose your color scheme, keep in mind any trees or shrubs in your garden that might bloom at the same time as the plants you're putting in. Some spring bloomers that make beautiful backdrops include flowering cherries (pinks, white), Western dogwoods (pinks, white), roses (rainbow hues), wisteria (lavender blue, white), and crape myrtles (reds, pinks, purples).

Plant	Bloom time	Colors	Companions, comments
Primula x *polyantha* English primrose	Jan–Mar	yellow, white, blue, purple	Great understory for azaleas and rhododendrons and overstory for spring bulbs.
Chrysanthemum multicaule	Jan–Apr, Oct–Dec	yellow	Handsome with white daffodils that have yellow or orange centers.
Matthiola incana Stock	Jan–May, Oct–Dec	white, pink, red, purple, blue, yellow	In winter, use purple stock with flowering kale and blue pansies.
Gazania Kiss series	Jan–Dec	yellow, bronze, orange, rose, white	Try it in a big pot with *Carex buchananii* and *Artemisia* 'Powis Castle'.
Felicia amelloides Blue marguerite	Mar–Jun, Sep–Nov	blue	At their best in front of perennial borders. Try with pink roses and gray dusty miller.
Limonium perezii Statice	Mar–Sep	purple and white	Goes well with 'Profusion Orange' zinnia, *Nemesia caerulea,* and purple heliotrope.
Scabiosa columbaria 'Butterfly Blue'	Mar–Oct	blue	Try with lavenders, catmint, and white 'Iceberg' roses. A very easy mixer.
Diascia 'Raspberry Parfait' Twinspur	Apr–May, Oct	pink, red, lavender, salmon	Combine with *Nemesia caerulea* 'Blue Bird' and orange and pink *Schizanthus*.
Nepeta x *faassenii* Catmint	Apr–Jun, Sep–Nov	blue	Excellent around other drought-tolerant perennials such as salvia, penstemon, and gaura.
Geum chiloense	Apr–Jul	orange and red	Pair with red and orange zinnias and black-eyed Susans. Also handsome with golden feverfew.
Begonia	Apr–Oct	pink, red, white, yellow	Mass bright orange tuberous begonias in shady garden beds with orange and hot pink impatiens.
Calibrachoa Million Bells	Apr–Oct	full range	Great in hanging baskets and pots. Pair hot pink–flowered kinds with *Salvia chiapensis*.
Impatiens walleriana	Apr–Oct	red, pink, white	The white ones light up shady areas; put lamium in front of them.
Salvia coccinea Tropical sage	Apr–Nov	red	Versatile bedding plant or border filler. Especially pretty in front of blue-flowered cape plumbago.
Salvia leucantha Mexican bush sage	Apr–Nov	purple	Plant in front of a *Solanum rantonnetii* standard, with penstemon 'Midnight' and red crocosmia.
Delphinium elatum	May–Jul, Sep–Oct	blue, white, lavender, pink	Plant with *Lavatera* 'Barnsley' and front with 'Flower Carpet' roses or yellow yarrow.
Convolvulus cneorum Bush morning glory	May–Sep	blue	Great ground cover for dry areas. Use with phlomis, salvia, and santolina.
Coreopsis verticillata	May–Sep	yellow	Mainstay of the summer perennial border. Pretty with variegated sage (*Salvia officinalis* 'Icterina').
Lavandula stoechas Spanish lavender	May–Oct	blue	Try *L.s.* 'Otto Quast' with *Penstemon* 'Midnight', *Phormium tenax* 'Atropurpureum Compactum'.
Lavatera thuringiaca 'Barnsley'	May–Oct	pink	Use in front of smoke trees or purple-leafed plums with pink roses and catmint.
Penstemon x *gloxinioides* 'Apple Blossom'	May–Oct	pink and white	Fine with salvias, lavenders, gaura, and other drought-tolerant perennials.
Rudbeckia hirta Black-eyed Susan	Jun–Sep	yellow, orange, rust	Plant with blanket flower, 'Coronation Gold' yarrow, and *Salvia farinacea.*
Solanum jasminoides Potato vine	Jun–Sep	white	Train on a trellis behind feverfew, white roses, and lime-colored nicotiana.
Dahlia	Jul–Oct	full range	Black-leafed plants with red blooms go well with dark canna or New Zealand flax leaves.

Plant	Bloom time	Colors	Companions, comments
Viola x *wittrockiana* Pansy	Jan–Dec	all colors, blotched and solid	Can bloom any day of the year. Border with gray-leafed perennials.
Helleborus argutifolius Corsican hellebore	Feb–Apr	chartreuse	Good naturalized under groves of deciduous trees such as tall Japanese maples.
Primula x *polyantha* English primrose	Feb–Apr	yellow, white, blue, purple	Great understory for rhododendrons and overstory for spring bulbs.
Anemone nemorosa 'Allenii' Blue wood anemone	Mar–Apr	blue	Plant as a creeping ground cover beneath and between tall rhododendrons and camellias.
Hemerocallis Hybrid daylilies	Apr–Oct	orange, yellow, red	Grassy leaves contrast well with broad-leafed evergreen shrubs.
Aubrieta deltoidea	May	lilac, purple, red	Great spreading plant for rock gardens and stone walls or between flagstones.
Papaver orientale Oriental poppy	May	red, white, pink	Interplant with blue and white peach-leafed campanula or with baby's breath or cosmos.
Astilbe x *arendsii*	May–Aug	red, white, pink, lavender	Plant in front of boxwood or use it to line a shaded woodland path.
Fuchsia triphylla 'Gartenmeister Bonstedt'	May–Oct	orange	Breathtaking when planted against a burgundy or bronze-leafed form of New Zealand flax.
Impatiens walleriana	May–Oct	red, pink, white	The white ones light up shady areas; put lamium in front of them.
Nepeta x *faassenii* Catmint	May–Oct	blue	Use it as a low border around rose beds. No plant fills in faster and few bloom longer.
Aurinia saxatilis Basket-of-gold	Jun–Jul	yellow	Use it as a foreground plant in perennial borders with 'Icterina' salvia and yellow 'Sunsprite' roses.
Coreopsis verticillata	Jun–Sep	yellow	Mainstay of the summer perennial border.
Begonia	Jun–Oct	pink, red, white, yellow	Surround bright orange tuberous begonias with orange and hot pink impatiens.
Delphinium elatum	Jun–Oct	blue, white, lavender, pink	Plant in front of *Lavatera* 'Barnsley'; edge with 'Flower Carpet' roses or yellow yarrow.
Fuchsia Angel's Earrings series	Jun–Oct	red	Put this knee-high shrub cover under Japanese maples; surround with white Accent impatiens.
Lavatera thuringiaca 'Barnsley'	Jun–Oct	pink	Use in front of smoke trees or purple-leafed plums or behind blue delphiniums.
Dahlia	Jul–Oct	all colors	Black-leafed plants with red blooms go well with dark canna or New Zealand flax leaves.
Helenium hybrids Sneezeweed	Jul–Oct	yellow, orange, rust, red	Try coppery red 'Moerheim Beauty' against smoke trees.
Rudbeckia hirta Black-eyed Susan	Jul–Oct	yellow, orange, rust	Plant with blanket flower, 'Coronation Gold' yarrow, and *Salvia farinacea* or with grasses.
Crocosmia 'Lucifer'	Aug	red	Plant in front of maroon barberry or behind *Heuchera* 'Palace Purple' (or both).
Sedum 'Autumn Joy'	Aug–Oct	green, aging to raspberry	Let red bee balm bloom among green buds or plant with 'Goldsturm' rudbeckia or daylilies.
Anemone x *hybrida* Japanese anemone	Sep–Oct	white, rose	Stately flowers are beautiful around tall, lacy–foliaged Japanese maples.
Aster novi-belgii Michaelmas daisy	Sep–Oct	blue, purple, white, pink	Plant behind ornamental cabbage and kale, with blue violas massed in front.

Winter and spring planting in Northwest gardens

A surprising number of trees, shrubs, and vines can be planted in winter or early spring as long as the soil is workable. (Such plants are naturally dormant at those times, which allows for a minimal amount of shock to their root systems.) Winter and spring are also the preferred seasons to plant many of the annuals and perennials, as well as some of the bulbs, between and around existing landscape plants.

SHRUBS AND VINES: Plant those sold bare-root (including roses) in winter. Potted plants that bloom in winter or spring—including azaleas, camellias, Chinese witch hazel, lilacs, mahonias, rhododendrons, winter daphne, winter heath, wisteria, and some viburnums—can go into the ground as soon as soil is workable.

TREES: Deciduous trees sold bare-root in winter and early spring, including flowering crabapples and flowering cherries, can be planted this month, as can those sold in pots.

BULBS: In February, plant summer bloomers, including tuberous begonia, canna, crocosmia, dahlia, gladiolus, and Asiatic and Oriental lilies, in low elevations. (Wait until April or May in colder areas.) In summer, plant bearded iris. From September to November, plant spring bloomers such as hyacinth, narcissus, and tulip.

Oriental poppies, Shasta daisies, and bachelor's buttons.

DAVID WINGER

Rose penstemon adds bright note to blue and white flowers.

Planning for spring planting in Mountain gardens

In intermountain and mountain climates, gardeners who order from catalogs during the winter will receive their plants as soon as the soil begins to thaw. Warmer weather also signals the time to start shopping for plants in person at local nurseries.

At low elevations (*Sunset* climate zones 3A and 3B), planting season for bare-root stock can begin as early as March. Perennials start to appear in April or May, and getting these plants into the ground early in the season will allow them time to establish before the relatively hot summers, which can cut bloom time short. Spring comes later at the highest elevations (zones 1A and 2A), but summer is cooler, so bloom season typically has a longer run.

When you choose your color schemes, keep in mind any trees in your garden that might bloom at the same time. Some spring-blooming beauties that thrive in mountain gardens include Cornelian cherry (*Cornus mas,* with yellow flowers), flowering crabapples (*Malus* hybrids, with pink, red, or white blooms; hardy to 6,000 feet), Colorado hawthorn (*Crataegus succulenta,* with white flowers; hardy to 9,000 feet), and Canada plum (*Prunus nigra* 'Princess Kay', with white flowers; hardy to 7,000 feet).

Plant	Bloom time	Colors	Companions, comments
Doronicum cordatum Leopard's bane	Apr–May	yellow	Fine choice for livening up a planting of hostas.
Aurinia saxatilis Basket-of-gold	Apr–Jun	yellow	Classic rock garden plant often used with evergreen candytuft and variegated iris.
Iberis sempervirens Evergreen candytuft	Apr–Jun, Sep–Oct	white	Excellent with blue bearded iris and *Penstemon digitalis* 'Husker Red'.
Iris Bearded iris	May	white, yellow, blue, rust, purple	Very good with *Crambe maritima* or underplanted with *Phlox subulata.*
Dicentra spectabilis Common bleeding heart	May–Jun	pink and white, white	Very impressive with *Heuchera micrantha* 'Palace Purple' and pink pansies.
Papaver orientale Oriental poppy	May–Jun	red, pink, white	Plant with baby's breath or cosmos, which cover fading foliage after bloom.
Phlox subulata Moss pink	May–Jun	white, pink, lavender blue	Makes a sheet of color in front of purple or white bearded iris.
Lupinus Russell hybrids	May–Jul	full range	Plant these behind Purple Wave petunias or pink and cream yarrow.
Penstemon	May–Jul	pink and red to blue	Red *P. eatonii* is striking behind blue *Nepeta racemosa.*
Chrysanthemum maximum Shasta daisy	May–Sep	white	Plant with pink cosmos and foxglove or with deep pink bee balm.
Geranium 'Johnson's Blue'	May–Oct	blue	Handsome accompaniment to potentilla, lamb's ears, and white or pink roses.
Erigeron x 'Pink Beauty'	Jun–Aug	pink	Very appealing with *Penstemon strictus* and orach (*Atriplex hortensis* 'Rubra').
Verbena 'Homestead Purple'	Jun–Aug	purple	Good with Mexican evening primrose, dwarf blue spruce, and artemisia.
Veronica spicata Speedwell	Jun–Aug	blue	Combines well with yellow daylilies and yarrow.
Oenothera speciosa Mexican evening primrose	Jun–Sep	pink	Try it with *Artemisia* 'Powis Castle' and red or purple penstemons.
Echinacea purpurea Purple coneflower	Jul–Aug	purple	Interplant with false sea holly (*Eryngium planum*), *Crambe maritima,* or white yarrow.
Lilium regale Regal lily	Jul–Aug	white flushed purple	Use it with white summer phlox and pink lavatera.
Lilium 'Star Gazer'	Jul–Sep	pink	Let variegated hop vine climb a trellis behind it.
Malva moschata 'Alba' musk mallow	Jul–Sep	white	Combine with feverfew and yellow columbine.
Rudbeckia hirta Black-eyed Susan	Jul–Sep	yellow	Handsome with yarrow and purple coneflowers or with white *Tanacetum niveum.*
Delphinium elatum	Aug–Sep	blue, pink, purple, white	Put blue ones behind pink petunias, red penstemons, and white Shasta daisies.
Aster novi-belgii Michaelmas daisy	Aug–Oct	blue	Try it with yellow chrysanthemums and columbines or in front of white delphiniums.
Zauschneria californica California fuchsia	Aug–Oct	crimson	Great with Dahlberg daisy.
Anemone x hybrida Japanese anemone	Sep–Oct	white, rose	Stately flowers are pretty in front of birches or maples or under high-branching trees.

Plant	Bloom time	Colors	Companions, comments
Justicia californica Chuparosa	Jan–Feb, Dec	red	Minimal water. Plant with deer grass, brittlebush, ocotillo.
Encelia farinosa Brittlebush	Jan–Apr, Dec	yellow	Minimal water. Plant with agave, globemallow, purple prickly pear.
Bulbine frutescens	Jan–May	yellow	Dry shade. Pair with aloe.
Justicia candicans Red justicia	Jan–May, Sep–Dec	red	Water weekly to prolong bloom. Plant with salvia, *Plumbago scandens,* bat-faced cuphea.
Tagetes lemmonii Copper Canyon daisy	Jan–May, Nov–Dec	yellow	Part shade in low desert, full sun in high desert. Plant with Texas ranger, deer grass.
Justicia spicigera Mexican honeysuckle	Jan–Dec	orange	Works well under light shade of palo verde, mesquite. Plant with turpentine bush, yellow bells.
Verbena pulchella gracilior Moss verbena	Jan–Dec	violet blue	Water twice a week in summer. Plant with agave, desert milkweed *(Asclepias sublata),* lantana.
Calliandra eriophylla Fairy duster	Feb–Apr	pink	Water weekly for more bloom. Plant with penstemon, desert milkweed, globemallow.
Tetraneuris acaulis Angelita daisy	Feb–Jul	yellow	Plant with gray santolina, turpentine bush, bush morning glory.
Baileya multiradiata Desert marigold	Feb–Oct	yellow	Minimal water. Plant with agave, globemallow, purple prickly pear.
Oenothera speciosa 'Rosea' Mexican evening primrose	Mar–May	pink	Plant with spotted emu bush, agave, penstemon.
Penstemon parryi Parry's penstemon	Mar–May	pink	Minimal water. Plant with California poppy, globemallow, brittlebush.
Sphaeralcea ambigua Apricot mallow	Mar–Jun, Oct	pink, orange	Minimal water. Plant with brittlebush, fairy duster, moss verbena.
Gaillardia aristata Firewheel	Mar–Nov	orange	Plant with Mexican hat, salvia, lantana.
Salvia coccinea Tropical sage	Mar–Nov	red	Water twice a week in summer. Plant with red justicia, *Plumbago scandens,* Mexican oregano.
Salvia greggii Autumn sage	Mar–Nov	red	Water twice a week in summer. Plant with *Plumbago scandens,* California fuchsia.
Ratibida columnifera Mexican hat	Apr–May	yellow	Plant with gaillardia, coreopsis, scarlet sage.
Salvia leucantha Mexican bush sage	Apr–May, Oct	blue purple	Plant with California fuchsia, Mexican oregano, white moss lantana.
Chrysactinia mexicana Damianita	Apr–May, Oct–Nov	yellow	Extra summer water prolongs bloom. Plant with gray santolina, black dalea, Texas ranger.
Penstemon baccharifolius Rock penstemon	Apr–Sep	red	Water twice a week in summer. Plant with salvia, gaillardia, lantana.
Poliomintha maderensis Mexican oregano	May–Oct	lavender	Water twice a week in summer. Plant with California fuchsia, *Ruellia* 'Katie', yellow bells.
Ruellia 'Katie'	May–Oct	blue	Plant with lantana, yellow bells, salvia.
Zauschneria californica California fuchsia	Aug–Nov	scarlet orange	Plant with red justicia, Mexican sage, gaillardia, or let it ramble around aloe or cactus.
Ericameria laricifolia Turpentine bush	Oct–Dec	yellow	Plant with Copper Canyon daisy *(Tagetes lemmonii),* Texas ranger, *Ruellia* 'Katie'.

Winter and spring planting in Southwest gardens

In the low and intermediate deserts (*Sunset* climate zones 12 and 13), January is an ideal month to plant bare-root roses as well as many kinds of trees and vines. It's also a good time to plant tulips that have been chilled in the refrigerator for six weeks, summer-flowering bulbs such as canna and gladiolus, and some bedding plants, including asters, chrysanthemums, coreopsis, pansies, and verbena. In February, plant perennials such as penstemons and salvias, and sow seeds of warm-season annuals.

Flowers that bloom through the summer in high desert often burn out in low desert. You can reduce the effects of extreme heat by planting in filtered shade or in places that are sheltered from western sun. Water is the other big issue; group plants by water needs.

When you choose your color schemes, keep in mind any trees or shrubs in your garden that might bloom at the same time. Beautiful backdrops for spring include desert willows (pink and rose to lavender blooms) and palo verde and mesquite trees (yellow blooms). For summer color, consider shrubs such as *Caesalpinia* (especially yellow-flowered *C. gilliesii* and orange red forms of *C.pulcherrima*) or oleanders with pink, red, and white blooms.

TOP: Purple moss verbena with pink penstemons. BOTTOM: Orange Mexican honeysuckles with scarlet hedge nettle.

TERRENCE MOORE (2)

FEBRUARY IS THE PERFECT TIME to plant long-stemmed annuals for spring and summer bouquets. For tips on creating a cutting garden of your own, see pages 48–53.

February

late-winter color beds in Seattle

■ Not all the floral splendor in Seattle is indoors this month at the Northwest Flower & Garden Show (see item on page 40). Just stroll through downtown Seattle, where municipal and corporate gardens brim with late-winter color. Last February, we spotted the beds pictured here near the corner of Sixth Avenue and Seneca Street.

In the bed above, deep pink primroses play off the purple-leafed heuchera, pale yellow daffodils, and pink azaleas. These evergreen Belgian Indica hybrid azaleas are forced in greenhouses, then sold in bud or bloom; their flowers stay perky as long as temperatures don't dip below 20°, which they seldom do in Seattle.

The bed at right is edged by sunny yellow primroses and filled with heuchera, rosy pink-and-white bleeding heart *(Dicentra spectabilis)*, tulips with swelling buds, and *Cornus alba* 'Argenteomarginata' with green-and-white foliage (right rear).

If you live in Seattle or one of the other relatively mild-winter climates west of the Cascades, try creating your own color beds by combining

cool-season flowers like primroses and pansies, spring bulbs, early-blooming perennials, and shrubs with striking flowers or foliage. Shop nurseries now for plants to bed out.

— *Steven R. Lorton*

bicolor
ranunculus

■ Until recently, traditional ranunculus have been admired for their clear, pure colors, whether yellow, orange, or scarlet. So breeders weeded out as undesirable any bicolors or blended shades that popped up in their crops. But the bicolor rose ranunculus pictured at right made Sakata Seed reconsider its selection process. Last spring, the company test-marketed plants in some local retail nurseries such as Roger's Gardens in Corona Del Mar, where the plants quickly sold out.

This year, Sakata is introducing two more bicolors: bicolor blue and bicolor orange. All three bicolor ranunculus are from the Bloomingdale series, a dwarf variety that grows 8 to 10 inches tall.

Southern California gardeners usually discard ranunculus at the end of the season and start over with new plants the following year. But if you grow these bicolors this year, you might want to try digging and storing the tuberous roots at the end of the season, as this strain is likely to remain in short supply for some time.

Wait until foliage turns yellow, then dig up plants, cut off the tops, and let the roots dry out for a week or more. Store the tuberous roots in a cool, dry place until you're ready to replant next fall.

— *Sharon Cohoon*

pruning shears designed for comfort

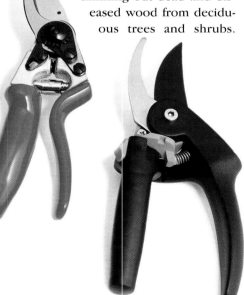

■ A good pair of pruning shears is imperative for all kinds of dormant-season pruning, from cutting back roses and trimming fruit trees to thinning out dead and diseased wood from deciduous trees and shrubs.

Good ones are sharp and sturdy. Great ones are also comfortable to use. If you do a lot of heavy pruning, consider buying a pair with one handle that rotates beneath your fingers as you squeeze the two handles together to make a cut. The rotating handle helps reduce hand and wrist fatigue. These two models have them.

Felco 7 professional quality pruning shears (far left). Both the upper, fixed handle and the lower, rotating handle are coated in plastic for additional comfort. All parts are replaceable; models are available for left-handers (Felco 10) and small hands (Felco 12). From $60 to $65. If you can't find them locally, order from A.M. Leonard (800/543-8955 or www.amleo.com).

Fiskars Bypass Pruner, model 7936 (left). The rotating handle (made of lightweight, reinforced nylon) has a gear mechanism that increases leverage and reduces cutting effort by 50 percent. Other features include an adjustable handle opening and a replaceable blade. The pruners cost about $30. For sources, call (800) 500-4849. — *Lauren Bonar Swezey*

E. SPENCER TOY; ABOVE: CLAIRE CURRAN

garden guide

'Thornton' grape

■ Most grapes are available as bare-root stock or container-grown plants, but one great table grape you won't find among the bunch is 'Thornton'. The only way to enjoy this elusive grape is to grow your own from cuttings.

'Thornton' produces clusters of small to medium-size golden green grapes. The seedless fruit has crispy-sweet flesh with a hint of spiciness. It ripens at midseason (from early September on) and is great for eating fresh or drying to raisins. Reportedly hardy to at least −15°, 'Thornton' is a self-pollinating variety with vigorous vines.

Cuttings are available from Oregon growers Nick Botner (541/849-2781) for $3 per cutting (minimum of three), plus $3.50 shipping, and Lon J. Rombough (503/678-1410 or www.bunchgrapes. com) for $1.25 per cutting (minimum of

RICK WETHERBEE

five), plus $6 shipping for the first 20.

When the cuttings arrive, soak them overnight in a vase of water. In a 1-gallon container filled with loose potting soil, plant cuttings so that only the top bud remains above the soil. Place the container in a sunny window or greenhouse,

and water to keep soil slightly moist. Roots will form in three to five weeks. Plant the rooted cuttings outdoors in spring near a trellis or other sturdy support for vines to climb. Vines should produce a full harvest in the third year.

— *Kris Wetherbee*

the Northwest show that grows and grows

DAVID McDONALD

■ The Northwest Flower & Garden Show just keeps growing larger. Now in its 14th year (2002), the show, February 6 through 10, has expanded from 5 to 8 acres of indoor space at the Washington State Convention Center in Seattle.

That means more room for show gardens, which run the gamut from exotic landscapes to wild forest scenes. Last year (2001), for example, Dianna MacLeod of Scotland Yards designed an award-winning garden (at left) edged by spring bulbs. Bring a notebook and camera to record landscaping ideas and plant combinations.

There's space for more than 100 additional exhibitors in the marketplace, where you'll find vendors selling everything from bulbs to books, plus enthusiastic members of Northwest plant societies, such as those devoted to dahlias and daylilies, ferns and fuchsias, rhododendrons and roses, and, of course, native plants. Also, the popular Orchid Pavilion is being completely revamped.

Once again, showgoers are invited to attend the free seminar series sponsored by *Sunset*. More than 100 demonstrations and lectures by expert horticulturists and designers, including Topher Delaney, Dan Hinkley, Ann Lovejoy, and Nancy Davidson Short, cover a full range of gardening topics. Seating begins 30 minutes before each seminar.

(Note: this article describes the February 2002 show. The event is held each year around the same time.)

— *Jim McCausland*

perfect gate for a desert garden

■ When landscape architect Peter Curé designed a gate for Connie and Craig Weatherup's property in Scottsdale, Arizona, he was inspired by classic Chinese moon gates that were popular elements in 18th- and 19th-century English gardens. But Curé, principal of the firm Arterra (602/569-9800), gave the Weatherups' moon gate a distinctive Southwest accent by incorporating the shapes of native plants into the design.

Forming a 270° arc, the gate was fabricated out of steel by Paco Saucedo of Art-Mex Iron Works in Phoenix (602/549-0665). Curé's design features the silhouettes of agave, ironwood tree, and saguaro, with a snake serving as the handle; the shapes were painted sage green. The gate swivels open wide enough for a small utility cart to pass through.

A masonry archway faced with native stone, which was gathered from a wash that runs through the site, frames the gate. Low walls extending from both sides of the arch are constructed of masonry block and are faced with more native stone.

The gate, walls, and some metal fencing surround an area planted with fruit trees and seasonal vegetables, protecting the crops from browsing deer, javelinas, and rabbits that roam through the rest of the Weatherups' property, which abuts the McDowell Mountains. On either side of the arch, Parry's penstemon provides splashes of springtime color. A flagstone pathway runs from the moon gate to the house. — *Nora Burba Trulsson*

garden guide

spiral fireplace planter in Tucson

■ Landscape designer Margaret West was asked to redesign this backyard in Tucson to create more seating area for entertaining, a smaller swimming pool, and a fireplace like the kind the owner had seen years ago in *Sunset*.

West decided to make the 8-foot-tall spiral fireplace the focal point of a larger new patio. To accommodate plenty of guests, West wrapped a seating wall around the fireplace and the planter extending from

it. Another planter is the backdrop for the pool and a rocky waterfall. West used Arizona flagstone to top the seating wall and to pave around the pool.

The owner fills the planters with seasonal flowers, like the pansies, petunias, and snapdragons pictured here. The flowers in the planters are color-coordinated with those in containers spotted around the patio. A built-in irrigation system waters the planters. — *S.C.*

BOOKSHELF
• *A Desert Gardener's Companion,* by Kim Nelson (Rio Nuevo Publishers, Tucson, 2001; $19.95; 800/969-9558), is a hardworking paperback specifically geared to the challenges of gardening in the desert Southwest. Drawing on her experience as a Master Gardener and former chair of the Plant Clinic at the University of Arizona Cooperative Extension in Tucson, the author offers page after page of garden-tested advice organized in a month-by-month format. — *S.C.*

roll-your-own seedling pots

■ With only a wooden mold and yesterday's newspaper, you can make your own biodegradable seedling pots in minutes. Simply wrap a strip of newspaper around the mold and press it into the wooden base to form the bottom— you'll produce a 2½-inch paper pot that's strong enough to hold soil and endure repeated watering. When the seedlings are ready to go into the garden, plant them intact, paper pot and all. You can buy the paper pot maker for about $15 from mail-order firms such as Gardener's Supply Company (800/955-3370 or www.gardeners.com). — *J. M.*

pacific northwest · checklist

PLANTING

☐ **BARE-ROOT STOCK. Zones 4–7:** Bare-root plants are cheaper than those sold in containers, and they adapt better to native soil. Choose from berries, grapes, roses, shrubs, and fruit trees. Don't let the bare roots dry out, and get them into the ground before the plant starts active growth. **Zones 1–3:** Plant as soon as bare-root stock is available but on a day when air and soil temperatures are above freezing.

☐ **CONTAINER STOCK.** *Evergreens:* Try camellia, Japanese andromeda *(Pieris japonica),* and rhododendron for showy blooms; sarcococca for tiny but very fragrant white flowers; English holly for bright berries; and heavenly bamboo for red winter leaves. *Deciduous:* For February bloom, plant Chinese witch hazel *(Hamamelis mollis),* cornelian cherry *(Cornus mas),* forsythia, flowering cherry like *Prunus* x *subbirtella* 'Autumnalis', flowering plum like *Prunus* x *blireiana,* viburnum, winter hazel, and wintersweet.

☐ **COOL-SEASON VEGETABLES. Zones 4–7:** Spinach and edible-pod sugar snap and snow peas such as 'Oregon Giant' will both germinate in cool soil. Sow seeds directly in raised beds from mid- to late February.

☐ **HARDY ANNUALS.** Direct-sow seeds of calendula, English daisies, godetia, pansies, many poppies (California and Iceland), snapdragons, and violas.

☐ **PRIMROSES. Zones 1–3:** Buy *Primula vulgaris* for indoor display (it does well on windowsills). **Zones 4–7:** Use *P. vulgaris* indoors or group them in outdoor containers. Plant taller, weather-resistant polyanthus primroses *(P.* x *polyantha)* in garden beds. *P. vulgaris* usually has one flower per stem, while polyanthus types have multiple flowers growing from a single sturdy stem.

☐ **SWEET PEAS.** Start seeds of flowering sweet peas indoors in 4-inch pots now for transplanting outdoors in March or April.

MAINTENANCE

☐ **CLEAN UP HOUSEPLANTS.** Feed any that flower or fruit indoors this time of year; wait until spring growth begins to fertilize other kinds. Give plants a lukewarm shower every month or two to wash dust off leaves and inhibit insect buildup. At the same time, prune off yellowing leaves and cut back plants (except palms) that are getting leggy to force regrowth from lower on the plant.

☐ **PRUNE ROSES. Zones 4–7:** Start by removing dead, injured, or diseased canes. Then prune hybrid teas for shape. Select the three to five strongest canes and cut them back by about a third. Each cane should be left with one robust, outward-facing bud. **Zones 1–3:** Wait to prune until new growth begins in spring. ◆

WHAT TO DO IN YOUR GARDEN IN FEBRUARY

PLANTING

☐ **CARROTS IN CONTAINERS.** Zones 7–9, 14–17: To avoid early spring's heavy, wet soil, plant carrots in containers. For small varieties ('Thumbelina'), use a wide, shallow (6 to 8 inches deep) container. For longer kinds (such as a Nantes-type), choose a container at least 1 foot deep. Fill the container with potting mix, add in a controlled-release or organic fertilizer, and wet the soil. Sow seed thinly (mix with sand to help distribute it) and cover with a fine layer of mulch. When watering before seeds come up, spray the soil gently to avoid washing seeds around.

☐ **EVERGREEN VINES.** Zones 7–9, 14–17: Good choices are fragrant, yellow-flowered Carolina jessamine *(Gelsemium sempervirens)*; white-flowered evergreen clematis *(C. armandii)*; purple *Hardenbergia violacea* 'Happy Wanderer'; pink *H. v.* 'Rosea'; fragrant, pinkish white *Jasminum polyanthum*; pink or white *Pandorea jasminoides*; and violet trumpet vine *(Clytostoma callistegioides)*. All are very vigorous, growing 15 to 20 feet or more.

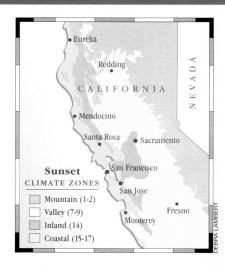

Sunset
CLIMATE ZONES
☐ Mountain (1-2)
☐ Valley (7-9)
☐ Inland (14)
☐ Coastal (15-17)

DEBRA LAMBERT

☐ **LILACS.** Zones 7–9, 14–17: These old-fashioned flowering shrubs bring a wonderfully sweet fragrance into the garden. Most nurseries carry them in containers at this time of year. You may also find some sold bare-root. In mildest climates (14–17), plant low-chill varieties such as 'Angel White', 'Blue Skies', 'Lavender Lady', or 'Sylvan Beauty'. If you can't find them at your local nursery, ask to have one ordered for you from L.E. Cooke Co. or Monrovia (both are wholesale only).

☐ **PERENNIALS.** Zones 7–9, 14–17: For spring-blooming perennials, try alstroemeria, bergenia, bleeding heart, brunnera, campanula, catmint, columbine, coral bell, dianthus, delphinium, diascia, evergreen candytuft, foxglove, *Linaria purpurea,* marguerite, poppy, scabiosa, and violet.

MAINTENANCE

☐ **CUT BACK FUCHSIAS.** Zones 7–9, 14–17: To stimulate lush new growth, cut back woody stems to main branches, then remove interior twiggy and dead growth. Container fuchsias can be pruned back to the edge of the pot rim.

☐ **FERTILIZE.** Zones 7–9, 14–17: Feed fall-planted annuals and perennials, and established trees and shrubs. Wait to feed azaleas, camellias, and rhododendrons until after bloom. Later this month, fertilize lawns.

☐ **PRUNE TREES AND SHRUBS.** Zones 7–9, 14–17: If you haven't pruned deciduous fruit trees, grapes, ornamental trees, roses, and wisteria, do so by midmonth. Wait to prune spring-flowering plants until after bloom.

PEST CONTROL

☐ **PICK UP OLD BLOSSOMS.** Zones 7–9, 14–17: Camellias and azaleas both are prone to diseases called petal blight (caused by two different organisms). Brown lesions develop and the flowers rot. Azalea flowers cling to the leaves or stems; camellia blossoms drop from the plant. The best way to control the diseases is to remove (or pick up off the ground) and discard infected blossoms and avoid overhead watering. Apply 4 inches of organic mulch beneath camellias to reduce spore survival. ◆

southern california · checklist

PLANTING

☐ COOL-SEASON VEGETABLES. In coastal (zones 22–24), inland (zones 18–21) and high-desert (zone 11) gardens, continue to sow seeds of beets, carrots, celery, chives, collards, endive, fennel, kale, leeks, lettuce, mustard, onions, parsley, peas, potatoes, radishes, spinach, Swiss chard, and turnips. Set out seedlings of cabbage-family plants like broccoli and cauliflower. Plant bare-root artichoke, asparagus, horseradish, and rhubarb.

☐ CYMBIDIUMS. Treat yourself or your Valentine to a cymbidium orchid, in peak bloom now. Enjoy the plant indoors while it is in flower, then move it outdoors.

☐ SUMMER BULBS. Plant agapanthus, amaryllis, caladium, calla, dahlia, daylily, galtonia, gladiolus, tigridia, and tuberose.

☐ SUMMER VEGETABLES. In the low desert (zone 13), plant eggplant, peppers, tomatoes, and other warm-season vegetables late this month. But be prepared to protect them with row covers or hot caps if a late frost threatens.

☐ WINTER-FLOWERING SHRUBS. Select camellias and azaleas at nurseries while in flower but resist planting if the ground is rain soaked. Wait until the soil dries out enough to be crumbly. Plant with rootball at least 1 inch above soil level, then mulch. Other shrubs that bloom this season include breath of heaven *(Coleonema), Erica canaliculata,* Geraldton waxflower *(Chamelaucium uncinatum),* and grevilleas.

MAINTENANCE

☐ FERTILIZE. Feed ground covers, shrubs, perennials, trees, and other permanent plants with a controlled-release fertilizer such as bonemeal, cottonseed meal, or well-rotted manure to provide gradual nutrition through the season. Or scatter a granular complete fertilizer and water in well. Also feed cool-season lawns. If you're within 10 miles of the coast, feed citrus and avocado as well.

☐ PRUNE ORNAMENTALS. Before new growth emerges, prune deciduous fruit and ornamental trees, grape and wisteria vines, roses, and summer-blooming shrubs. Wait to prune spring-flowering shrubs until after bloom. Don't prune hibiscus and other tropicals; it's still too cold to encourage growth.

☐ SET OUT RAIN BINS. Rainwater is too rare in Southern California to waste. Give your houseplants or container plants a break from municipal water by capturing any rainwater that does fall.

PEST CONTROL

☐ APPLY DORMANT SPRAY. While deciduous fruit trees are still leafless, spray with horticultural oil to smother overwintering insect pests such as scale, mites, and aphids. For fungal diseases such as peach leaf curl, add lime sulfur or fixed copper to the oil, following package directions. Spray the branches, crotches, trunk, and the ground beneath the tree to the drip line.

☐ CONTROL SNAILS. Reduce the population by hand-harvesting or baiting. If you have access to a liquidambar tree's prickly seedpods, try placing a barricade of them around the perimeter of the vegetable bed, a method used by Pasadena landscaping expert Tony Kienitz of Vegetare. ◆

WHAT TO DO IN YOUR GARDEN IN FEBRUARY

PLANNING AND PLANTING

☐ ORDER PLANTS BY MAIL. Check out the catalog offerings of these regional sources. High Country Gardens (800/925-9387 or www.highcountrygardens.com) specializes in drought-tolerant flowers and shrubs. One of their new introductions is *Eriogonum umbellatum* 'Shasta Sulfur', a yellow-flowered perennial with a long bloom season. Plants of the Southwest (800/788-7333 or www.plantsofthesouthwest.com) offers hardy native wildflowers, grasses, and shrubs; try Western blue flag *(Iris missouriensis)* in a sunny spot.

☐ SET OUT BARE-ROOT STOCK. As soon as your garden soil can be worked, plant bare-root stock. Many nurseries carry small fruits such as blackberries, grapes, raspberries, and strawberries; all kinds of ornamental, fruit, and shade trees; and perennial vegetables such as asparagus and horseradish.

☐ SHOP FOR SUMMER BULBS. Garden centers start stocking summer-blooming bulbs this month. Plant lilies as soon as your soil has thawed. Store other summer bulbs and tubers, including those of begonias, caladiums, cannas, dahlias, and gladiolas, in a cool, dry place until March, when they can be started indoors; or wait until May to plant them directly in the garden. If you can't find the bulbs you like locally, try mail-order specialists like Brent and Becky's Bulbs (877/661-2852 or www.brentandbeckysbulbs.com) or McClure & Zimmerman (800/883-6998 or www.mzbulb.com).

Sunset
CLIMATE ZONES
☐ 1-3   ☐ 10-11

DEBRA LAMBERT

☐ START COOL-SEASON CROPS. Indoors or in a greenhouse, start seeds of cool-season vegetables, including broccoli, cabbage, cauliflower, kale, and onion, for transplanting outdoors four weeks before the average date of the last frost in your area.

MAINTENANCE

☐ AVOID SNOW DAMAGE. To prevent broken or permanently bent branches, remove heavy snow from trees and shrubs after each storm. Use a broom to gently lift and shake all branches within your reach.

☐ PREVENT CROCUS DAMAGE. Stop sparrows and finches from shredding crocus blossoms by placing foil pinwheels—the kind sold for children's Easter baskets—every few feet among the flowers. The flashing foil frightens away birds.

☐ PRUNE SUCKERS. It's easier to remove suckering stems from the bases of trees and shrubs while the ground is still frozen and before new foliage emerges. If needed, leave a few well-placed suckers to replace broken or old woody stems.

☐ SPRAY DORMANT PLANTS. Spray dormant oil on deciduous fruit and ornamental trees and shrubs to kill overwintering insect eggs. Thoroughly wet all surfaces including the undersides of leaves and branches.

☐ THWART FUNGUS GNATS. Houseplants are frequently infested with these annoying flying insects. Their numbers can become bothersome in winter and early spring. To control them, use a soil drench of *Bacillus thuringiensis* (Bt) specially formulated to kill gnats. Two mail-order sources for Bt are Gardens Alive! (812/537-8650 or www.gardensalive.com) and Planet Natural (800/289-6656 or www.planetnatural.com).

— *Marcia Tatroe* ◆

WHAT TO DO IN YOUR GARDEN IN FEBRUARY

PLANTING

☐ BARE-ROOT PLANTS. Zone 10 (Albuquerque): Plant roses and deciduous shade and fruit trees (including apples), blackberries, grapes, peaches. pears, raspberries, and strawberries.

☐ GROUND COVERS. Zones 11–13 (Las Vegas, Tucson, Phoenix): Plant moss verbena *(V. pulchella gracilior)*, prostrate rosemary, sundrops, or trailing indigo bush *(Dalea greggii)*. Space plants 2 to 3 feet apart.

☐ PERENNIALS. Zones 11–13: For spring and early summer color, plant angelita daisy *(Tetraneuris acaulis)*, desert milkweed *(Asclepias subulata)*, lantana, Mexican evening primrose *(Oenothera speciosa)*, paper daisy *(Psilostrophe cooperi)*, penstemon, salvia, and vinca. Sow seeds of four o'clock late in the month.

☐ VEGETABLES. Zone 10: Direct-sow seeds of peas by midmonth. After midmonth, start seeds of cool-season crops (broccoli, cabbage, cauliflower, and lettuce) indoors for transplanting in six to eight weeks. Zone 11: Sow seeds of root crops (beets, carrots, radishes, and turnips), lettuce, spinach, and Swiss chard. Wait until the end of the month to plant potatoes. Zones 12–13: Set out transplants of tomatoes by midmonth: Cherry, yellow pear, and paste types do best; for slicers try 'Celebrity', 'Cherokee', or 'Pearson'. Sow seeds of cucumber, eggplant, melon, pepper, and squash indoors for transplanting in six to eight weeks.

DEBRA LAMBERT

☐ WOODY SHRUBS. Zones 11–13: Plant Arizona rosewood *(Vauquelinia californica)*, desert hackberry *(Celtis pallida)*, hop bush, jojoba, plumbago *(P. scandens)*, and Texas mountain laurel. Dig the planting hole as deep as the nursery container and three to five times wider.

☐ YUCCAS. Zone 11–13: Planted late in the month, yuccas will still have time to get established before blazing summer heat. Try *Yucca pallida* or twisted leaf yucca *(Y. rupicola)* for small gardens, or plant blue yucca *(Y. rigida)* or beaked yucca *(Y. rostrata)* where there's more space.

MAINTENANCE

☐ FEED ROSES. Zones 10–11: When nighttime temperatures are forecast to remain above freezing, water established plants, apply a complete fertilizer, and water again.

☐ FERTILIZE CITRUS. Zones 12–13: Spread granular fertilizer around the base of the tree and scratch it into the soil. Water trees deeply before and after application.

☐ PREPARE PLANTING BEDS. Zones 1–2 and 10: Get ready for spring planting by digging compost and other organic amendments into beds. — *Mary Irish* ◆

Plant now for spring
and summer bouquets

By Sharon Cohoon
Photographs by Christina Schmidhofer
Styled by Philippine Scali

Easy flowers

ABOVE: Cosmos bear their blooms atop long, strong stems, making them perfect for cutting. LEFT: Larkspur in shades of blue, with purple-tipped cerinthe and white and cream phlox.

9 unsung beauties

- **Bells-of-Ireland** (*Moluccella laevis*). Columns of apple green bells on long stems. Unusual color and shape; long bloom season. Flowers are also handsome when dried; the best drying method is right in the vase.

- **Cleome** (*C. hasslerana*). Large, rounded heads of pink or white flowers with long, protruding stamens. Dramatic flower, long season. Foliage has a strong, haylike scent. Dried seed capsules also useful in arrangements.

- **Cosmos** (*C. bipinnatus*). Daisylike flowers, 3 to 4 inches wide, with tufted yellow centers; available in shades of white, pink, and dark rose. Charming appearance, proliferation of bloom, long season. For longer vase life, cut while yellow center florets are still closed.

- **Love-in-a-mist** (*Nigella damascena*). Spurred, 1-inch-wide flowers in shades of blue, white, and pink; followed by decorative seedpods. Quick reward, but the flowers have a short season—in mild-winter areas, resow in fall for a second crop.

- **Love-lies-bleeding** (*Amaranthus caudatus*). Long (to 18 inches), pendulous ropes of red flower clusters. Handsome mixed with bold companions like zinnias and sunflowers. Good dried flower.

- **Phlox** (*P. drummondii*). Large clusters of small flowers in pastel and bright colors, some with contrasting eyes. Great mixer; long season; clean, pleasant fragrance. Make sure you select a tall (about 1½-foot) rather than dwarf (6- to 8-inch) strain.

- **Strawflower** (*Helichrysum bracteatum*). 2½-inch-wide papery flowers that look like prickly pompons. Available in pearly pastels and brights. Interesting shape, long season, excellent dried flower. Cut before the flowers are fully open or centers will turn brown.

- **Sunflower** (*Helianthus annuus*). Large (4- to 8-inch) daisylike flowers with black centers, plus chrysanthemum-like forms; mostly yellows, also bronzes and chestnut reds. Bold blooms, long season. To avoid pollen stains on tablecloths, select pollenless varieties like 'Valentine'.

- **Zinnia** (*Z. elegans*). Large (3- to 5-inch) dahlia-like blooms in every color (but blue) plus peppermint stripes. Long season. To prevent powdery mildew, allow for air circulation between plants and avoid overhead watering.

There are three grocery stores within a 10-minute drive where I can buy flowers anytime I want, and a farmers' market on Fridays that's close enough to walk to. So it's not like I *need* to grow my own blooms for bouquets. But I wouldn't think of letting a year go by without seeding some long-stemmed annuals in my garden for cutting. Try it for just one season and you'll understand why. The bouquets you make from garden-grown flowers always seem to have more personality, more cottage-garden softness than ones bought from the store. The occasional curving stem or bug-nibbled petal only adds charm. • There are also the advantages of immediacy and abundance. Having a bad day? Walk outside, cut some flowers for your desk, and you're over it. Having a *really* bad day? Cut enough blooms for every room. While you're at it, snip a bunch for a neighbor or friend—performing an act of generosity always lifts the spirits. Besides, when you grow your own, you can afford to be lavish. The more blooms you cut, the more the plants keep pumping out flowers, instead of setting seeds.

for cutting

easy flowers **for cutting**

Another benefit of growing your own flowers is variety. No matter how well stocked your supermarket is, there are some great cut flowers you aren't likely to see there—cleome, cosmos, and bishop's lace, for instance. Though they're too fragile to ship, they're a snap to grow. Indulge.

To come up with the list of the best flowers for cutting (see the previous page), we turned to Beth Benjamin, flower expert at Renee's Garden seed company. We asked her which varieties she would plant in a 5- by 12-foot bed—one small enough to fit into today's smaller yards but large enough to provide plenty of flowers from late spring into fall. Familiar summer classics such as cosmos, sunflowers, and zinnias make up the bulk of Benjamin's flower bed; some quick bloomers, plus some interesting fillers, round out her list. Summer flowers constitute most of the cutting garden Benjamin envisioned (see illustration below), but she also included a few early starters like love-in-a-mist and bishop's weed.

The best time to sow these varieties in most of the West is late March. In colder regions, wait until the danger of frost has passed. That gives you time to decide where you want to locate the flower bed, to prepare the soil properly, and to shop for seeds.

SEED SOURCES
Renee's Garden seeds are carried by many nurseries. To find one near you, call (888) 880-7228 or order seeds at www.reneesgarden.com. Mail-order catalogs with a good supply of annual seeds include Nichols Garden Nursery (541/928-9280 or www.nicholsgardennursery.com). Park Seed Company (800/845-3369 or www.parkseed.com), and Seymour's Selected Seeds (803/663-3084 or www.seymourseedusa.com).

'Valentine' sunflowers cut well; flowers are compact and pollenless.

A dream garden for bouquet makers

Front row: Purplish blue cerinthe and darker purple love-in-a-mist surround phlox. **Second row:** White cosmos are flanked by chartreuse bells-of-Ireland backed by white *Ammi majus,* sometimes called bishop's lace. **Third row:** Zinnias grow on either side of salvia in blue, rose, and white. **Fourth row:** Deep red love-lies-bleeding (left) and cherry pink cleome (right) flank cosmos in pink and rose shades. **Rear:** Sunflowers grow in the back, with strawflowers at far ends.

First to bloom are love-in-a-mist and *Ammi majus;* they'll be cut and gone before other flowers. As summer annuals decline, pull them out and sow spring-blooming annuals like larkspur *(Consolida ajacis)* and cornflower *(Centaurea cyanus).* DESIGN: Beth Benjamin. See above right for seed sources.

A

B

Planting and tending a flower bed

Choose a site that gets plenty of sun and protection from wind. To improve soil texture, work compost or other organic material into it; if necessary, correct the soil pH by adding peat moss to diminish excess alkalinity or lime for excess acidity (flowers grow best in sandy loam with a neutral pH). Several weeks before planting, force out weeds: Irrigate the soil, wait for weeds to emerge, then hoe them out; repeat at least once.

Decide how many plants will fit in your space. If you don't have room for the entire 5- by 12-foot bed described at far left, you can adapt the idea to fit your space by using fewer plants. Outline the boundaries for each variety by marking the soil with gypsum (**A**). Sow seeds according to package instructions. Water soil and keep it moist until seedlings emerge. Thin seedlings as directed on seed packets (**B**). If rainfall is scant, apply about an inch of water per week. Don't be shy about picking blossoms; it will only spur more production. Clip any faded blooms you missed (**C**).

Double flowers and delicate pink color give this lisianthus a softly old-fashioned look. Flowers last well over a week in water-filled vases if their stems are trimmed every few days.

How to extend vase life

When you're making a special gift bouquet or dinner party centerpiece, it's worthwhile to follow the rules.

■ Cut flowers early in the morning or just after sunset. Avoid cutting during the heat of the day.

■ Take a bucket of tepid water with you as you harvest. Place stems in it as you cut.

■ Indoors, fill the kitchen sink with cool water and recut each stem under water. Then pull off any foliage or flowers that will be below the water level in the vase.

■ Fill a vase with lukewarm water and a commercial floral preservative. Or provide the preservative's essential ingredients—sugar, acidifier, and biocide—with kitchen supplies: Mix one part regular (not diet) lemon-lime soda to three parts water, or stir 1 tablespoon sugar, 1 teaspoon vinegar, and a crushed aspirin into 24 ounces of water. ◆

Filler flowers

Choose from these annuals to place between bigger flowers in bouquets.

• **Annual clary** (*Salvia viridis* Claryssa). 18-inch stems covered with showy dark-veined pink, purple, and white bracts. Dries well.

• **Bishop's lace** (*Ammi majus*). Snowflake-shaped clusters of small, bright white flowers. Classic filler; looks good with everything. Short season but often self-sows.

• **Cerinthe** (*C. major* 'Purpurascens'). Purplish blue upper leaves and bracts, tubular purple flowers. Self-sows readily.

• **Lisianthus** (*Eustoma grandiflorum*). Striking single or double flowers of pink, cream, lavender, and purple. Plant from nursery pots; needs warm weather and well-drained soil.

TOP: Bouquet in the making contains snowy white phlox, cosmos, and bishop's lace. ABOVE: Cut blooms include pale pink Seashell (with rolled petals) and Sensation cosmos. Yellow and magenta zinnias are behind.

Scent-imental roses

Yesterday's roses with perfumes to perk up today's gardens

By Steven R. Lorton • Photographs by Norm Plate

■ Way back in most gardeners' memories, or perhaps their fantasies, is a grandmother's garden. It likely had a picket fence, an enormous old apple tree, a lollygagging lilac or buddleja, and a rose—a big old sticker bush with flowers so fragrant that the lightest breeze would carry their scent across the yard, through the open kitchen window, and into the house. Where are these wonderfully pungent old roses today?

They're still available, and their popularity is increasing. Most are antique roses—introduced from the 17th to the early 20th centuries—whose voluptuous blooms in shades of pink and apricot to red and white are celebrated as much for their informal exuberance as for their heady perfumes. To grow one in your garden is to establish a living link to yesterday's gardens.

February is the month to discover these dowager empresses of the rose kingdom. In California's mildest climates, bloom starts in late April or May; in colder climates it will begin between late May and July.

Some types put out a grand spring show, then speckle themselves with flowers throughout the season. Others cover themselves with a big flush of flowers just once a

Bench sits under the fragrant sweep of white-flowered 'Mme Plantier', a cold-tolerant climber or shrub. Large pink rose in foreground is 'Beautiful Carpet'; daintier rose to its left is 'Avon'. Close-up at left is of 'Reine des Violettes'.

year. But even those that flower only annually are handsome out of bloom, and the perfume of their flowers is so marvelous that they deserve a place in your garden.

Use one of these roses to fill a sunny corner. Settle one against a south- or west-facing wall or let it fountain out of the middle of an island bed.

Then some summer day, when you look out the window to see your grandchildren tearing around your backyard and you swing open the kitchen door to holler "Don't fall into that sticker bush," an unmistakable perfume will waft indoors. And it will remind you of the day, so long ago, when you planted that fragrant old rose.

14 fragrant old roses

Along with the other noteworthy roses shown on these pages, the following old roses are favorites of rosarians for fragrance.

'Alba Semiplena' (an alba rose). White, extremely fragrant semidouble blooms; plant is disease resistant. 6 feet tall, 4 to 5 feet wide. Not a repeat bloomer.

'Belle Isis' (Gallica). Medium pink, wonderfully perfumed. 4 feet tall by 3 feet wide. Not a repeat bloomer.

Cabbage rose (Rosa centifolia). The rose in paintings by old Dutch masters. Medium to deep pink, heady perfume. 6 feet tall by 5 feet wide. Not a repeat bloomer.

'Comte de Chambord' (Portland). Silvery pink blooms; pungent, old-fashioned scent. 4 feet tall, 3 feet wide. Continuous bloomer.

'Crepuscule' (Noisette), sometimes sold as Twilight. Double blooms of gold with ruffled petals, strong fragrance. 12 feet tall by 6 feet wide. Repeat bloomer.

"Darlow's Enigma" (ancestry unknown). Plant will grow in full shade. Small white blooms in clusters, richly fragrant. 8 feet tall by 6 feet wide. Repeat bloom.

'Ferdinand Pichard' (hybrid perpetual). Candy pink with stripes of deep crimson, aging to purple. 5 feet tall, 4 feet wide. Repeat bloomer.

'Francesca' (hybrid musk). Soft apricot semidouble blooms in clusters have the pungent fragrance of honeysuckle. 5 to 6 feet tall and as wide. Continuous bloomer.

'Henri Martin' (moss). Crimson red, many petals; strong, old rose fragrance. 5 to 7 feet tall by 6 feet wide. Not a repeat bloomer.

'Mme Hardy' (damask). White bloom with a green eye, very fragrant. 6 feet tall by 4 feet wide. Not a repeat bloomer.

'Mme Isaac Pereire' (Bourbon). Raspberry purple; one of the most fragrant of all roses. 5 to 6 feet tall by 4 or 5 feet wide. Continuous bloomer.

'Reine des Violettes' (hybrid perpetual). Deep violet purple, marvelously fragrant. 7 feet tall by 5 or 6 feet wide. Continuous bloomer.

'Rose de Rescht' (Portland). Bright fuchsia, wonderful fragrance. Compact, 4 feet tall, 3 feet wide. Repeat bloomer.

'Souvenir de la Malmaison' (Bourbon). Light pink, spicy sweet. Compact, 4 to 5 feet tall, and 4 feet wide. Continuous bloomer.

SOURCES

Arena Roses: (888) 466-7434 or www.arenaroses.com. Free catalog.

Edmunds' Roses: (503) 682-1476 or www.edmundsroses.com. Free catalog.

Heirloom Roses: (503) 538-1576 or www.heirloomroses.com. $5 catalog.

'Mme Isaac Pereire'

'Alba Semiplena'

'Belle Isis'

'Comte de Chambord'

Pink 'Lavender Lassie' entwines a trellis (above). At right, white 'Sombreuil' covers an arbor in Pam Seaburg's Kenmore, Washington, garden; its clouds of white blooms have a rich, fruity scent. Shrubby pink 'Wise Portia' grows beside it.

Planting and care

Plant bare-root roses as soon as possible after getting them home. Before setting them in the ground, soak the roots in a bucket of water for four hours or overnight. Amend the soil with compost or other organic matter to make sure it's rich and well drained.

bud union

■ **Dig a planting hole** at least twice as wide as the root system but a bit shallower (this will allow for settling). Roughen sides with a spading fork.

■ **Make a firm cone of soil** in the planting hole, then spread roots over it. Position the rose so the bud union (the thickened part toward the bottom of the stem) is above surrounding soil; measure the level by laying a shovel handle across the hole.

■ **Pack the backfill soil** around the roots as you hold the plant upright. When backfilling is almost complete, water to settle the soil around the roots. If the plant sinks too low, pump it up and down while the soil is saturated to bring it to the proper level. Finish filling the hole with soil, then water again.

■ **Water during the growing season** when the top 2 inches of soil is dry.

■ **Scatter a complete granular fertilizer** (such as a 12-12-12 formulation) around the base of plants in spring and midsummer. ◆

For more advice on caring for roses, go to www.sunset.com/garden/roses.html.

Grow your own blueberries

By Jim McCausland

'Toro' (above) bears plump fruits in dense clusters on a compact bush.

If you love fresh blueberries in your pancakes or on your cereal, why not raise basketfuls of fruit in your own garden? In mild-winter areas of the Pacific Northwest, you can set out bare-root or container-grown plants this month. In colder climates, order blueberries to ship for planting after the ground thaws.

Planting and care

Choose a site in full sun with well-drained soil. Blueberry roots don't grow too deeply (only a foot), so if you have heavy or alkaline soil, you can accommodate a bush by building a 16-inch-deep, 3-foot-wide raised bed.

Space northern highbush plants 4 to 6 feet apart; half-high types should be 2½ to 4 feet apart. Dig a hole about 2½ feet wide by 1 foot deep, amend the backfill with compost or peat moss, and plant. Blueberries need acid soil (a pH of 4.5 to 5.5 is ideal). East of the Cascades, where soil tends to be alkaline, you can acidify it by replacing 30 to 50 percent of the soil in the planting hole with moistened peat moss fortified with 2 cups of soil sulfur. After planting, cover the soil around the bush with 2 to 4 inches of mulch.

Water often enough during warm weather to keep the soil moist. Feed plants in spring with a half-strength dose of an acid-type fertilizer (often labeled for camellias and rhododendrons), or apply an organic fertilizer like fish emulsion. Feed established plants again after harvest.

Sources

Local nurseries may sell just a few kinds of blueberries. Two good mail-order sources are Raintree Nursery (360/496-6400 or www.raintreenursery.com) and St. Lawrence Nurseries (315/265-6739 or www.sln.potsdam.ny.us). ◆

Choice varieties

In recent years, breeders have developed plants that bear large crops of big, tasty berries. Most are self-fruitful and don't require a pollenizer.

In the coastal Northwest, northern highbush types are the most popular. You can extend the harvest season by planting early, midseason, and late-ripening varieties. Here are three outstanding varieties.

'Duke' (early). The most widely planted commercial variety in the United States, each 6-foot-tall bush can produce 20 pounds of medium to large, very sweet berries. It blooms late, so the flowers are less susceptible to frost damage—a plus for growers east of the Cascades.

'Toro' (midseason). Heavy clusters of extra large berries with a sweet flavor grow on a 4-foot-tall bush with glossy dark green leaves that turn brilliant red in fall.

'Chandler' (midseason to late). Delicious berries as big around as quarters are a bit too large for pancakes but are perfect for making jam and pies. The 6-foot-tall plant produces for about six weeks.

In cold-winter areas, try growing half-high types in a raised bed or half barrel. They're bred to tolerate extreme cold and carry heavy snow loads.

'Polaris' (early). Medium-size aromatic berries with delightful flavor are borne on an upright bush to about 4 feet. Benefits from a pollinator like 'Northblue' (see below).

'Northblue' (midseason to late). Large fruits with the flavor of wild blueberries are borne on a 2- to 3-foot-tall bush that produces heavier crops (3 to 7 pounds) as it matures. The plant can withstand temperatures to -35°.

Even in California?
You bet!

Raise tasty fruit in mild-winter areas

By Lauren Bonar Swezey

'Misty' (above) is a low-chill variety that bears medium to large fruits.

Choice varieties

Most of the blueberries listed below are self-fruitful and don't require a pollenizer. However, many southern highbush types will produce larger crops of bigger berries if at least two varieties are planted side by side. To extend the harvest, plant early, midseason, and late-ripening varieties. Low-chill types can be grown in coastal Southern California. The following are recommended by Garrison and/or Jiménez.

SOUTHERN HIGHBUSH

'O'Neal' (very early). Large, sweet berries on a spreading bush to 5 feet tall with gray green foliage.

'Misty' (early; low chill). Medium to large, flavorful berries on an upright bush to 5 feet tall with blue green foliage. Evergreen in mild climates. Benefits from a pollinator such as 'O'Neal'.

'Sharpblue' (early; low chill). Large, sweet-tart berries on a 4- to 6-foot-tall plant.

'Reveille' (late midseason). Small to medium fruit with crisp, sweet taste on a narrow bush 5 to 6 feet tall.

NORTHERN HIGHBUSH

'Bluecrop' (midseason). Large, sweet fruit on an upright bush 4 to 6 feet tall with great fall color.

S tarting in late spring, Nancy Garrison steps into her garden every few days to fill a bowl with sweet, succulent fruit from one of 15 productive blueberry plants. Surprisingly, Garrison doesn't live in "blueberry country"—the Pacific Northwest—but in San Jose.

Since 1997, Garrison, a UC Cooperative Extension horticulture coordinator, has tried 22 varieties and found that most of her favorites for flavor and performance are southern highbush types.

Meanwhile, in the San Joaquin Valley, Manuel Jiménez, a UC Cooperative Extension farm advisor in Visalia, has been equally successful with blueberries. For this mild-winter, hot-summer climate, Jiménez recommends only southern highbush types.

Sources

Look for plants at nurseries or ask the staff to order plants from Fall Creek Farm & Nursery (wholesale only), in Lowell, Oregon. Or you can order some varieties from Hartmann's Plant Company (616/253-4281 or www. hartmannsplantcompany.com) and Raintree Nursery (360/496-6400 or www.raintreenursery.com).

Planting and care

Choose a site in full sun with well-drained soil. In heavy soil, plant in raised beds. Space plants 4 to 6 feet apart. Dig a hole about $2\frac{1}{2}$ feet wide by 1 foot deep. Blueberries need acid soil (pH 4.5 to 5.5). If your native soil is alkaline, acidify it by replacing 30 to 50 percent of the soil in the planting hole with the same volume of moistened peat moss mixed with 2 cups of soil sulfur. After planting, cover the soil around the bushes with 2 to 4 inches of mulch. Water to keep the soil moist. Remove flowers the first year to allow plants to get established.

Feed plants in spring with a half-strength dose of an acid-type fertilizer (often labeled for camellias) or apply fish emulsion. Feed established plants again after harvest.

Blueberries bear fruits on the ends of canes that are at least one year old. In summer (after harvest from second year on), prune back wood that has borne fruit to brightly colored, smooth-stemmed new growth. In winter, while plants are dormant, cut out twiggy growth to foster good air circulation; remove low, prostrate growth to maintain vase shape. ◆

The look of love

Simply romantic Valentine's bouquets

By Lauren Bonar Swezey
Photographs by Thomas J. Story

Giving flowers is symbolic of the love and affection we have for one another. So every Valentine's Day, bunches of colorful blossoms exchange hands. Traditionally, red roses have been the most popular flowers to give. But surprisingly, women actually favor roses in pastel shades of peach, pink, and lavender, according to the California Cut Flower Commission.

Pink and red assortment

Who wouldn't adore getting this luscious assortment of pink and red blooms? This bouquet is easy to put together, using a grid of florist's tape to hold the flowers in place.

DESIGN: Jeffrey Adair, J Floral Art, 704 Santa Cruz Ave., Menlo Park, CA (650/322-4488)

MATERIALS
• White or clear florist's tape
• Casual vase, such as a small French floral bucket (the one shown is 6

Arrange flowers easily with a grid of tape across the top of the vase.

inches wide and 8½ inches tall)
• Foliage: about 5 stems of salal
• Assorted pink and red flowers: Adair used five stems *each* of red roses, pink hyacinths, pink callas, pink nerine, red anemones, hot pink ranunculus, plus 15 small red tulips.

Bouquet-making tips

■ Choose flowers with mostly tight blossoms—they'll last longer. As blossoms open, they will fill in gaps in the design.
■ Cut stems at an angle, preferably under water.

■ Arrange the greens first to create a base for the flowers.
■ Insert larger blossoms, then fill in spaces with smaller flowers.
■ For longer vase life, add floral preservative to the water (see page 53 for a preservative you can make).

DIRECTIONS

1 With florist's tape, form a grid across the top of the vase (see photo at left). Secure the ends by wrapping more tape around the rim of the vase.

2 Fill the vase with water. Add floral preservative, if desired. Insert stems of foliage, spacing them randomly in the grid.

3 Insert the roses, spacing them at random. Then add the hyacinths, callas, and nerine, in that order. The flowers in the center of the vase should be slightly taller than the ones around the rim to create a rounded form.

4 Fill in with anemones, ranunculus, and tulips.

A handful of jewels

Assemble this bold bouquet in your hands, then tie with twine or raffia.

DESIGN: Jeffrey Adair

• Assorted flowers in jewel tones: red gerbera daisies, red roses, blue delphiniums, burgundy snapdragons, purple irises, purple lisianthus
• Foliage: salal stems
• Rubber band • Twine or raffia

DIRECTIONS

1 Buy enough flowers to create the effect you want. Form the bouquet in your hands, starting with some stems of foliage. Then evenly space flowers. Set large ones, such as gerbera daisies and roses, inside the bouquet. Allow taller flowers (delphiniums, snapdragons, irises) to stick out. Lisianthus can bridge the gaps. Add more foliage as you go. Finish with an odd number of each type of flower.

2 Wrap a rubber band around the middle of the stems, then trim the bottoms so they're even in length.

3 Wrap several strands of twine or raffia over the rubber band and knot it at the end. ◆

Bravo, 'Altissimo'

Classic climbing rose steals the show

By Sharon Cohoon

When Carol Brewer selected 'Altissimo', one of the most popular climbing roses in the country, for her garden, she had no idea what a good choice she was making. "I'd just started gardening, and I didn't know many roses by name," she says. "All I knew was that I wanted to see a lipstick red rose leaning against my white picket fence, and this color was just what I had in mind."

Later, Brewer came to appreciate some of the other virtues that make 'Altissimo' a classic. Generosity of bloom, for example. This rose produces large flower clusters—up to a dozen flowers per cluster—and it produces them often throughout the season. The flowers last well, even in a vase. The foliage is superior too—it's a deep, dark green and highly disease resistant.

'Altissimo' is also very flexible. You can let it grow into a big climber, train it on a pillar, or let it ramble at will, which is more or less what Brewer did here. Beside the rose, the dead trunk of an ornamental cherry tree supports two delightful birdhouses that double as feeders. ◆

BOB WIGAND

'Mellow Yellow'

Yellow roses
that resist black spot

By Jim McCausland

In the late 1800s, a French horticulturist named Joseph Pernet-Ducher developed the first yellow in the hybrid perpetual class. The rose world swooned with delight, and other growers introduced Pernet-Ducher's hybrid into their own breeding lines. A trickle of yellows followed, then a river that soon swelled to a flood. Unfortunately, almost all these new hybrids inherited a trait besides yellow color: susceptibility to black spot, a pernicious leaf disease that defoliates and sometimes kills the plant.

Over time, the hereditary link between yellow roses and black spot weakened, and disease-resistant yellows started to appear. Here, we describe 10 yellow roses that have shown strong resistance to black spot in recent field tests around the West.

Bear in mind that even resistant roses need proper care to avoid disease. Mike Cady, a horticulturist with Jackson & Perkins, advises, "Plant roses in well-drained soil, in full sun where there is good air circulation, and fertilize regularly."

Sources

Most of the roses listed are available from nurseries and garden centers. You can also order several varieties from Edmunds' Roses (888/481-7673 or www.edmundsroses.com), Heirloom Roses (503/538-1576 or www.heirloomroses.com), Jackson & Perkins (800/292-4769 or www. jacksonandperkins.com), and Northland Rosarium (509/448-4968 or www.northlandrosarium.com).

For more on rose care, go to www. sunset.com/garden/roses.html. ◆

10 reliable varieties

'Baby Love'. This 3-foot shrub rose (breeders call it a shrublet) bears masses of single, buttercup yellow flowers with a hint of licorice scent. Considered more resistant to black spot than any other yellow rose on the market. Does well in all climates.

'Carefree Sunshine'. This 3- to 4-foot shrub carries lots of soft yellow flowers with little fragrance over light green foliage.

'Easy Going'. A fairly new floribunda (classed by some as a shrub rose), this 4-foot plant produces peach-yellow flowers with moderately fruity fragrance.

'Elina'. Quite vigorous, this hybrid tea can reach 6 feet tall; it bears abundant pastel yellow flowers with light fragrance. Does best in cool climates.

'Lord Mountbatten'. One of the English Legend series, this 4- to 5-foot shrub produces clusters of large, fragrant medium-yellow flowers whose edges go pink in cool weather.

'Mellow Yellow'. This 7-foot hybrid tea (a descendent of 'Midas Touch') carries moderately fragrant flowers of a brighter yellow than the name would suggest.

'Midas Touch'. When it was chosen as an All-America Rose Selection (AARS) in 1994, it was the first yellow hybrid tea winner in 19 years. This plant grows 4 to 5 feet tall and bears golden yellow flowers with fruity fragrance. Doesn't fade in heat.

'Morning Has Broken'. Even when surrounded by other roses covered with black spot, this shrub rose showed no sign of the disease. Semidouble flowers cover the 4-foot-tall bush, fading from rich yellow to pastel with age. Handles heat well.

'Sun Sprinkles'. A knee-high shrub rose, this 2001 AARS winner has double yellow blossoms with light spicy fragrance.

'Topaz Jewel'. This 4-foot hybrid rugosa bears soft yellow, sweetly scented blossoms. Vigorous, cold-hardy plant.

Wise-buy orchids

Moth orchids are beautiful, long-flowering, and unfussy

By Jim McCausland

'Happy Valentine'
x 'Carmelas Stripe'

PAUL BOUSQUET; BELOW: THOMAS J. STORY

During the past few years, orchids have taken the West's big flower shows by storm. There are so many, you hardly know where to begin.

Our advice: Try moth orchids *(Phalaenopsis)*. Able to hold flowers for months, they're well adapted to household conditions. And they're often as inexpensive as $15 or $20. They're available almost everywhere; you'll find them at nurseries, supermarkets, home and garden centers, and discount clubs.

More to choose from

As supply has increased, so has the variety of flower colors and forms. In addition to basic white, pink, and yellow, there are now mauve and purple versions and any number of lined, spotted, and bicolored flowers. Leaves can be green or patterned, often with red-tinged undersides or spotted with deep plum. There are also dwarf moth orchids, ones with multiple or branching stalks, and a few that produce more than 20 blossoms per spike. Named varieties usually have more flowers per stalk or more exotic color combinations (and a higher price) than seedlings.

Care and feeding

Place moth orchids indoors where they'll receive light from an east- or north-facing window. Daytime temperatures should be 68° or higher with at least 50 percent humidity. To raise the humidity, place pots atop pebbles in water-filled trays.

Feed moth orchids with half-strength liquid fertilizer twice per month during late spring, summer, and early autumn. Water whenever the top inch of growing medium dries out. Never let roots sit in water.

If pests like mealybugs or scale appear on plant foliage, carefully dislodge them with your thumbnail or a knife, or wash mealybugs from foliage using tepid water about once a week.

Sources

For the biggest selection, visit one of the West's major garden shows. The Northwest Flower & Garden Show (early February) stages a huge orchid show and sale, as does the San Francisco Flower & Garden Show (mid March). For details about both shows, visit www.gardenshow.com. One good mail-order source for moth orchids is Oriental Orchids (604/515-7133 or www.oriental-orchids.com). ◆

For more flowers

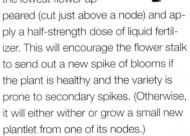

A single phalaenopsis spike usually flowers for two or more months. After the last bloom falls, cut the stalk where the lowest flower appeared (cut just above a node) and apply a half-strength dose of liquid fertilizer. This will encourage the flower stalk to send out a new spike of blooms if the plant is healthy and the variety is prone to secondary spikes. (Otherwise, it will either wither or grow a small new plantlet from one of its nodes.)

Most varieties flower in winter or spring. To trigger blooming, put plants where there's a 15° temperature difference between day and night. If your thermostat doesn't allow that, put the orchid next to a window, where temperatures fluctuate more (but be careful to diffuse strong sunlight).

COLORFUL PETUNIAS in an assortment of pots ring the fountain in this Phoenix courtyard. Though it looks as if it dates from the turn of the 19th century, the courtyard is only 11 years old. Learn how the aura of age was achieved on page 70.

March

a magnet for monarchs

■ Four years ago, Kathy Icaza bought butterfly weed from Heard's Country Gardens in Westminster, California, because Mary Lou Heard told her the plant was guaranteed to attract butterflies. What an understatement! That single *Asclepias tuberosa,* which reseeded generously, turned Icaza's backyard into monarch motel row.

The butterfly weed's orange and yellow flowers are a great nectar source, attracting butterflies to Icaza's garden all summer. But it's the plant's leaves that the fall-arriving monarchs are interested in (and the monarchs are what make this rather rangy-looking perennial so rewarding). Many butterflies have evolved to lay eggs on only a few species of plants; monarchs go to butterfly weed. Their eggs hatch into hungry caterpillars, which feed on the leaves.

The first year that Icaza's

daughter Alexis discovered a caterpillar, she brought it indoors so the family could watch its metamorphosis. She placed it in a glass jar with a few ventilation holes in the lid and fed the caterpillar butterfly weed leaves every day. After two to four weeks, the caterpillar enveloped itself in a jade green chrysalis, where it stayed for 10 to 14 days. Soon after the pattern of its dark wings began to show through the translucent case, the monarch emerged with the awesome perfection only new butterflies have. The Icazas were hooked. They've been growing butterfly weed and rearing monarchs ever since.

Heard's Country Gardens (714/894-2444) usually has some *A. tuberosa* plants in stock. Or start plants from seed; one source is Park Seed Company (800/845-3369 or www.parkseed. com). — *Sharon Cohoon*

about butterfly weed

■ Grows from a perennial root

■ Reaches about 3 feet tall, 1 foot wide

■ Needs full sun, well-drained soil, moderate water

■ Thrives throughout most of the West

hole-in-the-wall vines

■ If you like the look of a vine-covered wall but lack ground for planting, try growing vines through a hole in the wall. That's what Billy Spratlin did in his yard in Newport Beach, California. Paving at the base of a wall prevented planting in front of it. So Spratlin hired a professional concrete-coring company to bore 4-inch-diameter holes in the block wall 6 feet apart and 6 inches above grade. Holes this wide provide ample room for supple vines like the Carolina jessamine shown here. (For woodier vines or climbing roses, use 6-inch-diameter holes.) As the vines grew, Spratlin trained them up the back of the wall with hooks and wires, then wove them through the holes. — *S.C.*

STEVEN GUNTHER

BOOKSHELF

• **New guide for native plants.** *Trees and Shrubs of California,* by Humboldt State University professors John D. Stuart and John O. Sawyer (University of California Press, Berkeley, 2001; $45; 800/822-6657 or www.uc-press.edu), is a comprehensive field guide to the woody plants of California's wildlands. Intended for both amateurs and professionals, it includes 200 line drawings, 300 range maps, and easy-to-use plant keys.

• *Desert Landscaping for Beginners* is a hardworking guidebook aimed at gardeners in the low desert (zone 13, which includes Phoenix and Yuma). This paperback is packed with tips and techniques compiled by Arizona Master Gardeners in conjunction with the University of Arizona Maricopa County Cooperative Extension. There are extensive chapters on watering desert landscapes, growing citrus, and maintaining lawn grasses in an arid climate. An appendix lists the best rose varieties for the low desert. Look for this title in bookshops and nurseries, or order by mail ($14.95) from Arizona Master Gardener Press (602/470-8086, ext. 312).

TERRENCE MOORE

stroll amid desert wildflowers

■ Visitors to Desert Botanical Garden in Phoenix once had to search for spring wildflowers because the blooms were confined to small beds scattered among the other plant collections. Now, there's an expansive showcase devoted to desert wildflowers. The Harriet K. Maxwell Desert Wildflower Trail loops through 2 acres of habitats featuring the flowering herbaceous plants, shrubs, and trees of the Chihuahuan, Great Basin, Mojave, and Sonoran Deserts. During peak bloom in March or April, the ⅓-mile-long trail is adrift in arroyo lupine (*Lupinus sparsiflorus*), Mexican gold poppy (*Eschscholzia mexicana*), and the waist-high flower stalks of Palmer, or scented, penstemon (*P. palmeri*). Benches and a fountain designed by Phoenix landscape architect Christine Ten Eyck add to the wildflower-viewing experience.

Desert Botanical Garden is open from 8 A.M. to 8 P.M. daily during March and April; $7.50 adults, $6.50 seniors, $4 ages 5–12. 1201 N. Galvin Pkwy.; (480) 941-1225 or www.dbg.org.
— *Nora Burba Trulsson*

garden guide

'Sweetheart' cherry

■ Until recently, growing sweet cherries required a lot of space and a tolerance for split fruit if it rained near harvest time. Now, a new generation of self-fruitful cherries on dwarfing rootstocks is changing that. The latest variety is 'Sweetheart', developed in eastern British Columbia.

'Sweetheart' is usually sold on a rootstock called 'Gisela 5' (check the label). It gives 'Sweetheart' the ability to start bearing fruit when the tree is only two years old and produce heavily by the third year. Cold-hardy on both sides of the Cascades, the tree grows very slowly to 15 feet tall (on another rootstock, 'Sweetheart' would grow faster and taller). Because the tree is relatively small, the whole canopy can be covered with netting to keep birds from gobbling the harvest. The wine-red fruit is sweet, slightly tart, and a little softer than 'Bing'. This slight softness keeps 'Sweetheart' cherries from splitting after summer rains.

Look for 'Sweetheart' cherry trees in nurseries or order plants from Raintree Nursery (360/ 496-6400 or www. raintreenursery.com).

— Jim McCausland

MARK TURNER

bold garden visions

■ If you're looking for strong landscape design ideas, you'll find page after page of them in *Bold Visions for the Garden* (Fulcrum Publishing, Golden, CO, 2001; $30; 800/992-2908 or www. fulcrum-books.com), by Richard Hartlage, curator and director of the Elisabeth C. Miller Botanical Garden in Seattle.

In clear prose and superb color photos—all taken by the author—Hartlage presents the elements of good garden design, including architecture, color, form, and features. Many of the gardens he shows are the work of Pacific Coast designers, including Hartlage himself, whose planting at Miller Garden is pictured above. As Hartlage describes it, "*Phormium* 'Color Guard' in a large stoneware container...is captivating: great swords of leaves striped valentine crimson. In mid-May the *Geum* 'Red Wings' blooms, and the combination, which lasts two weeks, is a knockout. Scarlet dots hover like irradiated lightning bugs."

Inspired by such visions, you may view your garden in a bold new way. — *S.R.L.*

Aah! *Pieris* in the springtime

■ Clusters of jewel-like flowers account for its common name: lily-of-the-valley shrub. But *Pieris japonica* is also admired for its colorful new spring growth. Several cultivated varieties are standouts. The leaves of *P. j.* 'Bert Chandler' start out salmon pink before aging to cream, then white, and finally pale green. The juvenile foliage of 'Prelude' is rosy pink, while 'Mountain Fire' and 'Valley Fire' both flaunt bright red new growth. The young leaves of hybrid *P.* 'Forest Flame' (pictured here) are intense cherry red at the tips and rosy pink at the bases.

Shop nurseries now for container plants with new growth emerging. Plant in a site that gets high, light shade or morning sun and afternoon shade. These evergreens have the same basic cultural needs as rhododendrons. — *Steven R. Lorton*

PAUL BOUSQUET

'Blaze' of glory in Boise

■ Seven years ago, Jay and Rosemary Hill of Boise planted two 'Blaze' roses on each side of an 8-foot-tall, 8-foot-wide arch at the entry to their Boise garden. As they grew, the plants were trained by weaving new canes through the wrought-iron arch and tying them in place. The two plants took four years to cover the arch completely. Large clusters of 2- to 3-inch cup-shaped blossoms with slight fragrance cloak the canes during peak bloom in late spring, followed by sporadic flowers into summer.

First introduced in 1932, 'Blaze' ranks as one of the best climbing roses to plant on a fence or trellis. In addi-tion to its floriferous nature, 'Blaze' is very cold-hardy and resists disease.

Each spring, the Hills' roses are fed with a mix of controlled-release fertilizer, blood meal, and bonemeal. At the same time, the plants are pruned to follow the shape of the arch and thinned to improve air circulation. Once the roses finish blooming, spent blossoms are removed and the plants are fertilized again. During summer, the plants are watered for 20 minutes daily by a drip-irrigation system, supplemented by deep soaking with a hose once in a while, depending on the weather. — *Suzanne Touchette Kelso*

petunias aplenty in Phoenix

■ The Hirsches' residence in Phoenix is a venerable adobe dating to the turn of the 19th century. The site reputedly served as a watering station for the pony express, and the Hirsches' courtyard certainly looks as if it dates from that period. But, actually, it's only 11 years old. The aura of age is a result of the materials used in the garden's design, says landscape architect Greg Trutza of Phoenix. To visually echo the site's historic role, Trutza created a 10-foot-wide fountain in the courtyard. He capped the fountain with volcanic stone (called Piñon Adoquin) from Mexico, chosen for its graceful weathered appearance. For the sur-

rounding paving, Trutza used manganese-colored Saltillo tiles to match the stone.

The generous rim around the fountain gives the Hirsches plenty of surface area to display colorful annuals in an assortment of pots. "It's the traditional way to bring color into Spanish and Mexican landscapes," notes Trutza. Petunias are a particularly good choice, since they provide color over a long season. In the Hirsches' garden, petunias are planted in October and last through May, sometimes even into June.

— S.C.

shades of purple

Cineraria splashes this Oakland garden with vivid hues

■ Cinerarias in shades of purple, blue, and white fill this flower bed, where they complement a lavender-flowered wisteria growing nearby. Delicate though they appear, these plants are tough, often overwintering in the Bay Area's mild climates (*Sunset* climate zones 16–17). "They're the Godzillas of the plant world, and they reseed themselves everywhere," exclaims Oakland, California, owner–interior designer Karen Adelson, who often finds volunteers poking up from nearby sidewalks and parking strips. (In zones 1 and 2, grow them as annuals, or indoors).

Adelson planted a large-flowered dwarf form of florist's cineraria (*Senecio* x *hybridus,* usually sold as Hybrida Grandiflora) in the east-facing beds five years ago from sixpacks. Before planting, she dug fir-bark mulch into her garden soil—a procedure she repeats annually after the growing season. Rich soil and the location's filtered sun proved ideal growing conditions; the first year's flowers thrived. (In cooler summers, the color can last through early summer months.)

Each year, Adelson lets her favorite flowers set seed, then she shakes the seeds out in the bed and adds mulch. She digs the seeds under, then plants impatiens, which carry the color show through late fall. Invariably, some cineraria plants appear early or in the wrong place, so Adelson thins and cuts back often. When the impatiens are finished blooming, the spring crop of cineraria is well on its way.

Plants get infrequent watering in spring, daily irrigation in summer.

-— Peter O. Whiteley

PETER O. WHITELEY

Covered from spring into summer with 3- to 5-inch daisylike blooms, cineraria is an easy-care perennial (usually grown as an annual).

garden guide

an umbrella for tender crops

■ I failed to harvest a single eggplant in my Montana garden for 10 years. The plants just didn't ever mature in our cool mountain evenings. But last spring, I tried covering the seedlings with a solar umbrella, and I finally picked my first ripe eggplant later in the summer. In fact, the umbrella worked so well I wish I could find one big enough to put over my entire garden.

Essentially a miniature greenhouse, the umbrella protects tender, heat-loving vegetable plants, including peppers, summer squash, and tomatoes, until they mature. It can also be used in early spring to warm the soil before planting cool-season crops such as lettuce and peas. The 42-inch-diameter plastic dome is 22 inches high at the center, allowing plenty of room for plants to grow beneath it. When its shaft is pushed deeply into the ground, the umbrella is well anchored against strong winds and rain. If a hard freeze is predicted, the umbrella can be covered with a blanket to hold in the heat. Once plants are mature and the danger of frost is past, the umbrella can be removed and folded up until next year.

The solar umbrella sells for $16 from Irish Eyes-Garden City Seeds (877/733-3001 or www.irish-eyes.com). — *Amy M. Hinman*

hydrangea magic

■ Why are some hydrangea blooms blue, while others are pink? This is the number one question readers ask us about garden hydrangeas *(H. macrophylla)*. The answer lies in the soil.

In acid soils, pink and red garden hydrangeas often turn blue or purple, while in neutral or alkaline soils, blue hydrangeas turn pink. To make (or keep) flowers blue, apply aluminum sulfate (mix 1 tablespoon in 1 gallon of water) to the soil several times in spring and fall, at weekly intervals. To keep flowers pink or deepen their hue, add lime to the soil (apply ½ pound to every 5 feet of surface area under branches once or twice a year). Treatment needs to occur well ahead of bloom time to affect color.

CHRISTINA SCHMIDHOFER

BACK TO BASICS

Dig out deep-rooted weeds. Dandelions, mallows, and other deep-rooted weeds are difficult to hand-pull. Before weeding, water to loosen the soil, or do your weeding after a rain. Pry out the root with a screwdriver, or use the Angle

LINDA HOLT AYRISS (2)

Weeder shown here; it's available for $15.95 at nurseries or from Garden Works (425/455-0568 or online at www.createagarden.com). Its barbed tip also is useful for weeding between cracks in paving.

— *Lauren Bonar Swezey*

Tomato labels bearing any combination of V, F, N, or T indicate resistance to certain diseases and pests. Verticillium (V) and fusarium (F) are fungi that wilt and stunt or kill the plant, usually in hot weather. Nematodes (N) are microscopic worms that feed on roots (look for swollen root nodules) and stunt growth. Tobacco mosaic (T) is a virus that mottles leaves, stunts plants, and reduces yields. If one or more are a problem in your area (ask at your local nursery), choose a resistant tomato. — *J.M.*

out of Africa, to Irvine

Out of Africa

■ Most gardeners know how well freesias grow in Southern California. But what about *Moraea gigandra,* the violet blue flower in the bouquet shown here? It comes from Cape Province, the same area of South Africa as freesias, and would fare just as well in our similar Mediterranean climate. So would *Ixia dubia,* the apricot flower with dark eyes. Or *Sparaxis bulbifera,* the six-petaled, snowy white beauty. You can see these and hundreds of other early bloomers in a garden setting in the new South African Bulb Garden at the UC Irvine Arboretum's Winter Bulb Festival, usually held in early March.

The bulb garden, now in its second year, is the result of more than 11,000 volunteer hours, primarily from UC Master Gardeners of Orange County and arboretum volunteers. San Clemente landscape designer Vicky Bowles, herself a Master Gardener, contributed 150 hours alone.

Though the primary purpose of the event is to show off the garden, South African bulbs are also for sale as potted plants. In addition to many commercial hybrids, there are usually a limited number of wild species like the ones shown here (come early for these).

Festival hours are 10 to 4 on Saturday, March 9, and 11 to 3 on Sunday, March 10. Admission is $2. The UCI Arboretum is located just south of Jamboree Road at Campus Drive on the UCI North Campus in Irvine. For more information, call (949) 824-5833. — *S.C.*

in Escondido: Rock dams form planters

■ Two years ago, Christina Douglas tried transforming a pile of granite boulders alongside her newly built home in Escondido into a rock garden brimming with blooms. But, she recalls, "I'd plant between the boulders, and water would run off, even if I shoved a rock in to hold it." Undaunted, Douglas decided to create natural raised beds. Rocks were abundant, so workers used them to form terraces and V-shaped dams between boulders. Because the terrain was steep, pathways and steps of gray flagstone (used to supplement on-site rocks) evolved "wherever boulders allowed you space to get by."

Douglas poured commercial potting soil behind retaining walls and into the dammed crevasses, then planted heat-loving. unthirsty perennials, bulbs, and aloes. Ivy geraniums and nasturtiums provide cascades of bloom, while plants such as manzanita, salvias, and pride of Madeira soften the perimeter.

— *Debra Lee Baldwin*

tulip time in Oregon

■ Starting this month, swaths of circus-bright tulips paint the fields of the Wooden Shoe Bulb Company near Woodburn, Oregon. The Iverson family has been cultivating them here since 1974. And during the firm's annual Tulip Festival, usually held mid-March through mid-April, you're invited to stroll around 30 flowering acres of the bulbs.

On weekdays, take a quiet walk among the blooms. Look for unusual tulips like 'Red Riding Hood' (crimson flowers with mottled leaves) and 'Zombie' (carmine red petals fringed in yellow). The all-time best-selling tulips here are 'Angelique' (pink double flowers), 'Apeldoorn' (red), and 'Negrita' (deep purple). The farm also grows bulbs of allium, camass, crocus, daffodil, fritillary, hyacinth, scilla, and winter aconite. Plants are labeled, so it's easy to order your favorite varieties for fall delivery. Bulb buyers receive a complimentary bouquet of fresh-cut flowers. Pots of daffodils, tulips, and hyacinths, as well as cut blooms from the fields, are for sale.

On weekends, the festival tempo gets livelier with the addition of performances by local musicians, wooden-shoe carving demonstrations, displays of antique farm

implements, a crafts sale, wine tasting, and foods ranging from Dutch sausages to deep-fried onion blossoms.

To reach Wooden Shoe Bulb Company from Interstate 5, take the Woodburn exit #271 and drive east 6 miles to Meridian Road. Turn right (south) and continue 2 miles to 33814 S. Meridian Rd. For a schedule of events or a printed catalog, call (800) 711-2006. For field reports on tulip bloom as well as an online catalog, visit www.woodenshoe.com.

— *Mary-Kate Mackey*

pacific northwest • checklist

PLANTING

☐ **CAMELLIAS.** Zones 2–3 (Pendleton, Spokane): Try hardy camellia hybrids like 'Winter's Charm' (pink flowers), 'Winter's Dream' (pink), 'Winter's Hope' (white), 'Winter's Interlude' (lavender pink), 'Winter's Rose' (shell pink), and 'Winter's Star' (purplish red). In zones 4–7, spring-flowering japonica camellias are just coming into bloom. Plant on a mild day, or keep your camellia in a container and enjoy its blooms until they're spent; then plant in a place that gets midday and afternoon shade.

☐ **COOL-SEASON VEGGIES.** Zones 4–7: Plant bush and pole peas, cole crops (broccoli, brussels sprouts, cauliflower, kale, kohlrabi, mustard), leafy salad crops (lettuce, spinach, Swiss chard), onion family members (chives, garlic, leeks, onions, shallots), and root crops (beets, carrots, radishes, potatoes). Hurry to plant bare-root asparagus, horseradish, and rhubarb.

☐ **LAWNS.** This is the very best time of year to start new lawns and repair old ones. For new lawns, you get instant results by laying sod, but you can save money by starting from seed. Either way, till the top 6 to 8 inches of soil, pick or rake out roots and rocks, level the soil (a roller helps), then lay the sod or rake in seed and reroll. Don't let it dry out until grass is well established and growing strongly (rain will usually take care of this for you). To patch lawns, rough up the bare spots, rake in seed, cover with a thin layer of compost or peat moss, and water.

☐ **WARM-SEASON CROPS.** Indoors, start seeds of summer crops, including basil, cucumbers, eggplants, melons, peppers, and tomatoes, for transplanting outside in mid-May.

MAINTENANCE

☐ **CONTROL SLUGS.** Look for them during mild, rainy spells; deal with them while they're small. Iron phosphate slug bait is considered nontoxic to humans and pets, but isn't as effective as metaldehyde-based baits.

☐ **DIVIDE PERENNIALS.** Zones 4–7: This is the best time to divide summer- and fall-flowering perennials such as Shasta daisies, asters, and chrysanthemums. In zones 1–3, divide as soon as you see growth buds start to swell.

☐ **FEED LAWNS.** Zones 4–7: As grass starts to green up, apply ½ pound actual nitrogen per 1,000 square feet. This time of year, fertilizers that include iron do a good job of killing the moss that has come into the lawn over winter.

☐ **PRUNE CLEMATIS.** Zones 4–7: For summer- and fall-flowering clematis, cut back to the strongest stems now, then scratch fertilizer into the soil around the bases of the plants. In zones 1–3, prune after danger of hard frost is past. In all zones, prune back spring-flowering varieties immediately after bloom. ◆

WHAT TO DO IN YOUR GARDEN IN MARCH

PLANTING

☐ **EARLY TOMATO.** Zones 7–9, 14–17: You can't beat 'Early Girl' for flavor, production, and earliness (about 54 days to harvest). Most nurseries carry this reliable old-timer, introduced in the 1970s by Joseph Howland, retired chairman of PanAmerican Seed Company. For exceptionally sweet flavor, cut back on watering during fruit production.

☐ **GROUND COVERS.** Zones 7–9, 14–17: If you're fed up with mowing and caring for your lawn, consider replacing at least part of it with unthirsty ground covers. Try juniper (*Juniperus communis* 'Mondap', *J. conferta* 'Blue Pacific', *J. conferta* 'Emerald Sea', *J. horizontalis* 'Monber', *J. h.* 'Prince of Wales'), kinnikinnick (*Arctostaphylos uva-ursi* 'Wood's Compact'), lantana (*L. montevidensis* 'Mongen', 'Monma', and 'Monswee'), *Myoporum parvifolium*, or 'Huntington Carpet' rosemary.

☐ **LILIES.** Zones 7–9, 14–17: You can't beat lilies for sheer drama in the garden, for fragrance, and for long vase life. 'Casablanca' (white) and 'Stargazer' (dark pink with white edges) are two of the most perfumed. Other dramatic choices include 'Grand Cru' (vivid yellow with red markings), 'Italia' (deep pink with soft yellow throat), and 'Le Reve' (soft pink). All are available from www.tulipworld.com; the site also offers suggestions for companion plants, tips on bulb care, and more detailed information about all bulbs.

Sunset
CLIMATE ZONES
☐ Mountain (1-2)
☐ Valley (7-9)
☐ Inland (14)
☐ Coastal (15-17)

DEBRA LAMBERT

☐ **POTATO TUBERS.** Zones 7–9, 14–17: Try potatoes in different colors and flavors, like yellow 'Bintje' or 'Yukon Gold', red 'All Red' or 'Red Dale', blue 'All Blue', or lavender 'Caribe'. Order these or any of 87 other varieties (certified disease-free before shipping) from Irish Eyes-Garden City Seeds, Box 307, Thorp, WA 98946 (877/ 733-3001 or www.irish-eyes.com).

☐ **SCENTED GERANIUMS.** Zones 7–9, 14–17. Dozens of scented geraniums (a type of *Pelargonium*) are now available at nurseries or by mail from Geraniaceae (415/461-4168 or www.geraniaceae.com; catalog $4) or Mountain Valley Growers (559/338-2775 or www. mountainvalleygrowers.com). A few of the scents to try are apple, apricot, ginger, lemon, peppermint, nutmeg, and rose.

MAINTENANCE

☐ **CHECK DRIP SYSTEMS.** Zones 7–9, 14–17: Flush out sediment from filters and check screens for algae; clean with a toothbrush, if necessary. Turn on water and check to make sure all emitters are dripping water; clean or replace clogged ones. (If you can't get an emitter out, install a new one next to it.) Check for and repair leaks in lines. For supplies, visit your local home center or irrigation supply store. Or order by mail from the Urban Farmer Store (415/661-2204 or www.urbanfarmerstore.com).

☐ **DIVIDE PERENNIALS.** Zones 7–9, 14–17: Summer- and fall-blooming perennials such as agapanthus, coreopsis, daylily, and yarrow can be divided now, while they're still semidormant. Do this if clumps are crowded or if last year's blooms were sparse. Lift clumps with a spading fork and make a clean cut with a spade. Replant the young, outer portions of the clumps. ◆

WHAT TO DO IN YOUR GARDEN IN MARCH

PLANTING

☐ **CUTTING FLOWERS.** Cosmos, cleome, sunflowers, and zinnias all make great cut flowers, and their seeds germinate easily. Two companies in particular, Renee's Garden and Botanical Interests, offer seeds for several varieties of these and other flowers (widely available at retail nurseries). For more choices, try the mail-order company Van Dyke Zinnias @ Redbud Farms (517/851-8194 or www.redbudfarms.com), which sells mixes in single colors, such as rowdy reds or sultry salmons.

☐ **PERENNIALS.** Blooming perennials to plant now include brachyscome, campanula, columbine, coral bells, delphinium, geranium, kangaroo paw, lavender, limonium, penstemon, phygelius, salvia, Stokes aster, and yarrow.

☐ **SPRING ANNUALS.** Fill any empty spots in the garden with bedding plants. For a change of pace, try something out of the ordinary. *Echium* 'Blue Bedder', for example, grows 1 to 3 feet tall, with dense spikes of medium-blue flowers that appear over several months, and it often reseeds. We found it at M&M Nursery in Orange (714/538-8042); Burkard's Nursery in Pasadena (626/796-4255) also carries unusual plants.

☐ **SUMMER BULBS.** Plant acidanthera, agapanthus, tuberous begonia, caladium, calla lily, canna, crocosmia, daylily, gladiolus, tigridia, tuberose, watsonia, and, especially, dahlia. (For information on some exceptionally choice varieties, see the article on page 86.)

MAINTENANCE

☐ **CUT BACK FUCHSIAS.** Trim trailing varieties to the edge of their containers. Cut upright types back by two-thirds so that only two or three nodes (buds or leaf scars) remain on the stems. Then feed to spur new growth.

☐ **FERTILIZE MOST PLANTS.** As the weather warms, plants are raring to grow, but rain may have leached much of the nitrogen they need from the soil. Give all your hard-working permanent plants a boost with a little granulated fertilizer high in nitrogen. Annual and perennial flowers, all types of turf grass, container plants, houseplants, and citrus and avocado trees will welcome food now too. Wait until after bloom to feed camellias and azaleas, then give them an acid-type fertilizer such as cottonseed meal.

☐ **THIN FRUIT TREES.** Begin thinning apples, pears, and stone fruits when they are about ½ inch in size. Space them 4 to 6 inches apart or leave one fruit per spur.

PEST CONTROL

☐ **CONTROL APHIDS.** New growth attracts these sucking pests. Dislodge with a strong blast of water from a hose or strip from plants by hand. (Wear thin disposable rubber gloves if you're squeamish).

☐ **MANAGE SNAILS.** Look for them hiding under strap-leafed plants like agapanthus, phormium, and daylilies during daylight hours. Handpick and discard. Trap by allowing them to collect on the underside of a slightly elevated board, overturned grapefruit rinds, or lettuce leaves. Or set out commercial bait. Protect citrus trees by circling their trunks with copper bands. Vegetables or annuals in raised beds can be protected the same way. ◆

mountain · checklist

PLANTING

☐ **BARE-ROOT ROSES.** Remove packaging material and soak the rose in a bucket of water for as long as 24 hours. Dig a hole 2 feet deep and 2 feet wide. Plant the roots so the graft or bud union is 2 inches below the ground level. Mix a shovelful of compost into the backfill, refill the hole, then water. Mound soil over the canes to protect them from freezing. Later in the season, gradually remove the soil so that the canes are uncovered completely by the last frost date in your area.

☐ **COOL-SEASON VEGETABLES.** If you didn't prepare planting beds last fall, dig several inches of compost or well-rotted manure into the soil as soon as it is workable. Then sow seeds of beets, carrots, endive, kohlrabi, lettuce, onions, parsnips, peas, radishes, spinach, Swiss chard, and turnips.

☐ **LILY BULBS.** Asiatic hybrid lilies are hardy in cold-winter climates and are more tolerant of alkaline soil than other hybrid lilies. For a large selection of flower colors, try Van Bourgondien (800/622-9997 or www.dutchbulbs.com). Plant lilies in loose soil generously amended with compost, in a location that gets morning sun and afternoon shade.

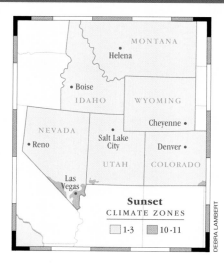

Sunset
CLIMATE ZONES

☐ 1-3   ☐ 10-11

DEBRA LAMBERT

☐ **STRAWBERRIES.** Cold-hardy varieties include everbearing 'Fort Laramie' and 'Ogallala', and June-bearing 'Guardian' and 'Honeoye'. Choose a site in full sun and amend the soil with all-purpose fertilizer and 4 inches of compost or well-rotted manure. Plant strawberries 1 foot apart in rows or in a block. Spread several inches of mulch (hay, pine needles, or straw) around plants. Keep the soil evenly moist. Cut off the first crop of flowers to encourage stronger roots, then allow fruit to develop thereafter.

☐ **WILDFLOWERS.** Scatter seeds of wildflowers directly into the garden where you want them to grow. Among the flowers that germinate best in cold, moist soil are annual coreopsis *(Coreopsis tinctoria)*, California desert bluebells *(Phacelia campanularia)*, lemon mint *(Monarda citriodora)*, mountain phlox *(Linanthus grandiflorus)*, Tahoka daisy *(Aster tanacetifolius)*, and Texas bluebonnet *(Lupinus*

texensis). Seeds of all these are available from Plants of the Southwest (800/788-7333 or www.plantsofthesouthwest.com).

MAINTENANCE

☐ **CARE FOR LAWNS.** If your lawn is covered with gray snow mold, rake it off. Dehydrated turf grass attracts winter mites; to control them, keep the grass well watered, especially along sidewalks.

☐ **GROOM GRASSES.** Trim ornamental grasses close to the ground before new growth starts. It helps to wrap an elastic cord around the whole clump and use a saw to cut the old stems below the cord.

☐ **GUARD AGAINST DAMPING OFF DISEASE.** Seedlings started indoors are especially susceptible to this fungal disease that causes young plants to suddenly wilt and die. There is no cure, but you can prevent the disease by using sterile potting soil. Place pots in a shallow container and let them wick water from the bottom up. Allow the soil surface to dry out slightly between waterings. — *M.T.* ◆

WHAT TO DO IN YOUR GARDEN IN MARCH

PLANTING

☐ **ANNUALS.** Zones 12–13: Set out warm-season flowers such as celosia, globe amaranth *(Gomphrena globosa)*, lisianthus, Madagascar periwinkle *(Catharanthus roseus)*, marigold, portulaca, and salvia.

☐ **GROUND COVERS.** Zones 12–13: Set out *Calylophus hartwegii*, dwarf periwinkle *(Vinca minor)*, Mexican evening primrose, trailing indigo bush *(Dalea greggii)*, and verbena.

☐ **PERENNIALS.** Zones 10–11: Plant aster, chrysanthemum, coreopsis, feverfew, hollyhock, maximilian sunflower *(Helianthus maximilianii)*, Shasta daisy, and statice. Zones 12–13: Set out blackfoot daisy *(Melampodium leucanthum)*, California fuchsia, lantana, penstemon, and salvia.

☐ **SHRUBS.** Zones 12–13: Plant frost-tender shrubs such as Baja fairy duster *(Calliandra californica)*, hibiscus, red bird of paradise *(Caesalpinia pulcherrima)*, ruellia, and yellow bells *(Tecoma stans)*.

☐ **SUMMER BULBS.** Zone 10: Set out gladiolus corms after all danger of frost is past and the soil warms to 65°. Zones 11–13: Plant amaryllis, caladium, canna, crinum, hymenocallis, and zephyranthes.

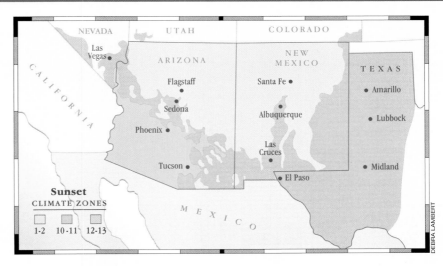

Sunset
CLIMATE ZONES

☐ 1-2 ☐ 10-11 ☐ 12-13

DEBRA LAMBERT

☐ **VEGETABLES.** Zones 1–3 (Flagstaff, Santa Fe): Start seeds of celery and onion indoors for transplanting in six to eight weeks. Plant garlic. Zone 10 (Albuquerque): Plant onion sets. Sow seeds of broccoli, cabbage, carrots, cauliflower, kohlrabi, lettuce, radishes, and spinach in prepared beds. Indoors, start seeds of eggplant, peppers, and tomatoes for transplanting outside in six to eight weeks. Zones 11–13 (Las Vegas, Tucson, Phoenix): Sow black-eyed peas, bush beans, cucumbers, lima beans, melons, okra, pumpkins, summer squash, and sweet corn. Set out basil, eggplant, and peppers.

☐ **VINES.** Zones 10–11: Plant Carolina jessamine, Lady Banks' rose, silver lace vine, trumpet creeper, and Virginia creeper. Zones 12–13: Plant any of the above, plus bougainvillea and coral vine.

MAINTENANCE

☐ **DIVIDE PERENNIALS.** Zones 10–13: Divide clumping perennials such as chrysanthemums and daylilies.

☐ **TEND PERENNIAL HERBS.** Zones 10–13: Cut back perennial herbs like mint and sage that look ratty, then fertilize and water.

☐ **WATER.** Zones 10–13: As days lengthen and get warmer, adjust irrigation schedules. Citrus and fruit trees need water every 10 to 14 days. ◆

home-grown herbs

These nine culinary herbs are indispensable for gardener-cooks. Here's how to grow and cook with them

By Lauren Bonar Swezey • Recipes by Linda Lau Anusasananan

Photographs by Thomas J. Story

■ Fresh herbs are simply the best flavorings for many foods and drinks. But there's nothing simple about the complex array of tastes they impart to dishes. "Fresh herbs open up the senses and invite one to cook in a looser, freer way," says Carolyn Dille, author of a book on cooking with herbs and the first chef at Chez Panisse Cafe in Berkeley. "The pleasure they bring to the garden and the kitchen is indispensable."

Dille, who gardens in Santa Cruz, says that dried herbs are no match for those that are freshly picked from the garden. "They're totally different creatures," she emphasizes. "Fresh herbs contain all of their complex volatile oils. Once the herbs have dried, some oils dissipate and flavors change."

Even herbs purchased fresh at the produce market have lost some of their essences by the time they're sold. "From a flavor perspective, it's a real plus to grow your own," says Dille.

Listed on the following pages are nine herbs that gardener-cooks won't want to be without.

parsley

lemon thyme

sage

Fettuccine with green herbs

PREP AND COOK TIME: About 20 minutes

MAKES: 2 or 3 servings

8	or 9 ounces **fresh fettuccine**
3	tablespoons **extra-virgin olive oil**
¼	cup thinly sliced **fresh chives**
2	tablespoons coarsely chopped **parsley**
2	tablespoons coarsely chopped **fresh oregano, basil, lemon verbena,** or **thyme** leaves (or a combination of two or three)
1	teaspoon grated **lemon** peel
2	tablespoons **lemon juice**
½	teaspoon freshly ground **pepper**
	Salt

1. In a 5- to 6-quart pan over high heat, bring 2 to 3 quarts water to a boil. Add fettuccine and boil, stirring occasionally to separate noodles, until barely tender to bite, 2 to 3 minutes.

2. Meanwhile, in a wide, shallow bowl, combine olive oil, chives, parsley, oregano, lemon peel, lemon juice, and pepper.

3. Drain pasta, reserving ⅓ cup cooking water. Pour hot pasta into bowl with herb mixture. Gently lift with two spoons to mix, adding salt to taste and as much of the reserved pasta cooking water to moisten as desired.

Per serving: 345 cal., 42% (144 cal.) from fat; 8.9 g protein; 16 g fat (2.3 g sat.); 43 g carbo (2 g fiber); 23 mg sodium; 55 mg chol.

FOOD STYLING: BASIL FRIEDMAN

9 essential herbs for a kitchen garden

■ **Basil** *(Ocimum basilicum)*. Sometimes referred to as the king of herbs (the name is derived from *basileus,* which is Greek for king), basil has fragrant, bright green leaves on 6-inch- to 2-foot-tall plants. Annual. All zones.

BEST CULINARY VARIETIES: 'Finissino Verde A Palla' bush basil, 'Italian Pesto', 'Lettuce Leaf', 'Mammoth Sweet', 'Mrs. Burns' Lemon Basil', 'Profuma di Genova', 'Red Rubin', 'Sweet Basil'.

GROWING TIP: Basil thrives when the soil is warm and nighttime temperatures are above 60°, so don't rush springtime planting. To encourage branching on young seedlings, cut back stems to just above the first set of leaves when plants have developed three pairs of leaves.

HARVEST TIP: Prune often to avoid flower formation. When a stem has developed four pairs of leaves, cut each stem down to just above the first set. Continue cutting plants back throughout the summer, or set out new seedlings in succession a month or so apart and harvest the entire plant for pesto.

USES: Eggs, fish, marinades, meats, pastas, pestos, salads, soups, stews, and tomatoes.

■ **Chives** *(Allium)*. Green, grasslike, 12- to 24-inch-long spears form in clumps. Clusters of rose purple or white flowers in spring. Perennial.

BEST CULINARY VARIETIES: Chives *(A. schoenoprasum);* all zones. Chinese or garlic chives *(A. tuberosum);* zones 1–24, H1–H2.

GROWING TIP: Increase the number of plants by dividing in winter every two years or so.

HARVEST TIP: Gather chives by snipping the spears to the ground (otherwise you'll have unsightly brown foliage mixed in with the green).

USES: Butters, cheeses, eggs, lamb, mayonnaise, potatoes, rice, salads, sauces, seafood, soups, sour cream, stews, and vegetables.

■ **Cilantro** *(Coriandrum sativum)*. Bright green leaves on foot-tall stems look similar to flat-leafed parsley. *Cilantro* refers to the leaves; the seeds are called coriander.

BEST CULINARY VARIETIES: Grow

How to grow herbs

The best place to grow herbs is near the kitchen, so you can easily duck outside to harvest them. If you don't have a convenient sunny spot in your garden, you can grow herbs in large containers and position them where the light is favorable.

Sun: For the best flavor and the most growth, herbs need six hours of full midday sun; four hours is minimum for adequate growth.

Soil: All of the herbs mentioned here grow best in slightly acidic soil (pH 6.3 to 6.8), but they'll also tolerate soil that's slightly alkaline. When growing them in the ground, provide loose, well-drained, moderately fertile soil. Dig in plenty of compost before planting. In containers, plant in a high-quality potting mix.

Air circulation: To help prevent disease, allow enough space between plants for good air circulation.

Fertilizer: For perennial herbs, mix an organic fertilizer (such as California Organics Fertilizer 7-5-7 available from Harmony Farm Supply & Nursery; 707/823-9125 or www.harmonyfarm.com) into the soil in early spring. For annual herbs, follow the guidelines above but also fertilize with fish emulsion every time you cut the plants back.

rosemary

sweet marjoram

oregano

types that are slow to bolt (go to seed), which are labeled as such or sold as a variety called 'Slow-Bolt'.

GROWING TIP: Cilantro grows best in cool weather. Plant in early spring after last frost (autumn in the low desert). If practical, start from seed; cilantro has a taproot and transplants poorly. Plant in succession every few weeks through summer. Once it goes to seed, the flavor changes.

HARVEST TIP: Cut off leaves as needed. Harvest the entire plant before it starts to flower.

USES: Beans, curries, fish, lamb, Mexican dishes, pork, poultry, salads, salsas, sauces, shellfish, and stir-fries.

■ **Oregano** *(Origanum).* Shrubby plant with 1½-inch-long leaves grows 2 to 3 feet tall. Perennial. Zones vary.

BEST CULINARY VARIETIES: Greek *(O. vulgare hirtum)* has gray green leaves; zones 8–9, 12–24. Italian *(O. x majoricum)* has milder bright green leaves; zones 4–24.

GROWING TIP: Needs especially good drainage. Plants thrive on little to moderate water.

HARVEST TIP: Oil is strongest when the plant is in bud but before flowers open. Cut back to 4 inches tall in late spring, summer, and fall.

USES: Beans, cheeses, eggs, meats, pastas, salsas, sauces, soups, stews, and vegetables.

■ **Parsley** *(Petroselinum).* Flat or curly green leaves grow in clumps. Flat-leafed types grow 2 to 3 feet tall, curly types to 1 foot. Biennial often grown as an annual. All zones.

BEST CULINARY VARIETIES: 'Giant Italian' is best for cooking; the curly type ('Extra Curled' or 'Green River') is good as a garnish.

Flavored vinegars

■ **Lemon Thyme Vinegar** (center, above). With a vegetable peeler, pare a thin spiral strip of peel 6 to 8 inches long from a **lemon.** With a chopstick or wooden skewer, push lemon peel and 6 rinsed sprigs (each 3 in. long) **fresh thyme** into a clean 12- to 16-ounce bottle. Fill bottle with **white wine vinegar** (vinegar should cover herbs completely) and seal. Store in a cool, dark place at least 1 week or up to 4 months.

VARIATIONS

■ **Lemon Verbena Vinegar** (left). Follow recipe for **Lemon Thyme Vinegar** (preceding), except replace the thyme with 2 or 3 sprigs (each 6 to 8 in. long) **lemon verbena;** omit peel, if desired.

■ **Purple Basil Vinegar** (right). Follow recipe for **Lemon Verbena Vinegar** (preceding), but replace verbena with 2 or 3 sprigs (each 4 to 6 in. long) **purple** or **opal basil.** Omit lemon peel.

This two-tiered container garden holds a selection of basic herbs. Trailers and fillers—chives, oregano (not shown), rosemary (which stays small in a pot), and thyme—tumble over the edges of the bottom pot (about 24 inches wide). Dwarf, purple, and sweet basils grow in the top pot (about 16 inches wide), with thyme filling in around the edges. To keep potted herbs healthy, fertilize and water them regularly.

How many plants?

Use this list as a guideline, adjusting the number to reflect your preferences. If you love to cook with basil, set out six plants to start with, then add more several weeks later to extend the harvest season.

- Basil, four to six plants
- Chives, three to four plants
- Cilantro, two to three plants
- Oregano, two plants
- Parsley, one to three plants
- Rosemary, one to two plants
- Sage, one to two plants
- Sweet marjoram, two to three plants
- Thyme, three to four plants

Mail-order sources

The herbs we list are available in well-stocked nurseries. But for large selections, order by mail from the following sources.
Mountain Valley Growers, 38325 Pepperweed Rd., Squaw Valley, CA 93675; www.mountainvalleygrowers.com or (559) 338-2775. Sells herb plants.
Nichols Garden Nursery, 1190 Old Salem Rd. NE, Albany, OR 97321; (800) 422-3985, (541) 928-9280, or www.nicholsgardennursery.com. Sells plants and seeds.
Renee's Garden, (888) 880-7228 or www.reneesgarden.com. Sells seeds.
Territorial Seed Company, Box 158, Cottage Grove, OR 97424; (541) 942-9547 or www.territorialseed.com. Sells plants and seeds.

Tips for buying herbs

To choose the right variety, use the sniff test

When you shop for herbs, keep in mind that within each group—oregano or rosemary, for instance—fragrances differ widely. Some oreganos are mild, almost scentless, and not great for cooking, while others are pungent and flavorful. Rosemaries, on the other hand, can be strong and piney or have a sweet, gingery taste.

Since flavor preferences vary, the best way to know if the aroma of a certain herb appeals to you is to give the plant a touch and sniff test. When shopping at the nursery, gently run your fingers over the foliage (don't hurt the plant), then sniff them. If you like the fragrance, buy the plant.

Keep in mind that plantings are never permanent. If you don't like the flavor of a certain herb after growing it and cooking with it, you can always remove the plant and try another variety.

Buying herbs by mail is another matter; there's no opportunity to sniff the foliage before the plant arrives on your doorstep. The varieties listed under "9 essential herbs," our favorites, can help you get started.

GROWING TIP: Start new plants each year. In mild-winter climates, plant in fall or early spring (provide partial shade in hot climates); in cold climates, plant in spring after last frost.

HARVEST TIP: Pick outside leaves so the center of the plant continues to develop new ones.

USES: Bouquets garnis, cheese sauces, pestos, soups, stews, stuffings, vegetables, and as a garnish.

■ **Rosemary** *(Rosmarinus)*. Short, narrow green leaves with grayish white undersides grow on woody stems ranging from 1 to 6 feet tall. Perennial in zones 4–24, H1–H2.

BEST CULINARY VARIETIES: Some of the best varieties for cooking are 'Blue Spires', 'Gorizia', and 'Tuscan Blue'. Avoid rosemary plants with strong pine or turpentine undertones. 'Arp' is hardy to –10°.

GROWING TIP: These are tough plants that take wind and salt spray, or inland heat if given moderate water. Too much fertilizer and water produce rank growth and woodiness.

HARVEST TIP: Prune regularly to encourage new growth.

USES: Beef, breads, cheeses, dressings, eggs, lamb, legumes, marinades, oils, potatoes, poultry, roasted game, seafood, soups, stews, stuffings, and vegetables.

■ **Sage** *(Salvia officinalis)*. Shrubby plant from 1 to 3 feet tall with 2- to 3-inch-long leaves. Perennial. Zones 2–24, H1–H2.

BEST CULINARY VARIETIES: 'Berggarten' produces few or no flowers and is considered the best culinary type by herb professionals. For a milder flavor, grow *S. officinalis*, *S. o.* 'Icterina', or *S. o.* 'Purpurascens'.

GROWING TIP: Keep plant on the dry side once established. Avoid planting near a lawn where the soil stays wet. Give afternoon shade in hot climates.

HARVEST TIP: Cut just above where new growth emerges; don't cut into old, woody growth.

chives

cilantro

basil

FROM GARDEN TO KITCHEN

FOOD STYLING: BASIL FRIEDMAN

Herb cheese log

On a 12- by 15-inch piece of plastic wrap, mix 1 tablespoon *each* minced **fresh chives, fresh cilantro,** and **fresh basil** leaves. Roll a 5½- to 6-ounce log of **fresh chèvre (goat) cheese** in herb mixture to coat evenly. Set on a small rimmed plate or serving dish and drizzle with 2 tablespoons **extra-virgin olive oil.** Serve with **baguette** slices.

USES: Apples, beans, breads, butters, cheeses, chowders, fish stock, game stuffings, gravies, lamb, marinades, pork, poultry, soups, stews, and tomatoes.

■ **Sweet marjoram** *(Origanum majorana)*. Oval gray green leaves on 1- to 2-foot-tall plants. Milder and more floral than oregano. Perennial in zones 8–24; annual elsewhere.

GROWING TIP: Same as for oregano.

HARVEST TIP: Same as for oregano.

USES: Cheeses, eggs, fish, gravies, meats, pastas, poultry, rice, sauces, soups, stews, and vegetables.

■ **Thyme** *(Thymus)*. Small, pungent leaves grow on stems up to 1 foot tall. White to lilac flowers appear in late spring to early summer. Perennial. Zones 1–24.

BEST CULINARY VARIETIES: English or common *(T. vulgaris)*, French *(T. vulgaris* variety), golden lemon *(T. x citriodorus* 'Aureus'), and lemon *(T. x citriodorus)*.

GROWING TIP: Use as a low edging for vegetable or herb gardens.

HARVEST TIP: For best flavor, cut back before flowers appear. Hold foliage like a ponytail and shear it to about 6 inches tall.

USES: Bouquets garnis, breads, casseroles, cheeses, eggs, fish, grains, marinades, meats, mushrooms, poultry, soups, stews, tomato-based sauces, and vegetables. ◆

dahlias
for every garden

By Lauren Bonar Swezey • Photographs by Christina Schmidhofer

■ Who can resist a pretty face like 'Sweet Lorraine' or the intriguing form of 'Anna Marie'? For that matter, who won't be seduced by any of the hundreds of magnificent dahlia blossoms that splash across the pages of catalogs and captivate us at garden shows and nurseries this month? The truth is, few gardeners can say no to dahlias: When you see them in bloom, you'll want to grow them. Perhaps that's why the dahlia is the city flower of both San Francisco and Seattle. • "Dahlias have never been as beautiful as they are today," says Erik Juul, award-winning dahlia hybridizer who, along with his wife, Gerda, grows hundreds of tubers in their San Francisco garden and at Golden Gate Park Dahlia Dell. "There are more colors, shapes, and sizes, and more people developing new dahlias than ever." • From the mammoth Cactus to the elegant Waterlily to the diminutive Pompon, there's a dahlia size that will appeal to almost any taste and style of garden. And the color range? You'll find every shade in the rainbow except blue, including gorgeous blends of two or more colors. • In the garden, dahlias are surprisingly easy to grow—and will brighten up beds and borders with brilliant blooms from summer through fall.

A bloom of 'Wildwood Marie' (at left). Four-inch-wide blossoms of 'Ted's Choice' grow on 4-foot-tall stalks; a sturdy metal obelisk supports the plant.

Shapely blooms, rich colors

Waterlily
'Alena Rose'

Formal Decorative
'Duet'

Cactus
'River Road'

Pompon
'Chick A Dee'

Informal Decorative
'Chilson's Pride'

Collarette
'Evan Matthew'

Fimbriated or Laciniated
'Show 'N' Tell'

Growers' favorites

To keep track of the thousands of varieties available today, the American Dahlia Society classifies the flowers according to color, flower size, and form. The largest blooms (classed as AA) can reach 14 inches or more across, while the smallest ones (Pompon and Mignon Single) bear flowers as small as 2 inches across.

The shape of the petals (called ray florets) determines the flower formation. Here we list dahlia flower forms, along with the favorite varieties of three Western dahlia specialists—Erik and Gerda Juul, Jennifer Eubank of Swan Island Dahlias, and Kim Connell of Connell's Dahlias—and their comments about them.

■ FORMAL DECORATIVE: Flat petals are uniform and arranged like shingles on a roof. 'Almond Joy' (lavender and white blend); good, strong stems. 'Canby Centennial' (deep rose red); named in honor of the 100th birthday of Canby, Oregon; 'Vernon Rose' (variegated pink and dark red); "everybody's favorite."

■ INFORMAL DECORATIVE: Petals are twisted, curled, or wavy, and their arrangement is irregular. 'Dana' (bright orange red with a bright yellow center); "very showy in the garden." 'Gitts Perfection' (delicate pink blending to white); "absolutely gorgeous show winner." 'San Francisco Sunrise' (very bright orange); outstanding color, good for cutting.

■ SEMICACTUS: Petals are broad at the base and rolled for up to half their length. 'Camano Regal' (purple); "exceptional flower." 'Dare Devil' (bright red); excellent cut flower. 'Kenora Sunset' (red and yellow blend); "very popular color," good for cutting.

■ CACTUS: Petals are rolled for more than half their length, straight or slightly curved downward; they radiate in all directions from the center. 'Glenbank Twinkle' (white and purple); "striking in the garden." 'Ruskin Marigold' (orange); "new, good in every way."

■ INCURVED CACTUS: Petals are rolled for more than half their length and curved upward. 'Bird's Nest' (pink); "swirls like a Ferris wheel—very interesting." 'Lilac Mist' (white blending to lavender); excellent in the garden and as a cut flower.

■ FIMBRIATED OR LACINIATED: Petals are split on the ends, giving the flower a fringed look. 'Al Almand' (orange); striking color. 'Fidalgo Climax' (clear yellow); "unusual shaggy look." 'Nenekazi' (red and pink blend); "beautiful color." 'Show 'N' Tell' (red tipped with yellow); "very showy like its name."

■ BALL: The fully double flowers are

Dahlia cutting tips

- Medium to small dahlias make the best cut flowers for arrangements. Avoid single-petaled dahlias, which tend to drop their petals. Large dahlias can be floated in a glass bowl.
- Cut flowers early in the morning or in the evening.
- Place stems in warm water (100°) for ½ hour, then place in cold water.
- Display in a cool location to extend vase life (about a week).
- Change vase water daily.

'Lemon Candy' and 'River Road' make a stunning bouquet. To plant (at right): Dig a 4- to 6-inch-deep hole; lay the tuber with growth buds facing up.

ball shaped and more than 3½ inches wide. 'Jessie G' (dark red); lots of blooms, great color, good for cutting. 'Kenora Fireball' (silvery red); striking color, good form. 'L'Ancresse' (white); excellent cut flower. 'Robin Hood' (orange and pink blend); unusual color combination.

■ MINIATURE BALL: It is like Ball but smaller, between 2 and 3½ inches wide. 'Downham Royal' (dark purple); "beautiful color." 'Robann Royal' (lavender); a popular variety.

■ POMPON: Also similar to Ball, but blooms are less than 2 inches in diameter. 'Poppet' (orange); beautiful color, good in the garden. 'Yellow Baby' (yellow); a favorite for arranging.

■ WATERLILY: Fully double blooms look like saucers from the side. The

What dahlias need

Plant after last frost.
SOIL: Well drained; mix in compost before planting.
EXPOSURE: Full sun.
WATERING: Start when growth is 6 to 12 inches tall. Thereafter, keep the soil moist.
FERTILIZER: Mix low-nitrogen fertilizer into the soil at planting time.

center should be closed. 'Juul's Lotus' (white blushed with lavender); "beautiful in bouquets." 'Snowflake' (pure white); one of the best whites for cut flowers. 'Wildwood Marie' (pink with yellow center); "beautiful colors."

■ PEONY: Open-centered flowers have two or more rows of petals surrounding a disc. 'Longwood Dainty' (orange); "a winner." 'Powder Gull' (pink); "a winning flower." 'Tasagore' (dark red); very striking green-black foliage.

■ ANEMONE: One or more rows of single petals surround a pincushion-like dome. 'Alpen Pearl' (lavender, yellow, and white blend); "stands out in the

garden and at shows." 'Goldie Gull' (yellow and pink); "another winner."

■ COLLARETTE: A single row of evenly spaced petals are a backdrop to smaller disc flowers emerging from the center. 'Alpen Cherub' (pure white with yellow in center); strong stems, prolific bloomer. 'Astrid Siersen' (purple and white); "a favorite with the public." 'Cher Ami' (red and yellow); small, "perfect bloom."

■ SINGLE: A single row of petals surround the center disc. 'Bashful' (deep purple with lavender tips); "it glows." 'Joshua Juul' (white, orange, purple blend); "very unusual color combination." 'Juul's Cosmos' (lavender); "unique color for a single—looks like a cosmos flower."

■ MIGNON SINGLE: Similar to Single, but it is under 2 inches in diameter. 'Matthew Juul' (orange and dark red blend) and 'Rembrandt' (dark red); "both are good for small gardens—as border plants or in pots."

■ ORCHID: Blossoms have a single row of tubelike petals. 'Juul's All-Star' (dark red), 'Juul's Star' (white), and 'Marie Schnugg' (red); "all have excellent form and color and are good for arranging."

■ NOVELTY: This is a dahlia that doesn't fit in any other class. 'Alloway Candy' (pink); a beautiful cut flower.

Dahlias by mail

Shop for tubers at nurseries or order from one of the sources below. For other sources and care tips, visit www.sunset.com.

Connell's Dahlias, 10616 Waller Rd. E, Tacoma, WA 98446; (253) 531-0292 or www.connells-dahlias.com.

Dan's Dahlias, 994 S. Bank Rd., Oakville, WA 98568; (360) 482-2406 or www.dansdahlias.com.

Elkhorn Gardens, Box 1149, Carmel, CA 93921; (831) 761-2280 or www.elkhorngardens.com.

Swan Island Dahlias, Box 700, Canby, OR 97013; (800) 410-6540 or www.dahlias.com. ◆

Urban renewal

Updating a garden takes vision and strategy

By Sharon Cohoon
Photographs by Bob Wigand

Imagine you're in the midst of landscaping that was pretty groovy when it was first installed in the '70s. The focal point is a Jacuzzi large enough to hold at least 14 people; everything else is woodsy and green. In the era when a hot dip after dinner was de rigueur, tubs like this were cool and perfect for parties.

But it's a new millennium now, and you'd rather sit outdoors and read than soak. Some of those sheltering trees have grown so much that they're starting to feel smothering. And you've seen enough green for a lifetime, thanks; you long for colorful flowers.

That's the situation Carol Brewer and her husband, Mike, faced three years ago. Though they loved their location in El Cajon, California, and had no desire to move, their landscaping lagged behind the changes they'd made in their lifestyle. They needed to move their yard from then to now, without breaking the bank. Their threefold strategy was to bite the bullet and get rid of the

solving the five toughest problems

#1: The Jacuzzi. It took four hours to heat and almost as long to clean.
SOLUTION: Get rid of it. Fill it in.

#2: Overgrown trees.
SOLUTION: Remove ones that crowd and darken the house.

#3: The stone-faced retaining wall that held their sloped backyard in place.
SOLUTION: Live with it. Carve a new series of terraces into the slope for easy planting. For continuity, edge them with more stones, unearthed from the property or recycled from nearby construction projects.

#4: No real structure to the garden.
SOLUTION: Add a picket fence to enclose the property and an elegant pergola at the top of the slope. Put up arbors and trellises; use boulders as foils for roses. Display flower-filled containers throughout the garden.

#5: Not enough color.
SOLUTION: Roses make great mainstays by providing color most of the year in mild climates. Plant them throughout the garden with annuals and perennials in complementary colors. Create color rooms: Put pastels in one place, bright primary colors elsewhere, and whites in another area.

TOP: White lantana billows beneath twin canopies of 'Iceberg' tree roses. White-flowered mound above the rose on the right is potato vine, which covers a gazebo. Red rose on the distant picket fence is 'Altissimo'; pink clump in front is a 'Dubonnet' regal pelargonium. ABOVE: Carol Brewer

ABOVE: Backyard roses include bright red 'Knock Out' (foreground), 'Red Simplicity', and white 'Sally Holmes'. TOP RIGHT: Potted plants encircle a pond. BELOW: In the front yard, 'Sun Flare' rose blends with lime-flowered 'Jade Dragon' euphorbia.

RENOVATION TIPS

1. Seek good advice, even if you don't follow all of it. Though the Brewers decided not to incur the cost of either a landscaping installation or a detailed landscaping plan, they had two professionals—Del Mar landscape designer Linda Chisari and El Cajon garden designer Chris Wotruba—look at their site and offer informal suggestions for a nominal fee.

2. Make the acquaintance of more experienced gardeners. Carol is an active member of four gardening clubs and has friends in additional clubs. "Some of the best ideas in this garden have come from club members," she says.

3. Read everything you can get your hands on, but take it all with a grain of salt. Some plants reported to do well in her climate limped along, says Carol, and some things that shouldn't have been happy thrived. In the end, she says, accept that you're always flying by the seat of your pants.

most egregious mistakes. Then, live with as much of the rest as possible. Finally, camouflage what they'd like to change but can't yet afford to.

Following this strategy, Carol created this showplace in a mere three years. She did much of the work herself, which saved money and, in the process, yielded the project's greatest reward—satisfaction. ◆

Daphne cneorum 'Ruby Glow'

Daphne x burkwoodii 'Carol Mackie'

Daphnes perfume the garden

By Steven R. Lorton

This month, daphnes start to perfume Western gardens. Here, we describe four kinds prized for their fragrant flowers. In mild-winter areas, shop nurseries for these shrubs now. In cold-winter areas, order daphnes for spring planting; two excellent mail-order sources are Forestfarm (541/846-7269 or www.forestfarm.com) and Greer Gardens (800/548-0111 or www.greergardens.com).

Once established, daphnes tend to grow steadily and evenly, so no major pruning is needed. A snip here or there is usually all you need to keep errant branches under control. Do this while the plant is in bloom, so you can take the cut stems indoors. (Note: All parts of the plant are poisonous if ingested.) ◆

Winter-blooming kinds

February daphne *(D. mezereum).* Deciduous. Sweetly scented, reddish purple flower clusters are borne along naked branches from February to April. This somewhat gawky shrub grows 4 feet tall and 3 feet wide. Plant it in front of fine-textured evergreens or tuck one among broad-leafed evergreens. Full sun or light shade. One of the hardiest daphnes, to –20°. *Sunset* climate zones 2–7, 14–17.

Winter daphne *(D. odora).* Evergreen. Intensely fragrant flowers, pink to rose outside with creamy pink throats, appear in February and March. The species has glossy green leaves to 3 inches long. 'Aureo-marginata' has yellow-edged leaves. Noted for its neat growth habit, the shrub reaches about 4 feet tall (sometimes 8 or 10 feet) and 6 feet wide.

Despite its reputation for being hard to grow, including a tendency to die suddenly for no apparent reason, this plant is widely grown. You can improve the odds by planting in porous, well-drained soil in a spot where it will get at least three hours of shade each day and no strong afternoon sun. Also avoid transplanting or otherwise disturbing the roots. If you have heavy garden soil, try growing it in a container or raised bed filled with organic soil mix. Zones 4–10, 12, 14–24.

Spring bloomers

D. x burkwoodii. Evergreen to semievergreen to deciduous, depending on the severity of winter cold. Small clusters of strongly fragrant flowers (white fading to pink) appear in late spring and again in late summer. It has rich green leaves and grows 3 or 4 feet tall and wide. The variety 'Carol Mackie' has gold-edged leaves and reaches 4 feet tall and 6 feet wide. Full sun or light shade. Hardy to –20°. Zones 2B–6, 14–17.

Garland or rose daphne *(D. cneorum).* Evergreen. Clusters of fragrant, rosy pink flowers appear in April and May. The species has dark green leaves, as does the variety 'Ruby Glow' (deep pink flowers); 'Variegata' has gold-edged leaves. Forming a mat less than 1 foot tall and 3 feet wide, this plant is well suited to containers or rock gardens. The variety 'Pygmaea Alba' (white flowers) grows only 3 inches tall and 1 foot wide. Full sun in cool-summer areas; light shade in warm areas. Hardy to –20°. Zones 2B–9, 14–17.

Half-dollar-size lewisia flowers, which come in sherbet colors like those shown left and right, are combined in a big pot by Seattle gardener Dave Peterson.

BURL MOSTUL, ANDREW DRAKE (2)

Lovely lewisias

Montana's state flower and its cousins are among the West's favorite natives

By Jim McCausland

In August 1805, one of the Lewis and Clark expedition's hunters surprised a band of Native Americans along the Missouri River. The startled group ran away, leaving behind a few roots they were about to eat. So the hunter took the roots back to Meriwether Lewis, who tasted them and pronounced them "bitter and naucious to the pallatte." (French trappers had named them well: *racine amère,* or bitter root). Eleven months later, though, when Lewis saw the plant in glorious bloom in the Bitterroot Mountains, he noted it in his acquisitions journal as a "singular plant." He gave a plant to German botanist Frederick Traugott Pursh, who renamed it *Lewisia rediviva,* after Lewis. The plant is now the state flower of Montana.

Among the toughest and most delicately beautiful Western wildflowers, lewisias are drought tolerant to a fault. (Fleshy, water-holding roots in *L. rediviva* are key to their drought

tolerance: On a mature plant, the main root can be thicker than your thumb.) You can easily kill *L. rediviva* and *L. cotyledon* by giving them summer water, but if you plant them in fast-draining soil or in pots, they can keep flowering for years.

Where to begin

All lewisias are native to parts of the West. If you've never grown them, plant a small colony of *L. cotyledon,* native to California and Oregon, which bears flowers in white, pink, red, yellow, and orange several times (if you pinch off faded blooms) between spring and fall.

If you're willing to sacrifice repeat bloom for more sensational flowers once (in late spring), try *L. tweedyi,* native to south-central Washington, whose starlike cream- to peach-colored blooms are 2 inches across. Especially intolerant of summer water, this one is almost immortal when planted in a chink in a rock wall.

Plant either *L. cotyledon* or *L. tweedyi* in fast-draining soil in an east-facing location. Morning sun is perfect (the plants will burn in hot south- or west-facing spots). To get essential drainage if you don't have a rock wall, plant in a mixture of two parts sand or gravel to one part potting mix. Or use a commercial cactus mix.

Throughout most of the high-mountain West, lewisias, once established, will usually survive on rainfall alone. In hot-summer lowlands, water plants in the ground once every two or three weeks in spring and fall, and monthly during June, July, and August. Protect container-grown plants from hot sun in summer; water them rarely. Avoid overhead watering.

Sources

Look for lewisia plants this month at retail nurseries or order by mail from Siskiyou Rare Plant Nursery (541/772-6846) and Rare Plant Research (www. theamateursdigest.com/rareplnt.htm). ◆

THE "MARATHON PERENNIALS" featured on pages 110–116 flower for months at a time, combining the staying power of annuals with the long-range reliability of perennials.

April

stop and smell the lilacs

■ Every spring, hundreds of fragrant lilacs bloom in the Hulda Klager Lilac Garden. Born in Germany in 1863, Klager moved with her family to a farmstead in Woodland, Washington, in the 1870s. She began hybridizing lilacs in 1905; 15 years later, she invited guests to see her creations in bloom. Today Klager's tradition of hospitality continues during Lilac Days, usually from mid-April through mid-May.

You can tour Klager's residence, now a museum filled with period furnishings. Stroll the 4½-acre garden, where grass paths lead you through groves of mature lilacs, their scented blossoms drooping overhead. A new wheelchair-accessible plaza behind the farmhouse affords a sweeping view of the grounds. You also can choose from more than 70 lilac varieties for sale, including many developed by Klager herself, such as intensely fragrant, purple-flowered 'Frank Klager' (named for her husband) and magenta 'Fritz Klager' (named for her son).

10–4 daily; $2. The garden is a half-hour drive north of Portland via Interstate 5. From I-5 take exit 21 and follow Goerig Rd. south until it becomes Davidson St. Go several blocks to S. Pekin Rd. and turn left to the Hulda Klager Lilac Garden at 115 S. Pekin Rd. For more information, call (360) 225-8996 or go to www.lilacgardens.com. — Mary-Kate Mackey

Seattle's classic rock gardens

■ This month, Seattle's Queen Anne Hill bursts into bloom. The springtime spectacle originated in the late 19th century when this steep south-facing slope was transformed into a fashionable neighborhood. After lots were leveled, grand houses were built atop retaining walls made from chunks of basalt.

Gardeners packed soil between the rocks and planted perennials that would spread and fill in the gaps. They chose hardy spring-blooming plants that would tolerate summer sun and drought and be easy to maintain. Five plants in particular were favored: common aubrieta *(A. deltoidea)*, pictured at left in full bloom; basket-of-gold *(Aurinia saxatilis)*, with brilliant yellow blooms and silvery leaves; coral bells *(Heuchera sanguinea)*, with airy coral red blossoms over scalloped leaves; evergreen candytuft *(Iberis sempervirens)*, with white flower clusters over shiny dark green foliage; and *Saxifraga umbrosa*, with clusters of tiny pink flowers over shiny green leaves. A century later, specimens of these plants still grace gardens here.

To view the rock gardens, drive north on Queen Anne Avenue North. Turn left on West Prospect Street; park and walk, zigzagging east and west on the streets that run horizontally along the hill.

— *Steven R. Lorton*

PAUL BOUSQUET

Jack-in-the-pulpit from Japan

■ Jack-in-the-pulpit *(Arisaema)* has long ranked high on the list of woodland wonders that thrive in Northwest gardens. Now *A. sikokianum*, a species from Japan, is gaining in popularity. And no wonder: The exotic-looking blooms suggest art nouveau versions of calla lilies. Each flower is composed of a sinuous purplish brown spathe poised like a cobra's hood over a pure white spadix with a rounded tip. Standing 20 inches tall, the plant bears handsome 6-inch leaflets.

Look for specimens in 1-gallon containers at nurseries this month. Or order tubers from mail-order specialists for fall planting; one source is Naylor Creek Nursery in Chimacum, Washington (360/732-4983 or www.naylorcreek.com). Plant in loose, rich, moist, acid soil. — *S.R.L.*

ANDREW DRAKE

- **Oregon-grown seed.** Silver Falls Seed Company has been producing seeds at Silverton, Oregon, for nearly 60 years. This family-run business, which grows most of the seed it sells, has been a wholesale supplier, but recently it began retailing flower and grass seed. Its catalog includes annual flowers, wildflower mixes, and lawn and pasture grasses. You can view the catalog at www.silverfallsseed.com or send $3 for a 48-page paper copy to Silver Falls Seed Company, Box 885, Silverton, OR 97381.

- **Head start for corn.** Most gardeners sow corn directly in the ground. But trials at Washington State University show that in a cooler climate like the Puget Sound, you can harvest three weeks earlier if you start with transplants. At WSU's Mt. Vernon Research and Extension Center in western Washington, Wilbur C. Anderson conducted trials with 'Krispy King', 'Super Sweet Jubilee', and 'Sheba' cultivars, planting seeds and transplants on the same day. The transplants yielded ripe corn three weeks earlier than plants sown directly in the ground. Buy seedlings at nurseries or sow your own in a cold-frame or greenhouse about three weeks before planting time (mid-May in most places west of the Cascades). — *Jim McCausland*

garden guide

concrete creations in Denver

■ Carlo Amato of Denver has been turning out ornamental garden decor since 1922, when the company was founded by Carlo Amato Sr., an immigrant from Italy. His grandson Carlo Amato now operates the business, which continues to craft high-quality decorative concrete pieces on the premises near the heart of downtown Denver.

Each spring, Amato's outdoor showroom comes alive with the splashing music of dozens of fountains and bursts of color from flower-filled urns and planters. Amato's inventory includes large birdbaths, statues, and surprisingly comfortable concrete benches and chairs. Prices range from $25 for a life-size rabbit sculpture to $9,800 for a multitiered fountain. Amato's offers delivery service and installs fountains and other sizable objects.

9–5 Mon–Sat, 10:30–4 Sun. 16th and Central Streets; (303) 433-1893. — Colleen Smith

---

Like celery? You'll love lovage

AMY HINMAN

■ One of my favorite culinary herbs is lovage *(Levisticum officinale).* This Mediterranean native grows luxuriantly in my Montana garden, with a single clump reaching 6 feet tall and over 2 feet wide. If you like celery as much as I do, you'll relish the intense flavor of lovage leaves and the stringless stalks.

In my kitchen, I use lovage all year in various ways. In the spring, I harvest tender young stems and blanch them with fresh asparagus shoots. In summer, I chop fresh leaves to season soups or to sprinkle over salad. Later in the season, when the flat-topped flower clusters form oblong seeds, I collect them to use like celery seed. For my winter cooking, I hang bunches of leaves to dry, then crumble and store them.

To get started, sow seeds indoors eight weeks before the last frost date in your area. Seeds are available from Territorial Seed Company (541/942-9547 or www.territorialseed.com). Or order plants from Full Circle Herb Farm (406/257-8133); set them out in late May or early June, protecting them from late freezes.

This herb does best in full sun. It prefers fertile soil and needs regular water. In my garden, lovage dies back to the ground in early winter; it sprouts anew each spring. — *Amy Hinman*

---

ice plant lives up to its name

■ Few perennial ground covers are as tough as ice plant (*Delosperma* species). This group of succulents from South Africa is extremely adaptable, according to Panayoti Kelaidis, curator of plant collections at Denver Botanic Gardens. Indeed, they tolerate extreme cold and heat, poor soil, and irregular irrigation. Despite this cast-iron demeanor, they bear delicate-looking flowers in brilliant carnival colors.

Over the last decade, yellow *D. nubigenum* has proven to be one of the best ice plants for intermountain gardens. This species reliably survives winters in *Sunset* climate zones 2A through 3B. In late spring, 1- to 1½- inch-wide daisies cover this ice plant. Its evergreen foliage forms a 2-inch-tall mat that's thick enough to keep out weeds.

In recent trial plantings in Denver, Kelaidis has found more than 30 new species of *Delosperma* that are winter hardy in zone 2B. This year, two varieties are being introduced through the Plant Select program cosponsored by Colorado State University and Denver Botanic Gardens. Salmon pink–flowered *D.* 'Kelaidis' (sold as Mesa Verde) and fuchsia-flowered *D.* 'John Proffitt' (sold as Table Mountain; shown below) are compact, long-blooming varieties.

— *Marcia Tatroe*

COURTESY OF COLORADO STATE UNIVERSITY

JAMES BOONE

hanging petunias at Elitch Gardens

■ When Elitch Gardens, Denver's venerable amusement park, moved from its old wooded home and relocated near downtown in 1995, the new site initially resembled a concrete wasteland. Creating a garden ambiance in the park, now known as Six Flags Elitch Gardens, presented a challenge for horticulturists like Shelley Cash. One solution she found is the Flower Pouch, a flexible plastic planter that adds instant color in otherwise unplantable vertical spaces.

Here's how it works. First, fill the pouch with a lightweight organic medium like moistened coconut pith fiber (a potting medium often sold in compressed bricks that expand in water). Next, tuck the rootballs of sixpack-size bedding plants through precut slits. Let the pouch rest on a flat surface for a week as the plants take root, then hang on a fence, wall, or porch railing.

The pouches shown here hold trailing petunias called Supertunias; impatiens, lobelia, and even strawberries also grow well in them. Like most containers, the pouches require vigilant watering: at least once a day in hot weather, possibly twice if they're hung against a brick wall in full sun. The flowers perform best if fed every other week with liquid fertilizer. Garden centers and mail-order nurseries sell the Flower Pouch and similar products under different names in various sizes. Thompson & Morgan (800/274-7333 or www.thompsonmorgan.com) sells one pack that includes three pouches for $10. — C.S.

Plum-colored 'Star of India' mingles with pink roses against an arbor. LEFT: *Clematis viticella* 'Venosa Violacea' with star jasmine and roses.

Clematis in mild climates?

Just follow these four tips from an expert

■ Contrary to popular belief, clematis do just fine in Southern California. Even the large-flowered hybrids—like plum-colored 'Star of India' (which shares arbor space with pink climbing roses in the photo above right), lavender pink 'Madame Baron Veillard', and carmine 'Ville de Lyon'—thrive in our mildest coastal climates (*Sunset* climate zone 24). That's the message Edith Malek, the "Clematis Queen," has been preaching since 1996, the year she founded what became the American Clematis Society. Her own garden in Irvine, where she pairs clematis with other plants in beautiful ways (two examples are pictured), is a splendid advertisement for her cause.

Forget the intimidating "head in the sun, feet in the shade" business, says Malek (one of her clematis thrives under a clothes dryer vent). Instead, follow the Queen's commands.

- **Invest in a well-established plant.** A 2-gallon plant is acceptable, says Malek, but a 5-gallon specimen is preferable. Choose a named variety recommended for this climate, such as 'Ernest Markham' or 'Lady Betty Balfour'.
- **Buy from a knowledgeable nursery.** Malek's favorites include M&M Nursery in Orange (714/538-8042), that will carry nearly 90 varieties this spring, and, for mail-ordering, Forestfarm (541/846-7269; www.forestfarm.com).
- **Dig a substantial planting hole—**24 inches deep by 24 inches wide. Mix the soil with generous quantities of soil amendments—up to half if you have heavy clay.
- **Plant deep.** Set the top of the rootball 3 to 5 inches beneath soil level.

For more advice, see Malek's book, *A Guide to Growing Clematis.* Visit www.clematis.org or send a check for $26.44 to Box 17085, Irvine, CA 92623. — *Sharon Coboon*

an arroyo runs right through it

■ Liz and Bob Gett's contemporary home in Scottsdale, Arizona, was designed by Phoenix architectural designer Bob Bacon to span an arroyo, which bisects their 1½-acre lot. Since the dry wash was to be a focal point, the couple asked Scottsdale landscape architect Pamela Graf to augment the indigenous plants on its banks for a lush but natural look.

Graf first tucked stones into the banks of the arroyo to stabilize the sides during occasional runoffs from nearby Pinnacle Peak. Working with a background of naturally occurring brittlebush *(Encelia farinosa)*, creosote bush *(Larrea tridentata)*, and bur-sage *(Ambrosia deltoidea)*, Graf laced the banks with other desert natives planted from 1- and 5-gallon containers. She chose autumn sage *(Salvia greggii)*, chuparosa *(Justicia californica)*, desert milkweed *(Asclepias subulata)*, tufted or white evening primrose *(Oenothera caespitosa)*, prickly pear cactus, and buckhorn cholla. Graf also planted several trees, including desert willow *(Chilopsis linearis)* and desert ironwood *(Olneya tesota)*.

The showiest plant is globemallow *(Sphaeralcea ambigua)*. Graf had a random mix of colors planted; in March and April these prolific native perennials produce cup-shaped blooms ranging from white and pale pink to coral, yellow, and lavender.

A drip-irrigation system was installed along the wash to help plants get established and to provide water during periods of drought. The owners added lighting to accent the landscape at night. — *Nora Burba Trullson*

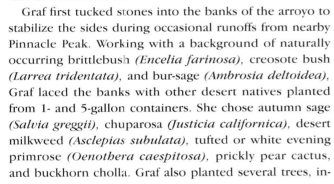

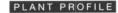

PLANT PROFILE

a torchy bougainvillea

■ 'Torch Glow', a variety of bougainvillea introduced by Monrovia, performs *almost* as promised in the Hirsches' garden in Phoenix. The flowerlike bracts certainly live up to the company's description: "beautiful torchlike reddish pink blooms atop upright branches." The plant's habit is just as advertised too: 'Torch Glow' grows upright naturally on sturdy, woody stems that need no support. This habit makes the plant useful for screening, which is how landscape architect Greg Trutza of New Directions used it here. He placed plants 8 feet apart and encouraged them to intertwine for a hedgelike effect. The bougainvillea hides the pool area behind the fence from the central patio shown in the photo.

However, at least in the Hirsches' garden, 'Torch Glow' has not proved to be a "moderate grower to 6 feet tall." In fact, it is twice that tall. But the homeowners, who love the bougainvillea's slightly overgrown appearance, don't mind the extra height at all.

— *S.C.*

STEVEN GUNTHER

bountiful raised beds in Las Vegas

■ As a Master Gardener in Las Vegas, Christina Cesaretti is well aware of the many problems posed by the poor native soil in this part of Clark County, Nevada. So when she and her husband, Luke, were landscaping their new house, they decided to overcome those problems by growing all of their vegetables and herbs in raised beds filled with an organically enriched soil mixture. The resulting design won a Southern Nevada Water Authority award for aesthetics and water efficiency.

The raised beds have two basic configurations. L-shaped herb beds (pictured above) are 18 inches tall and 44 inches wide, with arms extending 11½ feet and 8½ feet, respectively. Triangular vegetable beds (not shown), also 18 inches tall, measure 10 feet on each side and 15 feet at the base. Framed with untreated redwood, the beds are lined at the bottom with landscape fabric and along the sides

with polyethylene film to keep moisture from contacting the wood. A drip-irrigation system waters the plants.

The beds are filled with a blend of potting soil, sand, and organic compost. Twice a year, more compost is added along with a mixture of blood meal, bonemeal, cottonseed meal, and fish meal.

One pink-flowered 'Queen Margrethe' tree rose is planted in each herb bed, along with sage (*Salvia officinalis* 'Berggarten', 'Purpurascens', and 'Tricolor'), white-flowered English lavender (*Lavandula angustifolia* 'Alba'), Whirlybird nasturtium, Greek oregano (*Origanum vulgare hirtum*), yellow-flowered curry plant (*Helichrysum italicum*), scented geraniums, and several kinds of thyme.

The surrounding patio is paved with flagstone slabs set in decomposed granite. — *Gail Mueller*

BACK TO BASICS

How to orient a vegetable garden. To make sure all vegetables get optimum exposure to the summer sun, a standard rectangular bed should run along an east-west axis. Put tall plants, such as corn, pole beans, and sunflowers, on the north side, and shorter ones, like bush beans and peppers, on the south. In summer the sun arcs high across the southern sky for most of the day, so plants tend to cast shadows to the north. — *J.M.*

golden globes

■ Gourd plants are rambunctious by nature. But taming them is possible, as *Sunset's* test garden coordinator Bud Stuckey found out when he planted seedlings of mixed ornamental gourds at the base of an arching trellis last spring. Stuckey's plan: Let the plants race to the top of a trellis, then selectively pluck green leaves to maintain the arch shape and expose the blossoms (and ripening fruits) for better pollination.

At the nursery, he bought a 7-foot-tall by 11½-inch-deep iron trellis with a 3½-inch grid (about $70). For best exposure, he positioned the trellis facing south, then slightly splayed the two sides near the bottom as he sunk them about 1 foot into the soil. He planted seven seedlings around each of the trellis's two feet (you could direct-sow the seeds).

Through summer, the vine grew and covered itself with luxuriant foliage. The gourds fruited heavily from September into November

("like blown glass balls lacing the trellis," said *Sunset's* Northwest bureau chief Steve Lorton). And the colorful globes filled many harvest baskets to use as decoration.

Stuckey used soaker hoses to water the vines and fertilized every two weeks with dilute fish emulsion until fruits set.

— *Kathleen N. Brenzel*

---

a fair to remember

■ Early April is prime time to plant warm-season vegetables. Before you start, consider a visit to the Spring Garden Market, usually held in early April, at Emma Prusch Farm Park in San Jose. The market is sponsored by the Santa Clara County Cooperative Extension Service and Master Gardeners.

Among the large selection of plants and tools for sale, you'll find seedlings of more than 60 hard-to-find varieties of the Master Gardeners' favorite heirloom and hybrid tomatoes and the best hot and sweet peppers from their summer trials. You'll also find many annuals, perennials, and ornamentals.

Allow time to tour the high-density demonstration orchard, the rare fruit orchard, the pollinator garden, and the animal farm at the park, and treat yourself to food and beverages.

9–3, rain or shine; free. U.S. 101 at Story Rd. E; (408) 299-2635, ext. 1017.
— *Lauren Bonar Swezey*

garden guide

Weed-and-thin cutting garden

DIEDRA WALPOLE

■ From the look of his cutting garden, you'd think Chris Johnson had been gardening for decades. But the truth is, until he and wife Mary moved to their current home in Pasadena, his gardening experience was limited to container planting. This cutting garden, one of his first projects, is only three years old.

Johnson started it just the way we would recommend: choose a location, decide which varieties to grow, order seeds, use chalk or gypsum to mark areas for each variety on the soil, sow seeds. "I tried about twenty different things and about 75 percent of them came up," says Johnson. "It was easy." Then things got even easier. "About half the things that came up reseeded on their own," he says. "Now I mostly weed and thin."

Mary Johnson, the inspiration for the garden, is the bouquet maker in the family. "I've loved arranging flowers ever since I was a child," she says. However, the chance to make arrangements out of homegrown flowers is something special, says Johnson. "You get a lot more variety, and you—not the supermarket or florist—decide what you put together." Two of the Johnsons' star performers are annual phlox and delphiniums. — *S.C.*

CLIPPINGS

• **A book born in Laguna.** One of the advantages of being a member of the friends of the Hortense Miller Garden is reading Miller's colorful musings about her 40-year-old, slightly wild canyon-side garden in the friends' newsletter. Now the best of those pieces, from 1978 to the present, have been compiled into a book, *A Garden in Laguna* (Casa Dana Books, Dana Point, CA, 2002; $35; 949/248-0138 or www.casadana.com).

Miller writes: "One of the oddities about gardens throughout history is that they are associated with the rich, and the rich don't work. That's the whole point of being rich. … And yet it is curiously true that unless you work in the garden, it is not yours; it has only a most tenuous connection with you and you with it."

To join the friends ($15 per year), call (949) 494-1205.

Rx for broken pots

CLAIRE CURRAN

■ When Patty Christenson wanted to discard several damaged ceramic pots, her landscape designer, Frank Mitzel, had a better idea: Turn them on their sides, tuck them into a garden slope, and plant annuals that appear to spill out from the overturned pots. "I whacked [the pots] with a hammer so that about a third of each pot was removed," Mitzel says. Each piece sits on its own shelf of soil dug into the bank, about 3½ feet above grade. Mitzel clustered several pots together, pressing their broken edges into the ground to anchor them.

Verbena, ivy geranium, and sweet alyssum spill from the bright blue pots (trailing lobelia and Supertunias would be good choices too)—dazzling against a row of golden rudbeckia.

To enhance the cascade look, some of the annuals were planted within the pots, others in front. Before planting, the soil was amended with commercial potting mix. — *Debra Lee Baldwin*

pacific northwest • checklist

PLANTING

☐ **ANNUAL FLOWERS.** Continue to set out cool-season annuals such as calendula, English daisy, pansy, snapdragon, stock, sweet alyssum, and viola. After frost danger is past and the soil warms up, plant summer annuals like marigold, petunia, sunflower, and zinnia.

☐ **COOL-SEASON VEGETABLES.** Sow seeds or set out transplants of Asian vegetables, broccoli, cabbage, cauliflower, kale, kohlrabi, lettuce, spinach, and Swiss chard any time this month. Start carrots, peas, and radishes from seed only; plant seed potatoes.

☐ **FRUITS.** Zones 1–3: While bare-root stock is still available, plant blackberries, grapes, kiwis, raspberries, strawberries, and fruit trees. Zones 4–7: Bare-root stock is gone, but you can still plant all the above from containers.

☐ **HARDY PERENNIALS.** Look for basket-of-gold, bleeding heart, columbine, Corsican hellebore, evergreen candytuft, forget-me-not, leopard's bane *(Doronicum cordatum),* primrose, rockcress, sweet woodruff, wallflower, and many others. Plant immediately.

DEBRA LAMBERT (2)

☐ **HERBS.** Sow seeds or set out plants of chives and parsley now. Plant seedlings of lavender, marjoram, mint, oregano, rosemary, sage, tarragon, and thyme any time. Wait until frost danger is past to sow basil and cilantro.

☐ **LAWNS.** As soon as the soil is workable, start lawns from seed or sod.

☐ **TREES, SHRUBS, VINES.** Zones 1–3: Bare-root stock of many deciduous trees, shrubs, and vines is still available for immediate planting. Zones 4–7: Look for potted roses, flowering trees (especially cherries, dogwoods, and crabapples), and flowering shrubs like azaleas, rhododendrons, and lilacs. All kinds of climbing vines, from clematis to wisteria, are also ready to plant.

☐ **WARM-SEASON VEGETABLES.** In a greenhouse, coldframe, or on a sunny windowsill, sow seeds of corn, cucumber, eggplant, melon, pepper, and tomato.

PESTS AND MAINTENANCE

☐ **CONTROL APHIDS.** Spray them off tender new growth with a concentrated jet of water from the hose.

☐ **CONTROL SLUGS.** Metaldehyde is the most effective snail and slug bait, but iron phosphate–based bait is safer to use around kids and pets. You can also handpick slugs.

☐ **FERTILIZE.** While soil is cool, use a liquid fertilizer on vegetable and flower beds to give plants a quick boost of nutrients, or use an organic like blood meal with both quick- and controlled-release properties. Give lawns a granular formulation of about 2 pounds nitrogen per 1,000 square feet. ◆

northern california · checklist

PLANTING

☐ **COLOR IN THE SHADE.** Zones 7–9, 14–17: To brighten up a shady bed, try one or more of the following: astilbe, begonia, bergenia, browallia, brunnera, campanula, Chinese foxglove *(Rehmannia elata),* cineraria, coleus, columbine, coral bells, corydalis, cranesbill geranium, foxglove, francoa, impatiens, lady's-mantle, and lamium.

☐ **HERBS.** Zones 1–2, 7–9, 14–17: Nurseries usually carry many varieties of basil, chives, mint, oregano, parsley, thyme, and other basic herbs. For a huge selection of both unusual and traditional herbs (including culinary and medicinal), try Mountain Valley Growers (559/338-2775 or www. mountainvalleygrowers.com).

☐ **TOMATOES IN CONTAINERS.** Zones 1–2, 7–9, 14–17: If you don't have room (or proper sun exposure) to grow tomatoes in garden beds, try growing them in large containers. Start with a 24- to 30-inch-wide container that's at least 18 inches deep. Fill it with a good potting soil and mix in a controlled-release or organic fertilizer. If possible, use drip emitters to irrigate plants so the soil has a constant supply of moisture. Mix in water-absorbing polymers if you plan to water by hand. Remove the lower leaves on the tomato seedling and set it in the soil up to the remaining leaves; water well. If you didn't use a controlled-release fertilizer, fertilize regularly at half strength.

Sunset
CLIMATE ZONES
- ☐ Mountain (1-2)
- ☐ Valley (7-9)
- ☐ Inland (14)
- ☐ Coastal (15-17)

Eureka
Redding
CALIFORNIA
NEVADA
Mendocino
Santa Rosa
Sacramento
San Francisco
San Jose
Monterey
Fresno

DEBRA LAMBERT

☐ **WATER PLANTS.** To make a portable water garden, buy a glazed ceramic container with no drainage hole. Fill container with water and add a pump, if desired (drill a hole under lip of the pot for the cord to exit, or drape it over the pot edge and hide it behind plants). Add plants such as dwarf umbrella palm, floating heart, Japanese iris, primrose creeper, spike rush, water poppy, or white snowflake. (A good source for plants is Lilypons Water Gardens; 800/999-5459 or www. lilypons.com.) To raise the potted plants above the pot rim, set them on bricks or upside-down pots. Add mosquito fish.

MAINTENANCE

☐ **CARE FOR CUT ROSES.** To avoid bent-neck syndrome (drooping buds) and keep roses fresh and opening properly, recut stems underwater (removing about 2 inches) with sharp shears or scissors before arranging. Place the flowers in a well-cleaned vase with a solution of 1 cup nondiet citrus soda, 3 cups (preferably bottled or filtered) water, and ¼ teaspoon household bleach.

☐ **CLEAN BIRD FEEDERS.** Clean plastic feeders in a 3 percent bleach solution (2 cups hot water and 1 tablespoon bleach). Use a bottle brush to remove debris, rinse thoroughly, and allow to dry completely. Scrub wooden feeders with hot soapy water and a stiff brush, rinse, and allow to dry. Keep bird feeders filled with a high-quality bird seed. Natural seed sources are limited in spring.

☐ **SPRAY OLIVE TREES.** To prevent olive trees from setting fruits that will drop, staining driveways and sidewalks, spray trees with a fruit-control hormone like Florel when small white flowers appear. Or knock off blooms with a strong blast from a hose. ◆

southern california · checklist

PLANTING

☐ **ROSES.** Container-grown roses now outsell bare-root roses, according to Roger's Gardens in Corona del Mar and other local nurseries, probably because seeing roses in bloom is the easiest way to sort out the astonishing—and confusing—array of choices now available to home gardeners. It's not too late to plant potted roses, and it's a good time just to browse and identify varieties to buy bare-root next January. Other places to check out blooming roses include the Victorian Rose Garden at the Arboretum of Los Angeles County, the Huntington Botanical Gardens, and Rose Hills Memorial Park in Whittier.

☐ **SUMMER PERENNIALS.** Nurseries are well stocked with spring perennials, but to prolong color in your garden, shop for plants that will bloom into summer and beyond. Good choices include chrysanthemum, daylily, gaillardia, gaura, lion's tail, penstemon, phygelius, salvia, and yarrow.

☐ **VEGETABLES.** Coastal gardeners (zones 21–24) can continue to plant quick-maturing, cool-season crops like leaf lettuce, radishes, spinach, and Swiss chard. Inland (zones 18–21), switch to warm-season crops like beans, corn, cucumbers, eggplant, melons, okra, peppers, pumpkin, squash, and tomatoes. In the high desert (zone 11), frost is still a possibility; wait two to four weeks before planting.

Sunset CLIMATE ZONES

1-3 7-9 11 13 14-24

DEBRA LAMBERT

MAINTENANCE

☐ **FERTILIZE.** Fertilize trees, shrubs, ground covers, perennials, turf grasses, and other permanent ornamentals that you did not feed last month. Don't forget to fertilize your houseplants. They're growing again too.

☐ **SPRAY OLIVE TREES.** To prevent olive trees from fruiting and staining driveways and sidewalks, spray them with a fruit-control hormone like Florel when small white flowers appear. Or knock off blooms with a strong blast from a hose.

☐ **THIN FRUIT.** Continue thinning apples, pears, and stone fruit when they are about ½ inch in size. Space fruit 4 to 6 inches apart or leave one fruit per spur.

☐ **TREAT FOR IRON DEFICIENCY.** If camellias, citrus, gardenias, and other plants exhibit yellowing leaves with green veins, it's a sign of chlorosis; feed them with a fertilizer containing chelated iron.

PEST AND DISEASE CONTROL

☐ **MANAGE ROSE PROBLEMS.** To control aphids, dislodge them with a strong blast of water from a hose. To discourage sawfly larvae, which can leave rose leaves so skeletonized that they look like lace, spray foliage (including the undersides) with Green Light Rose Defense II, suggests Frank Burkard of Burkard Nurseries in Pasadena. Powdery mildew can appear on roses this month, especially along the coast; control it by spraying foliage with a baking soda formula—1 tablespoon baking soda plus 1 tablespoon summer oil to a gallon of water. Or try rose expert Jan Weverka's vinegar rinse: Fill a hose-end sprayer with inexpensive white vinegar and set the dial-a-spray to 2 tablespoons. The 4.5 pH acid spray that results kills mildew spores without damaging foliage, she says. ◆

WHAT TO DO IN YOUR GARDEN IN APRIL

PLANTING

☐ **ANNUALS.** Four to six weeks before the average date of the last frost in your area, start seeds indoors for warm-season annuals (ageratum, celosia, coleus, globe amaranth, and marigold) and vegetables (eggplant, melon, pepper, squash, and tomato). In mountainous areas, start seeds of cool-season flowers and vegetables this month. A good source for seeds is Botanical Interests Inc. (800/486-2647 or www.botanicalinterests.com).

☐ **EASTER LILIES.** After Easter lilies *(Lilium longiflorum)* finish blooming indoors, they can be planted in the garden where they will often come back for several years, blooming in late summer. Plant the bulbs 6 inches deep in good garden soil; water and fertilize regularly.

☐ **HARDY VEGETABLES.** Two to four weeks before the average date of the last frost in your area, set out transplants of broccoli, brussels sprouts, cabbage, and cauliflower. Protect plants from late frost for the first few weeks with floating row covers.

☐ **SUMMER BULBS.** Start begonias, caladiums, callas, cannas, dahlias, gladiolus, and hardy gloxinias in pots indoors on a sunny windowsill. Wait to plant them outside until all risk of frost is past.

Sunset CLIMATE ZONES
☐ 1-3 ☐ 10-11

DEBRA LAMBERT

PESTS AND MAINTENANCE

☐ **ATTRACT BENEFICIAL WILDLIFE.** As frogs, toads, salamanders, and snakes emerge from hibernation, encourage them to stay around your garden and help control pests. Set shallow bowls or birdbath basins on the ground and fill them with water. Rinse and refill regularly.

☐ **CARE FOR LAWNS.** Aerate lawns using a rental machine that removes plugs of soil; rake up the plugs and put them on the compost pile or leave them in place to decompose. To control crabgrass and dandelion seeds before they sprout, apply a corn gluten–based preemergent herbicide (available from Planet Natural; 800/289-6656 or www.planetnatural.com).

☐ **CLEAN UP BIRDHOUSES.** Remove old nests, clean the houses, and mount on poles or trees 6 to 20 feet from the ground.

☐ **DIVIDE PERENNIALS.** When new leaves appear, divide asters, bellflowers, chrysanthemums, daylilies, sedums, Shasta daisies, and yarrow. Dig plenty of compost into the soil before replanting.

☐ **PREPARE FLOWER BEDS.** Gradually remove winter mulch and debris around perennials, then topdress the beds with 2 to 3 inches of compost.

☐ **PROTECT CROPS FROM SPINACH LEAF MINERS.** Dark blotches and tunnels in the leaves of beet greens, spinach, and Swiss chard are the work of the spinach leaf miner. Protect plants against this pest by spreading floating row covers over these crops while new leaves are 2 to 3 inches tall.

☐ **PRUNE ROSES.** Toward month's end, after roses put out foliage, cut off dead and desiccated stems and canes. To prevent borer damage, seal each pruning cut with clear nail polish or white glue. As the weather warms up, remove last year's mulch and leave the soil bare until hot weather arrives. — *Marcia Tatroe* ◆

southwest · checklist

PLANTING

☐ **CITRUS. Zones 12–13:** Set out citrus trees appropriate to your garden's microclimate. Choose from these varieties, listed from most cold hardy to least hardy: calamondin (to 20°), kumquat, mandarins and tangerines, 'Valencia' orange, navel oranges, sweet oranges, limequat, tangelo, pummelo, grapefruit, lemon, and lime (to 28°). In cold-winter areas, grow calamondin, kumquat, or 'Bearss' lime in large pots and move to protected locations when frost threatens.

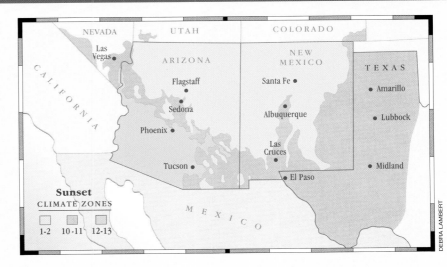

Sunset CLIMATE ZONES
1-2   10-11   12-13

DEBRA LAMBERT

☐ **LANDSCAPE PLANTS.** Plant native and desert-adapted species now, including *Caesalpinia, Dalea,* sages, and Texas ranger.

☐ **SUMMER FLOWERS. Zones 1–2 and 10 (Albuquerque):** Add instant color with pansies, petunias, and snapdragons. **Zones 11–13 (Las Vegas, Tucson, Phoenix):** Set out nursery transplants or sow seeds of celosia, coreopsis, cosmos, gaillardia, gomphrena, marigold, portulaca, and zinnia.

☐ **SUMMER VEGETABLES.** After the last frost, set out seedlings of Japanese eggplant, sweet and hot peppers, and small-fruited tomatoes, including such cherry varieties as 'Sweet 100' and 'Yellow Pear'. Sow seeds of other vegetables. Sweet corn performs well in the Southwest; proven varieties include 'Kandy Plus', 'Silver Princess', and heirloom 'Golden Bantam' (all available from the Cook's Garden, 800/457-9703). 'Ambrosia' and 'Venus' cantaloupes perform well, as do 'Klondike', 'Sugar Baby', and 'Yellow Baby' watermelons. Reliable summer squashes are 'Fordhook' zucchini and pattypans, including longtime favorite 'Sunburst'. Heirloom 'Acorn Table Queen' and newer 'Delicata' have proven to be good winter squashes.

MAINTENANCE

☐ **FERTILIZE.** The entire garden benefits from additional nutrients now. After a thorough irrigation, feed established plants and lawns with a balanced fertilizer, then water again. Give palms their first feeding using palm fertilizer, repeating monthly through summer. As roses enter peak blooming season, give them a dose of rose food every two weeks to increase flower size and yield. Pale foliage highlighted by dark green veins indicates iron chlorosis; correct this condition by applying chelated iron.

☐ **PRUNE.** Cut back frost-damaged plants, including bougainvillea, lantana, and perennials. Use clean, sharp tools to avoid damaging wood or spreading disease. Remove everything to the point from which new growth emerges. To maintain size and shape of prickly pears, remove young pads (nopales). You can cook them with onions and peppers. — *Kim Nelson* ◆

They bloom like annuals, but live on for years

marathon perennials

By Jim McCausland

T hough most perennials sprint through the bloom cycle in three or four weeks, a few are serious marathon runners: They flower for months at a time, combining the staying power of annuals with the long-range reliability of perennials. To get these star performers growing in your garden, start now, when nurseries and garden centers have more perennials on hand than any other time of year. By late spring, painterly combinations of color will start to catch your eye every time you look out the window, and by summer you'll discover that the long-flowering perennials you've added to the garden attract a lively array of birds and insects. • Which flowers will do the most for your landscape? There are a vast number of choices, so we've narrowed the list (page 113) to perennials that perform well throughout most of the West. Keep in mind, though, that hot weather can cut short the flowering season of many perennials, while mild summer temperatures common along the coast and in the high mountains can stretch out the bloom season.

Spilling over the path in an Idaho garden, 'Johnson's Blue' geranium (far left) is backed by pink dame's rocket and flanked by lupines, columbines, delphiniums, and more. Above, from left, scabiosa, *Nemesia caerulea* 'Blue Bird', and gaillardia show the range of perennial flower forms.

what is a perennial?

Perennials are flowering plants that live three years or more. Most are herbaceous (with soft or nonwoody tissue), dying to the ground in fall and reemerging in spring. But there are plenty of exceptions. Tender perennials, like the Million Bells *(Calibrachoa)* pictured on page 114, freeze out easily, so they're treated as annuals everywhere except in the mildest parts of the West. Other perennials, like Russian sage, are either evergreen or woody enough to never die back completely.

Creamy yarrow, barberry, and blue *Campanula persicifolia* crowd the birdbath in Elisa Corcoran's garden on Bainbridge Island, Washington.

Planting tips

For best performance, plant perennials in well-amended soil; dig the soil at least 8 inches deep (below left) and amend it with 2 or 3 inches of compost or well-rotted manure. Knock the plant from the nursery pot and loosen any coiled roots (center). Position plant, firming soil around it. Fertilize lightly three times during the bloom season and water regularly (when stressed by lack of water or nutrients, plants tend to force a quick, weak bloom then stop flowering for the season).

LINDA HOLT AYRISS (3)

Sneezeweed

Salvia confertiflora

THE PLANT LIST
western all-stars

The following perennials are grouped by peak bloom. Most grow throughout the West; some of the early-flowering perennials don't bloom until summer in cooler climates.

early flowers

AFRICAN DAISY
Osteospermum ecklonis 'Lavender Mist'. Midspring–fall. Foothigh mound of white daisies that fade to mauve. ZONES: 2B–24.

O. fruticosum. Intermittent year-round bloom. Trailing plants come with white, blue, pink, purple, or yellow blooms. ZONES: 8–9, 12–24, H1–H2.

AGASTACHE
A. 'Tutti Frutti'. Summer. Pink flowers favored by hummingbirds. ZONES: 2B–24.

A. mexicana. Spring–late fall. Hummingbirds are attracted to the pink flowers. ZONES: 3–24.

BEARD TONGUE
Penstemon Mexicali hybrids. Summer. Rose and violet flowers. ZONES: 1–3, 10.

P. x *gloxinioides* 'Firebird'. Summer. Scarlet flowers attract hummingbirds. ZONES: 6–9, 14–24.

P. x *g.* Kissed series. Summer. White-throated flowers with bright, warm-colored lips. Needs good drainage. ZONES: 6–9, 14–24.

P. heterophyllus 'Margarita BOP'. Spring–early summer. Electric blue flowers favored in Southern California. ZONES: 7–24.

BLEEDING HEART
Dicentra 'Luxuriant'. Spring–summer. Red flowers don't easily burn out in summer. ZONES: A1–A3, 1–9, 14–24.

D. formosa 'Zestful'. Everblooming in mild weather; rose-colored flowers. ZONES: 1–9, 14–24.

CATMINT
Nepeta x *faassenii.* Late spring–early summer. If plant is sheared when blue flowers slow down, catmint repeats in fall. ZONES: 1–24.

COLUMBINE
Aquilegia longissima. Late spring–midsummer. Large yellow nodding blooms. A Texas native. ZONES: 1–11, 14–24.

GERANIUM
G. 'Frances Grate'. Early spring–fall. Mauve flowers. ZONES: 14–24

G. 'Johnson's Blue'. Spring–fall. Blue violet flowers in loose clusters. ZONES: 2–9, 14–24.

G. incanum. Spring–fall. Light magenta. ZONES: 14–24.

G. sanguineum. Spring into summer; will rebloom in fall if cut down in late summer. Red to purple flowers. ZONES: A2–A3, 1–9, 14–24.

GEUM
G. chiloense 'Mrs. Bradshaw'. Spring–summer. Double red orange flowers. ZONES: 2–24.

later flowers

ASTER
Aster x *frikartii* 'Mönch'. Blooms summer–fall or nearly all year in mildest areas if you deadhead. Blue. ZONES: 2B–24.

BEGONIA
B. grandis. Summer. White or pink flowers; give it filtered shade. ZONES: 3–24.

BLACK-EYED SUSAN
Rudbeckia fulgida sullivantii 'Gold-sturm'. Summer. Yellow flowers keep on coming. ZONES: 1–24.

BLANKET FLOWER
Gaillardia x *grandiflora.* Blooms June until first frost. Yellow flowers banded with red, maroon, or brown. Interesting seed heads in winter. ZONES: 1–24, H1–H2.

G. x *g.* 'Goblin'. Blooms June until first frost. Dwarf form with yellow-bordered red flowers. ZONES: 1–24, H1–H2.

CAMPANULA
C. rotundifolia 'Olympica'. Summer. Bell-shaped blue flowers. ZONES: A1–A3, 1–10, 14–24.

COREOPSIS
C. verticillata 'Moonbeam'. Summer–fall. Pale yellow flowers; good tolerance for drought and neglect. Best in Northwest. ZONES: 1–24.

C. v. 'Zagreb'. Summer–fall. Golden yellow flowers. Good in Southern California. ZONES: 1–24.

CORYDALIS
C. lutea. Summer. Yellow flowers best in woodland settings, especially near water. ZONES: 2–9, 14–24.

DAYLILY
Hemerocallis 'Black-eyed Stella'. Summer. Yellow with red eye. ZONES: 1–24, H1–H2.

H. 'Pardon Me'. Summer. Red. ZONES: 1–24, H1–H2.

H. Starburst series. Summer. Many colors. ZONES: 1–24, H1–H2.

H. 'Stella de Oro'. Summer. Yellow. ZONES: 1–24, H1–H2.

GAURA

G. lindheimeri. Spring–fall or most of year in mild-winter climates. White or pink flowers. From Texas. ZONES: 2B–24.

PINCUSHION FLOWER

Scabiosa columbaria 'Butterfly Blue'. July–October or nearly all year in mild climates. Deadheading important. ZONES: 2–11, 14–24.

S. c. 'Pink Mist'. Same as 'Butterfly Blue'. ZONES: 2–11, 14–24.

PURPLE CONEFLOWER

Echinacea purpurea 'Magnus'. Summer. Pinkish purple flowers with orange-brown centers. Birds like the seeds. ZONES: A2–A3, 1–24.

E. p. 'White Swan'. Summer. White with orange-yellow centers. Birds like the seeds. ZONES: A2–A3, 1–24.

RUSSIAN SAGE

Perovskia. July–fall. Blue flowers. Can be an aggressive spreader in California; better in Northwest and mountains. ZONES: 2–24.

SAGE

Salvia confertiflora. Fall–winter in mild areas. Dark orange flowers have reddish brown velvet on stems and calyx tubes. Favored by hummingbirds, bees, and butterflies. ZONES: 16–17, 22–24.

S. nemorosa 'Ostfriesland'. Summer–fall if deadheaded. Violet blue flowers with pink to purple bracts. Favored by hummingbirds, bees, and butterflies. ZONES: 2–10, 14–24.

S. x *sylvestris* 'Blue Hill'. Spring–fall if deadheaded. ZONES: 2–10, 14–24.

S. x *s.* 'May Night'. Favored by hummingbirds, bees, and butterflies. ZONES: 2–10, 14–24.

SHASTA DAISY

Chrysanthemum maximum 'Esther Read'. Summer, with rebloom

if cut back after first round. White double. ZONES: A1–A3, 1–24.

C. m. 'Ryan's White'. Summer, with rebloom if cut back after first round. White single. ZONES: A1–A3, 1–24.

C. m. 'Snow Lady'. Summer–fall; nearly continuous. 10 inches tall with white flowers. ZONES: A1–A3, 1–24.

SNEEZEWEED

Helenium 'Moerheim Beauty'. Summer–fall. Coppery red flowers with brown centers. ZONES: A1–A3, 1–24.

H. autumnale. Summer–fall. Yellow flowers. ZONES: 1–24.

SPEEDWELL

Veronica hybrid 'Sunny Border Blue'. Late spring through first frost with deadheading. ZONES: 1–9, 14–21.

SUMMER PHLOX

Phlox paniculata 'Bright Eyes'. Dome-shaped flower clusters (rose pink with darker eye) through summer. ZONES: 1–14, 18–21.

VERBENA

Verbena 'Homestead Purple'. Late spring–fall. Spreading. ZONES: 2–24.

V. Tapien hybrids. Late spring–fall. Spreading, many colors. ZONES: 4–9, 12–24, H1–H2.

V. lilacina 'De La Mina'. Spring–fall or nearly all year in mild-winter climates. Purple flowers. ZONES: 12–24.

YARROW

Achillea 'Moonshine'. June–September. Deep lemon yellow. ZONES: A1–A3, 1–24.

Achillea filipendulina 'Coronation Gold'. June–September. ZONES: A1–A3, 1–24.

A. millefolium. June–September. Flowers come in rose, pink, lavender, salmon, yellow, and red. ZONES: A1–A3, 1–24.

regional favorites

A few plants deserve special mention because they are widely grown (and loved) as perennials only in the West's mildest climates; in colder regions, gardeners use them as annuals. Following are a few of the most popular, listed by region where they're grown as perennials.

FOR MILD PARTS OF THE NORTHWEST AND CALIFORNIA

Cape fuchsia *(Phygelius).* Warm-toned tubular flowers in summer and fall; also good for zones H1–H2.

Twinspur *(Diascia* 'Ruby Field'). Salmon pink blooms June through fall.

Wallflower *(Erysimum* 'Bowles Mauve'). Nearly continuous bloom in mild climates.

CALIFORNIA'S LOW ELEVATIONS ONLY (EXCEPT DESERT)

Canna. Red 'Firebird' or 'The President'; orange 'Tropicanna' has striped leaves. Cannas are also grown as perennials in zones 6, H1–H2.

Million Bells *(Calibrachoa).* Profuse, bell-like blooms.

COASTAL CALIFORNIA

Bacopa *(Sutera cordata).* Trailing white flowers; June to frost. Perennial in zone H2.

Heliotrope. Scented, deep violet to white flowers come most of the year in warm areas; perennial in zones H1–H2.

Kangaroo paw *(Anigozanthos).* Deadhead the red, purple, green, or yellow blooms to keep them coming from spring through fall.

***Nemesia caerulea* 'Blue Bird'.** Violet blue blossoms with yellow centers; perennial in zones 14–24, annual elsewhere.

Million Bells *(Calibrachoa)*

Heliotrope

'Tropicanna' canna

AT THE NURSERY

how to choose wisely

To stimulate the garden planning process and help avoid expensive mistakes, landscape designers usually match flowering perennials at the nursery.

■ **Arrange plants on a nursery cart** to see which ones work well together.

■ **Pair flowers for color**— whether hot and very summery (red, orange, and yellow) or cool and springlike (blue, lavender, peach, and pale pink).

■ **Check plant tags** to find out how big the plants will grow and whether they like sun or shade.

■ **Choose plants that will bloom together,** and—to prolong the bloom season—include early and late bloomers. In a border, for example, choose two or three great combos for each season.

■ **Consider plant size.** Gallon-size perennials (in 6-inch pots) will take hold faster in the garden than smaller stock, but they're more expensive. Buy smaller plants (4-inch pots) for container planting—you can really pack them in for a full display—or when you need larger quantities for massing in garden beds.

■ **Check plant health.** Avoid buying plants that have leggy stems, or lots of roots protruding through drain holes of the nursery pots—signs that the plants are probably rootbound and may perform poorly.

Supports for plants

Many tall perennials need help standing up straight; the trick is to avoid a lot of visible hardware. Sometimes you can plant tall, weak-stemmed perennials between woody perennials or shrubs that serve as subtle supports. For a few tall stems, it's simplest to use bamboo or metal stakes; keep ties loose. For larger, multibranching plants, set hoops in place when planting or use linking stakes later to corral long stems.

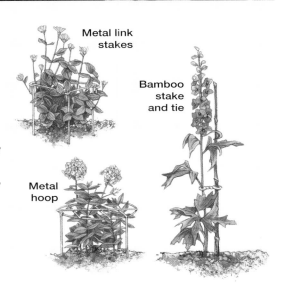

Metal link stakes

Bamboo stake and tie

Metal hoop

Drifts of Shasta daisies play off flower spikes of lupines and iris in Gene and Judy Whitmyre's Ketchum, Idaho, garden. Those are wild daisies on the right, yellow iris and columbines on the left.

mixing plants in borders

A border's design doesn't have to be complicated. Just keep taller perennials at the back and shorter ones up front. Decide which colors to plant side by side. Separate by several yards flowers whose colors clash, or divide them with a mass of blue or white flowers or gray foliage.

Plant perennials that have similar needs together. Pay attention to leaf texture and color.

Beyond that, the balancing principles of contrast and repetition come into play. "Put bold next to delicate and big next to small," says perennials expert Judy Wigand. "Contrast flower shapes as well, letting spiky, flat-topped, and pompom blooms play off each other."

For color inspiration, Wigand lets nature be her teacher. "Look at Anza-Borrego Desert, where miles of purple desert verbena grow with white desert primrose," she says, "or Arizona's Superstition Mountains, where orange poppies contrast perfectly with blue lupine." Wigand likes red flowers beside yellow ones, or orange and blue flowers side by side, with gray foliage around them.

But, admits Wigand, "I'm a fast-paced person, so I like my garden to calm me down. That's why I choose pastels—soft peach with blue interspersed with white, and maybe yellow as a distant highlight."

Repetition is another great workhorse of good design. Clumps of three or more gloriosa daisies repeated throughout a border unify the planting, as does placing side by side plants whose flower or foliage colors echo one another—a rudbeckia with a chocolate brown center beside a chocolate-bronze purple fountain grass. ◆

Postseason plant care

Cutting back. You can cut herbaceous perennials to the ground as soon as tops die back in fall (cut to lines shown at right). Let woody and evergreen perennials stand until spring, then cut plants back by about half to just above swelling buds.
Dividing. To keep flowering well, most perennials need to be divided every few years. You'll know it's time to divide plants when their centers start to die out or when the plants start producing fewer or smaller flowers each year. Divide spring bloomers in fall and summer-to-fall bloomers in early spring. Dig up each clump with a shovel (right), then tease its roots apart by hand (far right) or cut them apart with a knife or spade before replanting.

Small-lot orchard

Espaliered apple and Asian pear trees produce plenty of fruit

By Lauren Bonar Swezey

Apples and Asian pears are trained on a metal arbor to form a handsome and highly productive tunnel, shown here at 10 years old. Baby's tears grows between pavers, and *Geranium biokovo,* Japanese anemones, and lady's-mantle edge the walkway.

Here's a riddle: How do you fit an entire orchard of 24 fruit trees into a small San Francisco garden? For landscape designer Stephen Suzman, the answer is simple: Espalier the trees on an arched iron arbor, 6 feet wide by 56 feet long across the back of the garden.

Suzman, inspired by the works of English landscape designer Gertrude Jekyll, developed the structure (with designer John Dorr) as a support system for the trees—spaced 8 feet apart—and as a leafy tunnel for the owners' two small children to explore. Despite the lack of winter cold, six types of apples thrive here, 'Cox's Orange Pippin', 'Fuji', 'Lady', 'McIntosh' ('MacSpur McIntosh'), 'Pink Pearl', 'Red Astrachan', plus crabapple and two Asian pears. "We chose mostly heirloom varieties with a low chill requirement, because they're so much more interesting to grow," says Suzman. "'Pink Pearl' is lovely just to look at."

Before planting the young fruit trees (which were purchased as 4-foot-tall espaliers), Suzman first had to overcome a severe soil drainage problem. To correct it, the top 2½ feet of soil were removed, then a drainage system was installed and covered with new topsoil.

The trees produce a bountiful harvest, and the handsome arbor provides interest through the seasons.

How to care for an espalier

Landscape gardener Hilary Gordon has been caring for the tunnel of trees since 1992. Her approach is simple: Feed, thin, prune, and water regularly, and the trees will reward you with baskets of fruit starting in midsummer.

Fertilizing

Gordon applies Whitney Farms organic Rose & Flower Food three times a year.

- **Late winter,** before blossoms open. To make the soil more alkaline, she also applies lime around the base of each tree, 6 inches away from the trunk.
- **Late spring,** when fruit are setting.
- **Summer,** when fruit are maturing.

Pruning and tying

- **During the dormant season** (late December in San Francisco), Gordon prunes the trees for shape and to open up the top of the espalier so that sunlight and air can reach the inside of the tunnel; in addition, she cuts off any errant branches.
- **As the branches grow,** she secures them to the arbor with bonsai wire.
- **In summer,** she prunes lightly but frequently to remove suckers and maintain the trees' flat profile.

Thinning

To increase fruit size and reduce quantity, some of the fruits need to be thinned out. (Gordon doesn't thin 'Lady' apple, since the small clusters are very ornamental.)

- **In late spring,** when fruits reach dime size, she thins them down to one fruit per every couple of inches of branch. ◆

Feasts for the eye

Vegetable gardens can be beautiful as well as productive

By Lauren Bonar Swezey
and Jim McCausland

■ Six centuries ago, Saint Ignatius of Loyola offered these words of advice: "It is not enough to cultivate vegetables with care. You have the duty to arrange them according to their colors and to frame them with flowers, so they appear like a well-laid table." Heeding this advice, Europeans have long excelled at creating grand kitchen gardens (or *potagers,* as the French call them) that combine vegetables and ornamental plants in stunning designs.

Today, the concept seems more timely than ever, especially in the West, where ever-smaller yards give gardeners more incentive to make the vegetable patch an aesthetically pleasing part of the landscape.

On these pages, we show beautiful, productive vegetable gardens, each representing different approaches to design. Choose the style that suits your taste, and have fun experimenting. You'll be rewarded with a well-laid table—in the garden and in the kitchen.

THOMAS J. STORY

Focal points in a formal setting

"Vegetable gardening should be elevated to the level of a formal garden, where the beauty of the plants can be shown off to maximum potential," says designer Freeland Tanner, who gardens with his wife, Sabrina, in Napa, California. Inspired by the plants' delightful colors, textures,

and forms, the Tanners created a inviting garden room in which to show them off.

A formal allée of metal arbors draws visitors into the garden along a gravel path and culminates at a circular herb bed accented with a wooden obelisk.

Throughout the rest of the garden, raised beds with low

Bright green leaves of summer squash play off bluish cabbage backed by purple-leafed perilla and pink-flowered agastache.

stone columns at the corners form living tapestries of plants in complementary colors. "I stage each bed like a flower arrangement," Freeland explains. He starts with a focal point in the center, then builds a composition around it.

Large half-barrels, for instance, anchor most beds. In each barrel, the Tanners place an obelisk (planted with beans or peas, depending on the season) or a handsome blend of vegetables, herbs, and flowers. In other beds, variegated corn, *Agastache* 'Tutti Frutti' (shown above), or other tall plants serve as focal points. Below these, low-growing herbs and vegetables form patterns (as in a potager) or a more random mix of compatible colors

ABOVE: A wood obelisk supports 'Sun Gold' tomato. RIGHT: Parsley edges a bed of bronze and green lettuces.

and shapes.

Each bed is edged with overlapping hoops formed from small cuttings of apple, elderberry, and pear trees. The hoops are then underplanted with sweet alyssum, parsley, or violas.

The Tanners do mix in a few choice nonedible perennial flowers with their crops. "This way, we'll always have vegetables for dinner and flowers for the table," says Freeland.

THOMAS J. STORY

SAXON HOLT

Design tips

- **Create focal points.** Place a large container, an obelisk, a trellis, or a sculptural object in the center of the bed.
- **Arrange the bed like a container.** Place taller plants in the center and surround them with shorter plants.
- **Plant in patterns.** Arrange low-growing plants with interesting forms, colors, and textures (cabbages, herbs like basil) in circles or other patterns.

- **Echo colors.** Start with a colored vegetable (purple eggplant, for example), then echo the hue with similarly colored vegetables, flowers, or foliage.
- **Grow vegetables vertically.** Trailing types of cucumbers, melons, and squash are space hogs: Train them on an arbor or trellis. Pole beans, peas, and indeterminate tomatoes also need to be trained on some sort of structure.

- **Plan for seasonal change.** Consider the seasons so you can shift from cool- to warm-season plants and back again "like a seasonal migration," advises Freeland Tanner. When one crop is harvested, have something ready to plug in the hole.
- **Frame the space.** Surround the perimeter of the bed or garden with edging or a fence.

Arrayed like sunbeams, saplings form a gate. A bevy of birdhouses cap fence posts.

Fences frame the garden

Vi Kono of Redmond, Washington, started by framing a space with fences, then composing a garden within it. "I can see the vegetable plot from my kitchen," she explains. "The fence gives structure to the garden and gives me something to look at during the time of year when there's the least to see."

The rustic fence is composed mostly of bitter cherry saplings joined with wood screws. Three varieties of espaliered apples form a living fence along the south side. Fence-top birdhouses, as well as an arbor and gates made of unpeeled logs and twigs, convey the feeling that Hobbits inhabit the garden.

Inside the fence, assorted vegetables—carrots and garlic, Swiss chard and lettuce, squash and tomatoes—share informal, curved beds with dahlias, delphiniums, lavatera, perennial linaria, and a few annuals like cosmos and marigolds. Edible-pod 'Sugar Snap' peas and pole beans clamber up twiggy trellises, while a hop vine and porcelain berry (*Ampelopsis brevipedunculata*) grow up opposite sides of an arbor that runs along one side of the garden.

At planting time, every vegetable and flower seedling gets a sprinkling of controlled-release fertilizer. To maintain soil fertility, Kono digs in vast quantities of compost each year, supplemented with cow manure every third year.

(Continued on page 122)

Growing tips

• **Exposure.** Some vegetables (tomatoes and peppers, for instance) need six to eight hours of midday sun for best production and flavor. Slightly shadier areas can be reserved for plants like arugula, beets, kale, and lettuce that grow well with a little less light.

• **Air circulation.** To reduce the possibility of diseases, provide plenty of air circulation.

• **Soil.** Most vegetables prefer well-drained soil enriched with plenty of organic compost. If your garden soil is heavy and poorly drained, plant in raised beds.

• **Irrigation.** All crops need water to get established, but some need more than

others as they mature. Plant tomatoes in an area where you can cut back on water as the fruit starts to ripen. Greens, on the other hand, need constantly moist soil.

• **Fertilizer.** Use fish emulsion alone or in combination with a kelp-type fertilizer such as Maxicrop. Corn plants, which are heavy feeders, benefit from a side-dressing of dry organic fertilizer during the season.

STEVEN GUNTHER

Giving peas a rung up

Julie Heinsheimer of Palos Verdes, California, has a passion for old, weathered garden implements. So when she found this vintage ladder in a trash heap, she rescued it and put it to use as a support for vining vegetables. Peas climb it in spring (cucumbers take their place in summer). Wire wrapped around the ladder gives the vine tendrils plenty of places to twine around. Near the ladder, the rosy pink plumes of Jupiter's beard *(Centranthus ruber)* attract beneficial insects, including butterflies.
— *Sharon Coboon* ◆

More online: For your guide to growing the perfect tomato, go to www.sunset.com/garden/tomatoes.html.

Favorite colored plants

Check catalogs and nurseries for examples of the colored fruits, vegetables, herbs, and flowers listed below.

Blue gray: Broccoli, cabbage, cauliflower, Red or White Russian kale, 'Silver Shield' sorrel.

Bronze: Bronze fennel, 'Revolution' lettuce.

Orange: Beets, calendula, carrots, eggplant, marigolds, nasturtiums, peppers, pumpkins, Swiss chard, tomatoes.

Purple: Basil, beans, beets, broccoli, brussels sprouts, cabbage, eggplant, lettuce, ornamental alliums, peppers, perilla (shiso), scarlet runner beans, sweet alyssum, tomatoes, violas.

Red: Apples, beets, eggplant, 'Giant Red' mustard, lettuce, peppers, sunflowers, Swiss chard, tomatoes.

Silver: Artichoke, curry plant *(Helichrysum italicum)*, dianthus, dwarf garden sage,

'Ruffled Yellow' tomato

santolina, sea kale *(Crambe maritima)*.

Variegated foliage: Comfrey, raspberries, sage, salad burnet, strawberries, 'Sweet Dumpling' winter squash, thyme, variegated watercress, 'White Anniversary' oregano.

Yellow Swiss chard, 'Bright Lights' mix

SAXON HOLT (2)

Yellow/lime: Apples, beans, calendula, golden feverfew, golden hops, golden lemon balm *(Melissa officinalis* 'Aurea'), golden oregano, lettuce, lime thyme, marigolds, peppers, sunflowers, Swiss chard, tomatoes, violas, zucchini.

ROBIN CUSHMAN; BELOW: BOB WIGAND

Roasted Tomatillo Salsa

PREP AND COOK TIME: About 20 minutes

NOTES: This green salsa from Renee Shepherd makes an excellent dip or a topping for grilled chicken or fish.

MAKES: About 1¼ cups

- 1 pound **tomatillos** (about 8, each 2 in. wide)
- 1 **fresh serrano chili** (¼ oz.)
- ¼ teaspoon chopped **garlic**
- 1 or 2 **green onions**, rinsed, ends trimmed, and chopped
- 1 tablespoon **lime juice**
- 1 tablespoon chopped **fresh cilantro**
  Salt and **pepper**

1. Remove and discard husks from tomatillos; rinse tomatillos. Rinse chili; remove and discard stem. Place tomatillos and chili in a 9-inch square baking pan and broil 4 inches from heat, turning as needed, until browned well on all sides, 12 to 15 minutes total for tomatillos and 6 to 8 minutes for chili. Remove vegetables as done.

2. In a food processor or blender, whirl tomatillos, chili, garlic, green onions, and lime juice, pulsing just until mixture is coarsely chopped; do not overprocess. Stir in cilantro, then salt and pepper to taste.

Per tablespoon: 7.5 cal., 24% (1.8 cal.) from fat; 0.2 g protein; 0.2 g fat (0 g sat.); 1.4 g carbo (0.4 g fiber); 0.4 mg sodium; 0 mg chol.

Tangy tomatillos

Grow the main ingredient in *salsa verde*

By Sharon Cohoon

Tomatillos—those fruits that look like green cherry tomatoes wrapped in parchment— may be the most trouble-free summer crop to grow in this whole hemisphere. Renee Shepherd, owner of Renee's Garden Seeds, has been growing them in Northern California for more than 20 years. She has never seen a tomatillo plant suffer from fusarium or verticillium wilt, two soil-borne fungus diseases that affect tomatoes and other members of the Solanaceae family. Nor are tomatillos bothered by insect pests.

The most common use for tomatillos is in Mexican-style salsa verde. Try Shepherd's Roasted Tomatillo Salsa above: Spoon it over tacos, enchiladas, and huevos rancheros, or try it with grilled chicken or fish.

Planting and care

Tomatillos will grow in any climate. The plants set flowers earlier than tomatoes, and the fruits can be harvested sooner (they are usually picked while still green and tart). If you live in a mild climate, sow tomatillo seeds directly in the ground once all danger of frost is past. If you live in an area with a short growing season, start seeds indoors, then set out transplants at the same time you would set out tomato seedlings. Cage or stake plants or train them on a trellis if garden space is scarce. Initially, tomatillos look like little green paper lanterns. Harvest them when the fruit fills the husk but is still firm and green. Don't remove the husks until you're ready to use the fruits. Tomatillos can be stored in the refrigerator up to a month. They also freeze well.

Seed sources

Tomatillo seeds packaged by Renee's Garden Seeds (888/880-7228 or www.reneesgarden.com) are sold at many nurseries and online. You can also order seeds from Nichols Garden Nursery (800/422-3985 or www.nicholsgardennursery.com). ◆

Blooming in June: red sunrose backed by pink dianthus and purple catmint.

Year-round color in a dry Colorado garden

Water-thrifty plants brighten this easy-care Xeriscape

By Marcia Tatroe • Photographs by Charles Mann

Derived from the Greek word *xero,* meaning dry, the term Xeriscape was coined in 1981 by a team of Colorado landscapers and water providers as part of a campaign to encourage water conservation through creative landscaping. This worthy concept has a lingering problem with its image. Properly pronounced *zer*-i-scape, the term all too often sounds like "*zer*-o-scape," conjuring visions of unthirsty but ugly gardens covered with wall-to-wall gravel.

In fact, a well-designed Xeriscape garden is not only water-thrifty, but it's highly attractive as well. For dramatic proof, take a look at Mary Ellen Keskimaki's brightly colored Xeriscape garden in Golden, Colorado. Although it uses a fraction of the water of a conventional landscape, it looks good year-round. That wasn't always the case.

A Golden opportunity

When Keskimaki moved into her home at the base of North Table Mountain in 1988, her front yard had all the appeal of a gravel pile. The previous owner had buried the hillside under a foot of rock mulch. Before Keskimaki could plant anything in the 60- by 80-foot area, she had to get rid of all that rock. She posted a sign offering it free to anyone who wanted it, but after a few weeks, the takers had barely made a dent. Finally, Keskimaki called the city of Golden for advice. As it turned out, the city needed gravel for a public works project, so crews hauled away seven truckloads.

But even with the gravel gone, Keskimaki's problems weren't over. She discovered the newly exposed soil was heavy clay. To prevent the clay from becoming adobe brick, she dug in 15 tons of sand, 14 truckloads of composted manure, and 25 large bales of peat moss. The resulting soil is loose and fast draining, which encourages plants to root deeply, well away from the desiccating heat at the surface. With her neighbor's permission, Keskimaki retrieved dozens of boulders that had been dumped next door during her home's construction and distributed them on the hillside.

Through trial and error, she developed a palette of rugged, self-reliant plants. She has been ruthless, culling any plant that can't meet the site's formidable challenges. With its southern orientation, the hillside is subjected to extremes of heat and cold, as well as regular grazing by local deer herds. On top of all that, Keskimaki insists that every plant look good and cover the soil completely during all four seasons.

Keskimaki hand-pulls weeds and periodically cuts back the ground covers, yet she spends only one hour a week tending her garden. Irrigation is infrequent—only three or four times each year in the hottest part of summer, and then only when rain hasn't fallen for more than two weeks. When a ponderosa pine on the hillside drops its needles every fall, Keskimaki leaves them in place as a winter mulch to protect plants from extreme cold, then removes them in the spring.

Four seasons of color and texture

Throughout the front yard, ground covers are massed to form solid blocks of color. In May and June, bright hues splash the hillside. Daisylike flowers cover mats of hardy ice plant. Pinks, with their lavender blooms, spill around drifts of pink-flowered soapwort and rosy pink drumsticks of common thrift. The air is filled with the mouthwatering scent of old-fashioned tall bearded irises with lavender and purple flowers.

In late autumn, the hillside becomes a tapestry of textures in muted shades of gray, silver, and sage green, interspersed with burgundy and red. The ice plant's lime green foliage contrasts strongly with prickly silver mats of neighboring pinks. The glossy leaves of soapwort and finely textured carpets of Turkish speedwell stay green for most of the winter. A hardy form of English lavender (*Lavandula angustifolia* 'Munstead') and sunrose are ever-gray.

In winter, the garden is especially beautiful after a light snowfall dusts the slope, reminding Keskimaki of "powdered sugar on Christmas cookies." The ice plant's foliage undergoes a magical transformation, turning deep burgundy.

Tucked among the ground covers, bulbs herald spring. Dutch crocuses are followed by brilliant blue Greek windflower, 'King Alfred' daffodils, and orange, red, and yellow tulips. All of these bulbs have naturalized and spread across the hillside.

Rosy pink–flowered common thrift and light pink soapwort play off purple irises.

Swordlike yucca is a bold contrast to low-growing yellow ice plant.

Keskimaki's 10 favorite plants

Catmint (*Nepeta* x *faassenii*). Fragrant purple flowers in early summer; gray green foliage; 8 to 12 inches tall.
Desert beard tongue (*Penstemon pseudospectabilis*). Shocking pink flowers all summer; bluish green leaves; 3 to 4 feet.
English lavender (*Lavandula angustifolia* 'Munstead'). Fragrant lavender blue flowers in midsummer; gray green foliage; 18 inches.
Greek windflower (*Anemone blanda* 'Blue Star'). Blue daisylike flowers in early spring; 10 to 12 inches.
Greek yarrow (*Achillea ageratifolia*). Dainty white flowers in spring; gray green foliage; 4 to 10 inches.
Ice plant (*Delosperma nubigenum*). Bright yellow daisylike flowers in spring; succulent lime green foliage turns maroon in winter; 1 inch.
Soapwort (*Saponaria ocymoides*). Pink flowers in spring; glossy green foliage; 6 inches.
Sunrose (*Helianthemum nummularium* 'Wisley Pink'). Coral pink flowers in spring; gray green foliage; 6 to 8 inches.
Sunset penstemon (*Penstemon clutei*). Showy hot pink flowers June through August; bluish evergreen foliage; 3 feet. Note: a short-lived perennial.
Turkish speedwell (*Veronica liwanensis*). Blue flowers in spring; tiny deep green leaves; 1 to 2 inches.

For more Xeriscape help

Xeriscape Colorado, a nonprofit organization based in Denver, posts a list of Xeriscape demonstration gardens in Colorado and a bibliography of Xeriscaping sources on its website, www.xeriscape.org.

Two especially useful books are *Xeriscape Plant Guide* (Fulcrum Publishing, Golden, CO; 1999; $27.95, paperback; 800/992-2908) and *The Xeriscape Flower Gardener* (Johnson Books, Boulder, CO, 1991; $19; 800/258-5830). ◆

DAVID CAVAGNARO

'Meteor' bears clusters of deep red sour cherries.

Truly hardy fruit trees

Apples, cherries, plums, and other tree fruits for cold-winter areas of the West

By Lance Walheim

I n the coldest parts of the West, growing tree fruit has always been a risky proposition. Even if the trees survived the frigid weather, late spring frosts wiped out the blossoms before they could set fruit.

Luckily, that scenario has improved in recent years, as breeders in Canada, Minnesota, and the Pacific Northwest introduced some very hardy fruit trees. These varieties are the best choices for gardeners who live in really cold areas, including Alaska, eastern Montana, and higher elevations of the intermountain

West. Most of the varieties listed here can withstand temperatures of at least –40° (plums are slightly less hardy). Even so, they should be planted in the warmest part of the garden and given shelter from the wind if possible.

Apples

Only grow varieties grafted to hardy rootstock, and plant two varieties for cross-pollination. Apple-crabapple hybrids are the hardiest and, consequently, the best choices for the coldest areas such as interior Alaska (*Sunset* climate zone A1).

'**Breakey**', midseason. Medium-size fruit has yellow green skin striped or blushed with red; white flesh is juicy with mild, spicy flavor. Good fresh or cooked.

'**Heyer 12**', early to midseason. Medium-size fruit has greenish yellow skin; coarse flesh with tart taste. Good for pies and sauce. Very hardy apple.

'**Lodi**', early to midseason. Medium-size apple has greenish yellow skin

and tart flesh. Good for cooking; stores well.

'**Norland**', early. Medium-size fruit has greenish skin striped with red. Good fresh or cooked; stores well. Smallish tree. One of a series of very hardy apple-crabapple hybrids from Canada (others include 'Noran', 'Norda', 'Norsan', 'Parkland', and 'Westland').

'**Oriole**', early. Large fruit has yellow orange skin striped or spotted red. Excellent fresh or cooked. Susceptible to mildew.

'**Patterson**', midseason. Small to medium-size fruit has yellow skin blushed with red; excellent flavor and quality. Apple-crabapple hybrid.

'**Rescue**', early. Medium-size fruit has yellow skin covered with red; yellowish flesh is sweet. Apple-crabapple hybrid. A favorite in Alaska.

'**Summerred**', early. Medium-size fruit has bright red skin and tart flesh. Good for cooking until fully ripe, then good for fresh eating too. Sets fruit without a pollenizer.

Other hardy varieties include 'Carroll', 'Collet', and 'Goodland' apples, and 'Kerr', 'Trail', and 'Trailman' apple-crabapple hybrids.

'Oriole' apple is an early variety good for baking or eating fresh.

Apricots

Apricots are early-blooming trees and generally not as hardy as the other fruits described here. However, some hardier types have been developed from Asian and Russian species. Unfortunately, they are not widely available or fully tested yet in the West. They include 'Moongold', 'Sungold', and 'Sunrise', developed in Minnesota, and 'Scout' from Canada. 'Puget Gold', introduced by Washington State University, is described as having frost-tolerant blossoms; it might be worth a try.

Cherries

Sweet cherries are early-blooming trees and usually not good choices for the coldest climates. Much hardier are sour or pie cherries, which make great pies but can also be eaten fresh. The trees we list are self-fruitful.

'Evans' (also sold as 'Bali'), early. Dark red fruit; yellow flesh has excellent flavor. Smallish tree. The hardiest sour cherry (good producer in Anchorage).

'Meteor', midseason to late. Fruit has dark red skin; yellow flesh is firm and juicy. Tree reaches 8 to 10 feet tall.

'Montmorency', midseason. Bright red fruit; light yellow flesh is very juicy and tasty. The most popular sour cherry. Productive tree.

'North Star', early. Dark red fruit; yellow flesh is juicy and flavorful. Small tree is easily kept 6 to 8 feet tall with pruning.

Pears

Plant two varieties that bloom at the same time to ensure cross-pollination.

'Hudar', early to midseason. Medium-size yellow fruit with juicy flesh. Excellent fresh.

'Luscious', midseason to late. Medium to large fruit with yellow skin blushed with red; sweet, juicy flesh melts in your mouth.

'Luscious' pear

'Nova', midseason. Large round fruit can be used green or fully ripe. Self-fruitful.

'Summer Crisp', early. Small roundish fruit has green skin with red blush; crisp flesh is mildly sweet. Not quite as hardy as others listed here. Resists fireblight.

'Ure', midseason. Small to medium fruit with greenish yellow skin; flesh has good flavor when fully ripe. Resists fireblight. ('John' is a similar hybrid, but its fruit quality is not quite as good.)

Plums

Many native plums are very hardy, although fruit quality varies ('Norther' and 'Waneta' are two selections that have good-quality fruit). We list hybrid varieties with 1- to 2-inch-diameter fruit. Trees are small and bushy. Plant two varieties to ensure good fruit production.

'Hildreth', midseason. Small, but excellent quality. Developed in Wyoming.

'Opata', midseason to late. Reddish purple skin; yellow green flesh is sweet and juicy. Excellent fresh or in jams.

'Pipestone', early to midseason. Large, deep red skin with golden blush. Greenish yellow flesh is sweet and juicy. Good fresh or in jams.

'Superior', midseason. Large fruit with dark red skin; yellow flesh is juicy with sprightly flavor. Good fresh or preserved. Not quite as hardy as 'Pipestone' (above).

Other hardy plums that may be available locally include 'Assinboine' and 'Dandy'.

Sources

Local nurseries may carry a few varieties as bare-root stock in the spring, or ask the staff to order plants from Bailey Nurseries (wholesale only) in St. Paul, Minnesota. You can also mail-order many of the plants from St. Lawrence Nurseries in Potsdam, New York (315/265-6739 or www.sln.potsdam.ny.us). ◆

A winding path makes Christine Moore's garden seem larger. BELOW: A dining patio fits snugly in a corner.

Thinking small

In a tiny garden, every detail matters

By Sharon Cohoon • Photographs by Steven Gunther

Small rooms or dwellings discipline the mind, large ones weaken it.
—*Leonardo da Vinci,* Notebooks

If you have a huge backyard, da Vinci might argue, it's possible to approach landscaping casually— you have the latitude to absorb a few mistakes. If your garden is as small as Christine Moore's Los Angeles gar-

den, though, you can't afford that luxury. Step through her French doors and out onto her steps, and nearly every inch of her backyard is immediately visible—all 590 square feet of it. There is no room for error, no hiding place for clutter.

Faced with a situation like this, you could bemoan your lot. Or you could do what Moore did and embrace its limitations. Sure, a small garden has built-in restrictions, but there are also rewards.

Small makes it possible—as well as necessary—to think out every inch and detail. Which is just what Moore did. With research, planning, and care, she managed to squeeze into her minigarden three seating areas, a dining alcove, and a small water feature, not to mention a rich assortment of plants and a wealth of charm. Walking into this little polished space is like opening a locket and finding a miniature landscape inside. Small, yes, but perfect in every detail.

A tiled bench for two (top) and a fountain pool, both surrounded with foliage, are just big enough to make a splash.

A gallery of potted plants softens a terrace made of salvaged bricks.

planning a small garden

- **Determine your likes, down to the particulars.** Moore knew she wanted a Mediterranean-style garden compatible with both her Spanish-style stucco home and its Mexican folk art–inspired interior. But she didn't stop there. She read books, visited gardens, took notes, shot pictures, and kept track of it all in files organized by category until specific ideas emerged. The brick steps with broken tile inserts and matching bench, for instance, were inspired by a similar idea from the historic Adamson House in Malibu, California.

- **Devote a large portion of the property to hardscape.** It's irksome, but the reality is that the smaller the garden, the greater the ratio of hardscape to greenery. Fortunately, avid horticulturist though she is, Moore knew from the start that if she didn't include room for people as well as plants, she wouldn't have a garden.

- **Try it out on paper.** Once Moore knew what she wanted to include—a dining alcove, a water feature, and several places for guests to sit—the challenge was figuring out how to fit it all in. She measured the yard, drew it to scale, covered the sheet with vellum, and tried out designs until she came up with a configuration that pleased her. With this sketch and photos from her files, Moore was able to give clear instructions to the crew she hired to install the garden.

- **Indulge in premium materials where they'll count.** Moore opted for top-grade materials in select places. The Salmon Bay pebbles used in the pathway are a good ex-

ample. Moore chose this material over less expensive pea gravel because a pathway in a garden as small and narrow as hers—basically 10 feet deep by 50 feet across—was too prominent not to be decorative. Because they're so visible, the tiles in the garden, even the ones destined to be broken up, were also first-rate pieces.

- **Offset indulgences with savings elsewhere.** Moore saved money by not installing a sprinkler system. Because the yard is small and filled with plants that have low water needs, irrigating by hand isn't an onerous task, she says. All her outdoor furniture pieces were finds from swap meets. Most of the bricks, rescued from a house that had lost a fireplace from earthquake damage, were free.

- **Keep the color scheme restrained and flower and foliage size in scale.** When dealing with a small space, Moore realized, you have to simplify. She chose a strong color, red orange, as her main motif. But she used it judiciously, selecting primarily small-flowered plants like *Cuphea ignea,* the cigar plant. The few other colors she used—yellow, chartreuse, bronze—were harmonious, not contrasting.

- **Use vertical space.** Moore's garden is full of climbers like *Pyrostegia venusta* and 'Royal Sunset' rose. There's room for a sweetshade, two *Euphorbia cotinifolia* trees, and a pomegranate tree. And the fence that encloses her garden is ornamental in its own right. ◆

At Ron's R & R Nursery in Grover Beach, plants are beautifully displayed among pots of all sizes and shapes, stone benches, and iron wall ornaments.

Garden discoveries

On the Central Coast, nurseries, display gardens, and more

By Sharon Cohoon • Photographs by Steven Gunther

If you're a gardener with a hankering for adventure, hop in the car and head for San Luis Obispo County. Along this scenic stretch of the Central Coast in spring, with its beautiful beaches, farms, vineyards, and charming little towns, it's easy to convince yourself you're in England. Lush green hills are covered with wildflowers; weather is mild, if misty. Best of all, against this scenic backdrop, there are plenty of horticultural treasures—nurseries and display gardens—for garden aficionados. Following are some of our favorites, listed by area.

Grover Beach

Ron's R & R Nursery. This off-the-beaten-track nursery is well worth a detour off U.S. 101. Ron's looks small from the outside, but it's easy to spend several hours wandering around here contentedly. (The R

& R in the nursery's name, incidentally, stands for "rest and recreation.")

In addition to a large selection of plants, the nursery carries pots in many materials and styles, small fountains, garden furnishings, and other outdoor accessories—plus indoor items with an outdoor feel, like botanical prints and wicker chests. It's all displayed in beautiful vignettes to inspire creativity, not to mention avidity. *8–5 daily. 1207 S. 13th St.; (805) 489-4747.*

Cambria

Cambria Nursery and Florist. This small nursery has a large selection of unusual plants from specialty growers. Some of its stock comes from cuttings of plants at Cambria Pines Lodge. If you fell in love with a perennial you saw at the lodge, this would be a likely place to find it. *9–5 Mon–Sat, 10–3 Sun. 2801 Eton Rd.; (800) 414-6915 or (805) 927-4747.*

Garden Shed. Enter this little nursery through a rustic main street store,

and a wide selection of garden-related furnishings and accessories greets you. Step out back and wander among tables full of bedding plants. You'll find plenty to delight the gardener in you—not only plants and planting ideas but handmade bird feeders, one-of-a-kind birdbaths, great watering cans, birdhouses, wire furniture, and much more. *10–5 daily (until 6 Fri–Sat). 2024 Main St.; (805) 927-7654.*

Cambria Pines Lodge & Conference Center. The lodge is a hotel, but its grounds feel like a botanical garden. That's exactly what owner Dirk Winter (who also owns Cambria Nursery and Florist) hoped to achieve. Numerous floral borders connect a rose garden, hummingbird and butterfly garden, herb garden, and white garden. One of the prettiest vegetable gardens around, also on the grounds, supplies the hotel kitchen with certified organic produce. Even though you don't have to be a hotel guest to visit the gardens, you might want to stay for dinner.

2905 Burton Dr.; (800) 445-6868 or (805) 927-4200.

Heart's Ease Herb Shop & Gardens. The Herb Shop, which stocks herbal gifts and gardening books, is housed in an original Victorian cottage surrounded by a knot garden, gray garden, and other herb-themed gardens. Heart's Ease also carries a limited but choice selection of nursery stock. *10–8 daily (until 9 Fri–Sat). 4101 Burton; (805) 927-5224.*

Paso Robles

Sycamore Herb Farm. This sunny farm has a small herb garden, but the main attraction is table after table of culinary, medicinal, and landscaping herbs, including 33 different lavenders, 31 thymes, 18 rosemaries, and 41 scented geraniums. There's also a Bonny Doon Vineyard tasting room on the premises (the farm grows grapes for the winery). *10–5 daily. 2485 State 46 W; (800) 576-5288.*

San Luis Obispo

Leaning Pine Arboretum. This 5-acre display garden on the Cal Poly San Luis Obispo campus is devoted to plants from the world's Mediterranean climates, including California, South Africa, southwest Australia, New Zealand, and the Mediterranean basin. And, since early spring is the most floriferous time for these areas, this is Leaning Pine's glory period. *8–5 Mon–Fri, 9–5 Sat; free. Building 48 on Via Carta, Cal Poly San Luis Obispo; (805) 756-2279.* ◆

ABOVE: Bright golden nasturtiums and blue lobelia edge a bed of vegetables (including artichokes and Swiss chard) at Cambria Pines Lodge. LEFT: Planting at Leaning Pine Arboretum features unthirsty Mediterraneans—yellow-flowered santolina, lavenders, and purple *Teucrium cossonii majoricum* in foreground.

Standard dimensions and sturdy materials make the 64-square-foot structure easy to build and long-lasting.

Little house in the garden

This all-purpose shed fits on a patio

By Jim McCausland

Sometimes, one thing leads to another. For instance, this garden structure started with an unusable slope. Architect Bari Thompson of Lake Oswego, Oregon, first created a level terrace, then installed a patio. Thompson, an avid gardener, used the patio as the platform to build the little house shown above.

Instead of buying a barn-style prefabricated shed, Thompson chose to create a structure that would fit in with his home's architecture. To facilitate construction, he made it 8 feet square, which allowed him to use standard 8-foot materials; he cut the door down to 6 feet. All the materials came from a local home supply center.

So that the house would last a long time, Thompson says, "I wanted to use the most rotproof materials I could find." For the walls, he chose $1/2$-inch cement backerboard, instead of plywood, and, for the floor, concrete patio blocks. Standard stud-and-joist framing rests on pressure-treated 4-by-6 beams, which serve as footings for the load-bearing side walls.

The roof is covered with composition shingles. Gutters channel rainwater into a 44-gallon plastic trash container, which serves as a cistern supplying the sink inside—an inexpensive plastic storage bin with a drain hole drilled through the bottom. The flower-filled window boxes, irrigated with the rainwater, are made from $1/4$-inch backerboard screwed onto a cedar frame.

Painted with masonry paint, the little house holds tools and cheerful garden art. It's a place for potting up annuals and retreating from spring showers; in autumn, bunches of flowers dry on pegs in the rafters. ◆

MAY IS A GREAT TIME to choose your favorite bearded iris varieties for planting this summer or fall. (The beauty shown here is 'Seven Hills'.) For details on these versatile and nearly foolproof plants, see page 158.

May

Coloring lesson in Boise

■ Nancy Day of Boise describes her gardening style as "cottage garden casual." Despite the apparently arbitrary array of flowers, there's nothing random about her design. Day, a professional gardener, says she combines plants that "complement each others' bloom color, foliage, and texture." The red border shown here exemplifies her approach—from the ground all the way up to the eaves.

NORM PLATE (2)

At the front edge of the border, coral and salmon impatiens establish the color foundation. Above them, a miniature Old Glory rose provides bursts of red. Behind this rose, tree peony offers foliage contrast. A red-and-white-striped 'Fourth of July' climbing rose adds height to the border.

Day irrigates with a sprinkler for half an hour twice a week (three times a week in the hottest summer weather). As the roses fade, she removes spent blossoms. The miniature rose doesn't require any pruning; the climbing rose only needs thinning to improve air circulation. Every autumn, Day spreads a 2-inch layer of straw and manure-based compost over the border.

— Suzanne Kelso

top banana in Portland

In summer, banana trees all but hide the front of Burl Mostul's house in Portland. This jungly growth isn't a consequence of global warming; it's typical of Japanese banana *(Musa basjoo)*. This banana isn't grown for its fruit but for big, lush leaves and exotic flowers (one is shown above right). After seven years in the ground, Mostul's plants reach heights of 20 to 25 feet, undaunted by Portland's mild summer temperatures.

M. basjoo is hardy west of the Cascades and can even survive—with winter protection—in the harshest climates east of the mountains. It needs a sunny location and shelter from wind, which can shred the leaves. The plant grows vigorously in summer, dies back to the ground with November freezes, then reemerges in spring. Although the foliage freezes at 27°, the root has survived 6° in Port-land; it's reportedly hardy to –20° when protected by mulch.

M. lasiocarpa, another hardy banana sold by a few Northwest nurseries, needs plenty of summer heat to do its best. This species reaches 5 feet tall and can survive to 10° once established.

Both of these bananas need a steady diet of high-nitrogen fertilizer and plenty of water to thrive. Look for them at nurseries or order 1-gallon plants ($19.95 each) from Rare Plant Research (www.theamateursdigest.com/rareplnt.htm).

— *Jim McCausland*

CLIPPINGS

- **Azaleas in Maple Valley, Washington.** The most diverse public collection of native western azaleas *(Rhododendron occidentale)* has been assembled at South King County Arboretum in Maple Valley. The Smith-Mossman collection shows off dozens of mature azaleas. Plants are covered with fragrant blooms from mid-May through mid-June. *Open daily during daylight hours; free. 22520 S.E. 248th St.; (425) 413-2572 or (206) 366-2125.*

- **Berry Botanic Garden, Portland.** Tucked into a residential neighborhood, the Berry Botanic Garden is one of Portland's best-kept secrets. Originally developed by horticulturist Rae Selling Berry, the garden celebrates its 25th anniversary this year. Stroll the grounds to view fine collections of rhododendrons, primulas, and alpine plants (most of these will reach peak bloom this month and next). *Open daily by appointment only; $5. 11505 S.W. Summerville Ave.; (503) 636-4112 or www.berrybot.org.*

BOOKSHELF

fresh look at Northwest plants

Good garden writers aren't afraid to get dirt under their fingernails. Valerie Easton exemplifies that quality both in her Seattle garden and in her new book, *Plant Life: Growing a Garden in the Pacific Northwest* (Sasquatch Books, Seattle, 2002; $19.95; 800/775-0817 or www.sasquatchbooks.com). Easton leads you

through the gardening year month by month, highlighting plants and sharing her techniques for growing them successfully. In May, for example, she turns the spotlight on ornamental onions (*Allium* 'Globemaster' is shown at right): "I can't think of any plant that creates such a spectacle in so little space ... adding height and flamboyance to the late-May garden." The book is illustrated with sumptuous photographs taken by Richard W. Hartlage in Easton's garden. — *J.M.*

THOMAS J. STORY

Chaparral comes home

A San Mateo landscape mimics wild plant communities

■ As planting schemes go, the Chaparral Garden at Coyote Point Museum in San Mateo is sterling. Layers of trees and shrubs mingle together as they would on an untamed hillside—some mounding, some loosely informal, some upright—with lower plants stepping up to taller ones behind. The plants are native to California and other Mediterranean climates, so they adapt well to the Bay Area's summer-dry conditions and don't need much water once established. Flower and foliage colors and textures blend well too; brushlike lipstick red flowers of *Callistemon viminalis* 'Little John' and tiny deep rose leptospermum flowers, for instance, create high notes near the brooding bronze smoke bush *(Cotinus coggygria)* and the sprightly apple green manzanita foliage.

The Chaparral Garden is one of four plant display areas; there's also Hummingbird Garden, Butterfly Garden, and Nature's Marketplace Garden, featuring plants used by Native Americans to make baskets, dyes, and more.

"These are outdoor classrooms," says Suzanne Tognazzini of Plant Schemes, in Foster City, who designed the gardens and worked with head gardener Pierre Vendroux and volunteers to install them. "The garden is a masterpiece of textures," adds Vendroux. "It's also a labor of love." — *Kathleen N. Brenzel*

spring snow

■ The magnificent flowering tree shown at right, at the Grace Kallam Perennial Garden at the Arboretum of Los Angeles County in Arcadia, is a Chinese fringe tree *(Chionanthus retusus)*. Though not commonly planted, *C. retusus* is one of the best accent trees around for today's small gardens. To begin with, it's the right size—just 20 feet tall and as wide—and it's interesting to look at all year. In early spring, it unfurls soft green ovate leaves. Then comes the dazzling late-spring display—4-inch clusters of fragrant, fringelike, snowy-white flowers that cover the entire canopy. If you have both male and female trees, small clusters of olive-size dark blue fruits (that birds love) come after the flowers. In climates colder than Arcadia, the leaves may turn dark gold in fall. (The tree can handle temperatures to −10°.) When the leaves drop, a dome-shaped silhouette graces the winter garden.

To see the tree in full flower, visit the Kallam Garden at the arboretum. If you want the tree for your own yard

(fringe tree grows throughout Sunset zones 4–9 and 14–21), you'll probably need to have your nursery order it from a wholesaler. Or, if you're patient enough to start with a young plant, mail-order one from Forestfarm.

Kallam Garden: 9–4:30 daily; 301 N. Baldwin Ave.; (626) 821-3222. Forestfarm: (541) 846-7269.

— *Sharon Coboon*

'Pristine', a white hybrid tea rose with a soft pink blush, is lightly fragrant.

rosy outlook for South Coast

■ Though many visitors thought otherwise, South Coast Botanic Garden on the Palos Verdes Peninsula wasn't *really* closed most of last year—the front entrance was just shut down for renovations. Now that all the barricades are down, South Coast has a glamorous new entry, and the garden clubs are back. The South Bay Branch of the International Geranium Society usually has a show here this month, and the South Coast Rose Society's show is normally held in mid-June.

But another great reason to visit is the 10-year-old rose garden, which now looks pretty spiffy. Most of the decomposed granite path has been replaced with terra-cotta pavers, and poorly performing plants have been replaced with new ones. Some 150 varieties (1,400 plants) grow here, including recent All-America Rose Selection winners (the garden is an AARS test site). Peak bloom, in early May, should be spectacular.

9–5 daily; $5. 26300 Crenshaw Blvd., Palos Verdes; (310) 544-6815 or www.parks.co.la.ca.us.

— *S.C.*

garden guide

Angelic geraniums

■ Everyone who sees 'Veronica Contreras', the geranium pictured here, wants her. The same goes for two other geraniums in the same group—'Raspberry Ripple' and 'Wychwood'.

All three varieties are pansy-faced pelargoniums, or angels— crosses between scented pelargoniums and regals, some with a little species stock thrown in. Angels have a lot of small flowers, almost always splotched or streaked with a second color. Some of these varieties bloom nearly year-round in mild coastal gardens. To extend flowering time in warmer areas, give them a location with morning sun or light shade.

Angels vary considerably in growth habit. Some, like 'Veronica Contreras' and 'Wychwood', are loose and rangy, making them great candidates for trellis training (as shown above), window boxes, and hanging baskets. Others, like 'Madame Layal', are quite compact and make handsome border plants.

If you can't find angels at your nursery, order from suppliers such as Greenwood Garden (562/494-8944 or www.greenwoodgarden.com) or Geraniaceae (415/461-4168 or www.geraniaceae.com).

— *S.C.*

rose tricks

■ Floral designers know lots of techniques for creating beautiful bouquets. Twenty-year veteran Jill Slater offers this easy way to arrange a dozen roses in a slightly rounded bunch. "It's simple, quick, and will give everyone great results," she says.

1 For a dozen roses, choose a vase with a 5- to 6-inch-wide opening. Fill the vase with water and add floral preservative.

2 Strip off the lower leaves of the stems.

3 Clutching the flower stems in your hand, turn them upside down, then very gently bounce the flower heads on a tabletop, while slightly loosening your grip on the stems.

4 Once the flower heads are resting evenly on the tabletop, tighten your grip and turn the flowers right side up. Trim the stems with clippers and put the flowers in the vase. The roses should fall gently open into an attractive dome shape as shown in the photograph at right.

—*Lauren Bonar Swezey*

A fence grows in Tucson

■ When clients asked Tucson landscape designer Debra Huffman to create a secure fence for their front yard patio, she suggested using ocotillo *(Fouquieria splendens)*. Huffman drew inspiration from the traditional ocotillo fences once commonly used around adobe homes in Tucson's Barrio Historico. In the 19th century, Latino settlers stuck evenly spaced ocotillo canes in the ground to create a dense barrier with sharp thorns to keep livestock in and predators out.

For her clients' patio, Huffman first created a sturdy framework to support the fencing by sinking 6-foot-long steel posts into concrete footings at 5-foot intervals along the fence line. Huffman purchased 6-foot-tall lengths of

ocotillo that had already been wired together into 5-foot-wide panels by the supplier. The bottom ends of the canes were planted 6 inches in the ground between the posts. The panels were attached with another wire to a steel bar that runs between the posts.

The ocotillo canes took root. They get by on rainfall and runoff irrigation from the yard. The homeowners occasionally spray the fence with a hose to encourage the reddish orange blooms. Since the canes are actively growing, the owners keep them trimmed to about 5½ feet tall.

In addition to fencing the patio, Huffman installed two more ocotillo fence sections parallel to the street, providing greater privacy for the yard. — *Nora Burba Trulsson*

JIM McCAUSLAND

Rhododendrons reign supreme

■ Forty years ago, Alma Manenica and her husband started planting rhododendrons as understory shrubs in their woodland garden near Aberdeen, Washington. Eventually, they ran out of room and extended their planting onto property owned by three neighbors. Now, during peak bloom in spring, the spectacular 3-acre garden stops traffic in the street, and people jump out of their cars with cameras.

Alma Manenica's secrets for success

- **Plant for long bloom.** Individually, most rhododendrons are three-week wonders, but if you pick plants with staggered bloom times, you can extend the show for months. Manenica's garden flowers heavily from February until August, then sporadically again in fall.

- **Deadhead.** Manenica removes spent flowers from every rhody she can reach; it improves the plant's performance as well as its appearance.

- **Prune fearlessly.** When a plant grows too tall, Manenica cuts it back by half, pruning it into a Christmas tree shape. She prunes in April or May, during or right after bloom.

- **Chose companions carefully.** Manenica favors azaleas (deciduous Exbury and evergreen types), camellias (especially 'Brigadoon' and 'Donation'), Korean dogwoods, and *Magnolia* 'Star Wars'.

- **Eliminate competition.** She weeds constantly and cuts down most alders when they compete with rhodies. — *J.M.*

cheery entry in Colorado Springs

■ After building a studio in a century-old carriage house in the historic district of Colorado Springs, landscape architect Fawn Hayes Bell created an inviting entry garden. Shown here in late May, this bed is as saturated with color as the vivid Victorian paint scheme on the carriage house walls. The stately red spires of hybrid lupines steal the show; their palmate leaves demonstrate the value of attractive foliage. A drift of *Salvia* x *sylvestris* 'Mainacht' ('May Night') makes a quieter statement; their violet blue spikes harmonize with the lavender blue trim of the structure. The soft lavender pink flowers of *Geranium* x *cantabrigiense* in the foreground are echoed by the pink blossoms of *Rosa glauca* (right) at the back of the border. More bright accents come from the chartreuse foliage of common ninebark (*Physocarpus opulifolius* 'Dart's Gold'; at right) and the acid yellow flowers of 'Moonlight' broom. Orange Asiatic lilies provide a splash of contrasting color, like orange slices garnishing a green salad. — *Marcia Tatroe*

open house at an herb farm

■ Tammi and Chris Hartung cultivate more than 400 kinds of organically grown herbs at Desert Canyon Farm & Learning Center in Cañon City, Colorado. Tammi, an herbalist, and Chris, a botanist and horticulturist, started the wholesale business seven seasons ago, selling plants to retail nurseries and garden centers. Once each year, on Mother's Day weekend, the Hartungs open their gates to the public to celebrate the Farm Festival & Open House. The free event includes workshops on how to grow and use herbs and native plants in cooking and household cleaning. The festival also features display gardens and the chance to purchase heirloom vegetables, unusual herbs, and wildflower plants grown on the premises.

9–4. From U.S. 50 in Cañon City, take Field Ave. north. 1270 Field Ave.; (719) 275-0651. — Colleen Smith

Tammi Hartung's favorite herbs for pasta, salads, frosting, and drinks

'African Blue' basil has sweet and spicy leaves to use in pesto and pasta dishes.

Anise hyssop *(Agastache foeniculum)* flowers and leaves add licorice flavor to pasta dishes and a variety of salads, including fruit salad.

Calendula officinalis flowers add golden tones in foods ranging from rice dishes to cake frosting.

Cilantro *(Coriandrum sativum)* leaves are chopped to flavor soups, salads, and Mexican dishes.

Double bubble gum mint *(Agastache cana)* flowers and leaves sweeten iced tea and fruit salads.

Gotu kola *(Centella asiatica)* is a salad green with a slightly bitter undertone.

Hopi red dye amaranth *(Amaranthus cruentus* 'Komo') is used by Tammi to impart pink coloring to beverages and frostings.

Sunset hyssop *(Agastache rupestris)* has a minty licorice and root beer flavor that adds zing to lemonade, fruit dishes, and honey.

Trailing rosemary *(Rosmarinus officinalis* 'Prostratus') foliage flavors potatoes and poultry. And Tammi uses rosemary's edible blue flowers to decorate cakes.

garden guide

terraced oasis in Phoenix

■ Before John and Pat MacNeil renovated their Phoenix yard, a 60- by 20-foot swimming pool took up most of the space, leaving little room for anything else. Wanting more outdoor living space, the MacNeils decided to sacrifice the pool. So they sought help from landscape architect Chad Robert.

Robert replaced the pool with a series of terraces paved with Arizona flagstones. The terraces step down from the entrance to a railing at the rear of the property, which overlooks Camelback Mountain. The middle one shown here re-creates the mood of a desert oasis. Water spills from a boulder-rimmed spring into a pond. The island bed in the foreground is planted with cactus, purple verbena, and yellow angelita daisies. A circular spa is tucked on the far side of the waterfall.

The sitting areas are located to the right; a walkway along the left side connects them. When the weather is fair, the MacNeils like to open the sliding doors of their house and use the walk as an outdoor hallway as they move from one indoor room to another. In fact, the terraced space is "like having another room to live and entertain in," says Pat. It looks good at night, too, when uplighting creates dramatic shadows on the neighboring wall. — S.C.

NORM PLATE

mangoes in the low desert

■ The Sonoran Desert might seem like an unlikely place to cultivate mangoes, but Steve Flowers stocks 30 kinds at his Tropica Mango Nursery in south Phoenix. If you'd like to try growing your own mangoes, you'll probably want to start with one of the two varieties shown in the photo below left.

'Keitt', an Indian variety, has large round dark green fruit with great flavor and little fiber. Unlike the mangoes sold at supermarkets, 'Keitt' does not change color when ripe but stays green. This variety is used to dry heat and loves Sonoran Desert summers, says Flowers.

'Nam Doc Mai', a Southeast Asian variety, has kidney-shaped fruit that turns pale yellow when fully ripe. It is considered one of the best-tasting mangoes in the world. Like 'Keitt', it is nearly fiberless. Though this mango originated in the humid tropics, it adapts well to desert conditions, Flowers notes.

Provided they're supplied with enough water during warm weather, mangoes have few problems in the desert. "We don't have the insects or disease problems they do in the tropics," says Flowers. "Birds— even the cactus wren—leave them alone too."

Cold temperatures are the only real challenge, since mangoes tolerate little frost, especially when young. But even that's getting easier. "Once a mango is well established, it takes a major frost— eight hours or more at 32° or colder—to kill it," notes Flowers, "and we haven't had a freeze like that since November 1978."

Flowers also carries banana, guava, papaya, longan, and dozens of other subtropical edibles, plus many ornamentals. *Tropica Mango Nursery: 3015 E. Baseline Rd., Phoenix; (602) 576-6948.* — S.C.

TERRENCE MOORE (2)

pacific northwest · checklist

PLANTING

☐ **ANNUALS.** Zones 1–3: For instant color, set out nursery transplants after danger of frost is past. Zones 4–7: Sow or transplant any kind of annual. For sunny beds, use cosmos, geranium, marigold, petunia, and zinnia. For light shade, try begonia, coleus, impatiens, and violet.

☐ **FUCHSIAS.** Plant in large patio pots, hanging baskets, or garden beds. As they grow, pinch tips back to encourage bushy habit. Feed and water regularly through summer.

☐ **HERBS.** Basil makes a perfect companion for tomatoes and peppers; thyme makes a great edible ground cover; and oregano and marjoram look great spilling over rock walls. Plant chives and parsley as edgings.

☐ **PERENNIALS.** Set out spring-flowering plants such as astilbe, columbine, bleeding heart, lady's mantle, lupine, and poppy. For summer bloom, set out black-eyed Susan, coreopsis, and Shasta daisy.

☐ **SUMMER BULBS.** Set out cannas, dahlias, and all kinds of gladiolus.

☐ **VEGETABLES.** Zones 1–3: Plant cool-season vegetables right away and warm-season crops as soon as the danger of frost is past. Zones 4–7: Plant all kinds by midmonth. Sow seeds of beans and corn. Set out seedlings of eggplant, pepper, and tomato. Sow cucumber, melon, and squash in areas with long, warm summers; set out transplants in areas with short, cool summers.

MAINTENANCE

☐ **CONTROL APHIDS.** Blast them off with a jet of water from the hose. Spray severe infestations with insecticidal soap.

☐ **CONTROL SLUGS.** Track them down at night with a flashlight, or put out iron phosphate–based bait or beer traps.

☐ **FEED LAWNS.** Apply 1 pound actual nitrogen per 1,000 square feet of lawn early this month and water it in well. This is the last major feeding until September.

☐ **FERTILIZE PLANTS.** To save time later, add a controlled-release organic fertilizer to the backfill of planting holes you dig this month. Another option: Apply liquid fertilizer two weeks after planting, then every six weeks through summer.

☐ **MAINTAIN SPRING BULBS.** After bulbs such as daffodils finish blooming, fertilize lightly with a complete fertilizer. Keep watering until leaves start to die back.

☐ **PRUNE FLOWERING SHRUBS, VINES.** As soon as they finish flowering, prune azaleas, camellias, forsythias, lilacs, and rhododendrons.

☐ **SHEAR HEDGES.** As you clip, keep shape in mind: The base of the hedge should be slightly wider than the top to allow sufficient light to reach the lower part of the hedge and foster new growth. ◆

northern california · checklist

SHOPPING

☐ **PLANTS FOR MOM.** This Mother's Day, give a blooming gift that lives on for weeks or years. Every time she waters it, she'll think of you. Some lovely choices include azalea, calla, hydrangea, moth orchid, Oriental lily, rhododendron, and rose.

☐ **ROSES.** If you're having trouble finding a particular rose bush that you saw in someone's garden, check www.findmyroses.com. This website provides retail and mail-order sources for more than 6,100 varieties and species. Amity Heritage Roses (Hydesville; 408/768-2040 or www.amityheritageroses.com) and Michael's Premier Roses (Sacramento; 866/352-7673 or www.michaelsrose.com) are two of the sources you'll find there; they ship year-round.

PLANTING

☐ **DWARF LAVENDER.** For compact varieties to plant in containers or in the front of a border, try 'Grosso' (violet; 18 inches tall), 'Hidcote Compact' (violet blue; 12 to 15 inches tall), 'Jean Davis' (soft pink; 16 inches tall), 'Martha Roderick' (violet; 18 to 24 inches tall), and 'Nana Alba' (white; 8 inches tall). These varieties are available at nurseries or by mail from Nora's Nursery (phone and fax 360/379-3920 or www.norasnursery.com).

Sunset
CLIMATE ZONES

☐ Mountain (1-2)
☐ Valley (7-9)
☐ Inland (14)
☐ Coastal (15-17)

DEBRA LAMBERT

☐ **SUMMER FLOWERS.** Zones 7–9, 14–17: Set out sixpacks or 4-inch plants of ageratum, coreopsis, dahlia, gaillardia, globe amaranth, impatiens, lobelia, Madagascar periwinkle (vinca), marigold, nicotiana, penstemon, perennial statice, petunia, phlox, portulaca, salvia, sanvitalia, sunflower, sweet alyssum, torenia, verbena, and zinnia. Zones 1–2: Wait to set out warm-season annuals until after last frost. You can still plant cool-season flowers, such as calendula, pansy, and sweet pea.

MAINTENANCE

☐ **AERATE COMPACTED LAWNS.** If the soil under your lawn is hard and water doesn't penetrate well, it's probably time to aerate. You can rent an aerator from an equipment supply store (look in the yellow pages under Rental Service Stores & Yards). Rake up the cores and top-dress with a fine mulch, such as compost. If you haven't fertilized recently, apply a lawn fertilizer and water in well.

☐ **MULCH.** A 3-inch layer of mulch around trees and shrubs helps retain soil moisture, suppresses weeds, and keeps the soil cooler. To cover 100 square feet to a depth of 3 inches, you need 1 cubic yard (or 27 cubic feet) of mulch. For smaller shrubs and perennials, apply a 1 to 2 inch layer (9 to 17 cubic feet) around plants.

☐ **THIN FRUIT.** Zones 7–9, 14–17: In most years, apple, Asian pear, nectarine, and peach trees need excess fruit thinned so remaining ones develop to a good size. Gently twist them off, leaving 4 to 6 inches between fruit. Thinning may also help reduce insect and disease problems, since it eliminates touching fruit (insects can migrate from one to another) and improves air circulation around them. Zones 1–2: Thinning should be done in early summer. ◆

southern california · checklist

PLANTING

☐ **CULINARY HERBS.** Plant basil, chives, lemon grass, mint, oregano, parsley, rosemary, sage, tarragon, thyme, and other herbs. Greek columnar basil, named for its narrow habit, is a new one worth trying. It smells a bit like cloves, rarely flowers, outlasts other basils in the garden, and overwinters indoors more easily. If you don't find it at your nursery, order it from Shepherd's Garden Seeds (860/482-3638 or www.shepherdseeds.com).

☐ **LAWNS.** Plant subtropical grasses like Bermuda, St. Augustine, and zoysia. Lay sod or plant plugs.

☐ **SUBTROPICALS.** This is the best time to plant avocado, banana, cherimoya, citrus, guava, mango, and other tropical and subtropical fruit appropriate for your area. Planting now gives them a long season of growth before hardening off for the winter. Bougainvillea, ginger, mandevilla, palm, thunbergia, and other subtropical ornamentals can be planted now too.

☐ **VEGETABLES.** Set out heat lovers such as cucumber, eggplant, melon, pepper, and tomato. According to Frank Burkard Jr. of Burkard Nursery, good tomatoes to grow near the beach are 'Champion', 'Enchantment', 'Green Zebra', and 'White Beauty', and any cherry tomato. The best watermelon near the coast, he says, is 'Sugar Baby'. In the low desert (zone 13), plant Jerusalem artichoke, okra, pepper, and sweet potato.

Bishop
NEVADA
CALIFORNIA
San Luis Obispo
Bakersfield
Tehachapi
Santa Barbara
Lancaster
Los Angeles
Palm Springs
Sunset
CLIMATE ZONES
San Diego
1-3 7-9 11 13 14-24
MEXICO

DEBRA LAMBERT

MAINTENANCE

☐ **FERTILIZE PLANTS.** All actively growing plants will benefit from a feeding. If you want to go organic, try this recipe for "garden tea" from Yvonne Savio, manager of the Los Angeles County Common Ground Garden Program (part of the UC Cooperative Extension). Mix 1 tablespoon fish emulsion and $1/2$ teaspoon liquid seaweed or kelp concentrate in 1 gallon water. Irrigate root zones and spray onto leaves every two weeks during growing season.

☐ **PINCH BACK MUMS.** For abundant flowers and an attractive habit, continue pinching back the growing tips of chrysanthemums through July.

☐ **PRUNE.** If hibiscus, princess flower, and other subtropicals have become leggy and awkward, cut them back by as much as half. This is also a good time to cut back lavender, rosemary, santolina, and other Mediterranean perennials. After a few seasons, these plants tend to flop over and die out at the center. Hard pruning—up to half—keeps them shapely longer.

PEST AND DISEASE CONTROL

☐ **CONTROL INSECT PESTS.** To keep aphids, spider mites, and whiteflies under control, direct a strong stream of water from a hose to the susceptible plants, especially on the undersides of the leaves where the pests hide. For severe infestations, try insecticidal soap or horticultural oil.

☐ **PROTECT TOMATOES.** Watch for tomato hornworms—fat green worms that eat leaves and fruits. Pick them off of leaves. To prevent blossom-end rot, a calcium deficiency that can be triggered by sudden heat or over-fertilizing, mulch plants heavily to keep soil evenly moist, and reduce feeding. ◆

mountain · checklist

PLANTING

☐ ANNUALS. *At lower elevations,* plant heat-tolerant annuals such as ageratum, amaranth, browallia, cleome, cosmos, gazania, gomphrena, heliotrope, lantana, marigold, nicotiana, petunia, portulaca, sanvitalia, scabiosa, statice, verbena, vinca, zinnia, and zonal geranium. *At higher elevations,* start annuals indoors after May 1 for transplanting after June 1. Plants that perform well include begonia, clarkia, cosmos, Iceland poppy, lobelia, nasturtium, painted tongue, pansy, petunia, schizanthus, snapdragon, and sweet William.

☐ ORNAMENTALS. All evergreens, perennials, roses, shrubs, trees, and vines can go into the ground now. For the first two weeks, use floating row covers or evergreen boughs to shade plants imported from coastal nurseries and greenhouses. To help prevent transplant shock, apply liquid fertilizer diluted to half the recommended amount.

☐ SUMMER BULBS. When the soil warms up, plant acidanthera, calla, canna, crocosmia, dahlia, freesia, gladiolus, ixia, and lily.

Sunset
CLIMATE ZONES

☐ 1-3   ☐ 10-11

DEBRA LAMBERT

MAINTENANCE

☐ DIVIDE SPRING BULBS. After the leaves turn brown, dig up crowded clumps of daffodils, tulips, and other spring bulbs and gently pull the bulbs apart. Before replanting, till 2 inches of compost and a handful of complete fertilizer into the soil.

☐ FERTILIZE. After bloom, feed spring-flowering shrubs and start a monthly fertilizing program for long-blooming annuals, perennials, and container plants. Fertilize bluegrass lawns by midmonth. Feed roses this month, then once a month through mid-August.

☐ GUARD AGAINST WILDFIRE. In fire-prone areas, create a defensible zone around the house by removing brush and dead vegetation, trimming overhanging branches, and keeping plantings well watered. Clear dead leaves and pine needles from your roof and gutters.

☐ HARVEST ASPARAGUS. When spears are ⅜ inch in diameter, cut or snap them off at ground level. Leave thinner spears to develop into foliage to replenish the plants for next year.

☐ PROTECT ANNUALS. To protect newly transplanted annuals from frost, cover them with floating row covers on cold nights.

☐ SUPPORT PERENNIALS. When tall perennials, such as aster, delphinium, peony, and Shasta daisy, reach about 6 to 8 inches high, stake plants or place hoop supports over them.

PEST CONTROL

☐ APHIDS. Depending on the severity of the infestation, rub these pests off plants with your fingers, blast them off with a strong spray of water, or spray with insecticidal soap.

☐ OYSTERSHELL SCALE. These pests resembling oyster shells commonly infest aspen, cotoneaster, dogwood, and willow. They are nearly impossible to kill except in their newly hatched crawler stage, which usually occurs around Memorial Day. Beginning in mid-May, check adult oystershell scale weekly with a magnifying glass; if you find pinhead-size hatchlings, spray with summer horticultural oil. — *M.T.* ◆

southwest • checklist

PLANTING

☐ **ANNUAL FLOWERS.** Zones 1–2: Set out ageratum, coreopsis, cosmos, gaillardia, globe amaranth, portulaca, red and blue salvias, and zinnia. Zones 10–13: Sow seeds or set out transplants of coreopsis, cosmos, hollyhock, Mexican sunflower, portulaca, and zinnia. All zones: Try seed varieties grown for generations in the desert, such as 'Love-Lies-Bleeding' and 'Hopi Red Dye' amaranth (from Seeds of Change; 888/762-7333 or www.seedsofchange.com) and sunflowers like 'Apache Brown Striped', 'Hopi Black Dye', and 'Tarahumara White' (from Native Seeds/SEARCH; 520/622-5561 or www.nativeseeds.org).

☐ **HERBS.** When soil temperatures rise above 60°, sow seeds or set out transplants of basil, marjoram, mint, and oregano. Other herbs to plant now include bee balm, epazote, hyssop, lavender, lemon balm, lemon grass, sage, summer savory, and thyme.

☐ **LANDSCAPE PLANTS.** Zones 1–2, 10 (Albuquerque): Plant ground covers, shrubs, and trees. Zones 11–13 (Las Vegas, Tucson, Phoenix): Add color with agastache, artemisia, bougainvillea, hibiscus, lantana, and *Vinca major* or *V. minor*. Agave, cactus, *Dasylirion* species, and palms provide long-term interest.

DEBRA LAMBERT

☐ **VEGETABLES.** All zones: Set out transplants of Armenian cucumbers, chilies (try 'Big Jim', 'Chiltepin', 'Mirasol', 'New Mexico #6', and 'Peter Pepper'), and sweet peppers (pimiento is especially tasty). Sow seeds of melons and all kinds of squash. Along with traditional squash, try heirloom high-desert natives such as Hopi "Vatgna" and 'Rio Lucio' pumpkins or 'Tarahumara' squash (from Native Seeds/SEARCH; see "Annual flowers" at left). Sow seeds of okra (try 'Guarijio Nescafe' or 'Eagle Pass' from Native Seeds/SEARCH).

MAINTENANCE

☐ **CONTROL PESTS.** Watch for and handpick hornworms, grape leaf skeletonizers, and other caterpillars; treat heavy infestations with a spray of *Bacillus thuringiensis*.

☐ **FERTILIZE.** Feed citrus trees this month with a high-nitrogen fertilizer. Fertilize lawns now and every month through September. Continue to fertilize roses every two weeks while they're in bloom.

☐ **IRRIGATE.** Each time you irrigate, apply enough water to deeply soak the root zone of each plant: approximately 3 feet for trees, 2 feet for shrubs and vines, and 6 to 12 inches for annual flowers, vegetable beds, and lawns.

☐ **MULCH.** Apply a 4-inch layer of organic mulch beneath landscape plants, in vegetable gardens, and around tree bases. — *Kim Nelson* ◆

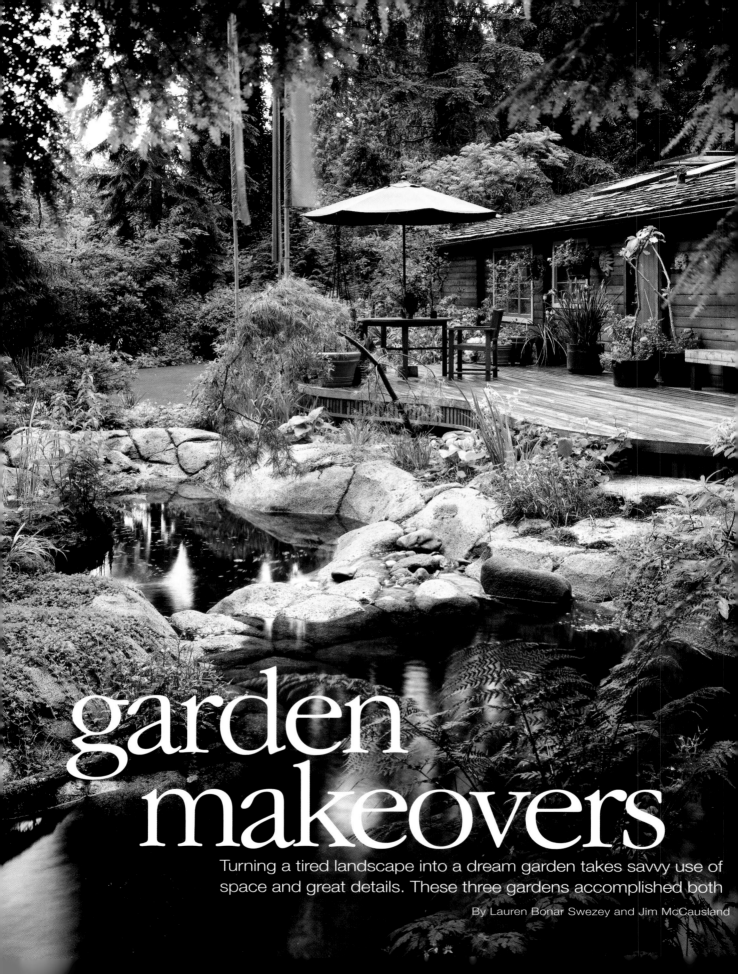

garden
makeovers

Turning a tired landscape into a dream garden takes savvy use of
space and great details. These three gardens accomplished both

By Lauren Bonar Swezey and Jim McCausland

Imagine lounging next to your own sparkling pond filled with multicolored koi.

Or gathering with friends in your private courtyard on a balmy summer eve with the heady scent of exotic flowers perfuming the air. Or throwing open the living room doors to hear the soothing sound of trickling water.

Such are the dreams of those who own a garden that's ripe for renovation. The owners and designers pictured on these pages made dreams a reality by completely overhauling their gardens. They banished scraggly lawns, tamed the tangles of overgrown shrubbery, and planted the patches of dirt. They added new recreation and entertaining amenities, and improved access into and around their gardens. These makeovers illustrate the ways that any area of the garden—front, side, or back of the house—can be transformed from wasted ground into attractive open-air rooms that make the best use of available space.

before

DESIGN CHALLENGES

Not enough light.

No room for outdoor entertaining.

Very limited plant palette.

Not enough time to do the whole job at once.

No irrigation system.

SOLUTIONS

Remove some trees to let in light; prune back English laurels.

Build a deck for entertaining and a pond for beauty (and for koi).

Add shade-tolerant plants in shadier areas. Create pockets for irises and water lilies in the pond.

Complete the work in stages over several years.

DESIGN: Élan Landscape Design & Build, Issaquah, WA (206/568-0220 or www.seattlelandscaping.com)

the backyard

"When we came to Tiger Mountain nine years ago," says owner/landscape designer Natyam Schraven of Issaquah, Washington, "we found our new property landscaped with a rotting little deck, overgrown English laurels almost coming through the kitchen windows, a struggling patch of lawn, and lots of large native hemlocks, firs, and maples. There was no place to entertain, and the whole property was dark."

Schraven and his wife, Leslie Wener, began the renovation process by deciding what they wanted in their garden—more light everywhere, a deck, and a pond— then coming up with a general plan.

The rear garden is the landscape's tour de force. Schraven and his business partner, Britton Shepard, built a clear cedar deck whose curved edge anticipated the line of the pond that would follow. They sculpted the pond's concrete edges, spattered the concrete with latex paint to mimic the color and texture of natural stone, and made in-the-pond planting pockets for water plants.

TOP: Schraven and Wener with Shepard. FAR LEFT: Deck nudges the pond. ABOVE: Iris and yellow corydalis bloom beside a meditating Buddha.

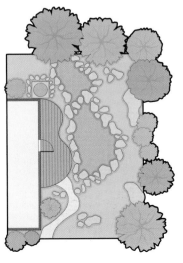

BEN WOOLSEY (3); ILLUSTRATIONS BY TROY DOOLITTLE TOPDOG ILLUSTRATION

garden makeovers

the front yard

before

Tim and Lisa Goodman. TOP CENTER: A large fountain with walls wide enough to sit on dominates the courtyard. FAR RIGHT: New path surrounded with dymondia leads through a striking mix of shrubs and trees, including cycads, bronze New Zealand flax.

Three years ago, Berkeley landscape designers Lisa and Tim Goodman purchased what Lisa calls a "confused Monterey colonial home" built in 1933. "Nothing had been done to the house or garden since that time," she explains. The Goodmans "decolonialized" the home by adding wooden beams and railings, which gave it a Spanish flavor and set the stage for a courtyard and flourishing Mediterranean garden in the front yard.

In an existing courtyard, the Goodmans removed an old boxwood hedge that cramped the area, tore out the lawn, and added a multilevel flagstone patio and fountain. They also saved a mature olive tree.

Outside the wall, they sacrificed two huge arborvitae trees, improving access to the front door. The two-story house still needed large trees to anchor it to its surroundings, so the Goodmans splurged on five tall palms, which gave the garden instant drama.

To replace the lawn, the Goodmans designed a meandering walk and surrounded it with plants chosen for their interesting colors, textures, and forms. Flowers and foliage of yellow and red predominate, with purple and white mixed in. *Maackia chinensis*, a deciduous tree with creamy white flowers, provides four seasons of interest. Yellow brugmansia adds fragrance all summer. Scattered throughout are *Coleonema pulchrum* 'Sunset Gold', desert spoon, dymondia, evergreen dogwood, and *Mahonia lomariifolia*. "We don't depend on flowers to make the garden look good," says Lisa.

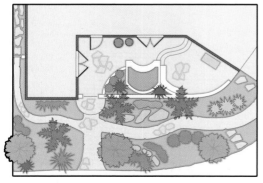

DESIGN CHALLENGES

A visually cramped courtyard, with no inviting space in which to gather.

No easy access to the courtyard.

No paths to allow strolling through the garden.

No cohesive design, no focal point.

SOLUTIONS

Open up the courtyard and make it more inviting—with flowers, paving, and a fountain.

Add paths to improve access into and out of the garden.

Visually connect the house and garden by using similar architectural details and colors.

DESIGN: Goodman Landscape Design, Berkeley (510/528-8950 or www.goodmanlandscape.com)

the side yard

"The yard was like a no-man's-land," landscape designer Shari Bashin-Sullivan says of Steven Bue and Trish Dilworth-Bue's old side-yard garden (18 feet wide, 70 feet long) in Oakland. "There was a step out from the kitchen door down to dirt and that's about it."

With two active kids and a desire to entertain outdoors, the couple needed to make much more efficient use of the space they did have along the side of the house. "We turned the side yard into a private space," Bashin-Sullivan explains.

The bold architecture and colors of the house determined the garden's tropical style. "Since the garden is small and the plants would be viewed from close-up, the plantings needed to be interesting," says Bashin-Sullivan. That meant using plenty of dramatic foliage and intense colors.

First, a 6-foot-tall wall was added to enclose the space, followed by a two-tiered flagstone

patio that connects the kitchen and living room doors and visually unifies the sloping garden. A fountain was positioned on the upper patio level so it can be seen and heard from the living room.

The planting beds are no more than 3 feet deep, but Bashin-Sullivan filled them with large plants such as 'Charles Grimaldi' brugmansia, honey bush, princess flower, and *Sambucus nigra* 'Madonna'. "The plants soften the walls so it doesn't feel like you're in a jail," she explains. Giant bird-of-paradise and 'Tropicanna' canna make striking accents against the house walls. Below the tall plants are coleus, dahlias, New Guinea impatiens, and tuberous begonias in "bright, yummy colors."

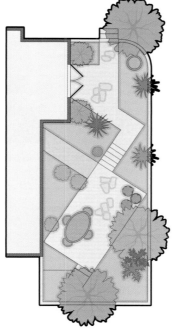

before

DESIGN CHALLENGES

No privacy: Side yard was small and open to the street.

No area for outdoor entertaining.

No access from the living room to the outdoors.

SOLUTIONS

Build a wall, turning the side yard into a private courtyard.

Create a two-tiered patio at an angle to the house to give the illusion of space, with the lower level for dining.

Remove a useless balcony off the living room to allow existing doors to open directly onto the upper patio.

DESIGN: Enchanting Planting, Orinda, CA (925/258-5500)

Tropical foliage unifies lower patio and upper patio. Splashes of color include 'Tropicanna' canna, red dahlias, orange flowering maple, and lime green flax. **LEFT:** The Bues and the Sullivans.

THOMAS J. STORY; SAXON HOLT (3)

Designers' tips

Choose a garden style and accessories that complement the style of your house—whether Tudor or Mediterranean. Here, mauve hellebores in a blue pot echo colors in nearby wall tiles.

Mix greens—evergreen and deciduous plants—so the garden looks good all year. Plant with upright, arching, trailing, and weeping forms. The result is richly textured, like this shaded path flanked with big-leaf *Petasites japonicus* and hostas.

Soften hard surfaces. *Miscanthus sinensis condensatus* 'Morning Light', planted 3 feet apart, form billowy mounds against 'San Diego Red' bougainvillea and the stucco wall.

Play up color contrasts. Here, ruby coleus pairs with impatiens and giant bird-of-paradise.

- **Plan what to keep.** If money's no object, you can start over with new structures such as walls. Consider altering the existing ones or camouflaging them with plants if you're on a tight budget. Large trees are probably worth keeping if they're healthy and can be assimilated into the new design. Or often they can be relocated; a designer or arborist can help you make that decision.
- **Consider grade changes.** Use raised beds or berms, a sunken patio, or seat walls to alter a flat garden.
- **Choose materials carefully.** They should tie in with the house. A warm-colored house, for instance, calls for warm-colored flagstone.
- **Give important elements the highest priority.** Put your money into structural elements (paths, decks) and slow-growing specimen plants first. You can save money by buying smaller, less important shrubs, perennials, and ground covers. ◆

Old-fashioned bouquets

Small and simple, they make great gifts

By Lauren Bonar Swezey

The month of May brings many reasons to head for the garden and pick a bunch of blooms: a little bouquet for Mother's Day, a gift for a favorite teacher at the end of the school year, a thank you to the friend who's invited you to a May Day garden party. Whatever the occasion, these old-fashioned bouquets are the perfect way to celebrate the season. If you don't have many flowers in your garden, use ones from a florist's shop or market.

DESIGN: Jill Slater

TIME: 20 minutes each (plus conditioning time)

COST: About $5 (plus cost of flowers if purchased)

MATERIALS: **Pruning shears** • One to two dozen stems of **flowers, foliage,** and **herbs** • **Bucket** • **Rubber band** • One **lace paper napkin** or two 8-inch-diameter paper doilies • **Scissors** • Roll of 1-inch-wide white **florists' tape** • 1 yard 1-inch-wide **decorative ribbon** • Several decorative **straight pins** • ½ yard **thin ribbon**

DIRECTIONS

1. Gather flowers. Select a focal point (a rose, for instance), then choose complementary blooms, foliage, and herbs to surround it.

2. Recut stems under water and strip off lower leaves; place stems in about 6 inches of water in a bucket. Let them sit in a cool place for several hours.

3. Surround the central flower with sprigs of smaller flowers, foliage, and herbs as shown. Add more materials until the bouquet measures about 4 to 6 inches in diameter.

4. Bind the stems together with a rubber band, then cut the stems to 3 or 4 inches long.

5. *If using a napkin:* On a table, fold two opposite corners of the napkin together to make a triangle, its tip pointed up. Lay the bouquet in its center, with the flower tops just below the tip. Bring the napkin's left corner loosely across the bouquet toward the top edges, then roll the bouquet and napkin toward the free corner, forming a loose cone around the bouquet. Arrange the corners outward and gather the napkin's bottom snugly around stems.

If using doilies: Place two paper doilies together; using scissors, make two 1½-inch cuts to form an X in the center of the doilies. Insert the flower stems through the X and fan out the doilies beneath the blooms.

6. Wrap the stems with florists' tape, starting at the top and catching the napkin or doilies' edges in the first few wraps (**A**). Stretch the tape taut and overlap its edges as you go.

7. Wrap the stems with 1-inch-wide ribbon as shown (**B**). Cut the ends to shorten as needed and secure with decorative pins.

8. Tie the thin ribbon around the wrapped stems. ◆

THOMAS J. STORY (4)

Visitors to Iris Test Garden in Eastern Washington can stroll and select among nearly 2,500 named varieties of bearded irises, including 'Seven Hills' at left.

Growing to love iris

Choose your favorite colors and styles to plant this summer or fall

By Jim McCausland

■ This is the season when the tall bearded iris reveals why it has won the hearts of so many admirers across the West. These nearly foolproof plants mix well with other perennials, grow in every Western climate, and multiply in the garden without becoming invasive. Chances are you probably don't live too far from a world-class iris grower, from whom you can choose your favorite varieties and order rhizomes to plant this summer for bloom next spring in your own garden.

A century of intensive breeding, much of it by amateurs, has transformed these irises from supporting players into the divas of the garden. Every season, growers flood the market with new varieties. One major grower told us that he replaces 50 or 60 of the 300 varieties of irises in his catalog every year. In such a fast-changing scene, how do you find the right iris? Start by looking at the past winners of the Dykes Memorial Medal, which has honored the best-looking and best-performing irises since 1927. The Dykes winners tend to stay around longer than more faddish varieties.

Price can also help you decide. A new introduction might sell for $50 per rhizome, but by the end of its commercial life span (5 to 10 years), the same rhizome will cost just $4 or $5.

Bearded irises have three major parts. Beauties from Iris Test Garden (left to right): 'Brimmed Satin', 'Jeweled Starlight', 'Flamenco'.

STANDARDS

FALLS

BEARD

Some growers welcome guests

The growers whose physical addresses appear below welcome visitors during iris bloom. Others are strictly mail-order sources for rhizomes. Call or check websites for catalogs and ordering information.

ARIZONA Shepard Iris Garden. Open for bloom 9 to 5 daily in April. 3342 W. Orangewood Ave., Phoenix; (602) 841-1231. Catalog $1.

CALIFORNIA Greenwood Irises + Daylilies. Open 9:30 to 4 on Saturdays, April through June. 8000 Balcom Canyon Rd., Somis; (562) 494-8944 or www.greenwoodgarden.com. Catalog online. **Maryott's Iris Gardens.** (877) 937-4747, (831) 722-1810, or www.irisgarden.com. Free plant list.

COLORADO Long's Gardens. Open for bloom 9 to 5 daily, May through June. 3240 Broadway, Boulder; (303) 442-2353 or www.longsgardens. com. Catalog online.

OREGON Cooley's Gardens. Open 8 to 7 daily (peak bloom May 19 to June 3). 11553 Silverton Rd. NE, Silverton; www.cooleysgardens.com or (503) 873-5463. Catalog $5.
Schreiner's Gardens. Open dawn to dusk daily during bloom (peak bloom late May). 3625 Quinaby Rd. NE, Salem; www.schreinersgardens.com or (503) 393-3232. Print catalog $5; online catalog free.

UTAH Zebra Gardens. Peak bloom in late May. 9130 North 5200 West, Elwood, UT 84337; (435) 257-0736. Catalog $3.

WASHINGTON Iris Test Garden. This 7-acre farm, 50 miles south of Spokane, is open May through June. 1102 Endicott-St. John Rd., St. John; (509) 648-3873 or www.iristg.com.

Breeders perform magic

COLOR. You can buy irises in every color except true rose red and lime green (there are pale chartreuse wannabes). Banded and bicolor types abound, but much current breeding is focused on color variegation—stripes and speckles, as in 'Batik' and 'Bewilderbeast'—which is gaining acceptance faster among serious gardeners than among iris show judges.

If you want to grow irises to view up-close, choose banded, bicolor, striped, and speckled kinds. But if you want to mass irises for concentrated color viewed across the garden, get solid colors.

FORM. Originally, most bearded irises had droopy falls (the petals that hang down). But as breeders have pumped more substance into them, the falls have flared out (some are nearly horizontal). The amount of flair and ruffling along petal edges is a matter of taste.

BEARDS. Resembling fuzzy caterpillars, beards are centered on the falls. Early on, growers spent a lot of time breeding beards with complementary or contrasting colors, but now they're selecting varieties with elongated beards shaped like spoons, horns, and flounces.

FRAGRANCE. The first time you sniff an iris that smells like grape ('Wild Thing' is one), you'll be enchanted. The scents vary in character and intensity.

BUD COUNT. Each flower lasts two or three days, so more buds translate into longer bloom. The most prolific irises produce more than a dozen buds per stem. The danger here is that spring rains can weigh down the flowers, so when strong winds follow, they can knock flower-laden stems to the ground unless they're staked. If you don't want the hassle of staking tall plants, choose intermediate or dwarf bearded irises, which tend to bloom earlier and stand up to the elements better.

LEAVES. A few irises, like 'Honky Tonk Blues', have a beautiful oxblood flush at the base of the leaves; someday, you may see whole leaves with that color.

Plant rhizomes 1 foot apart with leaf fans parallel. RIGHT: If you mail-order iris, you'll get a rhizome like this one.

E. SPENCER TOY (2)

Planting tips

Iris rhizomes (swollen underground stems resembling tubers) produce the fans of leaves that give rise to the flowers. Plant rhizomes so all the fans are parallel, and, if your garden layout allows, face them toward full sun.

Plant from July through fall in mild-summer climates; wait until October in Southwest deserts. Irises need fast-draining soil to avoid soft rot. Set rhizomes barely below the soil surface; in hot-summer gardens, cover them with about ½ inch of soil.

Irrigate from the time fans start growing in early spring until about six weeks after bloom. During summer, the rhizomes of most irises should be allowed to go somewhat dry. In hot climates, water about once a week if soil is light and about every other week if it's heavy; in cool climates, water half that much. However, continue watering remontant (reblooming) types as long they're actively growing.

Scatter a complete fertilizer over iris beds when growth starts in spring and again after the last flower fades.

How to use iris

Although bearded irises combine well with many other perennials, some gardeners put them at the back of the border, so that when the irises finish blooming, they'll disappear among the other plants. Other gardeners prefer to interplant them with spring flowers such as columbines, daisies, dianthus, Iceland poppies, lupines, and peonies. ◆

FLASHY FOLIAGE

An iris of a different stripe

DAVID WINGER; ABOVE: JANET LOUGHREY

In ancient times, the Romans used so-called orrisroot, derived from the rhizomes of certain irises, to flavor wine and for incense. In more recent times, orrisroot has been used in perfume and powder; some people even chew pieces of it as a breath freshener. The root comes from a plant we call *Iris pallida*. In modern gardens, this iris is valued for it variegated leaves, which brighten dull borders, as well as for its fragrant purple flowers. The most common form is often sold as 'Zebra' (creamy stripes); other forms include 'Argentea Variegata' (silvery white stripes) and 'Aurea Variegata' (golden yellow stripes; shown).

ABOVE: *Anthemis biebersteiniana* has 1-inch-wide daisies. LEFT: Border planting includes *Artemisia versicolor* 'Seafoam' at front right and yellow-flowered cranesbill behind. At front left are the spiky indigo flowers of *Salvia* 'May Night' and the lavender pink globes of *Allium christophii*.

Macho Mediterraneans

These ground covers and compact perennials stand up
to intermountain winter cold and summer drought

By Sharon Cohoon • Photographs by Charles Mann

We don't usually think of plants from the Mediterranean region as being particularly cold-hardy. But look at the topography of Southern Europe and North Africa—the regions that rim the Mediterranean Sea—and you'll notice mountainous areas throughout. Plants from high elevations in this part of the world are doubly challenged: They must survive freezing winter weather as well as long, dry summers. That double toughness makes them great additions to Western gardens, says David Salman, president of Santa Fe Greenhouses/High Country Gardens, a nursery and mail-order firm based in Santa Fe.

"Most of these plants can survive temperatures as low as –30° in the winter, and they're used to bone-dry conditions in the summer, so they actually handle drought as well as our Southwest natives," says Salman.

But these rugged plants aren't only for regions with harsh weather. Gardeners in more benign climates, like coastal areas of the West, will find them just as useful. As a group, they display foliage with the attributes gardeners have always admired in Mediterranean plants: gray green or silvery color, fuzzy texture, and often wonderfully aromatic scent. And, as is true of most mountain species, these plants tend to be more compact than other, less hardy garden varieties.

Salman has been testing high-elevation Mediterranean plants at his nursery for the last six years to determine which are the most adaptable to average garden conditions. On the facing page, we name some of his favorites, along with comments by garden writer Marcia Tatroe, whose work appears regularly in *Sunset's* Mountain Garden Guide. Tatroe has grown the same plants at her home near Denver, in one of the West's coldest climates (*Sunset* zone 2A).

Ground covers

GREEK YARROW *(Achillea ageratifolia)*. Dense gray green foliage; small white flowers in spring. "Very long-lived perennial—I've had it in my garden for 13 years," says Tatroe. Grows 4 to 10 inches tall by 18 inches wide.

HOREHOUND *(Marrubium rotundifolia)*. Soft green leaves with silvery white edges and undersides; insignificant flowers. 10 inches by 18 inches.

MOUNT ATLAS DAISY *(Anacyclus depressus)*. Feathery silver gray foliage; white daisylike flowers with dark red reverse. Needs good drainage. 3 inches by 15 inches.

WOOLLY THYME *(Thymus pseudolanuginosus)*. Tiny, fuzzy gray leaves. Takes considerable foot traffic. "All thymes are pretty tough, but this one is probably the toughest," notes Tatroe. 2 to 3 inches by 3 feet.

Mounding perennials

ANTHEMIS BIEBERSTEINIANA. Feathery silver foliage; showy yellow daisies in spring. "Very adaptable. Can be grown in a Xeriscape, but will also tolerate more water," says Tatroe. 10 inches by 15 inches.

ARTEMISIA VERSICOLOR 'SEAFOAM'. Frothy, curly silver foliage; occasional yellow blooms. Handles heavy clay soil well. Does best with occasional summer water. 8 inches by 24 inches.

CRANESBILL *(Erodium chrysanthum)*. Compact mound of silvery green, fernlike leaves; ½-inch-wide, pale yellow flowers. "One of my favorite plants," says Tatroe. 6 inches by 12 inches.

ENGLISH LAVENDER. *Lavandula angustifolia* 'Hidcote'. Gray foliage; deep purple flower spikes. With its aromatic blooms and leaves, this English lavender makes a sensual edging along paths. 15 inches by 18 inches. *L. angustifolia* 'Mitcham Gray' is also quite cold-hardy, and grows faster and slightly taller than 'Hidcote'. 20 inches by 20 inches.

NEPETA RACEMOSA 'WALKER'S LOW'. Billowy gray green aromatic foliage; lavender blue flowers. 15 inches by 24 inches.

SALVIA OFFICINALIS 'MINIMUS'. Dense mound of finely textured gray green leaves; lavender blue flowers. Tolerates more clay than most culinary sages. 15 inches by 18 inches.

STACHYS BYZANTINA 'BIG EARS' ('Countess Helen von Stein'). Fuzzy gray green leaves. "Grows in sun or shade; wet or dry conditions," says Tatroe. 6 inches by 24 inches.

TANACETUM DENSUM AMANII. Silvery white, felty leaves; yellow button flowers in summer. Likes well-drained soil, full sun. 6 inches by 15 inches.

Sources

Greek yarrow, woolly thyme, and *Stachys byzantina* 'Big Ears' are widely sold. All of the plants listed above are available by mail order from High Country Gardens (800/925-9387 or www.highcountrygardens.com). ◆

TOP: *Stachys byzantina* 'Big Ears' has velvety leaves. BOTTOM: Horehound has rounded whorls of flowers and woolly, aromatic leaves.

Versatile verbenas

These sun lovers add color to beds and containers from spring through fall

By Lauren Bonar Swezey

ABOVE: Babylon Blue Carpet verbena, Supertunia Lavender Pink petunia, and Symphony Crème osteospermum combine well in a hanging basket.
LEFT: Red Escapade verbena makes a great ground cover.

Some plants make handsome ground covers. Others provide nonstop bloom in beds and borders. And some are outstanding performers in containers. But very few plants perform all these tasks as well as some members of the genus *Verbena*.

This large category of perennials, including species native to Mexico, South America, and our Southwestern deserts, are superb colormakers. Their showy flower clusters appear with the onset of warm weather and generally bloom all summer long.

In recent years, there has been an explosion of patented verbenas developed by breeders from around the world, including California, Japan, the Netherlands, and the United Kingdom. "You can't beat these new verbenas for flower production," says Josh Schneider, a spokesman for Proven Winners, an international plant marketing firm that has introduced many varieties of verbena.

Another closely related group, garden verbenas, has its admirers too. Nurseryman Jeff Rosendale, of Watsonville, California, particularly likes the varieties 'Coral Red' and 'Pink and White'. "They're fairly resistant to mildew and have held up in our coastal garden for five years with only moderate water," he says.

How and where to use them

Most garden verbenas and patented hybrids are cold-hardy to 15° to 25°, but they can be grown as summer annuals anywhere.

Use any of these fast-growing spreaders to provide quick color in between shrubs, in the front of perennial borders, or along walkways. Planted in containers or hanging baskets, they form stunning cascades of color.

With so many kinds available, how do you choose which one to buy? First, consider the way you intend to use the plant. Some series, such as Escapade and Tapien, work better as wide-spreading ground covers. Others, like Patio Temari and Rapunzel, grow more upright, making them perfect for a container garden.

Choices are also determined by flower color and foliage type. If you live in a coastal area, choose one that is less susceptible to mildew, a white powdery-looking disease that infects the foliage of many plants.

Sources

Nurseries usually carry good selections of verbenas. To locate nurseries that sell Babylon, Patio Temari, Tapien, Temari, and Tukana, visit the Proven Winners website, www. provenwinners.com. For Twilight

Garden verbena (*V. x hybrida*)

Flat flower clusters up to 3 inches wide appear on bright green or gray green serrated foliage. Most grow 6 to 10 inches tall by 1½ to 3 feet wide. Some of the better colors include 'Coral Red', 'Hot Lips' (violet pink; grows up to 16 inches tall), 'Peaches 'N Cream' (pastel pink and cream), 'Pink and White' (white blushed pink), and 'Silver Anne' (pink). Garden verbenas tolerate mildew if given sun and good air circulation. These thrive in *Sunset* climate zones 8–24, H1–H2.

Patented hybrids

These hybrids are available in a number of series, which fall into two basic categories: fine-leaf and broad-leaf. All are hardy in zones 4–9, 12–24, H1–H2. Look for the series name on nursery tags.

FINE-LEAF TYPES. Developed from *V. pulchella gracilior,* their foliage has a delicate, fernlike appearance.

• Rapunzel. Upright spreading plant 10 to 12 inches tall by 30 to 34 inches wide. Two-inch-wide flower clusters come in burgundy, purple, and purple with a white eye. Useful in containers or as a ground cover. Less susceptible to mildew.

• Tapien. One of the first patented introductions, this spreading type grows almost flat (2 to 3 inches tall) and to about 2½ feet wide. Blue violet, pink, and salmon flower clusters are small (1 inch wide) but prolific. Best used as a ground cover along the edge of a border or path. Keep it away from vigorous plants that could overcome it. Less susceptible to mildew.

BROAD-LEAF TYPES. Typically developed from *V. canadensis,* these hybrids have wider serrated leaves.

• Babylon. Bushy, compact plant 8 to 10 inches tall by 12 to 14 inches wide. Large fragrant flowers come in eight colors. Blooms through winter in mild climates. Tolerates mildew.

• Escapade. Spreading type grows 12 inches tall by 38 to 40 inches wide. Two-inch-wide burgundy or red flower clusters. Use it as a vigorous ground cover or combine it with more upright annuals or perennials in containers. Less susceptible to mildew.

• Lanai. Spreading type 8 to 10 inches tall by 30 to 34 inches wide. Two-inch-wide flower clusters come in six colors, including vibrant pink. Useful as ground cover or in container plantings. Less susceptible to mildew.

• Patio Temari. Upright spreading plant 20 to 24 inches tall by 24 inches wide. Large (2- to 3-inch-wide) flower clusters come in blue, pink, hot pink, and rose. More floriferous than its cousin Temari (below). Tolerates mildew.

• Temari. One of the oldest patented introductions. Other verbenas, such as Patio Temari (above), are better bloomers.

• Tukana. Upright mounding plant 10 inches tall by 24 to 30 inches wide. Large (2½- to 3-inch-wide) flower clusters in blue, salmon, scarlet, and white. Blooms through winter in mild climates. Fills the top of a container first, then cascades down. Tolerates mildew.

• Twilight. Spreading plant 6 to 12 inches tall by 36 inches wide. Large (2-inch-wide) flower clusters come in seven colors, including Blue Spark (blue with a white star). Best used as ground cover, since blooms develop on outer growth. Tolerates powdery mildew. ◆

retailers, check the Flower Fields website, springplants.theflowerfields.com, and click on "Search."

What verbena needs

SOIL. Loose, well-drained soil amended with compost.

EXPOSURE. Full sun (at least six hours per day) with good air circulation.

WATER. Moderate to regular water; moisture-stressed plants are more susceptible to mildew. Use a drip-irrigation system, if possible. If using overhead irrigation, water in the morning.

FERTILIZER. Feed plants regularly, especially those in containers, with a balanced fertilizer.

PRUNING. To rejuvenate plants, prune back old growth before new growth appears in spring. During the season, shear off faded blooms or cut back plants if they look shaggy; fertilize afterward.

KURT REYNOLDS/GOLDSMITH SEEDS

Tiny white eyes dot flowers of purple Lanai verbena, a spreading type with serrated leaves. Try it in a patio pot as shown here.

Before & After

By Sharon Cohoon

A long, narrow bed made tending vegetables awkward. Smaller beds placed perpendicular to the walkway make all plants easier to care for.

Pretty and Productive

Paths, pots, and structures work wonders in this small vegetable garden

■ A few simple changes can make a huge difference in a garden's flow and appearance. Rita Sprinkel's vegetable garden in Newport Beach, California, is located in a sunny, south-facing side yard. Backed by a tall hedge that blocked out the wind, this plot yielded bumper crops of potatoes, tomatoes, and zucchini.

Still, Sprinkel wanted to increase production. And since she couldn't resist taking visitors back to her vegetable garden to admire her crops, she also wished the space were prettier. So she asked Lew Whitney of Roger's Gardens in Corona del Mar for help.

Better beds

Whitney's solution was to give the space more structure, by dividing the single bed into five smaller ones and separating them with 2-foot-wide

Details make the difference

BEDS. Each bed is outlined with 2- by 4-foot redwood header boards. Because the vegetable garden was trapezoidal (the 35-foot-long plot is almost 7 feet wider at one end than the other), Whitney did not make all the beds the same width. They start at 3 feet and widen to 6. This was done for balance, but it has other advantages. The variously sized beds lend themselves to different crops—the wider ones are great for sprawlers like potatoes, the narrower ones for tidy growers like leaf lettuce.

IRRIGATION. Ooze tubing (also called weeping soaker hose) handles the watering. It's flexible and can easily be rearranged to conform to any crop.

PATHS. Paths between beds are covered with Del Rio gravel and make it easier to plant, weed, and harvest all sides of the beds.

POTS. The bowls at the front of each bed are traditional Italian terra-cotta in style but made in China; nurseries sometimes sell them as terrachino.

VERTICAL STRUCTURES. The Texas Tornado tomato cages and bent-willow bean tepees from Roger's Gardens support sprawling plants and provide vertical interest.

gravel paths. To make up for some of the ground lost to the paths, he cut away 18 inches from the adjacent walkway and sacrificed some lawn in order to expand the bed by 4 or 5 feet. For visual interest and to maximize production, he brought in some vertical plant supports. Whitney placed a row of containers at the front of each bed and planted them with herbs, alpine strawberries, and edible flowers. Finally, to keep the bed looking good nearly all year, he added permanent foliage plants— artichokes, rosemary, thyme—that also yield a harvest.

"Because of the paths, I'm not sure I actually gained any square footage," says Sprinkel, "but the garden *seems* larger." And, she says, it's certainly simpler to care for. "The paths make it easier to plant, weed, and harvest. Now every inch is accessible."

The division of the plot into separate spaces of different sizes (see box at left) and the introduction of containers and supports for vertical crops also encouraged Sprinkel to experiment. "I've tried snow peas, arugula, and alpine strawberries—all new crops for me," she says. "That has been fun." Best of all, no matter what she grows, thanks to the structure now built into the garden, it looks good.

All of which proves it doesn't require a major overhaul to make a difference. Individually, the changes Whitney made to Sprinkel's garden were all small. Collectively, though, they converted a humble vegetable patch into a chic *potager*. ◆

Woven twig trellis adds height in a bed of low-growing herbs like parsley. Lemon tree behind dangles golden fruits.

Heavenly "hellstrips"

Turn barren spaces into lush oases that need little care or water

By Lauren Springer

I ronically, it is often the most visible part of your property that seems to offer the least hope for a successful garden planting. It might be an inhospitable area along the fence or by the driveway. Typically, it's the forsaken parkway strip—that trampled, parched ribbon of no-man's-land between sidewalk and street.

Yet with the right palette of plants, you can transform this wasteland into a floral oasis. These plants should fill in quickly and, once established, remain low enough so that they don't block traffic views or run afoul of height ordinances.

This kind of transformation not only enhances the look of your home, it can change the habits of passersby within a season of planting. Dog-walkers, skateboarders, joggers, even the most distracted group of teenagers stop intruding into the strip and may even linger to look.

Choosing "hellstrip" plants

As you make selections, look for plants that possess these traits.
- **Unthirsty**
- **Unfussy** about soil
- **Persistent** (bulbs, perennials, low shrubs)
- **Compact height** (under 3 feet)
- **Attractive foliage**
- **Tidy growth** (little pruning and primping needed)
- **Variety** of textures and shapes
- **Flower colors** to suit your taste
- **Varied bloom** times

Reborn parking strip is awash with pink stonecress, crimson dianthus, blue *Salvia jurisicii,* and pastel *Penstemon grandiflorus.*
DESIGN: Lauren Springer

Easy steps to reclaim a strip

1. **Remove weeds** and unwanted plants. Dig them up, smother with black plastic, or spray with a glyphosate-based herbicide.
2. **If the strip is long,** put a strategic path across it to guide pedestrians; steppingstones, bricks, and mulch all work well.
3. **If soil is compacted and lifeless,** dig or till in 2 to 3 inches of well-rotted manure or compost. Otherwise, dig or till the native soil to at least 8 inches deep, avoiding areas within tree drip lines.
4. **Pick a dozen or fewer species** and plant in drifts for a simple, classic look. A more adventurous, experienced gardener may be more flamboyant.
5. **For faster coverage,** space plants a bit more closely than normally recommended.
6. **Spread a 1-inch layer** of small-diameter mulch—such as pea gravel or crushed shells for sunny areas, shredded leaves or coarse compost in dry shade—around plants. Avoid growth-stunting organic mulches such as bark or wood chips.
7. **Water weekly** for the first few months unless there is regular rain. After that the plants should manage.
8. **Keep up with weeding,** which should be almost nil once plants fill in.
9. **Cut back spent flowers.** Remove any dead material from the previous season as new growth resumes.

LAUREN SPRINGER (2)

before after

Transforming a grim strip into a lush border took about two years in Colorado (the process goes faster in milder areas). Prominent flowers are blue flax, orange poppies, and red *Penstemon eatonii*.
DESIGN: Lauren Springer

Plant sampler

Unless noted, all do best in sun and are hardy in *Sunset* climate zones 2–9, 14–24, although many can survive in colder and hotter climates.

EARLIEST BLOOM
Bulbs
- *Crocus* **species.** Yellow, gold, white, purple, pale blue flowers.
- *Iris reticulata* (snow iris). Blue, purple. Hardy to zone 3.
- *Tulipa* **species.**

Evergreen perennials
- *Alyssum montanum* (mountain basket of gold). Yellow.
- *Veronica pectinata, V.* x 'Blue Reflection'. Blue.

LATE SPRING–SUMMER BLOOM
Bulbs
- *Babiana* **species** (baboon flower). Blue, lavender, purple, crimson, white. Hardy to zone 4.
- *Brodiaea* **species.** Blue. Zones vary.
- *Iris* **species.** All colors. Zones vary.

Perennials
- *Achillea* **species** (yarrow). Some evergreen. All colors but blue and purple.

- *Dianthus gratianopolitanus, D.* 'All-woodii' (pinks). Pink, crimson, white flowers.
- *Nepeta* x *faassenii* (catmint). Lavender blue; 'Snowflake' has white flowers.
- *Papaver atlanticum.* Orange.
- *Penstemon* **species.**

Low evergreen shrubs
- *Cistus* **species** (rockrose). White, pink, magenta. Choose compact species or hybrids. Hardy to zone 6.
- *Eriogonum* **species** (wild buckwheat). White, cream, yellow, pink, rose, or red. Zones vary.
- *Helianthemum* **species** (sunrose). All colors but blue or purple.
- *Lavandula angustifolia, L.* x *intermedia* (hardy to zone 4). Purple, pink, white.
- *Salvia dorrii* (desert sage). Blue.
- *Santolina* **species.** Yellow, cream. Zones vary.

LONG AND/OR LATE BLOOM
Perennials
- *Agastache* **species.** All colors but white and yellow. Zones vary.

- *Callirhoe involucrata* (wine cups). Magenta or white.
- *Gaura lindheimeri.* White or pink.
- *Limonium gmelinii.* Purple.

Low shrubs
- *Caryopteris* x *clandonensis* (blue mist). Blue.
- *Perovskia* (Russian sage). Lavender blue.

Ornamental grasses
- *Carex tumulicola* (Berkeley sedge).
- *Festuca californica* (hardy to zone 4) and *F. glauca, F. idahoensis* (to zone 1).
- *Nassella* **species** (needle grass). *N. tenuissima* is one of the hardiest, into zone 2B.

Sources

Bulbs: Brent and Becky's Bulbs (877/661-2852 or www.brentandbeckysbulbs.com).

Perennials: High Country Gardens (800/925-9387 or www.highcountrygardens.com). ◆

This heirloom sedum bears yellow flowers over succulent leaves. RIGHT: Reddish trailing sempervivum is a handsome contrast to spiky yucca.

Worry-free summer pots

Succulents and yuccas make ideal container plants

By Steven R. Lorton • Photographs by Norm Plate

Have you ever gone out of town for a fun summer weekend and then worried that your container plants would fry in the meantime? To avoid that scenario, we devised plantings that need little irrigation or any other care. In fact, the plantings shown here have lived happily for a decade. They feature specimens from three unthirsty groups of plants—sedums, sempervivums, and yuccas—all of which display handsome foliage year-round, with a bonus of seasonal bloom.

The cast-concrete containers were filled with a mixture of 2 to 3 parts potting soil to 1 part turkey grit, a material for raising poultry (sold at feed stores; if unavailable, substitute finely crushed gravel). Located on a sunny walkway in a Pacific Northwest garden, the plants get by mainly on rainfall, but during summer hot spells, they appreciate a good drink weekly.

After blooms fade, cut back the stems that bore flowers. Then, to promote dense, robust growth, fertilize with a balanced liquid plant food. Feed a second and even a third time in mid- and late summer. ◆

Sedums. West Coast native *Sedum spathulifolium* has spoon-shaped silvery gray to bluish green leaves blushed with deep rose, and it bears light yellow flowers in spring and summer. Hardy in *Sunset* climate zones 2–9, 14–24. Cousin *S. sieboldii* has blue green leaves with red edges and bears dusty pink flowers in autumn. Zones 2–9, 12, 14–24.

Sempervivums. These form rosettes of waxy evergreen leaves and star-shaped summer flowers. *Sempervivum tectorum,* commonly called hens and chickens, comes in dozens of named varieties that bear 2- to 5-inch-wide rosettes in colors ranging from gray green to purplish red; reddish flowers are borne on 2-foot-tall stems. Cousin *S. arachnoideum* has gray green rosettes crisscrossed with filaments resembling cobwebs (the plant's common name is cobweb houseleek); bright red flowers are borne on 4- to 6-inch stems. Both species grow in zones 2–24.

Yuccas. Named varieties of *Yucca filamentosa* and cousin *Y. flaccida* are available with variegated leaves having white or yellow stripes; pale yellow flowers appear in late spring and summer. *Y. filamentosa* grows in zones 1–24; *Y. flaccida* grows in 1–9, 14–24.

CHARLES MANN

Pretty, steep little garden in Denver

■ For years, Mary Samora couldn't figure out what to do with the very steep lot behind her cottage in Denver. From the back door, there was only 20 feet of level ground before the slope dropped abruptly toward an alley at the rear of the property. Then, one day while Samora was driving in the mountains, she spotted a gazebo with the builder's ad attached. She hired him to construct a similar one in her backyard. Built on pillars, the octagonal wood-frame gazebo juts out over the slope, extending the outdoor living area. In the summer, Samora furnishes the gazebo with white wicker chairs and a table.

To hide the gazebo's underpinnings, Samora surrounded the structure with lush plantings of shrubs and vines, including clematis. She also installed a water feature: two ponds linked by a streambed and spanned by a wooden footbridge leading to the gazebo.

The final problem she faced was a blank garage wall. Then, while she was sitting in a tearoom admiring an arch painted by artist Deborah Bays, serendipity struck again. Samora asked Bays to paint a mural on the bare wall. The trompe l'oeil scene depicts a cottage draped in wisteria. Bays also added rooftop planter boxes; Samora fills them with blue scaevola and waters with a hose-end wand. Her pastel color scheme is picked up by pink impatiens in the bed at right and pink petunias, lavender verbena, and purple heliotrope in pots. — *Marcia Tatroe*

Filled with soil and plants, large baskets can be heavy (they need a sturdy place to hang). This one rests inside a raised planter.

◀ Fanfare and filigree

Fanfare series trailing impatiens have stems that reach 8 to 10 inches long. Here, ones with lavender and hot pink flowers fill an 18-inch-diameter hanging basket (sold as Imperial Hanging Planter from Kinsman Company; 800/733-4146). The basket has a coconut fiber liner and rests in a larger (36-inch-tall) wrought-iron planter from a nursery.
DESIGN: Bud Stuckey

▼ Impatiens tree

At first glance, the 8-foot-tall "tree" in Lorraine and Glenn Fredriks's front yard in Ripon, California, looks like an ancient azalea putting on a summer-time bloom show. But closer inspection reveals that the tree is a steel frame that holds 23 pots of blooming impatiens. A product of Glenn's imagination and welding torch, it has a trunk fashioned from a 2-inch by 8-foot-long steel pipe and branches (as well as bracing beneath them) of 1-inch-square steel tubing. Rings that hold the pots are made of ⅛-inch-thick flat steel bar welded to the branch tips (for details, see www.sunset.com/garden/flowertree.html). The trunk is anchored in concrete.

Each spring, the Fredrikses plant pink impatiens in 12-inch plastic pots filled with potting soil. (At planting time, they mix ½ teaspoon controlled-release fertilizer into the soil.) Then they set the pots into the rings. A drip-irrigation system waters each pot 5 minutes a day throughout the blooming season. In addition, each pot is fed a dilute liquid fertilizer twice a month. ◆

Impatiens on high

Two fresh ways to use these handsome heat lovers

By Peter O. Whiteley

Impatiens are among the most versatile of summer plants, taking to life in hanging baskets, containers, and lightly shaded beds with equal aplomb. Their colorful flowers, in shades of lavender, pink, orange, and white, are so beautiful that some gardeners prefer to grow the plants at eye level. We show two ways to give impatiens a lift.

Plastic pots nest in steel rings on four tiers. Plants quickly fill out to form a blooming "tree," irrigated for 5 minutes a day by drip tubing that runs up the trunk.

before

Seeking shelter

This remodeled front yard adds privacy and an escape from the wind

By Peter O. Whiteley

Chilly winds and swirling fog prevented Sonja and Fred Conta from enjoying their backyard in Tiburon, California. The couple's more sheltered front yard seemed the most logical place for outdoor living, but it lacked privacy from the street, and a curving driveway filled most of it.

The solution? Move the driveway, reorganize the space, and build a privacy fence. Then bring in plants,

Before remodeling, the front yard was all pavement. Afterward, the azalea-edged lawn and a patio with fountain are invitations to outdoor living.
BELOW RIGHT: Trellis and fence conceal house from street; lavender offers a fragrant greeting beside the driveway.

a bench, and a gurgling water feature to mask noise from the street. Let the house keep the blustery wind at bay.

To reorganize the space, the Contas first relocated the garage door to face the street, then removed the old asphalt driveway. Then they put in a new driveway that's smaller, straighter, and made of interlocking concrete pavers set on compacted gravel and sand.

A trellis-topped privacy fence came next; built as close to the street as code would allow, it has a peaked pavilion framing the entry path to screen the street from the house and garden area. A new front walkway leads to a privacy gate.

Inside, the garden is divided into a couple of zones. A breakfast patio, which faces the garden and the morning sun, sits near the granite water sculpture in the garden's most wind-sheltered spot, where the old

garage door had been. A teak bench on a gravel path near a pair of raised planters offers views across the new lawn and flower beds.

Landscape architect Elizabeth Hutchinson provided the Contas with these outdoor living spaces and with a rich palette of plants: 4 kinds of trees, 26 shrub varieties, 9 different vines, and 11 types of perennials, plus ferns, palms, bulbs, and ground covers.

DESIGN: Elizabeth Hutchinson (415/ 488-4859). The fence, gate, and entry pavilion were designed by architect Thomas Bateman Hood of Larkspur, California (415/461-9490). ◆

A SHADE TREE, a comfy chair, and a blooming 'Trude Webster' rhododendron create the inviting backyard retreat shown here. For inspiration and advice on creating a garden sanctuary of your own, see pages 190–200.

MICHAEL S. THOMPSON

June

CHARLES MANN

Forest of columbines in Angelfire

From six plants, a self-sustaining spectacle in New Mexico

■ In 1985, when Kathy Kalen moved into her house in Angelfire, New Mexico, she bought a sixpack of columbines at an Albuquerque nursery and planted them on the property, at an elevation of 9,000 feet. Initially, the plants just sulked in the rocky soil, Kalen recalls, so she transplanted them into terraced beds amended with leaf mold and manure. The very next spring, the columbines put on a magnificent show. The following spring, hundreds of baby plants appeared. Every year thereafter, the self-sowing columbines have steadily multiplied into a multitude covering nearly 4,500 square feet. From mid-June through the Fourth of July, the columbines form a forest of flowers in shades of red, yellow, and violet. During peak bloom, Kalen invites friends and local garden club members to come see the array of color, which, she points out, is the natural result of bees, butterflies, and hummingbirds spreading pollen from one blossom to another.

Although Kalen didn't record which columbine she planted, horticulturists who have seen her plants believe they're the offspring of McKana Giants, a tall (to 3 feet) hybrid strain with long-spurred flowers. Kalen's plants thrive in the filtered shade of aspen, fir, and pine trees. She mulches around the columbines with pine needles or wood chips to help the soil hold moisture. — *Dick Bushnell*

Serenity with ease

STEVEN GUNTHER

■ The palette of silver, yellow green, and white plants shown at right is soft and soothing. It's also low maintenance. "Other than watering, you can leave it alone all summer and fall," says designer Barbara Deed.

The planting's reliance on foliage for interest is what makes it so easy, says Deed. "It's all about texture." The plant with the plush, silvery gray leaves and pink and white flower spikes on the left is *Plectranthus argentatus.* Needle-leafed *Westringia fruticosa* provides a sharp contrast next to it. The yellow green plant in the center, which looks a bit like ruffled celery, is variegated 'Prince Rupert', a scented geranium. "It

looks good with anything. It belongs in every border," says Deed.

Golden sage (in the foreground, at right) and *Carex comans* 'Frosty Curls' (the blond grass) repeat the colors of the geranium leaves. 'Star White' zinnia is the final touch. It blooms nonstop until Thanksgiving, and rarely needs deadheading. — *Sharon Cohoon*

PEST ALERT

Red imported fire ants (RIFA), serious pests in Southern California, are aggressive, reddish brown ants that bite people, pets, and wildlife while inflicting painful stings. Outside, they nest in lawns and gardens—look for a low mat of finely granular soil about 18 inches across—as well as under cracked pavement. Inside, they're often found in electrical and utility housings (causing short circuits). To eradicate them, California needs your help. If you find mounds or nests that could be RIFA colonies, report them to the hotline, (888) 434-7326. For details, consult www.ocfireant.com or www.cdfa.ca.gov.

Sweet pea time in Sebastopol

THOMAS J. STORY

■ Every spring, Glenys Johnson anxiously awaits the appearance of her first blooms—and the start of her spring-summer cut flower business—at Enchanting Sweet Peas farm in Sebastopol. "I am always amazed at how beautiful the frilly-edged blossoms are," says Johnson of those first blooms.

From April to August, Johnson supplies local florists and markets with these lovely blossoms. But one day a year, usually early in June, she has an open house at her farm, where visitors can see and smell her 30 varieties of English Spencer sweet peas growing on 400 feet of trellising.

At the open houses, visitors can take a self-guided tour through the garden, learn growing tips from Johnson, buy cut flowers, and purchase sweet pea seeds (at 20 percent discount) from the 18 types listed in her catalog, as well as other varieties she's experimenting with.

Call (707) 829-5284 to learn the date (and hours) of this year's open house. The farm is located at. 890 N. Gravenstein Hwy. (State 116).
— *Lauren Bonar Swezey*

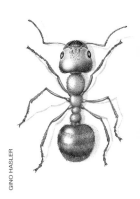

GINO HASLER

PLANT PROFILE
Japanese tree lilac

■ Imagine the beauty and fragrance of a lilac in a full-size tree. The Japanese tree lilac *(Syringa reticulata)* grows 20 to 30 feet tall and 15 to 25 feet wide and has a rounded canopy. From early to mid-June, the tree is covered with 6- to 12-inch-long clusters of sweetly fragrant white flowers. Even a young tree will carry enough blooms to make your yard smell wonderful.

Tree lilacs are hardy to –30° and tol-

erate drought well. Unlike most lilacs trained as trees, profuse suckering is not a problem. They can be grown in *Sunset* climate zones A2–A3, 1–12, and 14–15. Growth rate is 12 to 18 inches a year. They make ideal accent trees when planted on mounds or in beds. 'Ivory Silk' is a compact variety that blooms profusely at an early age.

Plant bare-root trees in spring and containerized or balled-and-burlaped specimens anytime the ground can be worked. As with all lilacs, tree lilacs prefer a sunny location and soil with a neutral pH. They don't do well in wet areas or in lawns unless drainage is excellent. Tree lilacs are available at many nurseries. A good mail-order source is Forestfarm (541/846-7269 or www.forestfarm.com). — *Dick Rifkind*

Secret gardens in Steamboat Springs

■ One of the best-kept secrets in the Rocky Mountains is the Yampa River Botanic Park in Steamboat Springs, Colorado. Opened in 1997, the 6-acre park is truly a community effort, built and maintained with the help of a large corps of dedicated volunteers. Twenty-seven theme gardens demonstrate the remarkable range of gardening possibilities in this ski resort (elevation 6,800 feet), where temperatures can drop to –30° in winter and only 60 frost-free days occur in a typical growing season.

Just inside the main entrance are four of the park's most colorful floral displays: the butterfly garden, the hummingbird garden, the summer sunshine garden, and the members' rock garden. Landscape timber steps planted with yellow-flowered *Potentilla neumanniana* lead visitors past clumps of yellow 'Stella de Oro' daylilies, drifts of lavender blue catmint, red-and-yellow *Gaillardia* x *grandiflora* 'Goblin', and two varieties of yellow-flowered sedums. Carpets of pink *Dianthus deltoides* dot the hillside.

The park is located south of downtown Steamboat Springs. From U.S. 40, turn west on Trafalgar Lane, south on Pamela Lane, and go to the parking lot at the far end. The grounds are open dawn to dusk May 1 through October 31. Admission is free. For information, call (970) 846-5172. — *Marcia Tatroe*

Porch pots in Boise

■ A pair of large containers extend a warm welcome all summer long on Randy Lancaster and Christine Yardas's front porch in Boise. Clockwise from top left are coral-colored pelargonium, burgundy-leafed coleus, pale pink petunia, white marguerite daisy, deep blue 'Crystal Palace' lobelia, 'Marguerite' sweet potato with chartreuse leaves, and pink baby's breath.

The 15-inch-diameter, 10-inch-tall glazed ceramic pots have saucers to catch the runoff from daily watering. To keep new flowers and leaves coming, the plants are fed with liquid fertilizer every few weeks.

— *Suzanne Kelso.*

1955 Chevy® Stepside Pickup

Park this revolutionary Chevy® in your collection!

1:32 Scale

Chevy's® innovative Stepside, powered by its first V-8 engine, was the hottest pickup on the market.

- Precision die-cast detail
- Egg crate grille
- Wraparound windshield
- Doors open

This item is not a toy. For adult collector use only. Made of diecast metal and plastic parts. Measures 5"L. Colors may vary.

4 PAYMENTS EACH ONLY $3.99

Keep chow time clean and tidy!

SAVE OVER 35%
Similar Items Sell Elsewhere for $24.95

Braided Doggie Bone Rug

A perfect placemat for your dog's dishes, this fun bone-shaped rug is colorful, texture-rich and ready to catch food and water spills. Made of durable 100% polyester.

4 PAYMENTS EACH ONLY $3.99

Hand Wash Only. Made of 100% polyester. Imported. Measures 30.3"L x 18.5"W.

8

STEVEN GUNTHER; BELOW: RICHARD SHIELL

Flying colors

Butterflies can't resist this swath of blooms in Cambria

■ This summer perennial border is pretty to look at, but its main purpose is to attract winged visitors like swallowtails, sulfurs, red admirals, and monarchs.

Shana McCormick, director of grounds and gardens at Cambria Pines Lodge, chose nectar-rich plants just for butterflies. And on her regular strolls through the garden, she has observed which flowers attract which ones. Swallowtails (shown right) love the tall, purple-flowered *Verbena bonariensis* at the back of the border. Sulfurs, on the other hand, are more likely to hang out by the *Aster pringlei* 'Monte Cassino', the fluffy cloud of small white flowers. Red admirals prefer or-namental oregano, the deep purple haze. And monarch butterflies love, above all else, bog sage *(Salvia uliginosa)*, a tall, blue-flowered plant not yet in bloom when the photo was taken. Every butterfly stops on the bright yellow landing pads at the center of the border, *Rudbeckia fulgida sullivantii* 'Goldsturm', says McCormick. And later in the year when the blooms turn to seed, they lure finches.

If you want to attract some of these winged guests to your own garden, head for a nursery. The plants shown here should be available.

Cambria Pines Lodge, 2905 Burton Dr.; Cambria. — S.C.

Clouds of rhododendron blossoms canopy a winding path through this green retreat.
RIGHT: Spouting water and potted hostas fill a grotto with sound and foliage.

Making the most of shade

■ Mature rhododendrons and an ancient ponderosa pine cast dense shade over most of Debbie and Jeffrey Ogburn's backyard in Eugene, Oregon. Pruned as small trees, the 20-foot-tall rhododendrons dangle pink and white blossoms over a basalt rock path leading to a granite bench. "The pine is really an old-growth tree that ought to be out in a forest somewhere," explains Debbie, "but we've been gardening here since 1986, and I've grown to appreciate the wonderful variety of plants that like low-light conditions."

Beside the path, Debbie wove a tapestry composed mainly of native sword ferns, bleeding heart, and *Geranium macrorrhizum,* a perennial ground cover that bears pink flowers in late spring and early summer.

The yard is filled with the splashing sound of water, which emanates from a grotto erected on a slate patio. The grotto is formed by a 7-foot-tall Douglas fir arbor covered with silver lace vine *(Fallopia baldschuanica).* Inside, wa-

ter spouts from a bas-relief sculpture of Poseidon into a matching faux-stone basin. The basin is nestled among the white-edged leaves of *Hosta sieboldii (H. albomarginata)* and pots of shade-loving coleus, impatiens, and ferns. Hanging baskets brighten the interior with a mix of white-flowered begonias, red pelargoniums, blue lobelia, and white bacopa *(Sutera cordata).*

The Ogburns prune the rhododendrons right after bloom, and in spring, they add a 3-inch layer of compost over the natural mulch of needles that continually drop from the pine. — *Mary-Kate Mackey*

Tillandsias
in the trees

■ Patrick and Julianne Mahoney display tillandsias the way they might appear in a real jungle. These epiphytic plants, which in the wild grow in the crotches of trees, are everywhere in the Mahoneys' tropical jungle garden in Anaheim, California—twining around branches, or in wire hanging baskets lined with sphagnum moss, like the one pictured here.

Tillandsias are available at most nurseries. For unusual varieties, contact Tillandsia International at (559) 683-7097 or www.airplant.com. — S.C

STEVEN GUNTHER

The Mahoneys' tricks for a natural look

• **Use Spanish moss to conceal** the basket's chain.
• **Insert the tillandsias facing in different directions** so all the interest isn't focused on just one side.
• **Mix** different shapes, sizes, and kinds of tillandsias.

CLIPPINGS

• **Conservatory of Flowers website.** To discover the latest details about the restoration of San Francisco's Conservatory of Flowers in Golden Gate Park and make a donation to help the effort, visit www.conservatoryofflowers.org.

BACK TO BASICS

LINDA HOLT AYRISS (2)

Cover drainage holes. To prevent soil from leaking out a drainage hole when repotting a plant, cover the hole with a fine mesh screen or pot shard before filling with soil. If using screen, cut a piece large enough to overlap the hole by several inches. If using a pot shard, select a curved piece and place it convex side up so it doesn't block the passage of water. Don't use gravel or charcoal in the bottom of a pot.

Summer lawn watering. To irrigate effectively with an underground system, you need to know how evenly your sprinklers deliver water. Check your system by placing a number of equal-size cans around the lawn, at regular intervals outward from the sprinklers. Turn on the water for 15 minutes, then turn it off and measure the amount of water in each can. If the containers fill unevenly, check the sprinkler heads; they may need adjusting or replacing.— L.B.S.

Lap pool made for a small yard

■ When Maggie White and Clair Cobb moved into their current home in Phoenix, they knew they wanted a lap pool long enough for serious swimming. They even knew what they wanted it to look like; White had already scoured home shows and decided on materials. Now all the homeowners had to do was figure out how to squeeze the pool into their modest 45- by 60-foot backyard.

Fortunately, White and Cobb's neighbor was landscape designer Carrie Nimmer. She envisioned a lap pool installed on the diagonal to fit the yard's tight confines. Once Nimmer had outlined the pool's perimeter on bare ground, White and Cobb saw that it would work.

La Paz Pools of Mesa, Arizona, designed the 35-foot-long, 8-foot-wide pool, with a small spa on one side. The deck around the pool is coated with an acrylic epoxy concrete compound called Lace, from Armor-Deck. The pool trim and the patio at front left are finished in a pattern called Saltillo that resembles Mexican pavers.

The surrounding garden is Nimmer's design. She placed intensely colored walls around the perimeter and planted equally flamboyant flowering plants, like the 'Superstition Gold' bougainvillea in the foreground. "It's very colorful and also very low maintenance," says White, "so that leaves us plenty of time to swim." — S.C.

NORM PLATE; BELOW: LINDA ENGER

Chocolate-scented blossoms

■ A perennial native to much of the Southwest, chocolate flower *(Berlandiera lyrata)* blooms over an unusually long season—from spring to fall—offering fragrance for human noses and nectar for butterflies, plus attractive seed heads for dried arrangements. To best enjoy the flower's chocolate scent, you'll want to plant it near patios or in containers.

Chocolate flower is hardy in *Sunset* climate zones 10–13. It forms a mound of grayish green foliage about 1½ feet tall and 2 to 3 feet wide. The drought-tolerant plant's 2-inch-wide blossoms wilt in the heat of the afternoon before perking up again in the cool of the evening. It takes full sun—but benefits from afternoon shade in the low desert—and while it grows largest in amended soil, it will still thrive in unimproved soil. To prune, simply cut back the plant in late fall or winter.

Start chocolate flower from seed or set out transplants in spring or fall. If rabbits are a problem, protect plants until they are established. Many nurseries carry the plant in 1-gallon containers. You can also order seed or transplants from Plants of the Southwest (800/788-7333 or www.plantsofthesouthwest.com) or seed from Wild Seed Inc. (602/276-3536). — Cathy Cromell

Season the border with

chives

■ Chopped chives are a traditional condiment atop baked potatoes. But in Judy Whitmyre's garden in Ketchum, Idaho, chives *(Allium schoenoprasum)* are an eye-pleasing ingredient of a mixed border. Whitmyre set out plants of this perennial herb three years ago. Starting in early spring, they bear rosy purple flowers over 2-foot-tall clumps of lush, grasslike foliage. Although Whitmyre simply removes the blooms as they fade, fresh chive blossoms are perfectly edible: They have a more intense onion flavor than the leaves and make a savory garnish for salads.

In this view of Whitmyre's border, the chives are surrounded (clockwise from bottom) by yellow-flowered lady's-mantle, Oriental poppies in bud, spikes of purple lupine, and tall bearded irises with multicolored columbines and pink dianthus behind.

Whitmyre irrigates the border with a sprinkler for half an hour daily and scatters granular fertilizer twice a month during the growing season. In autumn, she spreads a 2-inch layer of manure or compost over the border.

— *S.K.*

NORM PLATE

A pretty, lucky pot

■ Last summer, Cheryl Wilson of Kirkland, Washington, entered her first competition ever—the 2001 Supersoil Container Garden Contest. To Wilson's surprise, her entry (shown below) won the grand prize—a trip for two to Hawaii. Wilson, who has a background in both horticulture and interior design, filled a 23-inch-diameter ceramic pot with three perennials whose forms, colors, and leaf textures play off one another beautifully. If you'd like to try your luck in this year's contest, visit www.sunset.com/go/supersoil. html for more information.

Wilson's plant list

• Three 1-gallon myrtle spurge *(Euphorbia myrsinites)*. Its trailing stems are clad with spirals of succulent blue green leaves. Clusters of chartreuse to yellow flowers appear in late winter or early spring.

• Two 4-inch *Pelargonium* 'Mrs. Pollock'. This fancy-leafed zonal geranium has tricolored foliage and reddish orange flowers.

• One 5-gallon purple fountain grass *(Pennisetum setaceum* 'Rubrum'). Clumps of reddish brown leaves are topped by rosy flower plumes in summer. — *D.B.*

Birdproof tent for berry bed

■ Leave it to an architect to create an elegant yet practical garden structure with plain white PVC pipe. Bari Thompson managed this feat in his Lake Oswego, Oregon, garden. Using ³/₄-inch-diameter schedule 40 PVC pipe, he created a tentlike frame that he covers with netting to keep birds from gobbling his strawberries. The pipes are cemented at the joints with standard PVC glue. He slips the entire frame over one 3- by 12-foot raised bed, then ties bird netting across each end of the frame. The top and sides of the frame are covered with a single piece of netting draped over the ridgepole and tied to the pipes along each side of the frame. To harvest strawberries, Thompson simply lifts either side of the netting.

— *Jim McCausland*

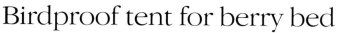

Northwest treasures in Tacoma

■ This month, you don't have to leave the Tacoma city limits to experience such natural wonders as a garden abloom with blue lupines, masses of fragrant Western azaleas, and a newly repaired pond edged with aquatic plants. These treasures and many more can be found in the Northwest Native Plant Garden at Point Defiance Park.

Opened in 1963, the garden is being revitalized by dedicated volunteers from the Tacoma Garden Club (www. tacomagardenclub.org). They've done a monumental job of weeding, pruning, and replanting sections of the 5-acre grounds.

You can walk through the gardens anytime. Before you wander the paths, pick up a take-home brochure that helps locate plants that will thrive under conditions similar to those in your own garden.

The native plant garden is just west of the rose garden near the main entrance to Point Defiance Park, at the north end of Pearl Street in Tacoma. The park is open daily during daylight hours; admission is free. — *J.M.*

NORM PLATE; LEFT: JIM WILSON; BELOW: JANET LOUGHREY

WHAT TO DO IN YOUR GARDEN IN JUNE

PLANTING

☐ **ANNUALS.** Sow seeds of cosmos, marigold, portulaca, sunflower, sweet alyssum, and zinnia right away for bloom in late summer and fall. But for instant color, set out nursery seedlings of all the above, plus coleus, geranium, impatiens, Madagascar periwinkle, and petunia.

☐ **BULBS.** While you can still get them, plant canna, dahlia, gladiolus, montbretia, tigridia, and tuberous begonia.

☐ **HERBS.** Plant seedlings of basil, chives, cilantro, mint, oregano, parsley, rosemary, sage, and thyme right away.

☐ **LAWNS.** Lay sod any time from March through September. Zones A1–A3: Sow seed or lay sod now so turf will have time to become established over summer.

☐ **PERENNIALS.** Plant aster, basket-of-gold, blanket flower, campanula, columbine, coreopsis, delphinium, erigeron, feverfew, foxglove, gilia, heuchera, Oriental poppy, penstemon, perennial sweet pea *(Lathyrus latifolius)*, potentilla, purple cone-flower, salvia, Shasta daisy, Shirley poppy, and Siberian wallflower. For filler, use artemisia, dusty miller, and golden or purple sage.

☐ **VEGETABLES.** Set out seedlings of cucumber, eggplant, pepper, squash, and tomato early in the month; sow successive crops of beets, bush beans, carrots, kohlrabi, lettuce, onions, parsnips, peas, radishes, spinach, Swiss chard, and turnips.

MAINTENANCE

☐ **CARE FOR APPLES.** *Prevent apple maggots.* If you noticed that last year's apples were riddled with tunnels, the culprits were apple maggots. For biological control, hang red sticky traps in the trees (red balls coated with a product like Tangle-Trap Insect Trap Coating by Tanglefoot). *Thin fruit.* Apples produce bigger fruit if you thin them after June drop, when trees spontaneously shed unpollinated fruit. Thin triple clusters to doubles, and double clusters to singles. Don't thin at all if you have an alternate-bearing tree and this is the light year.

☐ **CONTROL APHIDS.** Blast them off new growth with a hose and follow up with a spray of insecticidal soap or, in worst cases, pyrethrin-based insecticide.

☐ **CONTROL SLUGS.** Bait around susceptible plants, or hunt down snails and slugs on rainy days or at night.

☐ **DIVIDE PERENNIALS.** Immediately after bloom, dig and divide spring-flowering perennials. Oriental poppies can be separated root by root, but iris rhizomes need to be cut apart with a knife or spade. As you work, throw away woody or dead parts of the roots.

☐ **FERTILIZE.** Feed spring-flowering plants right after bloom. ◆

WHAT TO DO IN YOUR GARDEN IN JUNE

PLANTING

☐ CANNAS. Zones 7–9, 14–17: Set out 'Tropicanna', noted for its green-, pink-, red-, and yellow-striped burgundy foliage and bright orange flowers. If these colors don't work in your garden, try 'Black Knight' (red with dark burgundy foliage), 'Miss Oklahoma' (melon pink with deep green foliage), or 'Richard Wallace' (bright yellow with apple green leaves). If you can't find plants at your local nursery, have them order one for you from Monrovia Nursery (wholesale only). In zones 1 and 2, plant in large pots, or be prepared to dig and store plants next winter.

☐ HERBS. To make sure you have enough basil and cilantro to use fresh and for cooking through the summer and fall, plant successive crops of seeds every six to eight weeks. For basil, try 'Mrs. Burns' Lemon', 'Salad Leaf', or one of the wonderful aromatic Italian types, such as 'Italian Pesto' or 'Profuma di Genova'. Choose a slow-bolt (slow to set seed) variety of cilantro. (All types are available from Renee's Garden, sold on seed racks at nurseries or online at www.reneesgarden.com.)

Sunset
CLIMATE ZONES

☐ Mountain (1-2)
☐ Valley (7-9)
☐ Inland (14)
☐ Coastal (15-17)

DEBRA LAMBERT

☐ PLANTS FOR DAD. Nurseries carry a great assortment of interesting plants suitable for gifts on Father's Day. Consider a blooming bonsai, bougainvillea, daylily, or gardenia, or a citrus tree such as 'Clementine' tangerine, 'Improved Meyer' lemon, or kumquat.

☐ VEGETABLES. Sow seeds of beans (bush and pole types). For corn, try one of the super sweet or sugary enhanced varieties, which stay sweeter longer after harvest. New this year is 'Silver Princess', an early-maturing sugary enhanced white corn with great flavor (from Park Seed; 800/845-3369 or www. parkseed.com). Set out transplants of cucumbers, eggplant, melons, okra, peppers, pumpkins, squash, and tomatoes.

MAINTENANCE

☐ CARE FOR ROSES. To encourage growth and additional flushes of flowers, feed repeat bloomers with a complete fertilizer. If leaves are yellow with green veins, also apply iron chelate. Water deeply, after fertilizing, by running a hose into a basin of soil around the plant's drip line. Or use drip irrigation (place an emitter on each side of the plant). To conserve soil moisture and keep roots cooler, spread a 3- to 4-inch layer of mulch under the bushes (keep it away from trunks). Remove faded flowers.

☐ PICK HERBS. For the best flavor, harvest individual leaves or sprigs before flower buds open. If plants are blooming, use flowers to decorate foods.

☐ PROTECT JAPANESE MAPLES. Zones 7–9, 14: When temperatures rise, these sensitive trees often suffer from tip burn (leaves turn brown along the edges). One easy way to minimize damage is to spray the foliage with an anti-transpirant such as Cloud Cover (available at many nurseries and home improvement centers). Also, mulch the soil under the branches with an organic material such as ground or shredded bark (avoid piling it against the trunks) and water trees regularly. ◆

WHAT TO DO IN YOUR GARDEN IN JUNE

PLANTING

☐ **SHADE PLANTS.** For color, consider abutilon, begonias, brunfelsia, clivia, coral bells, fuchsias, hydrangea, and Japanese anemone. Variegated foliage plants such as aucuba, carex, pittosporum, and lamium will also add sparkle.

☐ **SUMMER PERENNIALS.** Look for plants that will bloom well into fall. Good choices include coreopsis, daylilies, gaillardia, lion's tail, penstemon, rudbeckia, salvias, and true geraniums. Helenium produces tons of daisylike flowers in golds, oranges, and reds. If you can't find it in your local nursery, order it from Digging Dog Nursery (707/937-1130 or www.diggingdog.com).

☐ **VEGETABLES.** Set out transplants of cucumbers, eggplant, melons, peppers, and tomatoes. Sow seeds of beans, corn, cucumbers, New Zealand spinach, okra, pumpkins, and summer and winter squash. In the high desert (zone 11), sow seeds of corn, cucumbers, melons, okra, squash, and watermelons.

☐ **VINES.** Indulge in a quick-growing annual like scarlet runner bean or morning glory. Or invest in something more permanent—bougainvillea, Carolina jessamine, Mexican flame vine, passion vine, or potato vine. Priscilla Stead, plant sale specialist at Fullerton Arboretum, says that Southern California can support more vining plants than any other climatic zone. For really unusual vines, like twining firecracker *(Manettia inflata)*, check out the arboretum's weekend plant sales.

MAINTENANCE

☐ **CONSERVE WATER.** Because this past winter's very dry and windy weather did not help our water supplies much, now's the time to start conserving. Call your local water district for helpful literature. Some districts also offer free water audits and water-saving tips by an irrigation specialist. To schedule an appointment in Orange County, call (714) 963-3058; in Riverside, (909) 789-5000; and in San Diego County, (888) 276-0800. Two useful websites are www.h2ouse.org and www.mwdoc.com.

☐ **FERTILIZE PLANTS.** Roses, lawns, annual flowers and vegetables, container plants, and just about anything actively growing except natives and Mediterraneans will benefit from fertilizing now.

☐ **RENEW MULCH.** To keep roots cool, preserve soil moisture, and discourage weeds, renew mulch around trees, shrubs, and established perennials. Homemade compost is ideal (partially decomposed is fine), or use wood chips.

PEST & DISEASE CONTROL

☐ **CONTROL GIANT WHITEFLY.** Look for the telltale white spiral of eggs on the underside of leaves of target plants—avocado, banana, hibiscus, and plumeria. Wash off with jets of water, still the best control. Pick off and discard leaves with long, waxy filaments.

☐ **MANAGE POWDERY MILDEW.** "June gloom," especially along the coast, creates ideal conditions for powdery mildew on roses and vegetable crops like cucumbers, melons, and squash. Combat by hosing off foliage in the morning to wash off spores. (Watering late in the day compounds the problem.) Or use a Neem oil product. ◆

WHAT TO DO IN YOUR GARDEN IN JUNE

PLANTING

☐ **BUTTERFLY GARDEN.** To attract many types of butterflies, plant aster, butterfly bush, gaillardia, milkweed *(Asclepias),* parsley, rabbitbrush *(Chrysothamnus),* sedums, and violets and leave a few dandelions in the lawn. Don't use insecticides. Place shallow bowls of mud near where butterflies feed.

☐ **COLORFUL COLEUS.** Sun-tolerant varieties of this tender perennial with showy foliage perform equally well in sun or shade. Look for 'Burgundy Sun', 'Crazy Quilt', 'Pineapple Prince', 'Plum Parfait', and 'Silver Sunrise'.

☐ **HANGING BASKETS.** Hang flower baskets on porches, lampposts, and tree limbs. Good plant choices for baskets include bacopa, ivy geranium, lantana, trailing lobelia, nolana, trailing petunia, and verbena. Baskets with plastic liners require less frequent watering.

☐ **SUMMER FLOWERS.** When the weather warms up, sow seeds of cosmos, marigold, morning glory, portulaca, sunflower, and zinnia. For instant impact, set out nursery seedlings of ageratum, amaranth, celosia, China aster, coleus, gazania, geranium, heliotrope, impatiens, Madagascar periwinkle, nierembergia, petunia, and scarlet sage.

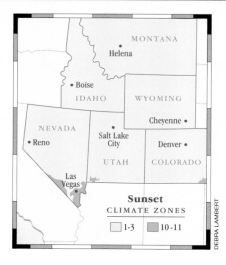

Sunset
CLIMATE ZONES

☐ 1-3 ☐ 10-11

DEBRA LAMBERT

☐ **VEGETABLES.** After the last frost date for your area, set out transplants of warm-season fruits and vegetables, including cucumber, eggplant, melon, pepper, pumpkin, squash, and tomato. Sow seeds of beans, corn, and tender herbs like basil and dill directly in the ground. Sow edible flowers such as anise hyssop *(Agastache foeniculum),* calendula, and nasturtium between vegetable rows, and harvest their blooms to garnish salads.

☐ **WATER GARDENS.** Put tropical water lilies and other frost-tender aquatic plants into outdoor ponds when the water temperature reaches 70°. Fertilize at planting time and monthly through September to encourage blooming.

MAINTENANCE

☐ **PINCH ASTERS AND MUMS.** To encourage branching, compact growth, and additional flowers, pinch or shear fall-blooming asters and chrysanthemums until mid-July. Remove the top few inches of each stem whenever the plant reaches 1 foot tall.

☐ **PRUNE ALL SPRING-BLOOMING SHRUBS.** If needed, prune beauty bush, bridal wreath spiraea, forsythia, kerria, lilac, mock orange *(Philadelphus),* quince, and wiegela immediately after flowering.

☐ **PUT OUT HOUSEPLANTS.** Move houseplants outside for the summer after all risk of frost is past. Cut back leggy growth and put the plants in a location sheltered from wind and direct sunlight (a covered porch or patio is ideal). During their outdoor stay, houseplants need more water than they do indoors; check the pots daily and feed every other week with a liquid fertilizer.

☐ **WATER TRANSPLANTS.** Recycle a 1-gallon milk jug to be a constant water source for small transplants until they get established. With a pin, poke a hole in one bottom corner of the jug, fill with water, and place the jug where it will drip over the plant's rootball. — *M.T.* ◆

WHAT TO DO IN YOUR GARDEN IN JUNE

PLANTING

☐ **ANNUAL FLOWERS.** Zones 1A–3B (Flagstaff, Taos, Prescott, Santa Fe): Plant marigold, salvia, and zinnia. Zones 10–11 (Albuquerque, Las Vegas): Plant four o'clock, geranium, larkspur, salvia, and verbena. Zones 12–13 (Tucson, Phoenix): Plant cosmos, gaillardia, globe amaranth, marigold, and zinnia.

☐ **HERBS.** Zones 1A–3B: Sow seeds of cilantro, dill, and parsley. Zones 10–13: Set out basil, marjoram, oregano, rosemary, and thyme in well-drained soil.

☐ **VEGETABLES.** Zones 1A–3B: Sow seeds of broccoli, cabbage, carrots, chard, radishes, and turnips. Zones 10–13: Sow seeds of Armenian cucumbers, black-eyed peas, corn, early-maturing green beans, melon, and summer and winter squash.

MAINTENANCE

☐ **FERTILIZE.** Lawns grow vigorously in the summer, so feed them monthly with a high-nitrogen fertilizer. If your roses are still blooming, continue to fertilize them every two weeks. Reinvigorate vegetable beds, annual color plants, and grape vines with twice-monthly applications of fish emulsion, compost tea, or commercial liquid fertilizer.

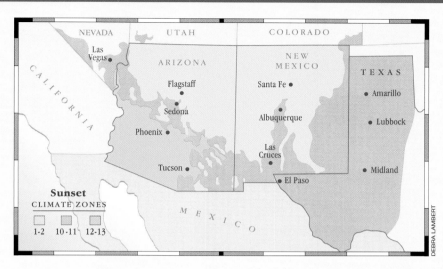

Sunset
CLIMATE ZONES
☐ 1-2 ☐ 10-11 ☐ 12-13

DEBRA LAMBERT

☐ **IRRIGATE.** A frequent cause of June plant loss is overwatering. Most desert-adapted and drought-tolerant plants, including acacia, citrus, dalea, lavender, rosemary, and salvia, don't like wet feet and are susceptible to root rot when hot, wet conditions persist. To conserve water and discourage fungal diseases, irrigate in the early morning, allowing the soil to dry out between waterings. On the other hand, small potted plants require twice-daily irrigation to keep the roots cool and the foliage hydrated.

☐ **MULCH.** If you haven't yet applied a 4- to 6-inch-layer of mulch around annuals, landscape plants, and vegetables, do so now. This insulating layer cools the root zone and keeps moisture in the soil.

☐ **PROTECT CROPS.** Protect vegetable crops and deciduous fruits from thirsty birds and the insects that follow by draping trees and plants with bird netting secured at the plants' base. Encase clusters of ripening grapes in knee-high nylon stockings. Watch for grape leaf skeletonizers: These tiny, brightly colored insects consume the tissue between leaf ribs and veins; what remains is a skeletal leaf that turns brown and drops off the vine. If you spot these symptoms, spray the vines with *Bacillus thuringiensis*.

☐ **SHADE TOMATOES, PEPPERS.** With tomato and pepper plants, you can prevent sunscald and reduce heat enough to increase blossom set and fruit production by sheltering them under 70 percent shade-cloth. — *Kim Nelson* ◆

How to make your escape: Seek shelter under a rustic ramada in Tucson; build your own gazebo; relax on a Seattle rooftop; enjoy a front row seat to a vegetable garden; and sink into a wicker chair, with a rhododendron for company.

CHRISTINA SCHMIDHOFER; CLOCKWISE FROM TOP LEFT: TERRENCE MOORE, THOMAS J. STORY, NORM PLATE, MICHAEL S. THOMPSON, JOHN GRANEN

Backyard
retreats

From the porch to the patio, for fun and for quiet, here are the inspiration and advice you need to create a sanctuary of your own

■ A Zen master could summon peace of mind on a packed city bus. The rest of us need help. Some privacy. Flowers. A little breeze ferrying the scents of a summer day. Whatever space you have outside that belongs to you, whatever its size or shape, it can be claimed as a place of refuge. On the following pages, you'll discover how homeowners from Seattle to Tucson made their escapes, and how you can too.

Tropical plants and container gardening blend with unusual artifacts and accessories. The Balinese temple umbrella is both decorative and functional, protecting plants from the noonday sun.

Living in
paradise

By Ann Bertelsen • Photographs by Christina Schmidhofer

Tropical plants, exotic accessories, and the right frame of mind create a personal resort in the suburbs

This sanctuary's features include temple carvings, antique columns from India, and Chinese slate tiles, with a pair of teak chairs the perfect complement.

At dawn on weekdays, Davis Dalbok tends his garden, then has breakfast "in the tropics" before dashing down the freeway to his city office. His tropical escape is his remodeled porch, which looks like it's in Bali or Hawaii.

Welcome to Fairfax, California, where Dalbok has created his own resort using subtropical plants and exotic accessories to capture the flavor of the South Sea Islands. "Many homeowners don't realize that they can take advantage of microclimates within their own gardens," says Dalbok, whose front porch was once a drab concrete slab.

A plantscape designer who travels the world to discover unusual plants and accessories, Dalbok says that it's

Dalbok (below) rotates brilliantly colored plants, such as this bright yellow canna, in and out of the garden, using ceramic containers for flexibility. A carved wood figure from the Ivory Coast is joined by a striped croton and a fanlike cycad.

possible to cultivate a subtropical oasis throughout the mild-winter West. The trick is to devise adequate sun shields with roofs, awnings, and tall plants to retain sufficient moisture throughout the garden.

To set the stage for his garden, Dalbok ripped out much of the original porch and added French doors and granite columns. He replaced the concrete with colorful slate tiles and used those colors in his palette.

The 8-foot-deep porch is edged by a 12-foot-long garden bed, where Dalbok planted tall banana and palm trees to act as a backdrop and provide shade for more delicate plants like maidenhair ferns. To get smaller layers in front for visual interest and as a way of framing the space, he placed bromeliads and philodendrons in a 5-foot-long wooden trough at the edge of the porch. The trough adds 2 feet of garden to the porch and offers excellent drainage for potted plants.

Spots of color and luscious foliage come from large ceramic pots and containers filled with blooming plants, which are changed with the seasons. A mix of bamboo and teak furnishings and artifacts like Indonesian and African figurines complete the illusion.

Create an exotic retreat

THOMAS J. STORY

• **Use overhanging eaves and awnings,** large trees, or decorative elements like umbrellas to provide partial shade.

• **Use troughs and containers to bring the garden onto a patio or deck.** Don't limit your "garden" to the existing dirt bed by your porch or deck.

• **Always layer plants,** using tall ones in the back and smaller ones in front to create different levels to stop the eye and enrich the composition. Experiment with plant combinations and container placement before making final decisions.

• **Rotate showy plants,** such as orchids, begonias, and bromeliads, into your garden for color all year.

• **Let plants grow full and loose** so your garden always looks lush.

• **Pay close attention to watering subtropical plants.** Some need more moisture than others. Bromeliads, for example, can survive up to a week without water, whereas maidenhair ferns need watering at least twice a week.

• **Look for exotic accessories** in your local stores—many now stock reproductions of antique statuary and wood carvings at reasonable prices.

DESIGN: Davis Dalbok, Living Green, San Francisco (415/864-2251 or www.livinggreen.com)

Bamboo chaise (page 191) from Bamboo Hardwoods, Seattle (800/783-0557 or www.bamboohardwoods.com)

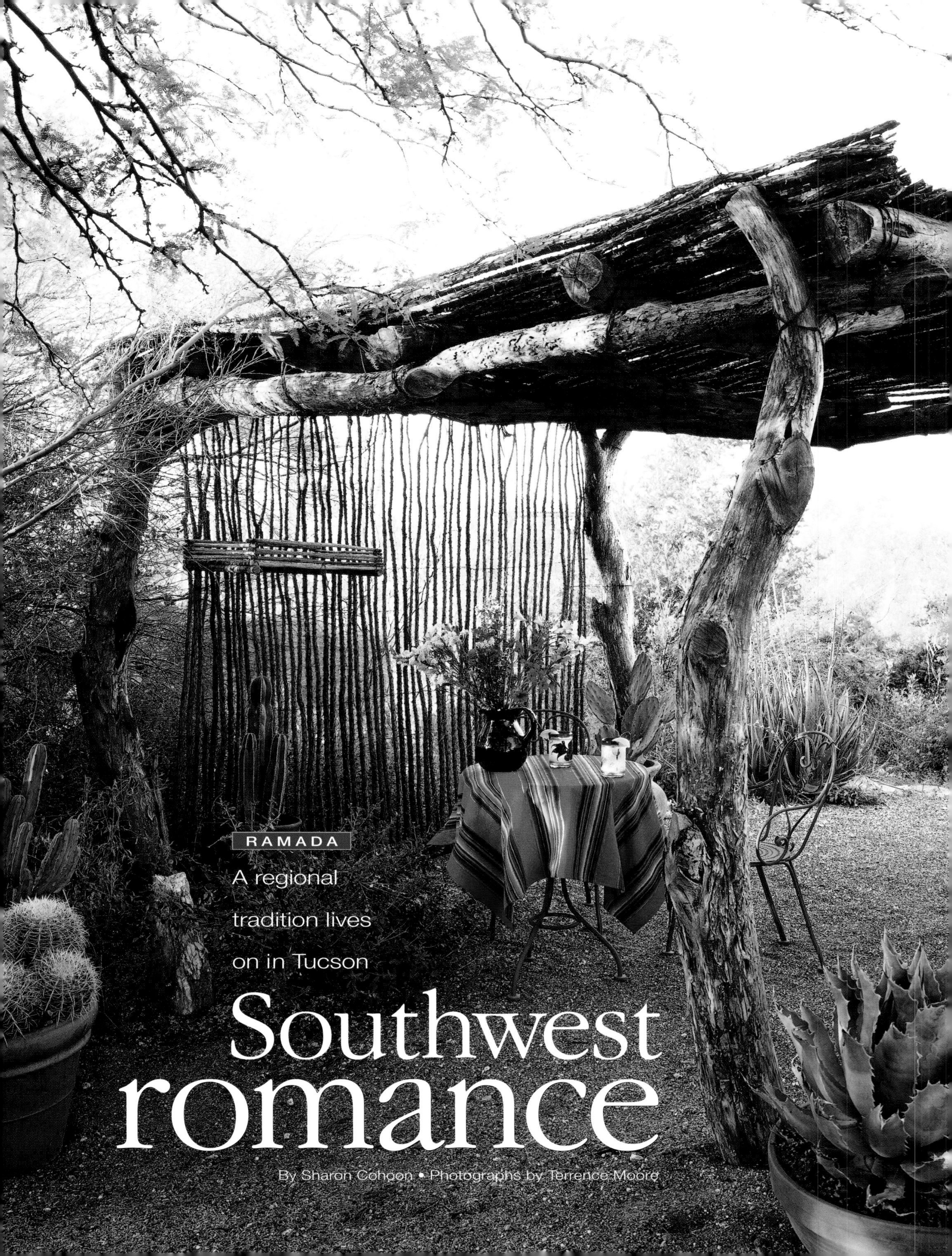

RAMADA

A regional
tradition lives
on in Tucson

Southwest
romance

By Sharon Cohoon • Photographs by Terrence Moore

A rustic ramada (along with the golden gate at right) has posts and crossbeams of mesquite and a roof of ocotillo canes. Accessories enhance its Southwest simplicity: a cobalt blue pitcher from Mexico, a bright tablecloth made in Guatemala. A living ocotillo fence screens an unwanted view.

When Ann and Mike Liebert throw parties in their Tucson garden, guests are always slipping away to spend time in the ramada. The structure, with a beautiful nighttime view of downtown Tucson, feels like a retreat and draws guests like a magnet. "It's irresistible," says Ann.

This twiggy shelter—open on three sides to let the breezes blow through—was designed and built by Ed Kisto, a member of the Tohono O'odham, in the authentic Southwest style. Native Americans have been constructing similar sun shelters in the Sonoran desert for centuries using natural materials.

Ann always admired these traditional ramadas, but the idea of having one in her own garden occurred to her while she was working as a docent at the Arizona-Sonoran Desert Museum. A fellow docent there, landscape architect Jeffrey Trent, told her about Ed Kisto and his artistry as a ramada builder, and he brought the two together. Though these structures were originally used to shelter workers from hot sun during harvest time, the Lieberts' ramada is strictly for leisure—eating pomegranates with their grandchildren or relaxing after dinner.

Much as the Lieberts like using it, they also love just looking at it. "I ask you," says Ann, "Could there be anything more Southwestern?"

■ Raise a ramada

• **Choose materials to reflect your region.** Though traditional ramadas were made with mesquite poles, ocotillo canes, and saguaro, these materials are not readily available in nurseries, and laws prevent harvesting from public land. Try eucalyptus, fir, or pine branches, or bamboo poles and palm fronds. Wood and stakes from a nursery or lumber-yard would work. Build a more permanent structure with a solid or partially open roof; some modern versions even incorporate fireplaces, ceiling fans, and chaises.

• **Anchor the posts firmly.** Kisto brushed the bottoms of the Lieberts' ramada posts with motor oil to discourage termites, then buried them 18 inches, tamping the soil firmly around them. In windy areas, you might want to secure the posts in concrete. He used barbed wire to attach crossbeams to posts and bailing wire to lash ocotillo canes to the crossbeams.

• **Let the ramada's style dictate the furnishings.** In keeping with the simplicity of their ramada, the Lieberts use only a few pieces of informal furniture.

DESIGN: Jeffrey Trent, Natural Order, Tucson (520/792-9274) and Ed Kisto.

Instant gratification

Use ready-made arbors to make an easy garden getaway

By Peter O. Whiteley • Photograph by Thomas J. Story

Few landscaping projects will have more of an impact on a garden than this instant gazebo, which is based upon a structure we found at Simpson House Inn, an elegant bed-and-breakfast in Santa Barbara. Since the gazebo's walls are four prefabricated arbors and its roof is an umbrella that rises from a garden table, there's almost nothing to build. In just a matter of hours, you can be enjoying a meal alfresco.

■ Build a gazebo

TIME: An afternoon
COST: About $450, not including plants
TOOLS AND MATERIALS

• String, a nail, and flour
• Four **garden arbors** (we found ours at a home supply center for about $80 each)
• Paint (optional)
• An **outdoor umbrella and table** sized to your space
• Shovel
• ½ cubic yard **decomposed granite**
• 1½-inch screws
• 30 feet **plastic** or wood **benderboard**
• Tamper
• Plants

NOTES

Our arbors—which are 8 feet high, 2 feet deep, and 54 inches wide and came painted white—required some finish work: We had to bolt the tops to the legs. We also repainted the arbors a soft sage green.

STEPS

Our gazebo forms a circle, roughly 13 feet in diameter, on a level site. An 8-foot-diameter umbrella is at the center, and the arbors stand 6 inches from the edge of the umbrella, fanning outward like spokes in a wheel.

1. Lay out the area needed (see plan) using string, a nail, and flour. Draw a 9-foot-diameter circle.

2. Determine the main entry point and lay out the locations for each of the arbors as if they were the four main points on a compass. Remember that the openings will likely be 54 inches wide (but check the width of your arbors' openings).

3. Open the umbrella to determine the height of the outer rim. You'll want to set each of the arbors in gravel-filled holes so their peaks will be at the same height. (Here, the height is 7 feet.)

4. Dig holes for arbor legs, place gravel in bottom, and insert the legs. Check that the sides are vertical and remain evenly spaced.

5. Screw an inner rim of benderboard to the front of the arbors that rises about 1 inch above ground level. This creates a low retaining wall for gravel.

6. Pack more gravel around the legs and fill the center area with decomposed granite. Dampen and compact the granite with a tamper.

7. Plant. We've trained star jasmine up the arbors and planted annuals in the remaining space.

FURNISHINGS: American Leisure (831/423-2425)

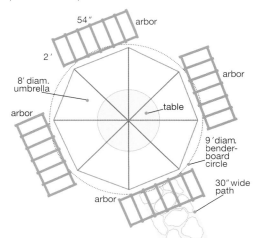

54″ arbor
2′
arbor
8′ diam. umbrella
arbor
table
9′ diam. benderboard circle
30″ wide path
arbor
arbor

The greatest appeal of this do-it-yourself gazebo—aside from the ease of construction—is that it creates a personal space that can be tucked into a lush garden setting or set on its own on a large lawn or meadow.

DECK

Up on the roof

Container gardening makes a great space anywhere

By Steven R. Lorton

Only one summer old, this lush Seattle roof garden is well on its way to becoming this family's favorite close-to-home hideout. Though most homeowners' getaways would more likely be a cantilevered deck or a patio, this rooftop provides lots of lessons in container gardening. Four things made it come together quickly and easily: large containers, 60-pound bags of potting mix, the availability of water—piping and an outdoor spigot were installed—and an enthusiastic owner. He makes daily rounds, watering and snipping off faded blooms and damaged foliage. When winter sets in, he'll cut back the garden, remove a few inches of topsoil from pots, and replace it with fresh mix. He's hoping that the big plants will stay happy for a decade.

NORM PLATE (2)

■ Create a garden on a deck

• **Get creative with containers.** The rooftop garden uses big glazed pots, imported from China and Vietnam, chosen for their size and bright colors. High-fired and glazed, these pots won't crack in winter. Be sure to fill them with a rich, sterile potting mix.

• **Feed and water frequently.** Plant roots quickly use up the nutrients in the small amount of soil in containers, so you have to feed often (every two weeks with half-strength liquid fertilizer) and water as soon as soil starts to dry out to keep things growing.

• **Freely mix annuals and permanent plants.** Repeat filler plants (like *Bidens ferulifolia* and ivy geranium) for visual continuity throughout the garden.

• **Don't be afraid to try trees and shrubs in containers.** The rooftop's denizens even include a crape myrtle. Smaller pots in various shapes and sizes are filled with small shrubs and woody plants: Algerian ivy, heather, *Hebe,* hypericum, and others.

• **Use upright perennials** such as gerbera, golden marguerite, and snapdragon for exclamation points of color.

• **Employ tender perennials and annuals,** like zinnia and helichrysum, as flowery fillers.

This small patio works, thanks to the dappled light and the partial sense of enclosure and privacy created by the greenhouse and foliage. The casual comfort of the two chairs seems to invite relaxation and intimate conversation.

JOHN GRANEN

PATIO

Watching the garden grow
Proper design and location make a patio a front row seat to nature

By Mary Jo Bowling

"Decks are architectural integrators; patios are landscape integrators," says landscape architect John Kenyon. "With a deck you have a rail and height separating you from the landscape. On the patio there's nothing between you and nature."

A patio can go anywhere on the lot—even off a small greenhouse facing the vegetable garden. Kenyon says watching vegetables grow is like watching television for gardeners. "A vegetable garden grows and changes daily—it almost makes other plantings seem static. It's fun to sit back, watch it happen, and appreciate your hard work," he says.

To soften the pavers and add interest to the space, Kenyon placed perennials around the irregular 8- by 8-foot stone shape. Willow trees (*Salix integra* 'Hakuro Nishiki') and fuchsia (*F.* x *hybrida*) add height and screen the greenhouse. Bronze New Zealand flax *(Phormium tenax)* adds a splash of color, and large squash leaves make the transition between patio and vegetable garden.

"It is the most successful spot in this garden," says Kenyon. "Everyone ends up hanging out there."
DESIGN: Sundance Landscaping Design/Build, Redmond, WA (425/881-5518 or www.sundancelandscaping.com)

▉ Plan a patio

• **Choose the site carefully.** Because the patio puts you close to the garden, locate it in an interesting area—facing a view of your garden or of rolling hills, for example.

• **Define the space.** Use plants to create leafy walls for privacy and a sense of place. Tuck ground covers between pavers to create a living carpet underfoot.

• **Establish a color scheme.** Coordinate your colors with those in the surrounding

area—the colors of your exterior walls, flowering shrubs, or trees—or if you want the patio to be an extension of an interior room, borrow from that room's palette.

• **Choose materials carefully.** In the garden above, designer John Kenyon used a mix of tumbled concrete pavers and bluestone for a more aged appearance. The color mix, along with the Corsican mint growing between the pavers, adds texture,

color, and pattern to the area.

• **Provide seating.** Be sure to group chairs, benches, or other pieces of outdoor furniture so that people can see each other and comfortably converse.

• **Add finishing touches.** Consider a fountain for the soothing sound of water, cushions for comfort and color, and garden art tucked among the plants to both surprise and amuse.

Sitting pretty

Indoor comfort and style move outside

By Mary Jo Bowling

In mild weather, many of us treat the backyard, deck, and patio like extensions of the living room. But when it comes to moving the equivalent of the living room sofa to the back patio, you can be stumped by the narrow selection of outdoor furniture. This season, outdoor furniture makers are introducing products that take seating to a new level.

A simple chair may be all you need to create a temporary retreat outdoors. Michael Thompson set his wicker furnishings (from an import store) within easy view of a 'Trude Webster' rhododendron's shimmery pink trusses.

MICHAEL S. THOMPSON

Furnish your retreat

Weather Master Laguna Chaise by Laneventure (www.laneventure.com)

Coastal Rope Rocker by Coastal Hammock (www.coastalhammock.com)

Sundance Collection by Laneventure

Ocean Collection by Richard Frinier, Brown Jordan (www.brownjordan.com)

TREND

■ **Increased comfort.** New outdoor furniture has actually been designed with people in mind. Features include cushions with springs and softer fabric. Chair backs are angled for comfort, and many chairs come with ottomans.

■ **More movement.** Outdoor furniture is rocking, rolling, reclining, and gliding in new ways. Bar carts, great for serving outdoor meals, are back. New accordion tables "grow" as needed, folding outdoor screens provide privacy, and even the tree-bound hammock has been rethought.

■ **Material mix.** There was a time when outdoor furniture was either teak, aluminum, or plastic. This year, you'll find furniture mixing all three. This allows the best traits from each material to be used: The warm good looks of teak are paired with the durability of plastic and aluminum.

■ **Contemporary lines.** Many new outdoor chairs and tables draw their design inspiration from modernism rather than Mom's picnic table. Lines are often sleek and curvaceous, not chunky.

WORDS OF WISDOM

More and bigger pads require extra storage space. Since many chairs have springs, you want to take extra care not to let them get wet, so use them in sheltered or semisheltered areas. Maintenance is required. To keep the upholstery looking fresh, dust frequently with a soft brush.

With a design emphasis on portability, these furnishings are perfect for the homeowner looking for privacy and the flexibility to create "rooms" within a large area. Keep in mind, however, that accessories such as screens and carts require large amounts of storage space during winter.

You could have one piece of furniture with two different maintenance needs. If you want teak to hold its color, you need to treat it with a special oil or stain. Aluminum and plastic need to be hosed off. Exotic woods can be endangered species—check for the Forest Stewardship Council tag to ensure there is responsible harvesting behind the product.

Use modern pieces in a setting where contemporary lines look at home. This furniture can sometimes be lightweight. While this can be an advantage in moving furnishings around, it does make them vulnerable to wind. Consider placing them in a protected place. ◆

For more information: American Furniture Manufacturers Association: www.findyourfurniture.com.

New shrubs for free

Create more plants by using cuttings from existing plants in your garden

By Lauren Bonar Swezey

Hydrangea, butterfly bush, and many other handsome deciduous shrubs can be propagated easily and quickly from softwood cuttings—pieces of stem that are neither too new nor woody. Deciduous shrubs generally reach this stage between early and midsummer. (Here's a test: A good softwood cutting will snap when bent. If it bends without breaking, it's immature; if it is dark and bends barely at all, it's too mature.)

Most softwood cuttings take from two to four weeks to begin making roots. Within six weeks, plants should have developed enough roots to make them ready for transplanting into a larger container.

THOMAS J. STORY (6)

TIME: 10 minutes or more (depending on number of cuttings)

COST: A few cents per pot

MATERIALS
• **Pruning shears**
• **Paper towels**
• **Gallon-size** or smaller **plastic bags**
• **2-inch pots** or other small containers
• **Potting soil** or propagation mix
• **Rooting hormone** (liquid or powder)
• **Thin stakes**

DIRECTIONS

1. Take cuttings early in the morning. Choose healthy lateral growth. Make cuttings 3 to 5 inches long, snipping just below a leaf node. (Temporarily store the cuttings between wet paper towels in a plastic bag. Keep them in the shade.) Fill pots with soil.

2. Remove the lowest set of leaves from each cutting. Dip the lower end in rooting hormone and shake off excess.

3. Poke a hole in the center of the soil with a stake. Set the stem in the hole and cover it with soil. Water gently but thoroughly.

4. Break or cut stakes into 5- to 6-inch long pieces. Place them at the corners of the pots to keep a plastic bag from touching the leaves. Place the pots in plastic bags and tie or zip closed. Set them in bright

light but out of direct sun. (If heavy condensation builds up in the bag, poke a few holes in it for air circulation or briefly open the bag every few days.) Keep the soil moist but not wet.

5. In three or four weeks, check for roots: If stems resist when very gently tugged, roots are developing. (Twenty to 30 percent of the stems may not root at all and will eventually wither.) Wait another few weeks to transplant the well-rooted cuttings into larger containers. ◆

THESE SHRUBS ROOT QUICKLY: Beautyberry, beauty bush, bluebeard, butterfly bush, crape myrtle, daphne, deciduous azalea, elderberry, enkianthus, flowering quince, forsythia, hydrangea, lilac, mock orange, redtwig dogwood, rugosa rose, serviceberry, smoke tree, viburnum, weigela

Penstemon parade

These showy perennials are naturally at home in Western gardens

By Lauren Springer

■ Penstemons are perhaps the quintessential Western flower. More than 250 species exist, almost all native to this region. It is the rare gardener who is not smitten by their array of brilliant colors and graceful forms. Luckily for us, they are easier to grow here than anywhere else in the world. There are penstemons for the hot desert, for the cool mountains, for the windy foothills. Many thrive in mild, maritime gardens, while others prefer the temperature extremes of the interior. All insist on good drainage, and the majority are truly drought-tolerant. What's more, their versatile looks combine well with the flashiest garden plants while still

LEFT: Fiery flowers of pineleaf penstemon (*P. pinifolius*) blaze around a pot of feather reed grass (*Calamagrostis* x *acutiflora* 'Karl Foerster'). DESIGN: Summer Kircher, Colorado Springs. RIGHT: *P. strictus* (above) is a Rocky Mountain native; *P.* 'Garnet' is a hybrid.

Red *P. eatonii* and purple
P. strictus bloom above yellow
daisies of *Thelesperma filifolium*.
DESIGN: Lauren Springer.

retaining that wildflower appeal.

Penstemons' tubular flowers are usually borne on long, upright stems. Aside from irises, no garden flower can boast the color range that penstemons offer. Pink-, white-, and lavender-flowered species attract bees and moths; red, orange, and crimson blossoms draw hummingbirds; deep blue, purple, and yellow species may host birds and insects alike. Flowering times range from the beginning of the growing season (as early as February in the low deserts) through spring and early summer, with species native to late-summer monsoon regions saving their show for August and September. Some species explode into full bloom for a couple of weeks, while others carry on well over a month or two.

(Continued on page 206)

Pick the right penstemon

■ Species for areas with hot, dry summers and cold winters

BRIGHTLY COLORED FLOWERS

This group includes flashy species that insist on dry conditions and hot summers. They are cold-hardy to at least *Sunset* climate zone 2B (from the *Sunset Western Garden Book*). They are not long-lived, lasting from three to five years. The brightly colored species are favored by hummingbirds. Bloom is midseason (late spring and early summer), unless noted.

Penstemon barbatus. Red orange flowers. 3 to 5 feet tall. Good cut flower. Selections include compact 'Elfin Pink' (18 inches) and 'Schooley's Yellow'.

P. cardinalis. Burgundy. 2 feet.

P. clutei. Rose pink. 3 feet. Nice waxy blue gray foliage.

P. eatonii. Red orange; early. 3 feet.

P. floridus. Bright pink. 3 to 4 feet.

P. grandiflorus. Very large flowers in lavender, pink, or white. 2 to 3 feet. Blue gray foliage shaped like florists' eucalyptus. Good selections are Prairie Jewel (same colors as species), 'Prairie Snow' (white), War Axe (deep pink and purple).

P. palmeri. Very large pale pink flowers. 3 to 6 feet. Blue foliage.

P. pseudospectabilis. Magenta. 2 to 4 feet.

P. rostriflorus. Red orange; late. 2 to 3 feet. Somewhat shrubby.

P. utahensis. Coral red. 1 to 2 feet.

P. virgatus. Lavender. 2 feet.

BLUE FLOWERS

Some of the best true-blue blossoms in the plant kingdom are found in this group. All are hardy to zone 2B, most even to zone 1. They prefer dry soil, cool nights, and low humidity. They bloom for several weeks at midseason.

P. cyananthus (Wasatch penstemon). Bright medium blue. 18 to 24 inches. Hardy to zone 1.

P. glaber. Large, bright medium blue flowers. 18 to 30 inches. Hardy to zone 1.

P. mensarum (Grand Mesa penstemon). Cobalt blue. 15 to 20 inches. Hardy to zone 2A.

P. neomexicanus (New Mexico penstemon). Indigo blue. 2 feet.

P. speciosus. Bright medium blue. 15 to 30 inches.

P. strictus (Rocky Mountain penstemon). Indigo blue. 2 feet. Hardy to zone 1.

P. virens (blue mist penstemon). Sky blue. 10 to 15 inches tall. Hardy to zone 1. Tolerates a bit more moisture and light shade than others.

■ Species for hot, dry areas with mild winters

This group includes some of the tallest species, all native to southern Arizona, California, and Mexico. Their thick, waxy foliage adds to their appeal. They need heat to perform well and are not winter-hardy in the intermountain region. Their life span is typically three to five years. Most are favored by hummingbirds.

P. centranthifolius. Red; early to midseason. 4 to 5 feet. Long bloom season.

P. clevelandii. Rose pink; early. 2 to 3 feet.

P. parryi. Rose pink; early. 3 to 4 feet.

P. spectabilis. Indigo blue; early. 4 to 5 feet.

P. superbus. Red; early. 5 to 6 feet.

■ Low-growing species

These species grow less than 1 foot tall and are hardy to at least zone 2B. They have attractive evergreen foliage and mounding or mat-forming

What penstemons need

- At least six hours of sun daily.
- Good air circulation.
- Soil that is well drained and relatively low in organic matter.
- To encourage plants in containers to establish in garden soil, remove most of the soil mix from around the rootballs of plants before setting them in the ground.
- Little competition from neighboring plants.
- Irrigation/rain before bloom, dry conditions thereafter.
- Prompt removal of spent flower stalks to prevent energy-robbing seed formation.
- Shrubby evergreen species need protection from drying winter winds.

LAUREN SPRINGER

ABOVE: *P. rupicola* grows only 4 inches high. RIGHT: Lavender *P. virgatus*, pink *P. palmeri,* and bluish purple *P. strictus* rise over pink evening primrose and *Artemisia* 'Powis Castle' (front right). DESIGN: Lauren Springer.

habits. All bloom mid-season, unless noted.

P. californicus. Deep purple. Silver foliage. Needs hot, dry conditions.

P. crandallii. Medium blue. Needs dry conditions. Prefers cool climates.

P. davidsonii davidsonii. Purple. Prefers cool climates. Protect from winter wind.

P. hirsutus 'Pygmaeus'. Pale lavender. Tolerates light shade.

P. linarioides coloradoensis. Lavender blue. Gray foliage. Needs dry conditions.

P. pinifolius (pineleaf penstemon). Red, orange, or yellow. Long blooming.

P. procerus tolmiei. Blue, lavender, pink, or yellow.

P. procumbens (*P. caespitosus*). Blue; early. Needs dry conditions.

P. rupicola. Rose red. Prefers cool climates. Protect from winter wind.

P. teucrioides. Light blue. Needs dry conditions.

■ Colorful hybrids for coastal areas

Sometimes referred to as garden penstemon or European hybrids, these showy plants were once bred mainly overseas. Best suited to coastal areas, they dislike intense heat and are not reliably cold-hardy in the interior West. As a group they are short-lived, but the darker-flowered selections tend to grow longer. They need regular water during the growing season and autumn. Typically, they grow 18 to 30 inches tall and bloom late.

BRIGHT REDS. 'Firebird', 'Flame', 'Razzle Dazzle', 'Red Ace', and 'Scarlet Queen'.

DARK REDS. 'Blackbird', 'Burgundy', 'Garnet', and 'Port Wine'.

PINK AND ROSE. 'Evelyn' (one of the hardiest), 'Hidcote Pink', 'Lynette', 'Patio Pink', 'Pennington Gem', 'Pink Endurance', and 'Wisley Pink'.

PURPLE. 'Hidcote Purple', 'Midnight' ('Russian River'), 'Papal Purple', 'Purple Tiger', and 'Raven'.

BLUE OR LAVENDER. 'Alice Hindley', 'Knightwick', 'Sour Grapes', and 'Stapleford Gem'.

COLOR BLENDS. 'Astley' (white–pale lavender), 'Mother of Pearl' (white-lavender), and 'Raspberry Flair' (lavender-rose).

Plant sources

High Country Gardens (800/925-9387 or www.highcountrygardens.com) has a good selection of species.

Joy Creek Nursery (503/543-7474 or www.joycreek.com) sells many garden penstemon hybrids.

Laporte Avenue Nursery (1950 Laporte Ave., Fort Collins, CO 80521; 970/472-0017) offers a large selection of species.

For further reading

A good reference is *Penstemons,* by Robert Nold (Timber Press, Portland, 1999; $29.95; 800/327-5680 or www.timberpress.com). ◆

Good companions

These plants are compatible with penstemons in mixed plantings. Zones vary.

Flowering plants
- *Achillea* (yarrow)
- *Anthemis*
- *Callirhoe involucrata* (wine cups)
- *Calylophus* (sundrops)
- *Cistus* (rockrose)
- *Dianthus*
- *Eriogonum* (wild buckwheat)
- *Eschscholzia californica* (California poppy)
- *Gaura lindheimeri*
- *Helianthemum* (sunrose)
- *Hesperaloe parviflora* (red yucca)
- *Iris* (bearded types and hybrids)
- *Linum* (flax)
- *Nepeta* (catmint)
- *Oenothera* (evening primrose)
- *Papaver* (poppy)
- *Salvia* (sage)

Foliage plants
- *Agave*
- *Artemisia*
- *Dasylirion* (desert spoon)
- *Yucca*

Grasses
- *Festuca californica, F. glauca, F. idahoensis*
- *Nassella tenuissima* (Mexican feather grass)
- *Stipa*

Hybrid penstemons: 'Firebird' (above) and 'Papal Purple' (right).

These kinds are well suited to Northwest gardens

Hybrid penstemons thrive in the mild coastal areas of the Northwest, while certain species are hardy enough to survive in cold-winter areas east of the Cascade Range.

Pick the right penstemon

HARDY KINDS FOR MOIST AREAS

These species and hybrids are adaptable to higher-moisture regimes and more humid air. They are hardy to at least *Sunset* climate zone 2B (from the *Sunset Western Garden Book*).

Penstemon cobaea. Very large flowers in white, lavender, or—rarely—purple; midseason (late spring and early summer). 2 feet tall.

P. digitalis. White, often purple-tinted flowers; midseason. 3 to 4 feet. To enjoy the attractive burgundy seed heads, refrain from deadheading this species after bloom. 'Husker Red' has burgundy foliage.

P. hirsutus. Pale lilac or white; midseason. 18 inches. 'Olinda Pink' is a special color selection.

Mexicali hybrids. Pink, red, purple, some with white throats; midseason to frost. 15 to 24 inches. Zones 1–3. Attractive foliage, shrubby habit. Flowers look similar to European hybrids. Named selections are 'Red Rocks' (crimson) and 'Pike's Peak Purple'.

Prairie hybrids. Midseason. Named selections are 'Prairie Dawn' (pink), 'Prairie Dusk' (purple), and 'Prairie Fire' (red).

P. rydbergii. Royal blue; midseason. 2 feet. Tolerates moister soil than most.

P. smallii. Lavender or rose; midseason. 2 feet.

COLORFUL HYBRIDS FOR COASTAL AREAS

Sometimes referred to as garden penstemons or European hybrids, these showy plants were once bred mainly overseas. Best-suited to coastal areas, they are not reliably cold-hardy in the interior West. As a group they are short-lived, but the darker-flowered selections tend to be tougher and longer-lived. They need regular water during the growing season and autumn, but they are prone to root rot in wet, heavy soil. Typically, they grow 18 to 30 inches tall and bloom late.

BRIGHT REDS. 'Firebird', 'Flame', 'Razzle Dazzle', 'Red Ace', 'Scarlet Queen'.

DARK REDS. 'Blackbird', 'Burgundy', 'Garnet', 'Port Wine'.

PINK AND ROSE. 'Evelyn' (one of the hardiest), 'Hidcote Pink', 'Lynette', 'Patio Pink', 'Pennington Gem', 'Pink Endurance', 'Wisley Pink'.

PURPLE. 'Midnight' ('Russian River'), 'Hidcote Purple', 'Papal Purple', 'Purple Tiger', 'Raven'.

BLUE/LAVENDER. 'Alice Hindley', 'Knightwick', 'Sour Grapes', 'Stapleford Gem'.

COLOR BLENDS. 'Astley' (white–pale lavender), 'Mother of Pearl' (white-lavender), 'Raspberry Flair' (lavender-rose).

Small-flowered spillers

Cascading plants for hanging baskets and more

By Kathleen N. Brenzel

Some plants are made for stardom; their big, bold, sometimes brassy flowers command the spotlight. Others are content with life in the chorus, creating beautiful effects when massed. Small-flowered though they may be, they're indispensable for their graceful, trailing habits. Tuck any of the six listed here into hanging baskets, in window boxes, or around a pot's edges, and they'll quickly drape curtains of living lace, adding to the drama.

Bacopa (snowy white blooms) and Million Bells (rosy orange flowers) add a lacy look to this hanging basket. Companions are lavender petunias, purple verbena, yellow strawflowers, pink and red ivy geraniums, and heliotrope. The soft blue green fringe trailing beneath the bacopa is *Lotus maculatus.*

Six terrific trailers

Bacopa *(Sutera cordata).* Small five-petaled white or lavender flowers resemble stars. 'Giant Snowflake' reaches 6 to 8 inches tall and spreads 3 to 4 feet in a growing season. 'Olympic Gold' has leaves splotched with golden yellow; it's pretty with pink or coral impatiens. All need good drainage, rich soil, and afternoon shade in hottest climates. Perennial in *Sunset* climate zones 15–17, 21–24, H2; annual elsewhere.

Italian bellflower *(Campanula isophylla).* Trailing or hanging stems to 2 feet long; loose clusters of upward-facing, light blue star-shaped flowers. 'Alba' has white flowers. For a refreshing patio planting, fill a big pot (18-inch diameter) with a single white florists' hydrangea and edge it with *C. isophylla* 'Alba'. Part shade; sun in cooler climates. Zones 4–9, 14–24; in Southern California, best near the coast.

Lobelia *(L. erinus).* Small flowers in white and shades of blue to lilac. Plants grow 3 to 6 inches tall; trailing types spread 1½ feet. One of the prettiest plantings we've seen was composed of 'Cambridge Blue' lobelia (sky blue flowers) tumbling over the edges of a stone birdbath. Annual. All zones.

***Lotus maculatus* 'Gold Flash'.** Bright yellow flowers with orange red markings. Needs cool nights to set buds; where nights are warmer, try 'Amazon Sunset', with bright orange red flowers. Grows 8 to 12 inches tall and 2 to 3 feet wide. Handsome with 'Tropicanna' canna. Sun or part shade. Perennial. Zones 9, 15–24.

Million Bells *(Calibrachoa).* A petunia relative with small bell-shaped blooms in white, pink, cherry, violet, terra-cotta, or yellow. Trailing and compact forms bloom prolifically all season. Sun or light shade. Perennial where frosts are light to nonexistent, zones 8–9, 14–24; annual in zones 2–7, 10–13.

Scaevola aemula. Lavender blue fan-shaped flowers. Trailing forms include 'Blue Wonder' and 'Colonial Fan' (8 inches tall trailing to 3 feet). Try a row tumbling over rocks around a pond or spilling from raised beds. Needs sun. Perennial. Zones 8–9, 14–24, H1–H2. ◆

A path fringed with hostas, ferns, and other greens winds through Nancy Short's "woodland" garden. RIGHT: Giant conifers rise behind her lakeside sun border. Nancy Short relaxes in one of her many viewing spots.

Sage advice

A veteran gardener shares ideas from her joyous Northwest landscape

By Steven R. Lorton • Photographs by Norm Plate

■ "There are very few places in life where you can do exactly as you please," says Nancy Davidson Short, an extraordinary gardener and former Northwest editor of *Sunset.* "Your garden is one of them!"

On a ¾-acre slice of lakefront in Bellevue, Washington, Short has done just that. Her tendency to experiment and play in the garden has led to a horticultural treasure.

Green and richly textured, Short's garden reflects decades spent scouting and reporting the best of

This elevated fern garden, an 85th birthday present from garden designer and author George Schenk, makes good use of Short's old metal-framed table. Schenk calls it "a garden party of small growing ferns." To plant it, he covered the cedar-plank tabletop with a 7-inch mound of potting soil, then set in ferns, dwarf perennials and conifers, and moss. The result is a lush, floating garden—simply framed in gravel—that thrives in soft dappled light. At right, rosy hydrangeas.

Northwest landscaping. Her gardening skills, inherent sense of good design, and all-embracing *joie de vivre* have made lasting marks here. (This month, when the American Horticultural Society holds its annual convention in Seattle, her garden will be one of the stops for AHS members from all over the country.)

Near the house's entry, ferns and other plants spread a leafy cover over a table (pictured above). There are a sunken garden; a sun border; a dry shade garden; a bog garden; a cutting garden filled with roses, lilies, and peonies; and big containers everywhere.

For Short, gardening is clearly a lifelong passion. Since she moved into her home, the cedars and Douglas firs along the property line have grown into timber-size trees, creating privacy and shade. (Lower limbs were

removed as the trees grew, allowing in some daylight under them.) Northwest natives such as sword and maidenhair ferns, flowering currant, and evergreen huckleberry weave a continuous thread throughout the garden. Among the plantings, benches and other seating perch on small landings and little terraces. "The garden looks and feels very different from different places," Short says. "I want to be able to sit and think and enjoy a new view as I move through the garden."

Over the years, Short has sought the advice of a dozen landscape designers. But since 1997, well-known horticulturist Jim Fox has lived and worked on her property. Nancy feels she's struck gold: "Jim is a master at bringing wonderful color and texture to the garden in all seasons—most as-

tonishingly, in winter." Plants in this garden are chosen for their leaf color, form, texture, year-round interest, and, lastly, for their bloom. "To choose a plant for its bloom," Short says, "is like marrying a woman because you like her Easter hat."

Short's garden basics

Be aware of a plant's needs. Group plants by their light, water, and soil requirements.

Be discriminating. As much as you'll want one of everything, hold off on buying plants just because you like them, or your garden will look like mulligan stew.

Go with nature. Look first at the palette of native plants around you. Design with and around nature.

Give plants enough room to grow. Think of the plant's ultimate size when you plant. You wouldn't want your teenager sleeping in a crib.

Plant for all-season interest. Include plants that look glorious in several seasons (as beautiful evergreens do) and ones that have seasonal appeal (flaming foliage in autumn, beautiful bark in winter).

Build a reference library. Ask for good garden reference books for birthdays and holidays. Start with the *Sunset Western Garden Book*.

Learn one genus at a time. Pick a plant group that you like (*Mahonia,* for example) and learn everything you can about it. Then move on to another genus.

Make daily rounds. Never miss a day walking through your garden to tell the plants how beautiful they are. It makes a difference. A garden is like a love affair—it thrives on attention.

Cherish winter. This is the time when the beauty of nature will do the most to cheer you.

Gunnera leaves fan over orange cannas, blue hydrangeas, yellow rudbeckia, yellowish Japanese forest grass, and sedum. 'Elk River Red' flowering currant accents a bench.

As the year turns

Nothing in this garden is wasted. In autumn, fallen leaves are raked back under the trees and shrubs ("the way nature does it," Short says). Prunings from trees, shrubs, and perennials—as well as spent annuals—are composted; the homemade compost most often ends up as top dressing around new plantings. In late winter and early spring, beds are covered with a 2-inch layer of organic mulch to cut down on weeds, enrich the soil, and help retain moisture.

Newly acquired shrubs or small trees might spend a few years in a pot before being planted in the garden. Potted shrubs are underplanted with bulbs or colorful annuals. In winter when the garden is defoliated, its structure is examined to see that plants are healthy.

Short advises new gardeners to be intrepid. "Fear is an inhibiting emotion," she says. "Look at [the garden] as an exciting challenge, a bold life experience. Reinvent it every year. Never come to the end of it. You'll never want to!" ◆

Urns are back

Here are three fresh ways to use the classic container

By Kathleen N. Brenzel

Long-necked and lovely, urns are the timeless beauties of garden containers, presiding over well-tended plantings with dignified grace. But stuffy they're not; nurseries are now selling them in a variety of sizes, shapes, and materials—from poured concrete and Italian terracotta to rusted iron. More gardeners are finding creative ways to use them in gardens of any size and style.

Keep in mind that the most durable terra-cotta is high-fired. Cast concrete generally lasts longer than terra-cotta, but it can be heavier. Much of it is gray too, but you can paint or stain it.

Most urns are handsome enough to display unplanted. But if you do plant one, make sure it has a drain hole. And put it where you want it before you plant, since large urns can be heavy. (One good solution to both problems: Nest plants already potted in plastic inside them.)

Rusted iron
18 inches in diameter
24 inches tall
$150

Terra-cotta
12 inches in diameter
16 inches tall
$43

Concrete
18 inches in diameter
16 inches tall
$150

▲ Higher ground

Freeland and Sabrina Tanner wanted height in a difficult, mostly shaded border in their Napa, California, garden. So they pulled what Freeland calls a "microclimate trick"—planting sun lovers in an urn raised on a pedestal "to grab more sunlight." Filled with fast-draining cactus mix, the large (30 inches across by about 2 feet deep) rusted iron vessel features fountainlike *Puya coerulea*, with *Helichrysum argyrophyllum* 'Moe's Gold' and lavender-flowered campanula tumbling out around it. A drip system handles the watering.

THOMAS J. STORY (2)

Urns in the landscape

- Use a single urn to mark a crossing of intersecting paths, as a sculptural accent in the center of a courtyard or formal pool, or at the end of a long strip of grass with a leafy hedge behind.

- Space several urns along the edge of a patio, terrace, or walkway. Put the same plant in each, like little kumquat trees.

- Near the base of a single urn, cluster three to five smaller pots of the same material. In each container, put the same kind of plant, whether a frothy sweet alyssum or a sculptural succulent like aloe. Or plant a single upright herb, like Salvia officinalis 'Icterina' or rosemary, in the urn and lower-growing kinds such as basil and chives in the smaller pots.

- Create a changing display by nesting plastic pots filled with plants inside an urn. Replace them as needed.

Looking through this tabletop is like peering into a tidepool with leafy greens at its depths. The succulents rooting here include hen and chicks, red-blushed *Aeonium arboreum,* a spiny aloe, and tiny sedums.

▲ Patio table greenhouse

When *Sunset's* test garden coordinator Bud Stuckey roots succulents, he puts them in an 18-inch-diameter urn filled to 6½ inches below the rim with potting soil, then centers a 24-inch round of tempered glass—sold as a tabletop—on the rim. The mini-greenhouse doubles as a table for a lightly shaded patio. To keep condensation from building up on the underside of the glass, he removes the glass tabletop every few days for an hour or so. Once the succulents are rooted (in four weeks), he transfers them to pots or garden beds.

Between periods of use as a mini-greenhouse, the urn displays objects such as glass balls.

◀ Living bouquet

Plantings as glorious as this one, in Karla Waterman's Seattle-area garden, deserve to be raised to eye level for close-up viewing. The concrete urn (21 inches tall and 11½ inches across) sits atop a brick pillar capped with Arizona flagstone to match the patio.

The plants, carefully chosen for color and texture, are arranged by height. A tall Mexican feather grass rises in the center; it's flanked with a green geranium and a frilly ruby red coleus. Lime green sweet potato vine, white-flowered bacopa, and small-leafed creeping Jenny *(Lysimachia nummularia)* spill over the urn's edges. Waterman chose the plants with Gail Halsaver of Foxglove Greenhouses; Halsaver did the planting. ◆

NORM PLATE; ABOVE: THOMAS J. STORY

LEFT: Downswept petals of purple coneflower play off misty sprays of blue Russian sage in a bed at Denver Botanic Gardens. DESIGN: Tom Peace. RIGHT: Checkerbloom bears clusters of 2-inch flowers resembling tiny hollyhocks.

Summer color standouts for intermountain gardens

These flowering perennials take heat in stride

By Lauren Springer

It's easy to have a knockout garden in late spring and early summer, but once the heat hits, things tend to get tired and dull. So make it a point to celebrate summer by planting perennials that save their best show for July and August.

First, consider your garden's exposure and watering regime, then select plants that will thrive in those conditions. Choose colors and textures that please you and play well off each other. Combine flowers with contrasting shapes, such as bold daylilies with delicate *Gaura lindheimeri,* or round coneflowers with spiky liatris. Include a smattering of plants with interesting foliage such as artemisia, lamb's ears, and ornamental grasses.

Another indispensable group of perennials look and act more like shrubs. They include butterfly bush (*Buddleja* species), hardy English lavender selections, and Russian sage. Since these plants suffer varying degrees of winter dieback, they benefit from being cut back by about half in early spring.

LEFT: Orange spikes of *Kniphofia* and purple plumes of *Liatris spicata* front gold circles of fernleaf yarrow. RIGHT: Pink blossoms of *Lavatera thuringiaca* pair well with yellow pincushion flower *(Cephalaria alpina)*.

Surefire combinations
The perennials listed below prefer sun unless noted.

LESS THAN 3 FEET TALL
Low water (1 inch rain/irrigation per month in summer)

• Pink-flowered *Diascia integerrima* 'Coral Canyon', deep lavender blue pincushion flower *(Scabiosa columbaria* 'Butterfly Blue'), silver-leafed lamb's ears *(Stachys byzantina* 'Silver Carpet')

• Magenta prairie wine cups *(Callirhoe involucrata),* purple English lavender *(Lavandula angustifolia* 'Mitcham Grey'), silver-leafed *Artemisia versicolor*

• White *Gaura lindheimeri,* yellow Ozark sundrops *(Oenothera macrocarpa incana),* purple skullcap *(Scutellaria resinosa)*

Moderate water (½ to 1 inch per week in summer)

• White or lavender calamint *(Calamintha nepeta),* rose purple *Liatris spicata,* blue, pink, or white balloon flower *(Platycodon grandiflorus)*

• Pale yellow *Coreopsis verticillata* 'Moonbeam', silvery blue *Eryngium* species, blue oat grass *(Helictotrichon sempervirens)*

• Purple coneflower *(Echinacea purpurea),* lavender *Limonium latifolium,* pink *Saponaria* x *lempergii* 'Max Frei'

• Purple *Geranium* 'Nimbus', yellow 'Happy Returns' daylily, golden feverfew *(Tanacetum parthenium* 'Aureum')

3 FEET AND TALLER
Moderate water

• Buff-flowered feather reed grass *(Calamagrostis* x *acutiflora* 'Karl Foerster'), yellow pincushion flower *(Cephalaria alpina),* blue globe thistle *(Echinops ritro)*

• Pink *Lavatera thuringiaca,* powder blue Russian sage *(Perovskia)*

Regular water (1 inch per week in summer)

• White mugwort *(Artemisia lactiflora),* white-flowered *Hydrangea arborescens* 'Annabelle', orange *Lilium henryi*

• Rose purple *Liatris pycnostachya,* rose pink bee balm *(Monarda* 'Marshall's Delight'), white *Phlox paniculata* 'David'

Light shade, regular water

• Dark blue garden monkshood *(Aconitum napellus),* white 'Royal Standard' hosta, rose lilac meadow rue *(Thalictrum dipterocarpum)* ◆

THIS LAVENDER-BORDERED PATH on Bainbridge Island, Washington, delights both the eyes and noses of garden strollers. For details on the two fragrant varieties shown here, see page 226.

216

July

Poway hideaway

■ Elan May was 10 years old when she asked her mother, garden designer Sharon May, to help her create a tea garden based on *Alice's Adventures in Wonderland,* by Lewis Carroll. That fantasy launched a mother-daughter project that took shape over the next three years in the Mays' backyard.

The gateway to this secret garden is a trellis cloaked with an exuberant climbing 'Joseph's Coat' rose and flanked with mounds of yellow-flowered *Asteriscus* 'Gold Coin' (that's yellow geum beside it). In the intimate sitting area beyond sits a boxwood topiary tea table designed to resemble the Mad Hatter's top hat; beside the table are two chairs (barely visible through foliage in the photo above).

To furnish the space, the two Mays hunted for "Alice stuff" at garage sales, thrift stores, and garden centers on Saturday mornings. They attached oversize blue plastic cups and saucers to green wooden dowels, then filled them with marigolds, lobelia, and alyssum. A ceramic rabbit from a garden center sits near the White Rabbit's hole—a black nursery pot buried at an angle.

Alice-themed plants include bunny tail grass *(Lagurus ovatus),* butterfly bush *(Buddleja),* butterfly weed *(Asclepias tuberosa),* and—one of Elan's favorites—chenille plant *(Acalypha hispida),* which has fuzzy red flowers that resemble caterpillars.

The garden delights neighborhood children who pass by on the trail beyond the fence. "We invite them to come in and explore Alice's Garden," Sharon May says.

— *Debra Lee Baldwin*

Benchmarks in landscaping

■ In the garden, a bench can serve not only as a focal point, but as a place from which to contemplate the scenery or maybe just take a snooze. In H. Joan and Mel Lindley's garden in Eugene, Oregon, two teak Lutyens benches are integrated beautifully into the landscape. Distinguished by its elaborate curves, this style of bench is named for its designer— Sir Edwin Lutyens, a 19th- and 20th-century British architect who collab-

orated with Gertrude Jekyll on many garden projects.

One 8-foot-long bench rests under an old magnolia in the Lindleys' side yard (above). The bench not only invites the viewer to enter the garden but also unites the design elements, says landscape architect Brad Stangeland, who remodeled the space. Concrete pavers set in crushed gravel lead to the bench. On either side, groups of arborvitae (*Thuja occiden-*

talis 'Emerald Green') add striking accents. Behind, a dark green trellis serves as a privacy screen.

In the backyard, a 6-foot-long bench sits on a gravel pad that projects into a garden bed (left). A 4-foot-tall privet hedge forms an alcove on three sides of the bench. Shaded by white birch trees, this bench is Mel Lindley's favorite spot to take a break and enjoy the garden.

— *Mary-Kate Mackey*

Good ideas at Mount Vernon

■ Collectively, the Skagit Display Gardens at Washington State University's Mount Vernon Research and Extension Center are becoming one of the most instructive horticultural venues in the Pacific Northwest. There are four gardens on this 11-acre complex. You can visit any day during the growing season.

Master Gardeners Discovery Garden is an expert blend of plants and landscape. It includes a pond, meadow garden, perennials, wildlife habitat, Japanese garden, and children's garden.

Native Plant Society Garden, which starts developing in earnest this summer, will eventually cover every western Washington habitat, from woodland to open meadows.

Skagit Valley Rose Society Garden (at left) has a collection of well-labeled roses that run the gamut from species to hybrid teas.

Western Washington Fruit Research Foundation Garden covers 5 acres and includes apples, pears, grapes, figs, kiwis, and other fruits suited to Northwest gardens.

From Interstate 5, take the Kincaid Street exit west. Turn right onto State 536 (Third St.) and follow it across the Skagit River Bridge; go about 2 miles to the center on your left. It's open daily dawn to dusk. Admission is free. — *Jim McCausland*

A charming mystery rose

■ As of last year, 78 varieties of historic roses had been discovered in Denver's 112-year-old Fairmount Cemetery. In 1999 a singularly beautiful mystery rose was found growing beside one of the old gravestones. Given the study name "Fairmount Proserpine," the charmer is very likely an early Bourbon rose, quite possibly the rare cultivar 'Proserpine' introduced in 1841. (In Greek mythology, Proserpine was the wife of Pluto, god of the underworld.)

From June through October, this repeat-blooming rose bears deep fuchsia and magenta flowers measuring 3 inches across. As each blossom unfurls, it is accented by a "knob" of unopened petals in the center. If you're lucky, the petals will pop open right before your eyes, especially if nudged by a finger. At that moment, the fruity, spicy old rose fragrance is particularly intense. In autumn, the flowers are transformed into small bright orange hips.

Cold-hardy in Denver, this upright shrub rose reaches 5 feet tall

MICHAEL MOWRY

and 4 feet wide. Even young plants are eager to bloom, and they are free of disease and pests if grown in full sun, deeply mulched, and fertilized in spring with fishmeal or fish emulsion. Frequently picking bouquets encourages even more blooms. Limited quantities of "Fairmount Proserpine" in 5-inch pots are available from High Country Roses in Jensen, Utah (800/552-2082 or www.highcountryroses. com). — *John Starnes*

Tropical summer pots in Denver

■ Lush containers can give an otherwise sedate front porch an exuberant tropical look. The containers shown here were created for a Denver client by landscape designer Bruce de Cameron of Great Gardens Inc. (303/321-4423). They showcase the sweetly fragrant yellow flowers of angel's trumpet *(Brugmansia* x *candida)* surrounded by a colorful tapestry of shorter flowers and foliage plants. The containers are set out on the porch in May and continue dazzling passersby long into autumn. During the season, they get about a half-day of full sun and dappled light the rest of the day.

Angel's trumpet is a frost-tender shrub: At season's end, it can be pruned back to a 6-inch stalk, repotted, and overwintered indoors in a sunny room for use again next year.

De Cameron used 2-foot square plastic containers. He mixed controlled-release fertilizer into potting soil.

PLANT LIST
- One 2-gallon *Brugmansia* x *candida*
- One 1-gallon *Salvia farinacea* 'Victoria Blue'
- Three 4-inch *Coleus* x *hybridus,* assorted leaf colors
- Two 4-inch 'Dragon Wing' semperflorens begonia
- One 2-inch Sprenger asparagus (*A. densiflorus* 'Sprengeri')
- Four 4-inch sweet potato *(Ipomoea batatas),* two *each* chartreuse- and purple-leafed varieties
- Three 2-inch variegated vinca (*V. major* 'Wojo's Jem')

DIRECTIONS
1. Fill the container with potting soil to within 6 inches of the rim. Mix in a controlled-release fertilizer, moisten soil thoroughly with water, and tamp down with your hand.
2. Arrange plants still in their nursery containers atop the soil. Use the angel's trumpet to anchor the composition, then place the shorter plants toward the edges, letting the trailers like sweet potato and vinca spill over the rim. When you're satisfied with the arrangement, knock the plants out of their nursery containers, fill around them with soil, and tamp down.
3. Keep the container evenly watered; you may have to water twice a day during the peak of summer's heat. Deadhead spent flowers throughout the season.
— *Colleen Smith*

PAUL BOUSQUET

NORM PLATE

"Ruining" the garden

A Fair Oaks family builds a new ancient wall

■ Some families take vacations in summer to stay connected to each other. Others play sports. But the Haleva family of Fair Oaks, California, constructed a ruined wall two years ago, with a pond in front, that looks like a relic of ancient times.

"It was one of our best summers together," says Sharon Ecker-Haleva, who joined her husband, Jerry Haleva, and sons Kevin, 22, and Michael, 15, on the project. "We all worked together trying out each other's ideas. We're very proud of it."

The project began after the removal of a dying oak tree left a large void in the family's backyard. Around the same time, Haleva acquired a pair of 300-year-old Tunisian doors from Sacramento landscape architect Michael Glassman. Glassman suggested the idea of a wall structure, but the Halevas created and built it.

They had no prior experience (she's a nurse and he's a lobbyist). "We had to learn how to work with cinder block, cement, and stucco," says Ecker-Haleva. "We built a 3-foot-tall test wall just to try out different materials and techniques."

To orient the wall properly, the family first built a wood frame, stapled cardboard to it, then rotated it so it faced the kitchen but didn't block views to the backyard. Then they built the permanent wall, including planting pockets for spots of color. (Irrigation lines run up through the cinder block.)

The pond came last. The Halevas dug out the hole, lined it with a pond liner, and surrounded the edges with rocks. Finally, they placed a statue, *Colonel Mustard*, on a rock in the pond's center.

"The kids worked hard on the wall all summer," says Ecker-Haleva. "Now they want to show it off to all of their friends." — *Lauren Bonar Swezey*

A find in the foothills

Lotus Valley Nursery offers a wealth of landscaping ideas

■ Anyone interested in plants—especially ornamental grasses—will find much that delights and inspires at Lotus Valley Nursery. Though this eclectic spot is off the beaten path in Lotus, California (between Auburn and Placerville), it's worth a detour on a weekend jaunt to the Gold Country or Lake Tahoe.

For starters, owners Bob Davenport and Joe House sell 126 varieties of grasses, along with Mediterranean plants and California natives. Their landscaped grounds are filled with interesting ideas for plantings, fencing materials, and displaying art and accessories. Bamboo grows in metal troughs. Recycled building materials, artifacts, and hypertufa (faux stone) pots made by Davenport are used as accents among plants. Adjacent to the parking area is a bamboo fence so simple that you'll want to rush home and build one just like it. There's also a wood arbor with drainpipe footings, and brick steps interplanted with ground covers.

"The garden is a 14-year work in progress," says Davenport. "We have no long-range plans. We just grow topsy-turvy."

During summer, Davenport and House hold two evening "moon sales" at the nursery, inviting customers, friends, and professionals to bring a picnic supper, listen to music, and enjoy the views. "We started them because [the weather is] so hot during the day," explains Davenport. Now, they're fun gatherings where gardeners can chat.

Located just minutes from Coloma and State 49. 9–5 Wed–Sun, March to November. 5606 Petersen Lane; (530) 626-7021.

— *L.B.S.*

A grand country garden in Montana

■ In 1898, Rose Gatiss built a homestead near Kalispell in northwestern Montana. An avid gardener, she planted beds with hardy perennials. During the 1930s her son, Bob, and his wife, Rowena, began planting the existing gardens using many of the perennials from the homestead. Eventually, their efforts grew into a grand estate garden dedicated to Rose. In 1990, Bob Gatiss sold the property to Paul and Elizabeth Siblerud. Today, the Sibleruds graciously allow visitors to stroll the gardens. Elizabeth explains, "We want to pass on the Gatisses' legacy of inviting people to share in this gift and, as Bob Gatiss once said, 'to make friends we may otherwise have never known.'"

Mill Creek meanders through the site's 5 acres, which offer stunning views of the Swan Range to the east and more distant Mission Range to the southeast. You might encounter wandering chickens or other pets of the Siblerud children.

The Sibleruds continue to display heirloom perennials such as peonies and summer phlox propagated from the original stock. From late June to the first week of August, delphiniums are in full bloom. Look for the majestic flower spikes of *D.* x *belladonna* 'Bellamosum' (dark blue), *D.* 'King Arthur' (blue with white bees), and Magic Fountains strain (mixed colors). Another knockout is queen of the prairie (*Filipendula rubra* 'Venusta'), whose lacy, rose pink blooms are perched on 4- to 6-foot-tall stalks. To partly defray the cost of maintaining the gardens, the Sibleruds sell transplants of selected perennials.

Gatiss Gardens is located at 4790 State 35 in Creston, about 10 miles east of Kalispell. The grounds are open from 9 to 9 daily, from Memorial Day to Labor Day. Admission is free. For more information, call (406) 755-2418. — *Amy M. Hinman*

NORM PLATE

Landscaping with cactus

There's an art to placing plants, as this Tucson garden shows

■ Tall, columnar cactus are a Tucson trademark. That's why landscape architect Jeff Van Maren of Studio Via Rotunda (520/322-5543) incorporates them into his designs whenever he can. Recently, Van Maren got the chance to weave cactus into his own landscape during a home remodeling project. To gain space for a playroom, Van Maren needed to remove a bunch of nondescript shrubs. In their place, he created a garden in which cactus are placed for maximum visual impact.

The three tall specimens at rear are Mexican fencepost cactus *(Stenocereus marginatus)*. The knobby-looking specimens in front are totem pole cactus *(Lophocereus schottii* 'Monstrosus'). Van Maren included a few smaller cactus as well. "In essence, all cactus are accent pieces,"

he explains. "You want to give them enough room to appreciate them individually." At night, uplighting gives the cactus an especially dramatic look. "I never get tired of looking at them. Their strong, simple shapes are timeless," he says.

For seasonal color, Van Maren added coral-flowered aloe. Closer to the house, he planted two trees with fernlike foliage—feather bush *(Lysiloma watsonii thornberi)* and jacaranda; they will eventually form a canopy of light shade. For contrasting foliage texture, he added Mexican blue palm *(Brahea armata)* and Sonoran palmetto *(Sabal uresana)*. Van Maren covered the ground with a mulch of decomposed granite and placed a few large rocks for interest. — *Sharon Cohoon*

PASADENA
Poolside surprise

■ When visitors to the garden shown here stroll around the corner of the house and discover the colony of rosemary spilling under and over the swimming pool's diving board, they inevitably break into a smile. There's just something so charmingly unexpected about the sight. Whimsical though it may appear, the rosemary was planted for a practical reason, says Chris Rosmini, the Los Angeles landscape architect hired to renovate the landscape.

"My client wanted me to soften this space and make it look more gardenlike," she says, "and my biggest challenge was what to do with this Olympic-size diving board." To make the board more a part of the garden, Rosmini planted beneath it, carving out a large planting pocket when she replaced the pool decking. Rosemary was chosen for the spot because of its toughness; it stands up to sun, reflected heat, and chlorine. Rosmini used two kinds—a prostrate form around the edges and semiupright 'Ken Taylor' in the middle to soften the diving board's edges. The gray foliage peeking through is *Plecostachys serpyllifolia* that reseeded from elsewhere in the garden.

One caveat: If you swim year-round (Rosmini's clients don't), prune off the rosemary's blue flowers in the winter; they attract bees. — *S.C.*

STEVEN GUNTHER (3)

CARPINTERIA
The place for pottery

■ Garden designers love the Eye of the Day in Carpinteria. The store gives them the chance to survey a wide range of garden ornaments from California and Europe in a less pressured atmosphere than the typical showroom. But you don't need to be in the trade to visit; the store is open to the public every day but Tuesday.

Eye of the Day owners Brent and Suzi Freitas keep the store well stocked with fountains, statuary, pots, and other garden ornaments from A. Silvestri Co., Al's Garden Art, and other California manufacturers. They also import pieces from England, France, and Italy, including Cotswold stone, English lead, and Impruneta terra-cotta. "To keep prices as reasonable as possible, we order by the truckload or ship carton instead of a few items at a time," says Suzi.

To reach the store from the south, take the Santa Monica Rd. exit off U.S. 101; from the north, take the Reynolds Ave. exit. *9–6 Wed–Sat, 10–5 Sun–Mon. 4620 Carpinteria Ave.; (805) 566-0778.* — *S.C.*

CLIPPINGS

• **Folktales for little gardeners.** Discover how morning glories came to blanket Kalihi Valley, Hawaii, or a peony saved a Japanese princess in a beautifully illustrated new book *Blossom Tales: Flower Stories of Many Folk* (Moon Mountain Publishing, North Kingstown, RI, 2002; $15.95; 800/353-5877 or www. moonmountainpub.com). Although the book is aimed at 5- to 9-year-olds, adults will also enjoy the 14 tales about well-known plants.

• **New resource guide.** Ten years in the making, the 700-page *California Master Gardener Handbook* (University of California Agriculture and Natural Resources, Davis, CA, 2002; $30; 800/994-8849) is an important reference for any gardener who wants to know more about soils, fertilizers, water management, pests, weeds, and the selection and care of many plants (including berries, citrus, houseplants, landscape plants, lawns, and vegetables).

• *Estate Gardens of California* (Rizzoli International Publications, New York, 2002; $50; 212/387-3400), by Karen Dardick, with photos by Melba Levick, celebrates the grand estate gardens of California in photos and prose. Dardick is a regular contributor to *California Homes, The San Diego Union-Tribune,* and *Garden Compass.*

SARATOGA
Passion for plumerias

■ "The secret to keeping plumerias healthy in the Bay Area," says Chi-Tao Yuan, "is to keep their roots warm in summer and dry in winter." Yuan should know. After starting plumerias from seeds and logs, he has coaxed cuttings into reflowering in his Saratoga, California, garden for years.

"My goal is to someday make a lei from my own plumeria flowers," he says. And because he grows more than 50 plants, "lei day" shouldn't be far off.

Most of Yuan's plants are grown in fast-draining soil in 1- or 5-gallon black plastic pots. They rest on his southwest-facing patio, where they get full sun until about 3 P.M., then shade. During the warm months, he waters them only when the soil dries out (usually no more than once a week) and feeds them every second watering with high-phosphorus liquid fertilizer formulated to promote bloom.

In late fall when the weather starts to turn cool and damp, Yuan moves all his plumerias under the wide house eaves.

E. SPENCER TOY (2)

(In colder inland climates, move plumerias indoors for winter.) "Plumerias can take some cold—even into the 30s—as long as they aren't wet," he explains. During winter, he doesn't water at all.

In spring, he brings his plumerias back out into the sun and starts watering again. Fragrant blooms start appearing in June.

Plumerias are sold in well-stocked nurseries during summer.

—*J.M.*

Sensual lavender path

■ A classic element of Mediterranean garden design, the lavender-bordered path is equally appropriate in the Pacific Northwest. The path shown on page 216 leads into Gregory and Sheila Kent's garden on Bainbridge Island, Washington. As visitors stroll along the gravel path, fragrant sprays of lavender delight their eyes and noses.

The Kents lined their path with two kinds of lavender. The taller one in the foreground is *Lavandula* x *intermedia* 'Grosso'. One of the most fragrant varieties, it grows 30 inches high and wide, bearing violet blue flowers and silvery foliage. The shorter one is *L. angustifolia* 'Hidcote', which grows 1½ to 2 feet tall, bearing deep violet flowers and medium green leaves. Cut flower spikes of both kinds are used fresh for wands or dried for sachets. The lavenders are backed by daylilies, Shasta daisies, and purple coneflowers.

The Kents own Frog Rock Lavender Farm. During bloom season, they open their garden and lavender fields to the public. *11–4 Wed–Sun. 14414 Madison Ave. NE, Bainbridge Island; (206) 780-2693.*

—*J.M.*

BACK TO BASICS

How to use summer oil.
This lightweight oil (sold under different brand names) provides good control of aphids, mealybugs, mites, scales, and a host of other insects by smothering them. Unlike dormant oil, it can be used year-round (even in warm temperatures), and it's not toxic to mammals. Mix according to label directions and spray it on foliage, including the undersides of leaves.

—*L.B.S.*

WHAT TO DO IN YOUR GARDEN IN JULY

☐ ANNUALS. For a late-summer show, plant seedlings of cosmos, marigolds, petunias, and zinnias as early as possible this month.

☐ HARVEST. To keep berries and vegetables producing, pick every second or third day. Pick or dead-head flowers every few days to stimulate continued bloom.

☐ LAWN. Alaska and zones 1–3: Sow seed or install sod for new lawns this month. Zones 4–7, 17: Wait until September to start a new lawn.

☐ VEGETABLES. For fall harvest, plant beets, broccoli, bush beans, carrots, Chinese cabbage, kohlrabi, lettuce, peas, radishes, scallions, spinach, Swiss chard, and turnips. You can also get an autumn crop of potatoes if you plant by the Fourth of July.

MAINTENANCE

☐ BATTLE SNAILS AND SLUGS. Apply a little bait in the cool, shaded parts of the garden to lure snails and slugs out of their hiding places. Hand-pick them in the evening or after a rain.

☐ DIVIDE BEARDED IRISES. Stop watering plants early this month. At month's end, trim back leaves into fans, then dig and divide the rhizomes. Let them heal in the shade for a few days, then replant.

DEBRA LAMBERT

☐ FEED CHRYSANTHEMUMS. Give plants a dose of high-phosphorus liquid fertilizer (often called a bloom formula) every three weeks until buds start to show color. When the first blooms open, feed weekly.

☐ FERTILIZE STRAWBERRIES. After harvest, feed June-bearing strawberries with 1 pound of 10-10-10 fertilizer per 50 square feet. Give everbearing strawberries half as much early in the month.

☐ MAINTAIN FUCHSIAS. Remove faded flowers to keep new ones coming. But expect bloom to slack off during hot weather before bouncing back in fall. Sustain fuchsias in containers with liquid plant fertilizer every two weeks.

☐ MAKE COMPOST. As the harvest comes in and early crops come out, add everything except diseased plant parts to the compost pile. Turn and moisten it a couple of times each week for quick compost.

☐ MONITOR HOUSEPLANTS. Check indoor plants frequently for aphids, mealybugs, mites, scale insects, and whiteflies. Treat infestations immediately before populations explode. Hose off dusty leaves periodically or rinse them in a lukewarm shower.

☐ MULCH SHRUBS. Spread a 3- to 4-inch layer of organic mulch under shrubs (especially azaleas and rhododendrons) to conserve moisture during the warm, dry months.

☐ WATER. Irrigate early in the morning to minimize evaporation and to allow plants time to dry off to discourage mildew. ◆

WHAT TO DO IN YOUR GARDEN IN JULY

PLANTING

☐ **FALL VEGETABLES.** Zones 1 and 2: For fall harvest (except in highest altitudes), now's the time to plant beets, broccoli, bush beans, cabbage, cauliflower, carrots, green onions, peas, spinach, and turnips. Below 5,000 feet, try planting winter squash between some of the spinach; the spinach will be ready to harvest before the squash grow large and start to sprawl.

☐ **GOPHER-RESISTANT PLANTS.** Starving gophers will probably eat anything green and growing. But according to the Bio-Integral Resource Center in Berkeley, where food is abundant, the munchers will usually avoid certain plants, including agapanthus, borage, bottlebrush, breath of heaven, catnip, ceanothus, coral bells, escallonia, fortnight lily, foxglove, fuchsia, grevillea, heavenly bamboo, hydrangea, lantana, lavender, oleander, penstemon, rosemary, salvia, and Shasta daisy.

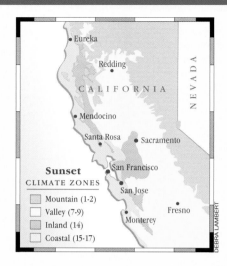

☐ **PERENNIALS.** To start new plants for fall, take 5-inch-long cuttings (without flowers) of geraniums, salvias, verbena, and other herbaceous perennials. Dip them in rooting hormone, then plant them in a mixture of one part perlite, one part peat moss. Enclose the containers in plastic bags and keep them out of direct sun (open them every few days for air circulation). Roots should start forming in about two weeks (allow cuttings to grow on for several more weeks before planting).

MAINTENANCE

☐ **BUILD A POND.** Dig a hole and line it with a flexible liner. Fill it with water and plants (available at many local nurseries) such as Japanese water iris *(Iris ensata),* parrot feather *(Myriophyllum aquaticum),* water lily, and water poppy *(Hydrocleys nymphoides).* Add mosquito fish and goldfish or koi, if desired. If you have no room for a pond, here's a simple alternative: Fill a large glazed urn that has no drain hole with water and plants (use bricks to elevate the plants above the water's surface if necessary).

☐ **CUT BACK CANE BERRIES.** After harvesting June-bearing blackberries, raspberries, and boysenberries, cut the woody spent canes back to the ground and tie up the flexible new canes.

☐ **DEEP-WATER TREES.** If you haven't watered mature trees (established three to five years), do so now. Deep-water flowering, fruit, and citrus trees once every week or two (use the higher frequency in hot, inland climates). Water drought-tolerant trees once a month or so, and newly planted trees regularly (don't let the soil dry out), gradually reducing frequency after a year or so. ◆

WHAT TO DO IN YOUR GARDEN IN JULY

PLANTING

☐ **ANNUALS AND PERENNIALS.** Asters, coreopsis, daylilies, gaillardia, lion's tail, marguerites, rudbeckia, salvias, and veronica are good summer-blooming perennials to plant now. It's not too late to add a few annuals, especially heat lovers such as celosia, marigold, portulaca, vinca, and zinnia.

☐ **SUBTROPICALS.** Flowering tropical shrubs—angel's trumpet, cestrum, hibiscus, princess flower—are plentiful in nurseries now. So are bougainvillea, passion flower, thunbergia, and trumpet vines. This is also the time to plant avocado, cherimoya, mango, and other exotic fruit trees, as well as tropical evergreens like palms, philodendron, and tree ferns.

☐ **SUMMER VEGETABLES.** Coastal (Zones 22–24) and inland (zones 18–21) gardeners can continue to plant summer vegetables. Set out cucumber, eggplant, pepper, squash, and tomato plants. Sow corn and snap beans. Or plant the year-round crops—beets, carrots, Swiss chard, and turnips. In the low desert (zone 13), start pumpkins and winter squash.

Bishop

NEVADA

CALIFORNIA

San Luis Obispo

Bakersfield

Tehachapi

Santa Barbara

Lancaster

Los Angeles

Palm Springs

Sunset
CLIMATE ZONES

1-3 7-9 11 13 14-24

San Diego

MEXICO

DEBRA LAMBERT

MAINTENANCE

☐ **ADJUST MOWING HEIGHTS.** To keep their roots shaded and conserve soil moisture, allow tall fescues to grow to 2 to 3 inches high. Warm-season grasses like Bermuda and St. Augustine, on the other hand, should be kept below an inch high to lessen thatch buildup.

☐ **FEED SELECTIVELY.** Feed annual flowers and vegetables, cymbidium orchids, ferns, fuchsias, roses, tropicals, and warm-season lawns. Also fertilize citrus and avocado.

☐ **MOVE HOUSEPLANTS OUTDOORS.** Houseplants look healthier and grow faster if they can spend all or part of the summer outdoors. Give them a shady spot protected from harsh sunlight and strong winds. Spray foliage with water occasionally to wash off dust.

☐ **RENEW MULCH.** To keep roots cool, preserve soil moisture, and discourage weeds, renew mulch around trees, shrubs, and established perennials. Homemade compost is ideal, or use shredded bark or wood chips.

☐ **WATER CAREFULLY.** It has been a long, dry spell and plants are stressed. Give shade trees a slow, deep soak monthly to ensure good health. Water established shrubs and perennials deeply too. Container plants need to be watered frequently—daily if necessary.

PEST & DISEASE CONTROL

☐ **CONTROL CATERPILLARS.** Spray or dust plants that have pest caterpillars (such as cabbageworm, tomato hornworm, or geranium budworm) with *Bacillus thuringiensis* (Bt). Since Bt kills *all* caterpillars, use only on problem plants so as not to harm the larvae of monarchs, painted ladies, swallowtails, and other welcome butterflies.

☐ **CONTROL GIANT WHITEFLY.** Examine the undersides of leaves of target plants—banana, hibiscus, plumeria—for white waxy spirals, where eggs are deposited. Wash away with jets of water. Pick off and discard leaves that have long filaments hanging from them.

☐ **WASH AWAY PESTS.** Keep spider mites and thrips in check by spraying plant foliage often, particularly the undersides of leaves. If water doesn't work, use insecticidal soap. ◆

WHAT TO DO IN YOUR GARDEN IN JULY

PLANTING

☐ DRESS UP PERENNIAL BEDS. When spring-blooming perennials such as bleeding heart, fernleaf peony, and Oriental poppy go dormant in summer, cut off their yellowed foliage and fill the gaps with container-grown annuals. Dig the planting holes for the annuals to the side of the perennials, being careful not to disturb their roots.

☐ PLANT IRISES. Set out rhizomes in soil amended with compost; water in well. One good mail-order source for irises, including bearded types and arilbred hybrids, is Willow Bend Farm (970/835-3389 or www.willowbendirisfarm.com), based in Eckert, Colorado.

☐ REPLACE COOL-SEASON ANNUALS. Cool-season annuals such as clarkia, Iceland poppy, lobelia, pansy, and stock can't stand intense summer heat. When they start looking ragged, pull them out and replant beds and containers with heat-loving annuals such as gazania, globe amaranth, gloriosa daisy, Madagascar periwinkle, marigold, petunia, portulaca, sunflower, and zinnia.

Sunset
CLIMATE ZONES
☐ 1-3 ☐ 10-11

DEBRA LAMBERT

MAINTENANCE

☐ CARE FOR CONTAINER PLANTS. In really hot weather, check containers daily and water when they start to dry out. Feed weekly with a liquid fertilizer. If annuals become leggy, cut their stems back by half to invigorate plants and restore their shape.

☐ CONTROL SLUGS. Slime trails and nibbled foliage are telltale signs that slugs have been eating your plants. Slugs are night feeders that hide out of sight in the mulch by day. To trap them, place damp, loosely rolled up newspapers in the garden at night. The next morning, dispose of the newspapers and the slugs hiding inside. Or try one of the iron phosphate–based slug baits that are safe for use around pets and wildlife.

☐ DIVIDE TALL BEARDED IRISES. The best time to divide overcrowded clumps of tall bearded irises is six weeks after they finish blooming. Lift and divide rhizomes with a knife or sharp spade, saving those with healthy new leaf fans. Before replanting, amend the soil by digging in compost or well-rotted manure and a handful of balanced fertilizer.

☐ RECOGNIZE SPRUCE GALL. Spiny brown growths resembling hollow cones that form at branch tips on Colorado spruce are caused by an insect called Cooley spruce gall aphid. However, since the insects rarely affect the health of the tree, spraying is not recommended.

☐ WATER WISELY. Most plants die from overwatering, not underwatering, so irrigate only when needed (check soil moisture first). To reduce evaporation, water when temperatures are cooler and air is still, usually in the early morning. Water deeply to moisten the root zone, but no deeper. Adjust irrigation systems so sprayers or sprinkler heads do not direct water onto pavement. Soaker hoses are an efficient way to deliver water along rows of vegetables or flowers. — *Marcia Tatroe* ◆

WHAT TO DO IN YOUR GARDEN IN JULY

PLANTING

☐ LANDSCAPE PLANTS. Plant trees and shrubs that are immune or resistant to Texas root rot (a.k.a cotton root rot) including acacia, *Caesalpinia* (poinciana), eucalyptus, mesquite, and palo verde. Add accent or specimen plants such as agave, dasylirion, dracaena, palm, sotol, and yucca.

☐ WARM-SEASON VEGETABLES. Zones 1A–3B (Flagstaff, Taos, Santa Fe): Set out transplants of early-ripening cucumbers, peppers, pumpkins, and squash. Plant a second crop of beans, cabbage, salad greens, and spinach.

Zones 10–11 (Albuquerque, Las Vegas): Plant beans, corn, cucumbers, and summer and winter squash. Try heirloom pumpkins resembling Cinderella's coach, such as 'Cinderella' (seed available from Roswell Seed Company; 505/622-7701) or 'Rouge Vif d'Etampes' (from Shepherd's Garden Seeds; 860/482-3638 or www.whiteflowerfarm.com).

Zones 12–13 (Tucson, Phoenix): Take advantage of summer monsoon rains by sowing seeds of melons and hard-shelled or winter squash, as Native American peoples traditionally do in July. Try these varieties (from Native Seeds/SEARCH; 520/622-5561 or www.nativeseeds.org.): 'Melon de Castillo' and 'Ojo Caliente' melon; 'Magdalena Big Cheese' squash has sweet flesh, and 'Silver Edged' squash is grown for its nutritious seeds, which are roasted.

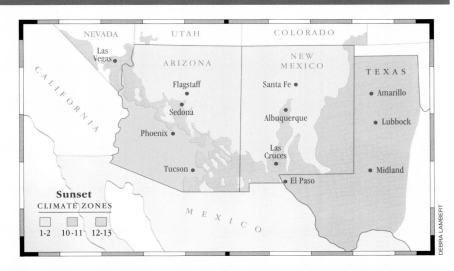

MAINTENANCE

☐ COLLECT RAINWATER. Summer monsoon rains erupt suddenly, so the soil has little time to absorb the moisture before it runs off. Keep more moisture on your property by implementing simple water-harvesting techniques. Mound soil berms to direct and hold rainwater in tree wells or on lawns, where it can soak into the ground, or channel roof runoff into large basins. Place buckets or barrels under downspouts and collect rainwater for potted plants.

☐ CONTROL COCHINEAL SCALE. If you see these white cottony insects infesting prickly pear pads, blast them off with a strong jet of water from the hose.

☐ DETHATCH LAWNS. Hybrid Bermuda grass needs to be dethatched every two or three years to remove the dense undergrowth that prevents water from soaking into the soil. After mowing, dethatch your lawn by vigorously running a hard-tined rake through it, pulling up runners and stolons; or rent a gas-powered dethatching machine and run it over the entire lawn twice in opposite directions. Follow with another mowing, fertilizing, and deep watering.

☐ FERTILIZE. Feed annual flowers, vegetables, and grapevines.

— Kim Nelson ◆

Three seasons, three uses

◀ Spring: Make the patio a focal point. Place a birdbath and pots of blooming annuals such as purple nemesia and bacopa in its center. Edge it with low mounders—New Zealand hair sedge 'Frosty Curls', 'Oriental Limelight' variegated artemisia—and add color makers such as breath of heaven, pink marguerites, pink and purple anemones, Swan River daisy, lilac, *Berberis thunbergii* 'Aurea'. Tuck low growers such as creeping thyme between the bricks.

▶ Summer: Bring out the bistro table and chairs. Tuck summer bloomers like purple verbena, yellow daisylike helianthus, purple coneflower, and coreopsis behind it. (Golden seedheads top eulalia grass behind chair).

Instant patio

It measures just 7 feet across. You can build it in a weekend for less than $200

By Kathleen N. Brenzel • Design by Bud Stuckey • Photographs by Thomas J. Story

■ Most patios take time, and days of effort, to build. But a small, detached patio like the one pictured here comes together quickly with minimal effort.

Think of the possible uses for this circle of bricks (we show three). You can tuck it into a perennial border. Or place it in a remote corner of your garden, where you can linger at day's end over a glass of wine, or on Sunday morning with a latte while perusing the papers.

Such flexibility was our goal when *Sunset's* Bud Stuckey installed this patio near the end of a wide flower border in our editorial test garden in Menlo Park, California, last summer. But we also wanted our tiny tuck-in to be relatively inexpensive to build, easy to install in a day or a weekend, and moveable. (Since heavy foot traffic wouldn't be an issue, we set the bricks in sand.)

You wouldn't want to walk on this patio wearing spiked heels. But if throwing fancy-dress garden parties is your style, set the bricks in mortar on a concrete base. Or arrange them on packed soil so you can grow plants such as creeping thyme in wider spaces between them. (You can edge the patio with bricks set on end in a trench around the outside, soil packed firmly against them. For other ideas, see *Sunset's Complete Patio Book*.)

If bricks don't match the other pavers in your yard, you can adapt the idea, substituting flagstone, slate, cobblestone, or colored concrete pavers. In place of a round slate paver in the center, you can use a concrete paver embellished with broken glazed tiles in pretty colors.

Locate your patio on level ground, out of wind and hot sun. Position it to take advantage of any grand views and create access to it with steppingstones. Then comes the fun part—styling your patio. Oh, and settling in with a tall glass of something cool to celebrate its completion.

BUILD IT YOURSELF
Installing the patio

TIME: 1 day (plus a day for planting)

COST: About $190

MATERIALS

Two 7-foot-long 2-by-4s • Two 1-foot-long stakes with pointed tips • String • Gypsum • 12 1-cubic-foot bags (about ½ yard) clean sand • One round slate or flagstone paver, about 17 inches in diameter (add two or more for steppingstones—optional) • 150 used bricks (includes a few extras for color matching)

Optional

One 80-pound bag Quikcrete mortar mix • 1 quart mortar color

TOOLS

Rotary tiller or spade • Rake • Carpenter's level • Tamper • Hose • Rubber mallet • Bench broom

Optional

Bucket for mixing mortar • Grout bag • Trowel • Rag • Burlap

▲ **Fall:** Make it your secret garden. Surround it with billowy bloomers like this *Tagetes lemmonii* for privacy, or—for fragrance—English lavender or mock orange *(Choisya ternata)*. Put a comfy Adirondack chair in the center.

8 A.M.

1. Rototill or dig the soil; rake it smooth. Lay the 2-by-4s about 7 feet apart to serve as temporary guides. Place a stake in the soil to mark the patio's center; tie a 7-foot-long piece of string to it, then tie the string's free end to the second stake. With the free stake, trace the patio's outline in the soil, pulling the string taut as you walk a wide circle around the center stake. Remove the stakes and mark the circle with gypsum. Remove the 2-by-4s from the sides; then place the carpenter's level on one of them to

make sure soil is level. (Recheck level at every stage.)

2. Pour six bags of sand evenly over the soil to about 5 inches beyond the gypsum mark. Smooth it with the edge of one of the 2-by-4s, then tamp it evenly to firm. Spray with a fine mist from the hose, then tamp it again into a layer about 2 inches thick.

3. Place the center paver on the sand base. Working from the center outward, set down the bricks (follow the pattern above), tapping

Number of bricks per row

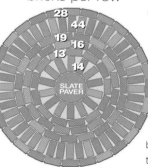

them into place with the mallet and butting them together as tightly as possible. Spread three bags of sand evenly over the surface of the finished paving, let it dry if wet, then sweep the sand into the joints be-

tween bricks. Mist lightly with the hose. Add sand until joints are full.

4. To mortar the center paver in place (optional, but recommended), mix the mortar and add color, if desired, according to package directions. Using a grout bag, apply the mixture between the bricks immediately surrounding the center paver (use a trowel tip to smooth it if necessary). Allow it to dry; wipe away excess with a clean, soft rag. For extra firming (also optional), mix 1 part mortar with 1 part sand, then brush the mixture into joints

between the outer bricks. Carefully sweep excess mortar off the bricks. Mist periodically over the next two hours. Scrub bricks with burlap to eliminate any mortar stains.

5. Pour the remaining sand around the patio's perimeter; mist it with the hose and pack it firmly with your hands or the back of the trowel.

5 P.M.

Finished! Planting can wait until tomorrow. To help reinforce the patio's edge, lay sod or plant low-growing ground covers as close to it as possible. ◆

Our sweet mix contains 3 stems of blue hydrangeas, 5 stems each of red zinnias and dahlias, 5 stems of white spray roses, yellow sunflowers, pale yellow roses, blackberries, and 10 stems of blue cornflowers.

Old Glory in a basket

Make a casual Fourth of July bouquet for a colorful centerpiece on your holiday table

By Lauren Bonar Swezey and Jill Slater

Summer flowers come into their bloom peak just in time for the biggest party of the season—Fourth of July. To dress up an outdoor table for a picnic, you can take advantage of the bounty by setting flowers of patriotic colors in a basket like the one pictured above.

Bold blue hydrangeas form the core of our arrangement. To fill the spaces around them, we used a luscious assortment of blooms in primary colors—about 50 stems total. (If your garden can't supply all the right colors, use blooms from a market or florist.) For longest life, display the arrangement out of direct sun.

TIME: 25 minutes

TOOLS AND MATERIALS

• Three bricks of florist's foam (4 inches wide, 9 inches long, 3 inches thick) • Clippers
• Assorted flowers (see list at left) • Floral food
• Round waterproof liner • Florist's tape
• Picnic basket (10 inches wide by 16 inches long) • Three handfuls of sphagnum moss
• Foliage: eight stems of salal, camellia, citrus, or other long-lasting greenery

DIRECTIONS

1. Soak two bricks of florist's foam in water for 30 minutes. While they're soaking, cut the flower stems and let them stand in a bucket of water mixed with floral food.

2. Cut both bricks to fit the plastic liner with 1 inch extending above the rim. Secure the foam to the liner by wrapping them together with florist's tape.

3. Cut the dry brick of florist's foam in half lengthwise. Place it in the bottom of the basket. Set the liner on top of it; the rim of the liner should be almost level with the basket rim. Add floral food to a quart of water, then fill the liner. Wedge moss between the rim of the basket and the liner.

4. Trim foliage stems to 8 inches long; insert them into the sides of the foam so that they extend beyond the basket rim.

5. To create depth, cut one hydrangea stem to 2 inches long and tuck it into the center of the foam. Cut two more hydrangea stems, each 4 inches long; insert them into opposite sides of the foam so they drape over the basket rim.

6. Cut the stems of three sunflowers and three pale yellow roses to 8 inches long. Insert one sunflower next to the handle on the left side of the basket; allow it to extend beyond the rim. Insert the other sunflowers, forming a triangle around the foam. Add pale yellow roses at each end and a third on the right side near the handle, so they drape over the basket edges.

7. To create height, cut the remaining flower stems 10 to 12 inches long, filling in between the shorter blooms. The tallest flowers should extend no higher than 2 to 4 inches above the basket handle. Poke in cornflowers.

8. Insert short blackberry stems to drape over the rim of the basket. ◆

THOMAS J. STORY (2)

Glazed French pots fill the shelves at A Garden of Distinction in Seattle (left). New and old furnishings mingle with fountains, bird cages, and more at Phoenix's On the Veranda (right).

Treasure hunting

For unique pots, benches, or trellises, try a garden art specialist

By Kathleen N. Brenzel with James Boone

"The garden is the bonus room of this century. Furnish it with things you love," advises Gail Chapman, who sells garden antiques and accessories from a south Seattle showroom.

Believing that plants and art go hand in hand to make a garden, Chapman is one of a growing number of Western entrepreneurs who are opening shops or warehouses to sell one-of-a-kind garden ornaments. Diane Egizii is another. Because gardens increasingly are places to dine, play, entertain, or just hang out, says this Phoenix garden decorator, they're being furnished and embellished as thoughtfully as indoor rooms. "You should be as comfortable outdoors as indoors," she adds.

For a gardener, browsing through the four stores listed here—a sampling of the many now opening throughout the West—may be the ultimate treasure hunt. Who knows what fun things you'll discover along the way.

SEATTLE
A Garden of Distinction

A head-spinning array of enticing items fills this 10,000-square-foot showroom. Glazed Asian pots huddle next to provençal bistro tables and antique French swings. Decorative ironwork from Tunisia and other countries hangs on a wall. Most of the items are displayed in vignettes designed to inspire.

"I search for and sell the things I love," says owner Gail Chapman, who regularly makes buying trips to France and Southeast Asia. "People come here looking for one-of-a-kind pieces."

WHAT'S HOT: Trellises, anything in iron, and shapely containers of all kinds. *10–5 Mon–Sat. 5819 Sixth Ave. S (one building south of the Seattle Design Center); (206) 763-0517 or www. agardenofdistinction.com.*

SAN JOSE
Artefact Design & Salvage

"I could never find the kind of garden art I liked, so I decided to start collecting," says owner David Allen, a high-tech drop-out from Silicon Valley, whose interest in architecture and garden ornaments blossomed into a business.

About two years ago, Allen opened his retail outlet in a 1920s corrugated steel warehouse. To keep it filled, he scours this country and Europe for old, handcrafted pieces he calls "lost arts"—items of Victorian terra-cotta, carved stone, wood, and pressed metal. There are stone benches, wrought-iron fences and gates, wall fountains, pots, pillars, and antique baskets.

"It's fun to discover great stuff in unexpected places," he adds, recalling the time he clung to scaffolding outside the 20th floor of a Manhattan high-rise slated for demolition just to check out decorative terra-cotta. Many of his offerings are pricey, but he sells inexpensive pieces too, like the oil jar, grape urn, and English terra-cotta pot pictured (inset on the facing page).

WHAT'S HOT: Turkish village oil jar, birdbaths, urns, and cast-iron benches with crusty finishes.

11–5 Wed–Sat, 12–5 Sun. 245 McEvoy St. (on the east end of Antique Row between W. San Carlos St. and Park Ave.); (408) 279-8766.

Brass bumblebee, $6, at Artefact Design & Salvage.

Shopping tips

- Ask yourself how best to show off the item you want to buy. Will it look good against an evergreen hedge? In the center of a patio or garden pool? Against a colored stucco wall?

- Think outside the box, says Allen. You can hang a chandelier over an outdoor dining table, fill a French washtub with flowers, or set three oil jars on their sides and plumb them to drip water into a pool.

- Before you buy, measure the space where you want to put garden art or furnishings, advises Huddle. Keep in mind the overall scale of the garden you're creating.

- Make your garden about you and what you like. Personalize it. "Mix up your favorite looks," suggests Egizii.

More fabulous finds

■ Many well-stocked nurseries, such as **Roger's Gardens** in Corona del Mar, California (949/640-5800), and **Swansons Nursery** in Seattle (206/782-2543) also sell garden art and furnishings.

Newly opened at Paradise Valley Marketplace in Phoenix is **Poppybox Gardens** (602/569-2087), a garden store and nursery. "We embrace gardening from a design sensibility," says Poppybox president Allison O'Connor. "Our look is contemporary." Designer containers are a specialty here. Poppybox also has two locations in Oregon—Portland (503/280-1228) and Tigard (503/968-8804).

Trio of square pots shows off desert spoon (tallest) and agaves at Poppybox Gardens.

PHOENIX
On the Veranda

Old meets new in this store tucked away at the rear of a shopping center. (Look for the green awning over the door.)

Owners Sharron Saffert and Diane Egizii describe their offerings as "eclectic," with garden ornaments and furnishings from France, England, and the East Coast rubbing shoulders with rock planters from Texas ("great for displaying desert plants") and ivy topiaries from California. Watch for decorating ideas among the patio tables displayed as though they've been set for parties.

WHAT'S HOT: Items in Old World, farmhouse, and shabby chic styles. "We're feathering our nests again," says Egizii, "with things like vintage porch swings, charming gates that open into secret gardens, and arbors for roses. Things that embrace us and recall sweet memories of

grandma's garden."
9–4 Tue–Sat. 4748 E. Indian School Rd.; (602) 955-8690.

DENVER
Paris Blue

"I keep my enthusiasm up by constantly looking for unique things," says Jim Huddle, who opened Paris Blue last December after quitting a hectic career in the cable news industry to sell antiques and garden art. "Customers like discovering something different every time they come in, and I love surprising them." Behind his store's brick façade, he displays everything from wrought-iron bistro tables and wall-mounted plant hangers to pots and urns.

WHAT'S HOT: Fountains of all kinds, including ones of glass, stone, ceramic, bronze, aged concrete, Italian porcelain, and stone look-alikes of resin.
10–5:30 Mon–Sat, 11–4 Sun. 350 Kalamath St.; (720) 932-6200. ◆

ABOVE: NORM PLATE; LEFT: THOMAS J. STORY

'Lady Scarlet' forms a sultry border in the sculpture garden at Norton Simon Museum in Pasadena.

Daylilies that win in the West

Plant the best performers for your region

By Sharon Cohoon

Why is the daylily (*Hemerocallis* hybrids) the most popular perennial in the West? For one thing, it grows in virtually all of our climates. In the moist Pacific Northwest, daylilies develop such luxurious foliage that it's wise to select tall-stemmed varieties if you want to see the flowers. In Northern California, nature supplies daylilies with the perfect balance of rainfall and sun. And daylilies bloom like the dickens in coastal Southern California, even outflowering roses. In California's Central Valley and other hot inland locations, the foliage may grow shorter, but the flowers come just as abundantly. Gardeners in colder intermountain areas can grow deciduous varieties hardy enough to stand temperatures as low as −35°. Even in Southwest deserts, where daylilies face more of a challenge, they do surprisingly well when given afternoon shade and plenty of water.

Another reason daylilies are popular is that they're so easy to grow. There are no disease or insect pests worth mentioning. Gophers leave them alone and deer usually do too. Even being trampled by kids or dogs or run over by a lawnmower doesn't faze them for long.

Variety is another plus. Though there is an abundance of yellow- and orange-flowered daylilies, there are also plenty of romantic pinks and lavenders, dramatic reds and purples, and exotic browns. The foliage can be as fine as grass or as coarse as corn.

Planting and care

In most Western climates, bare-root and container-grown plants can go in the ground anytime from spring through midautumn. In the desert, wait to plant until the soil cools down in fall.

In most areas, give daylilies the sunniest spot in your garden. In the desert, protect from afternoon sun by planting them in a spot where they'll get filtered shade or an eastern exposure.

For best performance amend the soil with organic matter such as compost before planting. Daylilies will survive considerable drought, but for generous bloom they need ample water during their growing period.

Star performers

Wherever you garden, there's a daylily that's just right for you. Some daylilies perform well in all climates. The most notable example is 'Bitsy', a variety with lemon yellow flowers, that outblooms any other daylily yet on the market, flowering up to 290 days a year in mild areas like Southern California and Hawaii.

Other daylilies, though, only put on their best show in certain climates. 'Stella de Oro', a deciduous variety, is an excellent choice for gardeners in colder areas like Colorado or Montana, but it doesn't perform well in Southern California.

We surveyed Western growers, landscape architects, nursery staff, and daylily society members to find out the star players in their areas.

Trio of beauties: 'Judith' (top), 'Lullaby Baby' (center), and 'Leebea Orange Crush' (bottom).

Winners for all Western regions

'Bitsy'. Lemon yellow. 2-inch flowers, 26-inch stems (technically known as *scapes*), 20-inch leaves; evergreen. 2002 All-American Daylily.

'Cranberry Baby'. Rosy red. 2¾-inch flowers, 15-inch stems, 10-inch leaves; deciduous. Compact habit.

'Judith'. Coral pink with rose eye. 5½-inch flowers, 30-inch stems, 18-inch leaves; deciduous. Heavy bloomer. 2002 All-American Daylily.

'Leebea Orange Crush'. Bright orange with darker eye and green throat. 6-inch flowers, 28-inch stems, 22-inch leaves; semievergreen. Fragrant. 2002 All-American Daylily.

Northern California

Any of the daylilies listed for other regions will do well here.

Coastal Southern California and Hawaii

'Dixie Land Band'. True red with white stripes and green throat. 7-inch flowers, 32-inch stems, 20-inch leaves; evergreen. Takes light shade.

'Joan Senior'. Near-white with yellow green throat. 6-inch flowers, 30-inch stems, 18-inch leaves; evergreen.

'Lavender Dew'. Lavender with green throat. 5½-inch flowers, 28-inch stems, 18-inch leaves; evergreen. Good repeat bloomer.

'Miss Victoria'. Clear yellow. 4-inch flowers, 24-inch stems, 20-inch leaves; semievergreen. Fragrant.

Inland Southern California and Central Valley

'Gingerbread Man'. Reddish brown. 6½-inch flowers, 34-inch stems, 24-inch leaves; evergreen. Very heat tolerant. Good rebloomer.

'Lady Eva'. Maroon purple. 6-inch flowers, 32-inch stems, 24-inch leaves; evergreen. Dramatic color. Reblooms readily.

'Lady Scarlet'. Red. 6-inch flowers, 22-inch stems, 20-inch leaves; semievergreen.

'Miss Victoria' (see under Coastal Southern California).

'TerraCotta Baby'. Rosy tan. 2¾-inch flowers, 22-inch stems, 15-inch leaves; evergreen. Blooms generously.

Southwest

'Aztec Chalice'. Brilliant velvety red. 5½-inch flowers, 36-inch stems, 26-inch leaves; evergreen.

'Cortez Cove'. Yellow with greenish cast. 4-inch flowers, 28-inch stems, 18-inch leaves; evergreen. Strong performer.

'Gingerbread Man' and **'Lady Eva'** (see under Inland Southern California).

Pacific Northwest

'Frans Hals'. Rusty apricot bicolor. 4½-inch flowers, 26-inch stems, 20-inch leaves; deciduous. Color deepens in summer and turns pastel again in spring.

'Joan Senior' (see under Coastal Southern California).

'Pandora's Box'. Near-white with large plum eye. 4-inch flowers, 20-inch stems, 13-inch leaves; deciduous. Exceptionally hardy.

'Pink Playmate'. Pink blend with white ribs and throat. 3½-inch flowers, 22-inch stems, 12-inch leaves; deciduous. Vigorous.

'Smoky Mountain Autumn'. Peachy rose with lavender halo. 5½-inch flowers, 22-inch stems, 18-inch leaves; deciduous. Fragrant.

Intermountain West

'Custard Candy'. Cream yellow with maroon eye. 4¼-inch flowers, 24-inch stems, 16-inch leaves; deciduous.

'Janice Brown'. Pink with rose eye. 4-inch flowers, 22-inch stems, 16-inch leaves; semievergreen.

'Lullaby Baby'. Pinkish white with yellow throat. 3½-inch flowers, 18-inch stems, 14-inch leaves; deciduous.

'Stella de Oro'. Yellow gold. 2-inch flowers, 20-inch stems, 16-inch leaves; deciduous.

'White Temptation'. Near-white. 5-inch flowers, 34-inch stems, 26-inch leaves; semievergreen.

Sources

Buy daylilies at well-stocked nurseries or from these growers.

Amador Flower Farm. Plymouth, CA; (209) 245-6660 or www.amadorflowerfarm.com. Catalog $3.50.

Caprice Farm Nursery. Aumsville, OR; (503) 749-1397 or www.capricenursery.com. Catalog free.

Cordon Bleu Daylilies. San Marcos, CA; (760) 744-8367 or www.buenacreekgardens.com. Catalog $2.

Greenwood Daylily & Iris Garden. Somis, CA; (562) 494-8944 or www.greenwoodgarden.com. Catalog free.

Shepard Iris Garden. Phoenix; (602) 841-1231. Catalog $1.

Snow Creek Daylilies. Port Townsend, WA; (360) 765-4342 or www.snowdaylily.com. Catalog $3. ◆

Meadow rue flowers perch like tiny butterflies on delicate stems above foliage that resembles maidenhair fern.

THREE'S COMPANY

Use three long-blooming perennials to form the backbone of the planting, then add smaller plants in complementary hues. The pot above, designed by Tina Dixon of Plants à la Cart in Bothell, Washington, and Cheryl Wilson of Kirkland, Washington, features *Rudbeckia* 'Goldsturm', chocolate cosmos, and 'Pardon Me' daylily. Dark-leafed 'Ace of Spades' sweet potato vine trails over the edge; its color echoes the dark eye of black-eyed Susan vine. The container also holds purple fountain grass, bronze fennel, *Sanvitalia procumbens* 'Orange Sprite', *Weigela* 'Magic Carpet', *Lysimachia nummularia* 'Aurea', and *Lonicera nitida* 'Baggesen's Gold'.

Potting perennials

Three approaches to low-care planting

By Kathleen N. Brenzel and Jim McCausland

You get a wonderful feeling when the potted perennials you've been ignoring all winter start to reappear in spring. Just when you've given up hope that new life will somehow spring forth from those clumps of strawlike twigs, fresh green growth appears, followed by robust stems, beautiful flowers, and a long summer show. It's the cycle of life and the seasons, being played out in a pot. And it's one of the joys of the low-care plantings pictured here, designed for beauty and simplicity.

Many perennials will come back pretty reliably for several years in the same container. You can grow them singly, pair a couple of compatible growers, or plant a medley of three or more comeback kids whose colors and textures complement one another.

For the first two years in pots, the perennials shown here need little care beyond watering, clipping spent blooms, and feeding (controlled-release fertilizer at the start of growing seasons works well).

But by the third or fourth year, mixed plantings can begin to appear crowded. Autumn is a good time to divide them.

Plant tall perennials (2 to 4 feet) in deep pots (at least 18 inches diameter and about 20 inches deep). Put low growers in wide bowls at least 8 inches deep.

SOLO SENSATIONS

A single, well-chosen plant can create drama in a pot. For example, take meadow rue, pictured at left. During summer, clouds of blooms cover its delicate stems, making this plant superb for creating an airy effect against a wall or dark green background. Many other perennials are showy enough to grow singly in pots; some are listed below.

To extend the season's show, fill several beautiful stoneware or Italian terracotta pots with perennials that peak at different times—late spring, early to midsummer, and midsummer into fall, for instance. You can move them out of sight after they've bloomed. Climate zones are from the *Sunset Western Garden Book.*

Aster (A. x *frikartii* **'Wonder of Staffa' and 'Mönch').** Clear lavender to violet blue single flowers on plants to 2 feet tall. Sun; early summer to fall. Zones 2в–24.

English lavender (*Lavandula angustifolia* **'Munstead', 'Hidcote', or 'Sharon Roberts').** Spikes of fragrant blooms. Sun; late spring. Zones 2–24.

Gaura lindheimeri. Wispy spikes of white flowers. Sun; late spring through summer. Zones 2в–24.

Geum chiloense **'Mrs. Bradshaw'.** Double scarlet blooms atop 2-foot stems. Part shade in hottest climates; late spring. Zones 2–24.

Meadow rue *(Thalictrum).* Clouds of small lavender blooms appear in late spring. Light shade. Zones 2–10, 14–17.

Santa Barbara daisy *(Erigeron karvinskianus).* Trailing plant 10 to 20 inches tall and 3 feet wide with dainty, daisylike flowers in white and pink. Plant in a low, wide bowl. Sun to light shade; rarely out of bloom. Zones 8–9, 12–24, H1–H2.

Stokes aster *(Stokesia laevis).* Large (3- to 4-inch) asterlike blooms of blue, purplish blue, or white on plants to 2 feet tall. Sun; summer or early fall. Zones 2–10, 12–24. Evergreen in warmer climates. ◆

NORM PLATE

TWO TO TANGO

Plant two perennials together—either a single tall one surrounded by low growers or two tall ones. In the pot pictured above, red *Geum* 'Mrs. Bradshaw' and white *Gaura lindheimeri* mingle their delicate blooms.

FRINGED BY FERNS and lacy Japanese maples, a waterfall creates a cool oasis in this Central Valley garden. For details on how to bring the soothing sound of falling water to *your* backyard, see pages 258–265.

August

CHARLES MANN

High-country collage

■ In July and August, a riot of flowers breaks out around the home of Bob and Jane Hendrix in Breckenridge, Colorado. Here, in a clearing of a lodgepole pine forest at an elevation of 10,000 feet, annuals, biennials, bulbs, and perennials all bloom simultaneously.

Jane refers to this exuberant design as an "alpine color collage." As she composes her plantings, Jane mixes flowers with harmonious colors (such as delphiniums in shades of blue, lavender, and purple) with vivid contrasting colors (such as orange pansies). Most of the garden is arranged in raised beds framed by stones or timbers. But Jane also places flower-filled half-barrels and other containers at strategic locations around the garden, such as beneath trees or at the edge the lawn.

The garden's framework is composed of flowering bulbs and perennials, including Asiatic lilies, bellflowers, columbines, delphiniums, *Geranium* 'Johnson's Blue',

lupines, and poppies. Jane overlays the permanent plantings with thousands of annual and biennial flowers, including cosmos, lobelia, marigolds, and pansies.

— *Marcia Tatroe*

Jane's color-making calendar

Winter. She orders seeds, reviews the garden design, and starts seeds of perennials to supplement existing plants.

March to April. She starts seeds of annuals and biennials indoors under lights.

May to June. She adds topsoil and peat moss to the beds as needed, and topdresses delphiniums with composted cow manure and blood meal.

Mid- to late June. She plants beds and broadcasts granulated all-purpose fertilizer.

July to August. During bloom, she deadheads faded flowers and feeds plants twice with liquid all-purpose fertilizer.

September to October. She cleans up beds.

Sensual orange jessamine

■ Diane Egizii, co-owner of On the Veranda garden shop in Phoenix, says, "Orange jessamine is a total sensual experience." To begin with, its flowers smell heavenly. The scent, which Egizii describes as a combination of orange blossoms and jasmine, intensifies as the day heats up, so that by night "it seems to be suspended in the air." You get to enjoy the fragrance often, since orange jessamine *(Murraya paniculata)* reblooms every six to seven weeks, bearing clusters of white, bell-shaped flowers. With its slender trunk, graceful branches, and glossy leaves, the evergreen shrub is also pleasing to the eye.

It's a surprise to find this Southeast Asia native growing outdoors in the Sonoran Desert, but Egizii has kept potted specimens in her garden for several years now without any frost damage. And landscape contractor John Sheridan, who introduced her to orange jessamine, has successfully grown it in the ground even longer. "My plants get full sun until about 3 in the afternoon, and they look just fine," he says.

Still, the safest way to grow orange jessamine is in containers. In colder climates, you can treat it as an indoor/outdoor plant. Use a coarse, fast-draining potting soil and give the plant a location where it will get a mini-

TERRENCE MOORE; BELOW: CHARLES MANN

mum of four hours of sun every day, advises Sheridan. Water and feed it frequently.

On the Veranda sells 14-inch potted specimens ($150; in the store only). You can order a tabletop plant in a $2\frac{1}{2}$-inch pot ($7.95) from Logee's Greenhouses (888/330-8038 or www.logees.com). — *Sharon Coboon*

A cool summer place

■ Ann and Larry Andersen of Denver transformed a boring backyard into an inviting garden retreat with the help of landscape architect Belinda Arbogast of Centennial, Colorado. In summer, the couple uses the space as a dining area.

Arbogast relocated an existing brick patio, then extended the paved area by adding randomly shaped red flagstones. The surface is softened by carpets of woolly thyme planted between the stones. In the surrounding beds, hollyhocks soar and golden columbines provide splashes of yellow. Containers are planted with geraniums and petunias in Ann's favorite colors—pink, lavender, and cerise.

A garage wall serves as a backdrop for the flower beds. Inspired by vivid painted walls they'd seen in the Southwest, the Andersens finished the stucco wall with a brilliant blue wash. First, they painted the stucco with a primer undercoat, then applied medium blue latex house paint. After it dried, they applied cobalt blue paint in streaks using a water-filled spray bottle to keep the surface wet while brushing the paint until they achieved the effect of falling water. The blue hues are echoed by a gazing ball, cushions on a chaise longue, and a ceramic birdbath. — *M.T.*

Peak time at Betty Ford Alpine Gardens

■ Founded in 1987, the Betty Ford Alpine Gardens has recently added several horticultural attractions, expanding its size to nearly 3 acres in Vail's Ford Park. The ambitious new Alpine Rock Garden features stone walls, waterfalls, and ponds, all constructed of local materials to harmonize with the spectacular scenery surrounding Vail Valley.

The site, at an elevation of 8,200 feet, encompasses every facet of alpine gardening. Nearly 3,000 different varieties of plants, including collections of peonies, primroses, and saxifrages, are displayed throughout the complex. Peak bloom comes in July and August. Bring a camera and notebook to make a record of plants you'd like to try. The gift shop, located in a restored 1922 one-room schoolhouse, offers a selection of books on alpine gardening.

Earlier this summer, the new Children's Environmental Garden opened. Youngsters follow a 150-foot nature trail that simulates a hike from the valley floor to the top of the Gore Range with demonstrations of Rocky Mountain ecosystems along the way.

Ford Park is east of Vail Village on South Frontage Road. The wheelchair-accessible grounds are open daily during daylight hours from May through October, when the gardens close for the season. Admission is free; donations are appreciated. For information on guided tours (Thursdays and Saturdays at 10:30) and events, call (970) 476-0103 or go to www.bettyfordalpinegardens.org. — *M. T.*

CHARLES MANN; BELOW: PAUL BOUSQUET

Bountiful border in Vail

■ At higher altitudes, summer makes a brief but glorious appearance. Flowering perennials, which relish the sunny days and cool nights, often bloom longer and more profusely than their counterparts do at lower elevations. That's certainly the case in this border in Vail, Colorado. At front left, snow-in-summer (*Cerastium tomentosum*) lives up to its name, producing such a flurry of white flowers that they nearly obscure the plant's silver foliage. In the center, blue and purple columbines nod gracefully over lacy green foliage. At right, Maltese cross (*Lychnis chalcedonica*) carries dense scarlet flower clusters. In the rear, red-hot poker (*Kniphofia* hybrids) shows off sizzling orange-and-yellow torches.

For his design work in this garden, John Rosenfeld of Johnie's Garden in Minturn, Colorado, won a grand prize in a competition sponsored by the Associated Landscape Contractors of Colorado. — *M. T.*

A summer living room in Tacoma

■ Wedged between a shoreline road and Tacoma's Commencement Bay, Barbara Berntsen's waterfront house offered only one possible garden spot: a sunny, west-facing deck that is as wide as her house and about 15 feet deep. It had the advantages of abundant sun, humidity, and temperatures moderated by water, but more than its share of wind, and no access to the ground—everything would have to live in containers.

From the beginning, Berntsen decided that this garden should be as diverse and complex as any conventional backyard garden: She wanted trees, shrubs, vines, perennials, and annuals; visitors would see plants above, below, and beside them.

She began putting flowers on the deck two decades ago, adding more containers every year: half-barrels, boxes, crates, a canoe, and a bathtub. Each holds permanent plants—small trees, shrubs, and perennials—that give her garden its backbone and provide some year-round screening. She fills out the containers with annuals in summer, putting shade lovers like begonias on the north sides of the containers and sun lovers like bidens facing south.

During summer, the deck serves as "my living room," Berntsen explains. "The sliding doors from the cabin to the deck are open all summer. When people come over, they don't even stop inside; they walk straight out onto the deck." To make entertaining easy, she arranged a table and chairs under an arbor that holds hanging baskets of flowers. Wisteria and grapevines emerge from pots and clamber over the arbor to give shade in summer, as well as flowers and fruit in season. —*Jim McCausland*

Water-smart in Las Vegas

■ Architect Jeffrey Dacks drew from a palette of drought-tolerant plants to create a natural landscape around his home in Las Vegas. The project demonstrates that water-thrifty gardening can be beautiful and practical at the same time.

In the front yard (shown at right), a mesquite tree *(Prosopis chilensis)* forms a feathery canopy over yellow-flowered lantana and *Dalea capitata* 'Sierra Gold' and spiky desert spoon *(Dasylirion wheeleri)* near the house. In front of the low stucco wall is wispy deer grass *(Muhlenbergia rigens)*. Behind the wall are tufts of blue fescue and red-flowered *Hesperaloe parviflora.*

In the backyard (above), Dacks wanted a lawn but limited it to 450 square feet. To give a sense of depth, the lawn of dwarf fescue grass was installed 6 to 16 inches lower than the surrounding ground. Mesquite trees are planted on two sides of a 12- by 14-foot concrete patio, where Dacks and his family frequently dine. Dotted around the landscape are more unthirsty trees and shrubs, including sweet acacia *(A. smallii)*, red bird of paradise *(Caesalpinia pulcherrima)*, desert cassia *(Senna nemophila)*, and specimens of the same plants used in the front yard.

For help with plant selection and irrigation design, Dacks consulted Las Vegas landscape architect Rich Marriotti. The permanent plants are watered by a drip-irrigation system. The lawn is irrigated by pop-up spray heads. To finish, Dacks laid down a 2- to 3-inch-deep layer of gold-toned decomposed granite as a ground cover, then placed boulders and smooth river rocks over the top.

— *Gail Mueller*

NORM PLATE (2)

Hidden spa in Scottsdale

■ Viewed from the front (see photo above), the water feature in this Scottsdale backyard looks like a series of boulder-studded waterfalls that cascade into a small pool. But the rocky façade actually hides access to a crescent-shaped spa, shown at right.

Steven Rogers of Sonoran Desert Designs (480/595-6400) designed the spa; Phoenix pool expert John Sensabough built it. The spa's curvy shape makes it seem more like a desert stream. Owners James Grassman and Mary Lynn Stenzel-Grassman appreciate the spa's 5½-foot depth. "It's lovely to be able to fully immerse yourself," says Mary Lynn. The steps descending into the spa are outlined by fiber-optic lighting, which "creates a magic effect at night," she says.

A desert ironwood tree *(Olneya tesota)* casts shade over the spa. At the base of the boulders, soil-filled planting pockets hold seasonal color like the red geraniums, white petunias, and yellow marguerite *(Argyranthemum frutescens)* blooming here. — *S.C.*

TERRENCE MOORE

Privacy wall with Southwest flair

■ Kelly Frink and Tag Merrick of Tucson wanted privacy from a nearby street as well as a sense of enclosure for their dining patio. So the couple sketched a design for a 7-foot-tall, L-shaped wall that would wrap around one end of the patio. To build the wall, they hired John Mikiska of Star Masonry (520/325-3724) in Tucson. Mikiska used burnt adobe blocks. While traditional adobe blocks are dried in the sun, burnt adobe is fired at low temperatures for greater durability. He laid the blocks in a running-bond style, using generous amounts of mortar in the style of the region's Hispanic-influenced walls. The wall is topped by a decorative coping made of 4-inch square glazed artisan tiles from Mexico set between two rows of blocks.

Other design elements:

• Grilles made of weathered redwood slats allow glimpses of mesquite trees on the street side of the wall.

• A curved platform made of blocks provides a spot for an adobe *chimenea,* which the owners use to roast hot dogs and to take the chill off a cool evening.

• Potted plants and ristras of dried red chilies create an inviting dining area.

• Low-voltage downlights built into the wall illuminate the space after dark. — *Nora Burba Trulsson*

NORM PLATE; FAR LEFT AND BELOW: JIM McCAUSLAND

This color combo is nothing to sneeze at

■ Sneezeweed is an unlovely nickname for a handsome group of summer-flowering perennials belonging to the genus *Helenium.* In her Washington garden, author and nurserywoman Ann Lovejoy planted *Helenium* 'Coppelia', a 4-foot-tall hybrid with coppery red flowers. She backs it up with a smoke tree called *Cotinus* 'Grace', which has burgundy-shaded leaves and puffy pink flowers. In the foreground are seedlings of pink-flowered *Spiraea japonica* 'Goldflame'.

Sneezeweed grows in *Sunset* climate zones 1 through 24. Although it really won't make you sneeze, it does irritate the skin of some people, so it's smart to wear gloves when you plant it. — *J. M.*

Borders underscore the view

■ When Charlene Towne and Nolan Gimpel moved into their new home in West Seattle, they inherited a nondescript rear garden with an awesome view of Puget Sound. They knew the old garden had to go, but they wanted to preserve the panorama. So they turned to Seattle landscape designer Brett Aalderink (Landscaping Plus: 206/767-8096). His approach was to keep the garden low by creating a series of mixed perennial borders that underline the view without blocking it. Because the site is windy, Aalderink chose plants that would withstand the wind or let it pass through.

In the foreground, black-eyed Susans and Shasta daisies mingle with lavender, gayfeather, and Mexican feather grass. Near the house, but placed away from the windows, are red-flowered montbretia, purple coneflower, lilies, and more ornamental grasses.

The entry to the rear garden was originally through a wooden gate that made the house look like a fortress. So Towne hired Vashon Island gate maker D. George Wright (206/567-0038) to create the heron shown at left; Wright fabricated the design from steel overlaid with brass for yellow highlights and copper for green tones. — *J. M.*

Floating flowers

■ When floral designer Laurie Connable throws backyard parties, she transforms her swimming pool into a floating garden. Bunches of blooms, arranged in the centers of foam rings, glide silently over the water's surface.

For each bouquet, Connable uses two foam rings (one 10 inches in diameter, the other 12 inches). She gathers flat green leaves such as citrus or ivy (enough to cover the smaller ring), 8 to 10 fern fronds (leatherleaf is ideal, with stems 18 to 24 inches long), and long-stemmed flowers like dahlias or roses.

Five large dahlias and several clusters of roses, ageratum, and cranesbill geraniums are usually enough for one bouquet. "I also add a fine-leafed variegated ivy, which I leave long so it trails along the water," she says.

To make a bouquet, Connable places the smaller ring on the larger one, secures the two together with toothpicks, then sets the stacked rings in a bucket filled with water. She adds the citrus or ivy leaves first, arranging them around the top ring so that they overlap with tips downward, to conceal the foam. The larger ring, which will stay be-

low the water's surface, remains uncovered.

Next, she inserts long-stemmed fern fronds through the center hole so that they cross underwater, forming a "frog" that will hold flower

stems snugly. Finally, she adds the flowers.

Connable makes the bouquets a day in advance and stores them in water-filled buckets in cool shade.

— *Debra Lee Baldwin*

CLAIRE CURRAN (3)

SONOMA COUNTY

Sculpture garden

■ Several years ago, Ricardo and Sara Monte decided it was time to rejuvenate the gardens adjacent to Wildwood Farm, their specialty Japanese maple nursery near Kenwood, California. Ricardo redesigned paths and renovated planting beds, but the couple soon realized that something was missing. "Eventually we figured out what it was—sculpture," says Sara. That's why the Montes now display and sell sculptors' works. So far, they have acquired more than 100 pieces representing 20 emerging and established California artists. The

sculptures, of ceramic, steel, coated resin, and other weather-resistant materials, range from shorter than 30 inches to taller than 16 feet. Lovely mature trees and flowering plants frame them "just like in a home garden," says Sara.

Twice a year (in spring and late summer), the Montes host a reception to bring the artists and the public together; it's a good time to view the sculptures in glorious settings and to meet their creators. Call for the date of their next party.

2–5 Sat; free. Also open 8:30–2 Tue, 9–4 Wed–Sun. 10300 Sonoma Hwy.; (707) 833-1161 or www.wildwoodmaples.com. — Lauren Bonar Swezey

CLIPPING

● **Book scene.** *Houseplants & Indoor Gardening,* by Julie Bawden-Davis (Creative Publishing International, Minnetonka, MN, 2001; $12.95; 800/328-0590). Bawden-Davis, a local garden writer, includes details on planting and care, an encyclopedia of plants, and ideas for choosing and arranging plants to complement your decor.

A handle on the side of the showerhead turns on the cooling spray. Plants in the foreground are yuccas.

Afternoon showers predicted

■ Think twice before you toss out *anything*. This smile-inducing outdoor shower, at the California home of George Martin and Jim Watterson, didn't start life as a shower. Martin, the creative director for a merchandising company, dreamed it up to add spice to a New York mannequin showroom. The bottomless cage, made of metal tubing bent and twisted in a whimsical fashion, originally housed a mannequin perched on a swing. When the cage outwore its novelty and was sent back to the warehouse, the company was going to discard it. But Martin envisioned how it could be recycled and had it shipped back to California. After a bit of plumbing, the couple had an outdoor shower. Or, as Watterson prefers to think of it, a *folie.*

Flagstone underfoot is interplanted with clumps of grass. Flowering vines twisting up the cage, and colonies of monkey flower nearby, add charm to the scene.

— *S.C.*

WHAT TO DO IN YOUR GARDEN IN AUGUST

PLANTING

☐ **ANNUALS.** Zones 4–7: You can still plant annuals for color that lasts almost to frost. Impatiens, marigolds, and pelargoniums are good candidates.

☐ **BULBS.** When you see autumn crocus *(Colchicum)* at nurseries, buy corms for bloom in late summer or early fall. Spring-flowering bulbs can go into the ground anytime after Labor Day. If you shop by catalog, order soon so you can plant by mid-October.

☐ **COOL-SEASON CROPS.** Zones 4–7: Early in the month, set out beets, Chinese cabbage and other cole crops, lettuce, onions, peas, radishes, and spinach. Planted now, early peas, lettuce, radishes, and spinach will be ready for harvest this fall, while beets, broccoli, cabbage, collards, kale, and kohlrabi can be harvested through winter.

☐ **LAWNS.** Zones A2–A3: Sow new lawns or repair old ones before midmonth. Zones 1–3: Sow seed now through mid-September, or lay sod anytime. Zones 4–7, 17: Wait until September to sow lawn seed or lay sod.

MAINTENANCE

☐ **COMPOST.** As you tear out spent summer flowers and vegetables, combine them with grass clippings and nonmeat kitchen waste to make compost for the fall garden. Don't throw diseased plants or weeds with seed heads on the compost pile.

☐ **HARVEST HERBS FOR DRYING.** Pick herbs in the morning just after dew has dried. You can dry the leaves in a food drier or, alternatively, arrange them on a clean window screen and set it in a cool, dry spot out of direct sunlight until the foliage is completely dry. Store the dried herbs in airtight containers.

☐ **PROPAGATE SHRUBS.** Grow new plants from the cuttings of existing shrubs. Candidates include evergreens such as azalea, camellia, daphne, euonymus, holly, and rhododendron, as well as deciduous plants like hydrangea. Take 4- to 6-inch cuttings in the morning and strip off all but the top three or four leaves. Dip the cut ends into rooting hormone and insert them into 4-inch pots filled with sterile soil. Place the cuttings out of direct sunlight and keep them constantly moist. Before frost hits, move them into a greenhouse or sunny room. Next spring, you'll have rooted plants ready to transplant into the garden.

☐ **PRUNE CANE BERRIES.** On June-bearing plants, remove all canes that produced fruit this season. On everbearing plants, cut back by half canes that have already borne fruit. Next year, plants will bear fruit on the remaining halves.

☐ **WATER.** Soak moisture-loving plants like rhododendrons every 7 to 10 days (more often in extra-hot weather or in fast-draining soil). Spray the foliage too; it washes dust off leaves and helps stressed plants absorb water quickly. ◆

WHAT TO DO IN YOUR GARDEN IN AUGUST

PLANTING

☐ LATE-SUMMER AND FALL COLOR. Many perennials reach their bloom peak in spring and summer, but there are plenty of flowers that will carry a border into late summer and fall. Choices include aster, cape fuchsia, chrysanthemum, coreopsis, daylily, gaillardia, gaura, Japanese anemone, lavatera, *Nemesia fruticans,* rudbeckia, Russian sage, salvia, and summer phlox. Before shopping, check to see which plants are adapted to your climate.

☐ SOW COOL-SEASON CROPS. Zones 7–9, 14–17: Start broccoli, cabbage, cauliflower, lettuce, spinach, and Swiss chard seeds in containers. Fill flats or pots with a well-drained potting mix and moisten the mix thoroughly. Direct-sow carrots, onions, peas, and radishes. Before planting, rotary-till the soil, mix in compost, soak with water thoroughly, and plant. Sow fine seeds about ¼ to ½ inch deep, larger seeds (peas) about 1 inch deep. Zones 1–2: Where frost isn't expected until late October, sow seeds of beets, carrots, radishes, and spinach; they should be ready to harvest by fall.

☐ TREES FOR SHADE. For optimum cooling effect, plant a tree in front of windows on the southwest side of the house. Use a deciduous tree for shade in summer and sun in winter. Zones 7–9, 14–17: Try Chinese hackberry, Chinese pistache,

flowering pear, Japanese pagoda tree, Raywood ash, and red oak. Zones 1–2: Try American hornbeam, Eastern redbud, honey locust, Japanese pagoda tree, littleleaf linden, and Marshall seedless green ash.

MAINTENANCE

☐ FEED ROSES. Zones 7–9, 14–17: Now's the time to feed roses to get a big fall flush of blooms. Use an organic or conventional fertilizer designed for roses and apply it to moist soil according to label directions. If your soil is very alkaline, also apply ½ cup sulfur (either iron sulfate, Ironite, or soil sulfur) to each established rose; mix it into the soil. Water well after fertilizing.

☐ PICK UP FALLEN FRUIT. Collect decaying fruit, such as peaches and nectarines, that could be harboring disease. Toss them in the garbage; don't compost them.

☐ RECYCLE GRASS CLIPPINGS. Every time you mow your lawn, allow the grass clippings to remain where they fall. They decompose quickly, releasing nutrients back into the soil, which reduces the need for fertilizer and promotes a healthy lawn. Recycling clippings also helps reduce the amount of green waste that otherwise would end up in landfills.

PEST AND WEED CONTROL

☐ CONTROL POWDERY MILDEW. These diseases, caused by fungus, infect leaves, buds, flowers, and stems, depending on the host plant. The first symptoms are white or gray circular patches on plant tissue, followed by large powdery areas. For nontoxic mildew control, mix 2 teaspoons baking soda and 2 teaspoons lightweight summer (horticultural) oil in 1 gallon of water and spray plants thoroughly. You can also purchase ready-made fungicides to control powdery mildew. Some, such as Safer Garden Fungicide (available at many nurseries or by mail from Peaceful Valley Farm Supply; 888/784-1722 or www. groworganic.com), are not very toxic to mammals. Others (triforine, for instance) are more toxic. ◆

WHAT TO DO IN YOUR GARDEN IN AUGUST

PLANTING

☐ **IRISES.** Iris rhizomes arrive in nurseries this month; plant them immediately. Along the coast, plant them so that the rhizomes show slightly above the soil surface. In hot inland areas, bury them slightly to prevent sunburn.

☐ **SOUTH AFRICAN BULBS.** Freesia, sparaxis, watsonia, and other Cape bulbs, which naturalize beautifully in our climate, start showing up in nurseries this month. See page 266 for details about buying and planting these bulbs.

☐ **SUMMER CROPS.** Coastal (zones 22–24), inland (18–21), and low-desert (13) gardeners can sow a final crop of beans and corn. Coastal gardeners can also set out transplants of eggplants, peppers, squash, and tomatoes. 'Celebrity', 'Champion', and 'Early Girl' are the most reliable tomatoes for fall harvest.

☐ **WINTER VEGETABLES.** Coastal, inland, and high-desert (zone 11) gardeners can start germinating cool-season vegetable seeds in flats. In six to eight weeks, the seedlings will be ready to transplant in the garden. Choices include Asian greens, broccoli, brussels sprouts, cabbage, cauliflower, collards, kale, kohlrabi, peas, spinach, and Swiss chard. Direct-seed beets, carrots, and turnips, or start in peat pots and transplant to garden, pots and all.

Bishop

NEVADA

CALIFORNIA

San Luis Obispo

Bakersfield

Tehachapi

Santa Barbara

Lancaster

Los Angeles

Palm Springs

Sunset
CLIMATE ZONES

1-3 7-9 11 13 14-24

San Diego

MEXICO

DEBRA LAMBERT

MAINTENANCE

☐ **CUT BACK PELARGONIUMS.** To improve appearance and encourage winter bloom, cut back pelargoniums to new basal growth. Do the same with impatiens.

☐ **DEEP-WATER ORNAMENTALS.** Trees and shrubs will appreciate a deep soaking now, even if they are watered regularly by a sprinkler system. (Most systems don't run long enough to penetrate the soil deeply.) Set a regular hose to water slowly into a basin around the plant. Or lay a soaker hose—one that slowly emits water through holes along its length—around the plant within the drip line. Run the water until the soil is soaked to a depth of 12 to 18 inches. (The larger the plant, the deeper the water needs to penetrate.) Check the moisture level by digging down with a trowel.

☐ **REMOVE WATER SPROUTS.** Citrus and stone-fruit trees may put out rampant growth (strong vertical shoots called water sprouts or suckers) this time of year. Prune that growth flush with the branch or part of trunk from which it sprouted. If wisteria puts out suckers, pull them off from the base of the plant.

PEST & DISEASE CONTROL

☐ **CONTROL INSECT PESTS.** Warm weather seems to bring out spider mites, scale, and thrips, which suck plant juices from houseplants. Mist the plants frequently to increase humidity and reduce stress. Treat infestations with insecticidal soap or horticultural oil.

☐ **FIREBLIGHT.** This bacterial disease makes the foliage of apple, cotoneaster, crabapple, hawthorn, pear, pyracantha, toyon, and other susceptible plants look like it has been scorched by fire. (Shoots and sometimes entire plants blacken and die suddenly.) To control its spread, remove the infected branches and twigs, cutting back 6 inches below the visible damage, and discard. ◆

WHAT TO DO IN YOUR GARDEN IN AUGUST

PLANTING

☐ GROUND COVERS. Consider replacing heat-stressed lawns on south-facing hillsides and along sidewalks and driveways with a heat-tolerant ground cover. Good candidates include creeping juniper, daylily, rock cotoneaster, 'Silver Carpet' lamb's ears, snow-in-summer, and woolly thyme.

☐ PEONIES. This is the best time of the year to divide established peonies or to plant new ones. To divide, cut the clump into large sections and replant the divisions in amended soil at the same depth at which the mother plant grew. A good mail-order source for more than 200 varieties of peonies is Adelman Peony Gardens in Salem, Oregon (503/393-6185 or www. peonyparadise.com).

MAINTENANCE

☐ CARE FOR ANNUAL FLOWERS. Cut off faded flowers daily to keep blooms coming. If petunias grow leggy and stop producing flowers, cut plants back by half and continue to water and fertilize.

☐ CARE FOR ROSES. Continue irrigating deeply once or twice a week until midmonth, then gradually cut back on water and stop fertilizing to start preparing plants for winter dormancy. If aphids are a problem, blast them off with a strong spray of water from the hose. Treat black spot, mildew, or rust with fungicidal soap spray or sulfur.

Sunset CLIMATE ZONES

☐ 1-3   ☐ 10-11

DEBRA LAMBERT

☐ COLLECT RAINWATER. Barrels placed under downspouts can collect copious amounts of roof runoff during summer storms. Pure rainwater is perfect for potted plants. Gardener's Supply Company (888/ 833-1412 or www.gardeners.com) sells plastic rain barrels with capacities of 40, 54, and 75 gallons for $90, $120, and $130, respectively, plus shipping.

☐ CUT BACK PERENNIALS. When summer-flowering perennials such as bellflower, geranium, Maltese cross, and Shasta daisy finish blooming, cut back stems to the rosette of new foliage at the base of the plant.

☐ HARVEST FLOWERS FOR DRYING. Cut flowers and air-dry them for everlasting summer bouquets. Try amaranth, baby's breath, cockscomb, globe amaranth, globe thistle, hydrangea, lavender, sea holly, sea lavender, statice, strawflower, and yarrow. Harvest blossoms before they open fully, strip off the leaves, bind the bunches with rubber bands, and hang them upside down in a cool, dark place such as a basement, closet, or garage.

PEST CONTROL

☐ TRAP YELLOW JACKETS. These yellow-and-black wasps can be serious nuisances as their numbers increase in late summer. Several kinds of traps, using attractant or food bait, are sold at garden and home supply centers. At *Sunset's* headquarters, gardeners have had good results with Rescue! Yellowjacket Trap by Sterling International (800/666-6766). Place any trap well away from heavily trafficked parts of the patio or garden.

☐ WATCH FOR CANE BORERS. Wilted or dead canes on blackberries, raspberries, and roses are often caused by the burrowing larvae of various insects, including rose stem girdler, stem-boring sawfly, raspberry crown borer, and currant borer. Watch for distinct swelling on canes and remove and destroy the affected ones to stop the pests from spreading. — *M. T.* ◆

WHAT TO DO IN YOUR GARDEN IN AUGUST

Editor's note: *As this issue of* Sunset *goes to press, parts of the Southwest are experiencing the worst drought in decades. Among the most severely impacted areas is Santa Fe, where homeowners are limited to watering outdoor landscapes once a week. Although an El Niño episode could bring above-average rainfall this summer, forecasters expect the drought to persist. That's why it's always wise to use unthirsty plants and follow water-saving practices.*

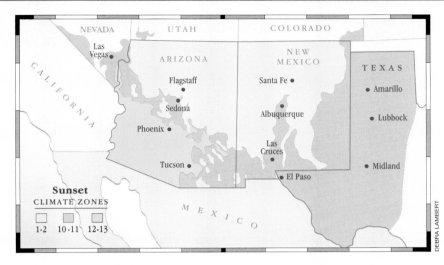

PLANTING

☐ **FLOWERS, HERBS.** Zones 1A–3B (Flagstaff, Prescott, Taos): Plant catmint, chives, and ornamental onion. Set out transplants of calendula, marjoram, oregano, rosemary, and society garlic. Zones 10–11 (Albuquerque, Las Vegas): Plant basil, bee balm, lemon balm, pineapple sage, and zinnia. Zones 12–13 (Phoenix, Tucson): Set out basil, blue salvia, chives, lemon verbena, nasturtium, and zinnia.

☐ **LOW-WATER LANDSCAPE PLANTS.** Select native or desert-adapted species that require little irrigation, including agave, aloe, bear grass *(Nolina microcarpa),* desert spoon *(Dasylirion wheeleri),* red yucca *(Hesperaloe parviflora),* and yucca.

☐ **VEGETABLES.** Zones 1A–3B: Plant carrots, radishes, salad greens, spinach, and turnips. Zones 10–13: Plant beans, corn, pumpkins, and squash.

MAINTENANCE

☐ **CONTROL OLEANDER GALL.** Sucking insects spread this bacterial disease that causes malformed flowers, split branches, and warty growths. Remove the affected branches several inches below the damage. After each cut, wipe the blade with a bleach solution (1 part bleach to 10 parts water) to avoid spreading the disease.

☐ **FERTILIZE.** Feed annual flowers and vegetables with a fertilizer high in phosphorous (15-30-15, for example). Feed citrus, shrubs, and trees with a high-nitrogen fertilizer.

☐ **RECONSIDER LAWNS.** When drought prevails, irrigating turf grasses becomes a low priority. Consider replacing water-intensive grasses with unthirsty buffalo grass *(Buchloe dactyloides)* alone or blended with blue grama *(Bouteloua gracilis).* Or remove the lawn altogether and install a Xeriscape.

☐ **WATER WISELY.** Irrigate when water-use regulations permit and then only when plants need it (check soil moisture first). To reduce evaporation, apply mulch around plants and water in the early morning, when temperatures are cooler and the air is still. Water deep enough to moisten the root zone but no deeper. Adjust irrigation systems so that water is not directed to pavement. Soaker hoses are an efficient way to deliver water along rows of vegetables or flowers.

— Kim Nelson ◆

a little water music

How to add the magic of falling water to your garden

By Jim McCausland

Perhaps it's the music of burbling water that is so enchanting about backyard waterfalls, or the tiny rainbows that form in the mist above them, or the ribbons of clear water, sparkling in sunlight, that cascade off rocks. But one thing is certain: Waterfalls cast spells, beguiling and entrancing anyone who sees them. And gardeners in increasing numbers are installing them.

Some hire waterfall specialists to do the work; others do it themselves or buy preformed waterfalls from pond equipment suppliers or well-stocked nurseries and just plug them in (the easiest and often the least expensive option).

No matter which strategy you choose, once the water starts to tumble over rocks, you'll fall under its spell too. And you'll discover that the greatest joy of owning a waterfall is the tranquillity it brings to your garden.

A cool oasis in California's Central Valley, this cascade is fringed by ferns and lacy Japanese maples in Mel Solomon's garden.
Landscape contractor: Rick Conger, Conger Construction (916/747-2887).

Before you start

Unless you're a contractor, installing a waterfall may seem like a huge undertaking. But pond equipment suppliers have gone to extraordinary lengths to help even first-timers succeed. They offer packaged kits, complete with instruction manuals, videos that describe the installation, and filters, pumps, and pond liners. Or you can buy individual parts to piece together.

Your water garden can be a tiny tuck-in like the one pictured on page 265, or a large complex with many falls, like the one pictured at left. But before installing a large water feature yourself, learn all you can about the process and the equipment options. Take a class (offered by some pond suppliers), and peruse books such as *Garden Pools, Fountains & Waterfalls* (Sunset Publishing, Menlo Park, 2001; $14.95; 800/526-5111).

For design ideas, check out other water gardens in your neighborhood. Many pond suppliers sponsor tours of residential water gardens early each summer to benefit charities; for details, ask your pond supplier about Parade of Ponds. Other factors to consider are the following.

THE SOURCE. In nature, waterfalls come from somewhere—a meandering stream that disappears into the woods, for instance. To avoid the "spilling from the wall" look and to create the illusion of a waterfall's source, angle the falls and flank them with boulders or plants.

PUMP. Before you buy a pump, you'll need to know how many gallons of water your pond will hold and the height of your waterfall. Here's why: Industry standards call for all of a pond's water to be recirculated every two

Left: Water courses down a series of stone ledges in the hillside garden of Gordon and Michele MacMillan in Albuquerque. Landscape design and installation: John DaCamara, Zia Scapes (505/350-8765); Consultant: Beth Rekow, Rekow Designs (505/345-5336). **Above:** Aquatic plants and koi thrive in a boulder-edged stream spanned by a footbridge in a Saratoga, California, garden. Design: Barbara Jackel (831/427-2042); Installation: Kurt Christiansen, Christiansen Associates Organic Garden and Design (831/458-2005).

The sound
of water
tumbling
over rocks
soothes
and cools.

hours. Pumps are rated in gallons per hour (gph), but in practice this rating declines for every foot the pump has to lift the water. Most pumps come with a chart that lists gph for each of several discharge heights (called "head height"). To calculate the number of gallons of water your pond will hold, multiply its volume in cubic feet by 7.48.

ROCKS. Rocks are often sold in "head" sizes (as in the size of a person's head). For most ponds, one- and two-head rocks work best. Blend different colors; in a pond we built in our test garden (see page 264), we mixed white cobbles with blue ones and brought in some large boulders for accents (all from Graniterock; 831/471-3400). Remember that big rocks can be heavy. Some suppliers will deliver and position them for an hourly fee (in advance of delivery, plan where you want them to go). If there are naturally occurring rocks on your site, try to include some of them.

FISH. Koi are beautiful and easy to keep. To protect them from raccoons and herons, provide enough plants to cover at least two-thirds of the water's surface; plants will also create hiding places among rocks. If marauders still come after them, switch to less expensive goldfish. For protection, some people stretch bird netting or a fan of clear fishing line over their garden pond.

COST. The pond/waterfall combinations shown here and on the following pages range in price from about $500 for the preformed pond shell pictured on page 265 to $25,000 or more. Choose the right system for your budget.

Anatomy of a waterfall & pond

The best site for a water garden is on level ground and in a spot where you can see and hear it from the house, patio, or garden bench. It should be within reach of electric power (plan to have an electrician wire it for you). Make it deep enough for plants and fish—18 to 24 inches in most regions. Though local codes sometimes vary, national codes require fencing for any pond more than 2 feet deep.

Waterfall
Terraced soil or stacked stones provide a place for the water to spill over. New waterfall boxes combine a waterfall and biological filter in a single box.

Pond plants

They work with filters and fish to reduce algae. They also consume carbon dioxide, which helps keep water clear. You can grow a wide array of plants in and near the water. Just keep them clear of the splash from the waterfall.

Marginal plants, such as cannas, flowering rush, Japanese iris, and papyrus, grow in boggy soil at pond's edge or very shallow water (underwater shelves give you a place to set these plants).

Deep-water plants rest at least 18 inches below the surface (2 feet is common), but their leaves and flowers float on the surface. One beautiful example is parrot's feather *(Myriophyllum aquaticum),* a lacy-foliaged plant. Water lilies *(Nymphaea)* add a lovely splash of color when they bloom in warm weather. Choose from hardy varieties or exotically colored tropicals (in cold climates, bring them into a greenhouse or sunroom during winter).

Free-floating plants, such as water lettuce *(Pistia),* dangle their roots in the water, from which they take up nutrients.

Rocks

Choose ones that are angular enough to be stackable but rounded enough that they won't poke holes in your liner.

Gravel

It fills spaces between rocks. For a natural look, use two sizes (3/8-inch and 5/8-inch); mix them in a wheelbarrow.

Beach

Include a shallow, gravelly section accented with larger stones. Birds love it!

Pump and filters

Pumps recirculate water in a garden pool and deliver it to the head of a waterfall. Filters trap small debris and help keep the water clean.

Liner

The best kind is a flexible, UV-resistant material such as 45-mil EPDM rubber, which is fish-safe, patchable, and warranted for 20 years or longer.

Plant shelf

This is a ledge for potted plants. Generally, make it 1 foot below the waterline and at least 1 foot wide, although it can vary based on plants' needs.

Underlayment

This is a sheet of woven plastic padding. It helps protect the liner from punctures by rocks or other sharp objects in the soil beneath the pond.

Fish

They dine on mosquito larvae and help keep the pond water balanced and clean. A rule of thumb: Stock your pond with 1 inch of fish for every square foot of water surface. Add them three or four days after the pond is filled with water.

THOMAS J. STORY (8); ILLUSTRATION: BARBARA JACKEL

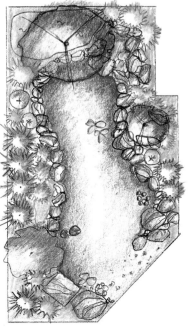

Create a waterfall garden in 6 steps

To show us the fine points of installing a waterfall using a kit (from Aquascape Designs; www. aquascapedesigns.com), *Sunset* test garden coordinator Bud Stuckey worked with experts to build one at our headquarters in Menlo Park. The water garden took our five-person crew eight hours to install. A pond this size would cost about $8,000. Two first-timers could build the same thing for a third of the price, but it would take about four days of labor, plus a couple of hours of an electrician's time to bring power to the pump. **Design and installation:** Kirk Samis of Pondsaway (800/353-4957); landscape designers Barbara Jackel (831/427-2042) and Kurt Christiansen of Christiansen Associates Organic Gardens and Design (831/458-2005); and Kim Kirby of Graniterock (888/762-5100 or www.graniterock.com).

Our pond measures 13 feet by 6 feet. Skimmer filter sits on an angle at lower left (in plan at left); waterfall is at the opposite end. Pebbly beach is perfect for wading birds.

See it in motion: Watch the installation of the *Sunset* waterfall at **www.sunset.com/garden/waterfall.html**.

Big splash on a small budget

This natural-looking creek works its way down a gentle slope—by trickling over terraces of stone—before spilling into a backyard pond in San Mateo, California. For an investment of about $500 and the equivalent of three days of labor, owners Barbara Carey and Mike Phinney got a gurgling chorus, a garden focal point, and a watercourse that delights their young sons as well as visiting birds.

Except for the rocks, which they selected "for the best lichen growth" at a building materials yard, all the supplies (including a rigid preformed pond shell) came from a home improvement center. The creek bed is formed with a pond liner and stones; some stones are mortared together to make smooth ledges. A pump submerged in the 90-gallon preformed pond sends water up through a flexible pipe to the creek's top.

Barbara's best advice for beginners? "Don't be in too much of a hurry to get digging. First, consider your point of view." Then orient your waterfall so you can see it from a patio or a favorite room.

The pond is not filtered, so Mike flushes it out periodically with fresh water and liberates from the depths a trove of Tonka trucks, Lego pieces, and leaves that the boys have launched down the falls. Pots of papyrus nestle in the pond; white-flowered bacopa *(Sutera cordata)*, pink-flowered penstemons, and grasses soften the edges. — *Alan Phinney* ◆

1. Outline the pond. Use a hose to try different shapes before committing to the final pond shape. Then outline it with bright spray paint.

2. Dig the hole. Use a shovel to excavate the soil to about 8 to 12 inches below grade. Also dig holes about 2 feet deep outside the pond, at opposite ends, for the waterfall box and skimmer; position the waterfall box. Then, with spray paint, mark a marginal shelf inside the pond rim for bog plants; dig it about 1 foot below the waterline and at least 1 foot wide. Dig out the pond's center (check its depth by setting a carpenter's level on a 2-by-4 spanning the hole; measure from the bottom of the hole to the bottom of the 2-by-4).

3. Position the skimmer-filter box, heap backfill around it, and connect flexible PVC hose following kit instructions.

4. Add the liner. With padded underlayment in place, line the hole with the pond liner. Place the folded liner at the waterfall end, then unfold it toward the shallow beach end (a two-person job for large ponds). Adjust the liner to follow the contours of

the pond and shelves. For a beach area, overlap the liner as needed, smoothing out the folds. Leave the edges untrimmed until after the pond is filled with water.

5. Cover the liner with rocks. Position light-colored rocks, which show up better than dark ones, around the bottom of the pond (covering the bottom first also keeps the liner from getting too tight). As you work, tilt and arrange them to fit snugly together and to show off beautiful coloring or mossy surfaces. Bigger rocks go in the bottom's deepest corners, smaller ones higher up, and flat ones on shelves.

6. Add gravel. Use a shovel to scatter it among rocks; brush it into the spaces between them with gloved hands. Toss a few cobbles into the pond, letting them stay where they fall. Hose off all rocks to wash away any dirt, pump the water out of the hole, and refill the pond. Trim the liner, leaving about 12 inches excess around the edges. Fold under the excess liner (tuck it beneath rocks if possible); if there's any settling after a few days, you can unfold it.

Ixia

Babiana sambucina

Garden gems

Cape bulbs look exotic but grow like natives in our climate

By Sharon Cohoon

■ If you live in California, you ought to read bulb catalogs in reverse. Why? Hidden in the back of the book under some grab-bag category like "exotics" are freesia, sparaxis, watsonia, babiana, and the rest of the Cape bulbs (named after a former province of South Africa). These are, without a doubt, the easiest bulbs to grow in mild climates and the ones most likely to naturalize here. The front of the book is devoted to page after page of tulips and hyacinths—bulbs that don't understand our mild winters and have to be stored in the refrigerator for at least six weeks in order to be coaxed into bloom for a season. In our Mediterranean climate, *they* are the exotics.

This year, make it easy on yourself. Save the vegetable crisper for lettuce and carrots, and try growing some of the wonderful Cape bulbs shown here. Plant them and they'll come back year after year, with no need for chilling.

On page 268 you'll find two bulb lists. The first includes the species you're most likely to find at your local nursery. Though other Mediterranean plants such as artemisia, lavender, rockrose, and santolina would be their ideal companions, the bulbs in this group are flexible and can handle moderate summer irrigation without rotting. (Use the sand sandwich planting technique described on page 268 for extra insurance.)

The bulbs in the second list need drier conditions. Plant them where they'll get no summer water, or try growing them in containers, as we did. You'll probably need to order these by mail. All take full sun, except where noted.

Sparaxis

Geissorhiza radians

Cyanella orchidiformis

Watsonia

Easy to find in nurseries

These tolerate light to moderate summer watering.

African corn lily (Ixia). Cup-shaped, 2-inch flowers in white, pink, red, lavender, and yellow with dark centers. Plants grow 18 to 20 inches tall. *Sunset* climate zones 7–9, 12–24.

Baboon flower (Babiana). Mostly blues and purples; also white. From 8 to 12 inches tall, with 2-inch tubular flowers. Some varieties are fragrant. Zones 4–24.

Flame freesia (Tritonia crocata). Funnel-shaped flowers of bright orange or red are long-lasting in vases. Grows 12 to 24 inches tall. Zones 9, 13–24.

Freesia. Tubular flowers come in a full range of colors—yellow, orange, red, pink, lavender, purple, blue, and white on plants 12 to 18 inches tall. Many varieties are fragrant, especially creamy white *F. alba.* Zones 8–9, 12–24.

Harlequin flower (Sparaxis). Blooms have red, orange, yellow, purple, or white petals around a yellow center outlined in black. Good cut flowers. Plants grow 10 to 12 inches tall. Zones 9, 12–24.

Watsonia. Flowers similar to gladiolus but smaller and more numerous; pink, rose, apricot, and white. Excellent cut flowers. Zones 4–9, 12–24.

Rare treats from catalogs

These cannot tolerate summer irrigation.

Cape cowslip (Lachenalia). Hyacinth-like flowers come in reddish orange, yellow, purple, and cream on plants 4 to 10 inches tall. Best in pots; appreciate light shade. Zones 16–17, 23–24.

Chasmanthe. Tubular flowers of orange red, occasionally yellow, attract hummingbirds. Plants grow 4 to 6 feet tall. Zones 13, 15–24.

Cyanella. Mostly lavender, but also yellow flowers. Grows 9 to 29 inches tall, depending on species. Zones 4–24.

Geissorhiza. Cup-shaped, 1-inch flowers are mostly blue, with contrasting center color. Very showy. Grows 5 to 10 inches tall. Zones 9, 12–24.

Homeria. Flowers come in yellows and soft oranges. *H. collina* and *H. flaccida* naturalize easily. Plants grow 18 to 30 inches tall. Can't be shipped out of California. Zones 4–24.

Spiloxene (Hypoxis). Star-shaped, 3-inch flowers are mostly yellow on plants 8 to 12 inches tall. Zones 9, 12–24.

Candy pink watsonias rise above clumps of grassy foliage in late spring.

Hot pink ixias pair with purple ones.

Planting and care

To ensure the widest choice, buy or order bulbs this month, but wait until late September or October to plant and water. If bulbs have already begun to sprout, however, plant and water immediately.

Dig a hole two to three times deeper than the bulb height. Plant with the pointed side up, indented side down. To improve drainage, encase the bulb in a sand sandwich: Add a ½-inch layer of construction-grade sand atop the soil in a planting hole, place

the bulbs on top, then cover them with another ½ inch of sand. If you're planting in containers, use a fast-draining mix, such as 40 percent fir bark, 40 percent sand, and 20 percent pumice.

Water regularly during the active growing season. After bloom when the foliage begins to yellow, start reducing irrigation for several weeks to encourage dormancy, then stop watering. Store potted bulbs in a shady location after the potting soil is dry.

Sources

Jim Duggan Flower Nursery. Carries everything listed and more. (760) 943-1658 or www.thebulbman.com. Catalog $2.
McClure & Zimmerman. *Lachenalia,* sparaxis, and watsonia. (800) 883-6998 or www.mzbulb.com. Free catalog. ◆

Edible pods of 'Oregon Giant' snow pea reach 4 to 5½ inches long.

THOMAS J. STORY

Peas as sweet as sugar

By Jim McCausland

Veteran pea growers can't resist nibbling peas right off the vine. That's because peas, like sweet corn, are at their sugary peak the moment you pick them. From that time on, the sugar starts converting to starch, and sweetness declines.

Tall vining types, which bear over a long season if you keep picking them, need support: a trellis, wire or nylon mesh, or poles. Bush types, which top out at 30 inches and usually don't need support, mature earlier and tend to produce most of their crop at once.

Keep in mind that to reach maturity, peas need three months of growing time before the average date of the first frost in your area. They also need cool soil and air temperatures. In mild-winter areas of California, you can plant peas anytime from August to February. In the desert, wait until October. In the coastal Northwest, sow peas in August for a fall crop. In colder areas, wait until next spring, then plant as soon as the ground can be worked (usually March or April).

Best varieties

Peas for shelling

They're ready to pick when their pods fill with sweet, plump peas.

'Dual' is a new variety that produces 10 to 14 peas per pod, compared to 8 to 10 peas of most other varieties. A bush type, it bears many pods in pairs, instead of singly.

'Garden Sweet', another new variety, contains 25 percent more sugar than most peas and stays sweet longer after picking (up to 48 hours) than other peas. A vining type, it reaches 3 to 4 feet.

'Maestro' also produces many double pods on a bush-type plant over a relatively long season. Excellent disease resistance.

'Novella II' is a semi-leafless bush type. Excellent disease resistance.

Peas with edible pods

You eat them pod and all.

Snow peas. Bred to be harvested young, their flat pods are perfect for stir-fries. The two most widely sold varieties, 'Oregon Giant' and 'Oregon Sugar Pod II', are bush types. If you wait too long to harvest most snow peas, they develop a string that you have to remove before eating, but 'Oregon Sugar Pod II' is virtually stringless.

Snap peas. These are ready to pick as soon as the peas swell the pods. If you leave them on the vine too long, most snaps develop a string. 'Sugar Snap' and 'Super Sugar Snap' are extra-sweet vining types (to 6 feet). 'Sugar Ann' and the stringless 'Sugar Sprint' are bush types. 'Mega', also a bush type, handles both colder and hotter weather better than many others.

Seed sources

Burpee Seeds: (800) 888-1447 or www.burpee.com.

Nichols Garden Nursery: (800) 422-3985 or www.nicholsgardennursery.com.

Territorial Seed Company: (541) 942-9547 or www.territorialseed.com.

Vermont Bean Seed Company: (803) 663-0217 or www.vermontbean.com.

West Coast Seeds: (604) 952-8820 or www.westcoastseeds.com. ◆

LEFT: Arched entry to the belvedere is flanked by a weeping Atlas cedar (far left) and a tile mural above a fountain. RIGHT: A sofa-shaped adobe bench is the inviting centerpiece of the meditation garden.

Summer suites in Taos

Plants and furnishings define spaces for meditating, entertaining, and relaxing

By Linda Thornton with Dick Bushnell

Photographs by Charles Mann

■ Born in England "with a trowel in my hand," as she puts it, Susan Blevins honed her horticultural skills in the Alban hills near Rome after moving to Italy in 1965. Then, a decade ago, she moved to northern New Mexico and began creating a landscape around her restored adobe house (circa 1830) in Ranchos de Taos. Here, Blevins has designed a suite of intimate garden rooms, decorated them with eclectic plants and furnishings, and linked them with archways and paths.

Blevins uses blue as the unifying color because it works so well with the apricot-colored walls of her house. Adobe walls also enclose many of the garden rooms. The walls, which absorb solar heat by day and release it at night, allow her to push the planting envelope here at an elevation of 7,000 feet (Taos is located in *Sunset* climate zone 2B). Blevins can't resist growing many of the frost-tender Mediterranean plants she came to love in Italy, including agapanthus, bougainvillea, lemon, oleander, and rosemary, which she keeps in containers and brings indoors during the cold, snowy winters. *(Continued on page 272)*

Susan Blevins's favorite color makers

The following flowers are annuals or tender perennials grown as annuals, unless noted.

- African daisy (*Arctotis* hybrids). Creamy apricot and yellow.
- Bachelor's button *(Centaurea cyanus)*. Blue. Self-sowing.
- California poppy *(Eschscholzia californica)*. Orange. Self-sowing.
- Common heliotrope *(Heliotropium arborescens)*. Fragrant purple flower clusters.
- Cosmos. Pink and white.
- *Geranium* 'Johnson's Blue'. Perennial.
- Larkspur *(Consolida ajacis)*. Blue.
- Pelargonium. Crimson.
- Perennial blue flax *(Linum perenne)*.
- Petunia. Lavender, burgundy, pink.
- Portulaca. Creamy yellow and peach.
- Snapdragon. Pink.
- Sweet alyssum. Fragrant white flower clusters.

ABOVE: A cobblestone path leads to the Japanese pavilion, which is shaded by clematis and grapevines.
LEFT: Carved posts are accented by lobelia, sweet alyssum, and red ivy geraniums; columns of scarlet cardinal climber trained up tomato cages grow in the center.

Stroll through three rooms

Step into the sunken meditation garden, where an adobe *banco,* or bench, is fringed by California poppies growing between flagstones. Fitted with a single mattress, the sofa-shaped bench is heaped with Middle Eastern pillows. Blevins likes to sit here, sipping a glass of wine while dangling her other hand in the pool behind and listening to the soothing splash of waterfalls. This garden is landscaped with a variety of deciduous and evergreen shrubs and trees, including aspen, Colorado blue spruce, crabapple, lilac, juniper, rose, and viburnum.

In the belvedere, essentially a summer terrace of the kind traditionally seen in Europe, Blevins serves drinks and hors d'oeuvres to guests before they adjourn to a nearby dining area. Framed by adobe planters, the belvedere is adorned with glazed and terracotta pots and furnished with a few benches and tables. An archway frames a pair of rustic wood doors Blevins found in Santa Fe. On one side of the arch, two deciduous vines (fiveleaf akebia and porcelain berry) drape over the wall above a Turkish tile mural and a small fountain. On the other side of the arch, a weeping Atlas cedar forms a twisty living sculpture.

Winding through drifts of California poppies, a path of concrete cobblestones leads to the Japanese pavilion, where a 5-foot-wide wood swing seat is suspended from the roof. "It's the most restful part of the garden. When I swing, it's like being on vacation," says Blevins. Built of rough-sawn timbers, the pavilion is entwined by clematis and grapevines and flanked by black locust, espaliered dwarf peach trees, and redbud. ◆

Trickle fountain

Water drips down plant-topped columns into a dreamy pond

By Jim McCausland

NORM PLATE

A fountain doesn't have to be a splashy affair. In fact, artists George Little and David Lewis (206/842-8327 or www. littleandlewis.com) have perfected a trickle fountain that flows just a drop at a time. One of their creations is pictured at right in a garden on Bainbridge Island, Washington.

The pond is made from poured steel-reinforced concrete. Three square pedestals are set in the bottom of the pond to support the hollow concrete columns—formed in sections and assembled on site—that rise above them. The capitals are filled with soil, planted (each with a different plant), and irrigated with pond water channeled through ½-inch copper tubes hidden in the column centers. (It's the ultimate drip-irrigation system.) A low-volume pump supplies enough water to soak the soil and trickle over the sides, where it drips from the tops of the capitals and back into the pond.

Papyrus *(Cyperus papyrus)* grows in the pond (it's in an underwater container that sits atop another inverted container). Every autumn, the owner brings the frost-tender papyrus into her greenhouse, where it lives through the winter in a bucket of water. Goldfish, koi, and plants keep the water clean enough that filters do not have to be used. Though clear water would seem to put the fish in danger of being seen by predators, overstory trees conceal the pond from passing herons, and it is too deep for raccoons.

Landscaping around the pond was

Water trickles from drip tubing hidden beneath plants atop each column. (Gardeners tend the plants that grow there by placing a ladder on the pond's bottom.)

CAPITAL PLANTS. That's dwarf cattail *(Typha minima)* sending up straight green wands from the tallest column, and creeping Jenny *(Lysimachia nummularia),* which "drips" stems of lime green foliage from the shortest one.

POND RIMMERS. Baby's tears and creeping Jenny mingle at lower left beside strappy green agapanthus and *Persicaria microcephala* 'Red Dragon'. At lower right is *Rehmannia elata* with rose pink flowers, next to oval-leafed *Bergenia* 'Winter Glut'. Assorted primulas and lime-flowered lady's-mantle fill in around the pond. Rhododendrons and Douglas firs create a leafy backdrop.

a collaboration of the homeowner; her lead gardener, Nathan Priddis; and David Halsaver of Foxglove Greenhouses in Kingston, Washington (360/ 297-0410). They used baby's tears *(Soleirolia soleirolii)* and creeping Jenny, both of which make low mats of soft leaves, to conceal the pond's concrete edges. The creeping Jenny is covered with yellow flowers in summer. An array of perennials also surrounds the pond. ◆

Foliage
carries the show

These leafy plants
may tempt you to
forgo flowers

By Steven R. Lorton

Photographs by
Norm Plate

ABOVE: Red-splashed coleus (left) and tricolored zonal geranium 'Mr. Henry Cox' (right) show the range of variegated foliage. FACING PAGE: Woven like a tapestry, this border blends the gold-striped foliage of *Acorus gramineus* 'Ogon', at front left, the soft chartreuse leaves of *Hosta* 'Gold Standard', and the dark red leaves of Abyssinian banana (*Ensete ventricosum* 'Maurelii') with purple allium and white coneflower. DESIGN: Tina Dixon, Bothell, Washington.

■ There's a horticultural trend sweeping the West. You might call it foliage frenzy and refer to its devotees as leaf lovers. It's all about creating colorful gardens using foliage plants almost exclusively.

When you rely on foliage to carry the show, you needn't worry about matters like bloom time or deadheading. Unlike flowers, which come and go, leaves hang on all summer, all season, or even all year. For the true leaf lover, flowers, if and when they appear, are merely a bonus.

Designing with foliage is much like assembling a perennial border or a bed of annuals. First, choose plants that have similar needs for light and water, then mix leaf colors, shapes, and sizes to suit your taste, pairing plants with contrasting foliage characteristics. Play blue leaves off silver ones, for example, or variegated leaves off solid-colored ones. Contrast spiky leaves with round or frilly foliage with hard-edged leaves.

At right and on page 276 we list some of the most versatile and dependable summer foliage plants. Experiment with them in beds, borders, or containers. Soon you will become a foliage connoisseur, mixing broad-leafed evergreens, conifers, deciduous shrubs, trees, and ground covers in spectacular compositions.

Leaf lover's wish list

Annuals and tender perennials

Coleus x hybridus. Tender perennials treated as annuals, they grow 1 to 2 feet tall. Leaves (some with lobed or frilled edges) come in a range of shades from chartreuse to salmon. Most coleus do best in bright, indirect light (some types tolerate sun). Regular water.

Fancy-leafed zonal geraniums. Actually members of the *Pelargonium* genus, these tender perennials have leaves with color markings ranging from cream and green to burgundy and orange red. Showy varieties include 'Mr. Henry Cox', 'Mrs. Pollock', and 'Vancouver Centennial'. Full sun. Moderate water.

Perilla frutescens. Commonly called shiso, this fast-growing annual (to 2 or 3 feet tall) bears bronzy purple leaves, which are edible. Full sun or light shade. Regular water.

(Continued on page 276)

Perennials from tubers and rhizomes

Caladium bicolor. Large arrow-shaped leaves are banded and blotched in shades of green, red, rose, pink, white, cream, silver, and bronze. Full or partial shade. Regular water. Dig and store tubers indoors where soil freezes in winter.

Canna. Large lance-shaped leaves resembling those of banana are borne on stalks ranging from 18 inches to 6 feet tall, depending on variety. Look for 'Minerva' or 'Pretoria' (yellow-striped leaves) and 'Tropicanna' (purple foliage striped with green, yellow, pink, and red). Full sun. Regular water during growth. Dig and store rhizomes indoors where soil freezes in winter.

Fancy-leafed sweet potato *(Ipomoea batatas).* Heart-shaped or lobed leaves 2 to 4 inches long cascade from trailing stems. 'Blackie' (blackish purple) and 'Marguerite' (chartreuse) are widely available. Let the vine spill over the rims of containers. Full sun. Regular water.

Iris pallida. Swordlike leaves to 18 inches tall have colored stripes running down the center. Look for 'Argentea Variegata' (silvery white stripes), 'Aurea Variegata' (golden yellow), and 'Zebra' (cream). Full sun. Low to moderate water. The rhizomes are hardy enough to stay in the ground over winter.

Japanese sweet flag *(Acorus gramineus* 'Ogon'). This grasslike perennial forms tufts of golden yellow leaves to 10 inches long. Light shade in hot inland climates. Ample water.

Hardy perennials

Artemisia. For foliage that shines like sterling, choose one of these. *A. ludoviciana albula* 'Valerie Finnis' forms a 2-foot spire of fernlike silver leaves. *A.* 'Powis Castle' forms a 3- by 6-foot mound of delicate, gleaming leaves. *A. schmidtiana* 'Silver Mound' forms a 1-foot dome of finely cut, silvery leaves. *A. stellerana* (often sold as dusty miller) is a classic filler that grows 2 feet tall. Full sun. Little to moderate water.

Bugbane *(Cimicifuga simplex).* Lacy leaves are borne on 2-foot stems. Two varieties with dark purple leaves are 'Brunette' and 'Hillside Black Beauty'. Full sun in cool coastal climates, partial shade inland. Regular water.

Heuchera micrantha. Roundish, toothed leaves 1 to 3 inches wide are borne in clumps. The Northwest-native species has gray green leaves. Hybrid forms include 'Palace Purple' with purple maplelike leaves and others in shades of purple, burgundy, brown, or dark red, sometimes with intricate silver veining. Full sun in cool-summer climates, light shade in hot-summer areas. Moderate to regular water.

Hosta hybrids. With rounded, lance, or heart shapes, leaves range in width from 3 inches to more than 1 foot. Colors run from chartreuse to turquoise, with variegations in shades of blue green, yellow, cream, or white. Named varieties include 'Guacamole' (chartreuse center with dark green margin) and 'Sum & Substance' (greenish gold). Full or partial shade. Regular water.

TOP: Like seams of gold, yellow stripes infuse the leaves of *Canna* 'Pretoria'. CENTER: Coleus makes a colorful splash in a mostly green shade garden. LEFT: Puffy clumps of blue fescue play off pale green sedum and purple heliotrope.

Ornamental grasses

Blue fescue *(Festuca glauca).* Fine leaves in shades from blue gray to frosty silver form dense tufts 8 inches to 2 feet tall. Tolerates some shade. Moderate water. Perennial.

Blue oat grass *(Helictotrichon sempervirens).* Wispy steel blue leaves form fountainlike clumps 2 to 3 feet tall and as wide. Full sun. Regular water. Perennial.

Japanese forest grass *(Hakonechloa macra* 'Aureola'). Arching leaves to 14 inches tall have yellow stripes (they turn chartreuse in the shade). Full sun in cool coastal climates, light shade inland. Regular water. Perennial. ◆

Under control

Automatic watering is easy with an inexpensive battery-operated timer

By Lauren Bonar Swezey

In the dry-climate West, watering lawns and garden plants is often our biggest challenge during summer (it's vacation time, after all). To keep plants irrigated automatically, you could install a highly efficient, multivalve automatic irrigation system. But there's a simpler option for small or isolated areas of the garden that can be irrigated from a single hose bibb: a battery-operated timer.

Unlike an automatic controller that must be wired to automatic valves, a timer attaches directly to a hose bibb (between faucet and hose) and can operate a soaker hose, a simple drip-irrigation system for beds or containers, or, in some cases, a mist system.

We tested several brands in a home garden last year and found that all are reliable, as long as you follow the basic operating guidelines below and care for them properly. Prices given are approximate.

Timer tips

• Use alkaline batteries, not rechargeable ones. Change them once a year.
• Program the timer before attaching it to the faucet or hose.
• To prevent damage, avoid excessive pulling or tugging on any hose attached to a timer. Remove the timer from the hose bibb if temperatures drop below 32°.

Where to buy timers

Timers are sold at home improvement centers, some nurseries, and

Dial timers
• Easy to operate, with only two dials to set
• Cost between $25 and $70; manufacturers not shown include Melnor and Rainbird

Orbit, $40

Run-time dial
How long the water will run in minutes—from 1 minute to 120

Frequency dial
How often, in hours or days, the water will turn on and off

Gardena, $60

Arzin, $25

Digital timers
• Allow the most flexibility in programming
• Cost between $35 and $90

Basic
To program them, press a few buttons to reach the preset watering times and schedules of your choice (Mondays, Wednesdays, and Fridays from 5 A.M. to 6 A.M., for instance). Manufacturers not shown include Gardena ($50) and Melnor ($35).

Gilmour, $60

Melnor, $45

Advanced
Designed for flexibility, these models allow you to make up your own schedule. On Melnor model 3060, for example, watering times can be scheduled to run for as long as 3 hours and 59 minutes on any day of the week. Because of this flexibility, timers can also be used to mist plants, using short cycles that repeat once or several times during the day. Most of these timers also offer preset schedules. Not shown are DIG ($40), Gardena ($85), and Orbit ($50).

irrigation supply stores. You can also order by mail from these sources.
Amazon.com. Sells Gardena, Gilmour, and Melnor. *www.amazon.com; search "Tools and Hardware."*
DripWorks. Sells DIG, Gardena, Orbit, and Rainbird. *(800) 522-*3747 *or www.dripworksusa.com.*
Lee Valley Tools. Sells Arzin. *(800) 871-8158 or www.leevalley.com.*
Urban Farmer Store. Sells Gardena and Orbit. *(415) 661-2204 or www.urbanfarmerstore.com.* ◆

The outdoor fireplace, clad with Boston ivy *(Parthenocissus tricuspidata)*, warms the trellis-covered patio on chilly evenings. Nearby, a rock-edged pond appears as an extension of an elevated spa (right).

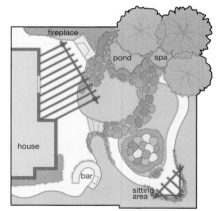

Four corners, four kinds of outdoor living

A Los Angeles garden
offers places to be together and apart

By Peter O. Whiteley • Photographs by John Granen

When all you have is a broad expanse of lawn for your backyard, you start dreaming of possibilities. The owners of this garden saw themselves entertaining, cooking, growing roses, relaxing in a spa, and simply stretching out in the sun. Their subsequent remodel offers lessons for anyone who wants to incorporate a variety of activity areas into the backyard.

Landscape designer Nick Williams removed the lawn and divided the bare, rectangular yard into quadrants corresponding to the owners' needs. The center of the garden is filled with flowering plants and slender paths connecting the sections. The plan gives the overall impression of a densely planted garden with distinctive destinations in each corner.

The main entertaining spaces—a covered dining area with a large freestanding outdoor fireplace, and a horseshoe-shaped barbecue center—lie closest to the two-story house. The elegant fireplace is near

This intimate getaway space is nearly hidden from view by a densely planted bed of roses, poppies, ranunculus, and stock. The triangular arbor, which projects from a plastered wall, supports downlights for use at night. Closer to the house is a barbecue area (below) that is notched into raised beds; a tall lattice panel behind obscures views of the neighboring house.

the edge of a pergola. The area faces the interior rooms and creates an inviting gathering spot for alfresco meals. The arched barbecue center with a tiled counter sits in an open area at the other end of the house.

Two secluded areas are positioned in the two quadrants farthest from the house. A spa with a raised bench lies out of sight beyond the fireplace; it's hidden by the rocks of an elevated recirculating brook that spills into a pond with water plants and fish. A triangular arbor, which catches the afternoon sun, defines the most remote area of the garden. The arbor's gas-fed firepit adds to the intimacy of evening conversations.

Williams points out that each quadrant offers a different experience and view and that the connecting paths meander past the rich colors and sweet scents of the flower bed. "You might not realize what you can pack into a relatively small space and still create a sense of grander scale," he says. It's a garden designed for exploration.

DESIGN: Nick Williams and Associates, Tarzana, CA (818/996-4010) ◆

A SENSUAL CELEBRATION OF COLOR and climate, the Mediterranean way of gardening is winning the West. For ideas you can incorporate into your own garden, see pages 296–301.

September

ROBIN CUSHMAN

A mini apple orchard

■ In this backyard in Eugene, Oregon, a 7-foot-tall stucco wall hides a view of an alley behind. At the foot of the wall, a soil-filled planter holds two espaliered apple trees, plus an assortment of colorful flowers. A ledge along the planter provides extra seating when the owners throw a party on the adjacent patio.

As part of a garden remodel, the owners retrofitted an existing cement block wall by inserting rebar into the blocks and filling the spaces with concrete. They textured the wall's stucco finish to match the house. Solar heat absorbed by the west-facing wall during the day radiates back into the space in the evening, making the patio a cozy place to sit on cool Northwest nights.

They built the raised planter 2½ feet wide and 20 feet long with a 20-inch-tall retaining wall. Atop the wall, a 9-inch-wide ledge is capped with the same tiles used to pave the patio.

Each semi-dwarf apple tree is grafted with four different varieties ('Gravenstein', 'Jonagold', 'Liberty', 'Yellow Delicious'). To train the espalier, the branches are tied to horizontal wires strung through eye hooks. The planter, shown here in late summer, is anchored at each end by pink-flowered *Lavandula angustifolia* 'Jean Davis', with a bright mix of black-eyed Susans, marigolds, yellow snapdragons, and red petunias and zinnias in between.

— *Mary-Kate Mackey*

Easy digging. Tool expert Bob Denman of Orange, California, offers this advice for preparing beds. When using a spade, don't take more than a 2½-inch slab of soil each time you push the blade into the ground. Most people take a thicker slab of soil, which is heavier to lift and doesn't crumble as easily. After the bed is dug, shovel the soil (and amendment, if any) back in, soak it with water, let it settle overnight, and you're ready to plant.

E. SPENCER TOY (2)

Composting components. Composting is a great way to re-cycle yard and kitchen waste. In return for your efforts, you get a valuable soil conditioner. **Do compost:** coffee grounds, fruit trim-mings, tea bags, plant trimmings, and washed and crushed eggshells. **Don't compost:** bones, dairy products, fish, grains, grease, meat, pet feces, or sawdust from plywood or treated wood.
— *Lauren Bonar Swezey*

Surprising garden art

■ Artists George Little and David Lewis of Bainbridge Island, Washington, create botanical sculptures that draw surprised smiles from onlookers. Two of their pieces decorate a border in Ed and Harriet Vincent's garden on Bainbridge Island. The 22-inch-diameter pomegranate (shown below) is downright Brobdingnagian, while the 60-inch-wide *Gunnera* leaf (left) is life-size. Both are made of color-washed concrete and are weatherproof. The leaf has become something of a trademark piece for Little and Lewis, though other artisans now make similar pieces.

In addition to the pomegranate and *Gunnera* leaf, which start around $1,000 per piece, Little and Lewis make garden benches, mirrors, and painted fragments that look like sections of excavated Pompeiian walls. For information call (206) 842-8327 or visit www. littleandlewis.com.
— *Jim McCausland*

NORM PLATE (2)

Grand-prize water feature in Boulder

■ It could be a wilderness scene high in the mountains. But this landscape is really an artful solution to a drainage problem on a small, narrow city lot in Boulder, Colorado. A series of rock-rimmed ponds, fed by recirculating waterfalls, serve as catch basins for runoff from the high water table. On one side of the lot, massive granite boulders form a retaining wall to hold the slope and visually echo the Flatirons formation in the distance. A patio paved with Colorado buff flagstone overlooks the ponds. For this innovative design, landscape architect Martin Mosko won his firm, Marpa & Associates, a Grand Award in a statewide competition sponsored by the Associated Landscape Contractors of Colorado.

Tucked into soil-filled pockets among the boulders are easy-care flowers, ground covers, and ornamental grasses. In summer, white Shasta daisies bloom next to yellow-flowered sedum and tufts of blue fescue grass. Mosko chose dwarf alpine fir and spruce trees so they would be in scale with the lot but give the illusion of a greater space. — *Marcia Tatroe*

Back to the prairie

■ Before Denver's landscape gave way to residential neighborhoods and skyscrapers, the area was part of a vast prairie that stretched across the Great Plains to the Rocky Mountains. Today, visitors can get a taste of that lost prairie at Denver Botanic Gardens.

The Laura Smith Porter Plains Garden represents seven prairie types that were prevalent in eastern Colorado a century ago. This ever-changing tapestry of native grasses and wildflowers is alive with birds, bees, and butterflies like the sulfur feeding on sticky aster

(Machaeranthera bigelovii) in the photo at left.

Dan Johnson, curator of native plants, says the plains garden largely survives on the moisture that nature provides. New transplants are irrigated a couple of times to get them started.

If you're inspired to try a similar planting on your property, you'll find good advice in a new book: *Gardening with Prairie Plants: How to Create Beautiful Native Landscapes,* by Sally Wasowski (University of Minnesota Press, Minneapolis, 2002; $29.95; www.upress.umn.edu).

Through Sep: 9–8 Sat–Tue, 9–5 Wed–Fri; $5.50. Oct–Apr: 9–5 daily; $6.50. 1005 York St.; (720) 865-3500 or www.botanicgardens.org. — M. T.

Unthirsty perennials in Santa Fe

■ Maintaining a garden during a severe water shortage is not impossible—provided you use the right plants. The garden of Susan and Walter Blake in Santa Fe, shown here, offers dramatic proof. Santa Fe, like much of the Southwest, is experiencing the worst drought in decades. But the Blakes' garden is able to tough it out because the plants in it are either very xeric (they survive with only occasional supplemental water) or drought-tolerant (they can get by on one watering a week or less).

In the foreground, the plant loaded with the lavender-blue plumes—*Perovskia* or Russian sage (*Sunset* climate zones 2–24)—is very xeric. In fact, says David Salman, owner of Santa Fe Greenhouses,

Russian sage is so tough you can even plant it during a drought. It only takes 1 to 2 gallons of water, applied once a week, to establish a 1-gallon plant, he says.

In the drought-tolerant category are orange-flowered *Zauschneria californica latifolia* 'Arizonica' (zones 2–11) just behind the Russian sage, the graceful grass *Miscanthus sinensis* (zones 2–24), yellow-and-red blanket flower (*Gaillardia grandiflora;* zones 1–24), and blue *Salvia transylvanica.*

Good Xeriscape principles also help keep the Blakes' garden alive. They installed a water-saving drip-irrigation system and they spread mulch around plants to conserve soil moisture.

— *Sharon Cohoon*

More unthirsty choices

Apache plume (*Fallugia paradoxa*). Semievergreen shrub bears white roselike flowers that turn to showy seedheads. Zones 2–23.

Chamisa or rabbitbrush (*Chrysothamnus nauseousus*). Gray-leafed shrub is covered with yellow flower clusters in late summer or fall. Zones 1–3, 10–11.

Globe mallow (*Sphaeralcea*

munroana). Perennial produces salmon to reddish orange flowers from midsummer on. Zones 1–3, 7–10.

Red yucca (*Hesperaloe parviflora*). Evergreen perennial with spiky leaves sends up red flower spikes from late spring on. Zones 2B, 3, 7–16.

Zinnia acerosa. Perennial produces white flowers sporadically from spring to fall. Zones 10–24.

Rock garden tapestry

■ Despite the lush connotations of its name, Evergreen, Colorado, is not the most conducive place for gardening. Located in the foothills west of Denver, at an elevation of about 8,000 feet, Evergreen has a short growing season. Snow may fall as late as June and as early as August. Summer temperatures can soar into the 90s during the day, but drop to the mid-40s at night. The soil is poor and rocky, and dry conditions persist. As if that weren't enough, deer and elk graze on plants. Yet those daunting elements didn't stop Lori Lapp from cultivating a showy alpine rock garden in her southwest-facing front yard.

Lapp, who is a Master Gardener, makes extensive use of hardy succulents, including several kinds of sedums. Nearly 100 plant varieties—all low-maintenance, drought-tolerant troupers—are arrayed on a berm that Lapp and her husband, Jack, built 12 years ago using a heap of rubble and subsoil excavated from the basement of their home. They terraced the berm with lichen-encrusted rocks gathered from the area, amended the soil with compost, and started planting. Over the years, the plants have spread to fill in the nooks and crannies. The result is a colorful quilt of textural foliage and seasonal flowers.

Taken in late summer, the photo shows some of Lapp's favorite sedums. They include, from front right to left, pink-flowered *Sedum spurium* 'Dragon's Blood', *Sedum kamtschaticum,* goldmoss sedum *(S. acre),* and above it *Sedum* 'Vera Jameson' and *Sedum* 'Ruby Glow', both blooming next to the stone slabs. — *Colleen Smith*

Organic bounty in a high desert canyon

■ Guests at Garland's Oak Creek Lodge come to enjoy its bucolic setting near Sedona, Arizona. They also come for the pleasure of dining on organically grown vegetables and fruits harvested from the lodge's bountiful vegetable garden and orchard, located in a sheltered canyon at an elevation of 5,000 feet.

Mario Valeruz oversees the lodge's 1/4-acre vegetable garden and a greenhouse, plus herb beds filled with everything from basil to tarragon. He orders seeds in January from the Cook's Garden (800/457-9703 or www.cooksgarden.com) and Johnny's Selected Seeds (207/437-9294 or www.johnnyseeds.com). He starts seeds in the greenhouse in March and transplants the seedlings into the garden mid-May. His longtime favorites include 'Aria' cucumbers, 'Celebrity' tomatoes, 'Fortex' pole beans, 'Neon' eggplants, 'Sunburst' pattypan squash, 'Blue Hubbard' winter squash, 'Gold Rush' zucchini, 'NuMex Joe E. Parker' chile peppers, and 'Yankee Bell' sweet peppers.

Valeruz uses drip-irrigation tape to water seedlings when they're first planted. He mulches the garden with straw to keep soil moisture in and discourage weeds. Valeruz intersperses insectary plants throughout the garden, such as carrots, chives, dill, and marigolds, to attract beneficial insects which provide natural pest control.

Garland's Oak Creek Lodge, State 89A, 8 miles north of Sedona; (928) 282-3343. — *Nora Burba Trullson*

Stone-flower fountain

■ Enjoying a water feature during a drought year isn't necessarily an irresponsible act, especially if you opt for a fountain like the one Marcia and Tom Bent enjoy in their garden. The water source is underground and, except for a small opening for the fountainhead, completely covered with tightly fitted, vertically stacked flagstones. Consequently, the evaporation rate is very low. "I only have to add water about three times a year," says Marcia Bent. "That's less than I'd use to keep a ground cover alive."

A metal grid supports the flagstone flower (chrysanthemum petals inspired the design); concrete footings support the grid. A pond liner covers the excavated space below. Access to the water pump is hidden underneath one of the flagstones in the path.

The fountain, near the Bents' entrance, is visible from the kitchen. "The front of the house faces south, and it gets very hot and dry here during summer and early fall," says Marcia, "so the sight and melody of the fountain is very refreshing." The birds love it, too, she says. "Lots of small birds live in our bougainvillea, and as soon as the fountain's on, they're out there."

Fountain design by Mark Bartos and Tony Exter of BEM Design Group, South Pasadena, California. — *S. C.*

A dream comes true

■ Catherine Burns wanted to remodel her Oakland garden, so she sought estimates from professionals. Put off by the high bids, she and her husband, Michael Monroe, decided to tackle the project themselves. It took about six months of weekend work, but eventually they completed their dream garden.

Before beginning, Burns and Monroe searched how-to books for landscaping ideas. After making a wish list, they sketched a rough plan for placement of various features. "The garden consisted mostly of dirt and weeds," explains Burns, "but fortunately there were lovely mature trees and rhododendrons we could incorporate into our design."

The couple's biggest accomplishment was building a tiered concrete pond, which a mason had discouraged them from attempting themselves. They had to hand-dig the soil since there was no access for machinery, then make laminated forms to create the pond's curved edge.

On the opposite side of the patio, a flower bed planted

with annuals and perennials mirrors the shape of the pond. The rest of the garden is filled with shade- and sun-loving subtropical and Mediterranean plants—abutilon, bougainvillea, datura, giant bird of paradise, and princess flower *(Tibouchina)*. "The garden's been my haven away from the chaos of work," says Burns. "And the daily feeding of the koi has become one of my greatest pleasures."

— *Lauren Bonar Swezey*

LOS OLIVOS

Charm store

■ Locating a retail nursery in a community of only 900 people does not seem like a sound business decision. But J. Woeste in Los Olivos (about 5 miles north of Solvang) is making it work. The appealing nursery, which wraps around a 100-year-old beige frame house, celebrated its fourth anniversary this spring, and business has never been better. From the start, the local population supported the nursery. Then tourists in the Santa Ynez Valley for wine tasting started dropping in to explore and began telling friends about their discovery. And soon J. Woeste became a destination all by itself.

The nursery carries a lot of ready-to-enjoy material. Rose standards of good size, clipped boxwood, twisted cypress, finished topiaries—all are potted up in handsome containers. "Stage-setting stuff," Jerry Nielsen, one of the owners, calls it. "Take it home, and the garden's done." If you're a do-it-yourself type, though, the nursery also has all the components. Elegant statuary and fountains, scaled for smaller gardens, are other specialties. Inside the house, you can shop for botanical prints, baskets, houseplants, and other merchandise with a garden theme.

10–5 daily. 2356 Alamo Pintado Ave., Los Olivos; (805) 693-1951. — S. C.

CLAIRE CURRAN; ABOVE: STEVEN GUNTHER

ARCADIA

Fern fest

■ Ferns have been around since the dinosaurs—long enough to develop into a huge, complex family. "There are thousands of species and at least that many cultivars," says Tony Barrett, Los Angeles International Fern Society publicity show chairman. You wouldn't guess that from visiting nurseries, he says. "What you see there is just a drop in the bucket."

To get a better idea of the true range of this prehistoric plant family, visit the annual Fern and Exotic Plant Show and Sale at the Arboretum of Los Angeles County in Arcadia on Labor Day weekend. Among the unusual ferns on display and for sale is 'Can Can', pictured here, which looks like a sword fern wearing petticoats. In addition to ferns, plants on sale include palms, bromeliads, and orchids.

9–3 Aug 31, 9–4:30 Sep 1; $5 (in 2002). 301 N. Baldwin Ave., Arcadia; (626) 821-3222. — S. C.

A dogwood for all seasons

■ Dogwoods make attractive spring-flowering trees for Northern California gardens. The species most commonly planted is Eastern dogwood *(Cornus florida)*. And the statuesque Pacific or Western dogwood *(C. nuttallii)*—a species native to Northern California and the Pacific Northwest—is well-known too; it's taller and bears larger blooms than many varieties of Eastern dogwood. Much less familiar, but one of the showiest of all dogwoods, is *C. n.*

'Goldspot', a variety of Pacific dogwood with shapely, gold-splashed leaves and 4- to 5-inch-wide, dazzling white bracts.

"The tree is very adaptable and a must for every garden," says Ricardo Monte of Wildwood Farm Nursery & Sculpture Garden in Kenwood, California. Monte's 25-year-old tree is 12 feet tall and as wide. It thrives even when temperatures soar to 110° (when watered regularly) and blooms twice a year—mid- to late

spring and again in fall, when it produces the heaviest display. The leaves turn brilliant rust orange in late fall, even in mild climates. 'Goldspot' is very slow growing, but it blooms at a young age.

Dogwoods are available from Wildwood Farm Nursery (888/833-4181 or www.wildwoodmaples. com). A 2-year-old tree in a 2-gallon can costs $50; an 8- to 10-year-old tree in a 15-gallon can costs $250 (shipping not included). — *L. B. S*

For the birds

■ There are times when nature alters the most carefully thought-out designs. When garden designer Laurie Connable installed a bird feeder atop a 6-foot-high 4-by-4 post in her front yard and surrounded it with annuals, for instance, dropped seeds soon took root among the annuals. So she bowed out gracefully and "let the birds plant their own garden."

In late winter, millet sends up slender green leaves. By summer, the millet's seed heads mingle with tall sunflowers. Birds feast on both. In January, everything gets pulled out, and the cycle starts again.

Most birdseed mixes are formulated with seeds that songbirds love. But a few mixes include thistles and grasses that can become weeds, so check labels before you buy.

— *Debra Lee Baldwin*

WHAT TO DO IN YOUR GARDEN IN SEPTEMBER

PLANTING AND HARVEST

☐ **HARVEST FLOWERS, CROPS.** Cut fresh flowers for bouquets and deadhead faded blossoms—both actions keep new flowers coming. Pick fruits as they ripen to keep rot from becoming established, and to keep plants like beans and ever-bearing berries producing.

☐ **PLANT SPRING-FLOWERING BULBS.** Crocus, daffodils, fritillaria, grape hyacinth, hyacinth, and tulips appear in nurseries after Labor Day. Try species tulips (*T. bakeri, T. batalinii, T. greigii, T. kaufmanniana, T. saxatilis,* and *T. tarda,* to name a few) for many years of repeat bloom. In *Sunset* climate zones 1–3, plant bulbs now through November; in zones 4–7, plant anytime from now through the first part of December.

☐ **SET OUT COOL-SEASON CROPS.** You can still sow seeds of arugula, cabbage, kale, leaf lettuce, mustard greens, radishes, and spinach, but do it before Labor Day. Or set out nursery seedlings of most of these, plus purple-sprouting broccoli for spring harvest and onion transplants for harvest next summer.

☐ **SET OUT LANDSCAPE PLANTS.** Autumn is the best time to set out trees, shrubs, vines, ground covers, and perennials.

☐ **SOW COVER CROPS.** Zones 4–7: Sow seeds of cover crops such as Austrian field peas, crimson clover, and vetch over bare vegetable and flower beds to help prevent soil erosion during winter. In spring, till the plants into the soil to enrich it organically.

☐ **START LAWNS.** Zones 1–3: East of the Cascades, sow grass seed from mid-August until mid-September; lay sod through mid-October. Zones 4–7: Sow grass seed or lay sod. If your lawn has thin spots, overseed them with the same kind of grass that originally grew there.

MAINTENANCE

☐ **CARE FOR ROSES.** After the last round of bloom, let roses produce hips to help prepare them for winter dormancy.

☐ **CLEAN GREENHOUSES.** Wash benches, containers, and glass with a solution of bleach and water to get rid of moss and algae. Check and replace weather-stripping; test heating and venting systems.

☐ **DIG AND DIVIDE PERENNIALS.** Divide and replant spring- and summer-flowering perennials now, but wait until spring to divide fall-bloomers like asters.

☐ **MAKE COMPOST.** Mix fallen leaves and lawn clippings to make compost for use this fall or next spring.

☐ **MULCH.** Zones 1–3: Apply a 3-inch layer of organic mulch like pine needles around perennials and shrubs to minimize winter freeze damage and reduce soil erosion.

☐ **WEED.** Keep the garden hoed and mulched to keep cool-season weeds like chickweed and dandelions from taking root. ◆

WHAT TO DO IN YOUR GARDEN IN SEPTEMBER

PLANTING

☐ ANNUALS. *Sunset* climate zones 7–9, 14–17: To get cool-season annuals off to a good start, plant after midmonth in cooler areas, at the end of the month in warm inland areas. If the weather is hot, shade new seedlings temporarily. Keep the soil moist. Set out calendula, forget-me-nots, larkspur, Iceland and Shirley poppies, ornamental cabbage and kale, pansies, primrose, snapdragon, stock, sweet peas, toadflax, and violas. In coastal areas, plant cineraria, nemesia, and schizanthus.

☐ BULBS. Shop soon for the best selection of healthy bulbs; choose firm ones without soft or moldy spots. Plant anemones, crocus, daffodils, Dutch iris, freesias, homeria, hyacinths, ixia, leucojum, lycoris, oxalis, ranunculus, scilla, sparaxis, tritonia, tulips, and watsonia (zones 1–2: some bulbs aren't hardy; choose from what's available in nurseries). In zones 8–9, 14–15, it's not critical to chill bulbs in the refrigerator for six to eight weeks before planting, but performance will be superior (tulip stems will grow one-sixth to one-third taller).

☐ COOL-SEASON GREENS. Zones 7–9, 14–17: Mesclun mixes, colorful selections of salad greens, are easy to grow at home. Try one of the 11 collections from Renee's Garden that are suitable for fall planting, including Baby Cutting Mix, Italian Misticanza, and Crispy Winter Salad. All are available on nursery seed racks, or order online at www.reneesgarden.com.

Sunset
CLIMATE ZONES

☐ Mountain (1-2)
☐ Valley (7-9)
☐ Inland (14)
☐ Coastal (15-17)

DEBRA LAMBERT

☐ NATIVE PLANTS. Zones 7–9, 14–17: You don't need a big garden to accommodate native plants. Any small bed away from heavily irrigated plants can make an attractive native border. Try bush anemone, *Arctostaphylos,* blue-eyed grass, fremontodendron, coral bells *(Heuchera maxima* or *H. micrantha),* lyme grass, mahonia, monkey flowers, Pacific Coast iris, *Penstemon heterophyllus purdyi, Salvia clevelandii*, and Western columbine. A few good sources for native plants are Intermountain Nursery in Prather (559/855-3113), Larner Seeds in Bolinas (415/868-9407), Mostly Natives in Tomales (707/878-2009), and Yerba Buena Nursery in Woodside (650/851-1668).

☐ SNAP PEAS. Zones 1–9, 14–17: If you can't get your kids to eat their green vegetables, just plant some snap peas. Soon they'll be eating them right off the plant. The best? Try 2-foot-tall 'Sugar Sprint' (from Nichols Garden Nursery; 541/928-9280 or www.nicholsgardennursery.com) or 5-foot-tall 'Super Sugar Snap' (from Renee's Garden, above).

MAINTENANCE

☐ FEED ROSES. Zones 7–9, 14–17: If you haven't fed your roses recently, give plants a shot of a fertilizer now to encourage a flush of autumn blooms. Choose one that's formulated for roses. Then, before applying it, make sure the soil is moist. Water it well afterwards.

☐ RENOVATE LAWNS. Zones 7–9, 14–17: Late September is a good time to start. Dethatch, then aerate compacted areas (rent dethatchers and aerators from equipment rental companies). Afterwards fertilize with a complete lawn fertilizer—try the slow release organic pelleted fertilizer from Peaceful Valley Farm Supply (888/784-1722 or www.groworganic.com); water in well. ◆

WHAT TO DO IN YOUR GARDEN IN SEPTEMBER

PLANTING

☐ **CARROTS.** If you've had trouble growing carrots in heavy clay soil, try planting them in containers. California Organic Gardening Club member Carol O'Brien grows hers in 20-gallon plastic tubs (she drills drainage holes in them before planting). 'Babette', a baby carrot, and 'Thumbelina', a short round one, are ideal candidates for growing in containers. Botanical Interests, whose seeds are widely available in area nurseries, carries both varieties.

☐ **PERENNIALS.** If your garden could use color, shop for fall-blooming perennials. Good candidates include asters, California fuchsia *(Zauschneria),* chrysanthemums, coreopsis, daylilies, gaillardia, Japanese anemone, and salvia.

☐ **SWEET PEAS.** For blooms by Christmas, plant seeds of an early variety like 'Winter Elegance' or Early Multiflora by mid-September. Other varieties should be planted now, but most won't bloom until early spring. Sow seeds in a sunny spot away from reflected heat. Water at least once a day for two weeks until all have sprouted. Letting the soil dry out temporarily during the germination period is the most common mistake gardeners make. If you can't keep the planting bed moist because you're away during the day, start seeds in small starter pots in filtered sun and transplant to the garden later.

Sunset CLIMATE ZONES

1-3   7-9   11   13   14-24

DEBRA LAMBERT

☐ **VEGETABLES.** From midmonth on, coastal (zones 22–24) and inland (zones 18–21) gardeners can plant winter crops. Sow seeds or transplant seedlings of Asian greens, beets, broccoli, brussels sprouts, cabbage, carrots, cauliflower, collards, kale, lettuce, onions, peas, potatoes, radishes, spinach, Swiss chard, and turnips. In the high desert (zone 11), plant lettuce, radishes, and spinach.

MAINTENANCE

☐ **DIVIDE PERENNIALS.** Dig and divide overgrown or poorly performing perennials. Good candidates are agapanthus, coreopsis, daylilies, and penstemon. Use a spade or spading fork to lift clumps, then cut into sections with pruning shears or a spade. Replant immediately. Keep soil moist.

☐ **PREPARE FOR SANTA ANA WINDS.** Move hanging baskets and water-sensitive container plants into a sheltered area. Thin dense trees to prevent wind damage to limbs. Stake young trees.

☐ **PROTECT AGAINST WILDFIRE.** Dead vegetation fuels flames. In fire-prone areas, before the onset of Santa Ana winds, cut and remove all dead branches and leaves from trees and shrubs, especially those near the house. Clear leaves from gutters and remove woody vegetation that is growing against structures.

☐ **PROTECT CABBAGE CROPS.** Squadrons of little white butterflies—called cabbage whites—seem to descend on cabbage and other brassica crops the minute you plant them. The easiest way to deal with cabbage whites is to cover the seedlings with floating row covers right after planting. The next best option is to spray with *Bacillus thuringiensis* (Bt) to kill the caterpillar larvae.

☐ **REPLENISH MULCH.** Add fresh mulch as needed to maintain a 3- to 4-inch-thick layer. Keep mulch away from crowns, stems, and trunks of plants. ◆

WHAT TO DO IN YOUR GARDEN IN SEPTEMBER

PLANTING

☐ SPRING-BLOOMING BULBS. Crocus, daffodils, tulips, and other spring bulbs are widely available this month. Plant them from now until the ground freezes.

☐ TREES, SHRUBS, PERENNIALS. Cool fall weather is ideal for planting hardy varieties of container-grown plants. After planting, apply several inches of organic mulch around each plant and don't let the rootballs dry out over the first winter.

☐ VEGETABLES. Sow seeds of lettuce and other salad greens, radishes, and spinach for late fall harvest. Prepare the bed by digging in 2 inches of compost or well-aged manure into the soil to a depth of 6 to 8 inches. Keep the bed evenly moist until the seeds germinate, and use a floating row cover to protect the plants from early frosts. Spinach can be left in the ground over the winter for harvest in late winter or early spring; protect the plants with a thick blanket of hay or straw.

MAINTENANCE

☐ HARVEST VEGETABLES. Pick beans, eggplants, peppers, summer squash, and tomatoes before first frost. Green tomatoes will continue to ripen indoors if stored in a dark, cool place. When frost threatens, pull out the whole tomato plant and hang it in the garage, or store picked green tomatoes in cardboard flats, taking care that

Sunset
CLIMATE ZONES

☐ 1-3 ☐ 10-11

they do not touch. Beets, carrots, parsnips, and turnips can be left in the ground for winter harvest if mulched with 6 to 12 inches of hay or straw.

☐ LIFT AND STORE SUMMER BULBS. After frost kills their foliage, dig up callas, cannas, dahlias, gladiolus, tuberous begonias, and other tender bulbs. To save time next spring, replant the bulbs in fresh potting soil in containers. Store the containers in a cool, dry place and keep the soil slightly moist all winter. In the spring the bulbs will be ready to start under lights or in a sunny window.

☐ OVERWINTER TENDER PERENNIALS INDOORS. Take cuttings from coleus and geraniums to overwinter indoors. Root the cuttings in moist vermiculite or sterile potting soil. Bedding or wax begonias, heliotrope, impatiens, and Madagascar periwinkles can be moved indoors and grown as houseplants over the

winter. Clean up the plants, cut them back by one-third, place them in containers in a sunny window or under lights, and fertilize.

☐ REVAMP FLOWER BEDS. Perennial flowers benefit from having their beds reworked every few years. Lift out all of the clumps and place them in a shaded spot. Spade the soil deeply and mix in several inches of compost and a balanced fertilizer. Divide any clumps of perennials that are overcrowded or have died out in the center; replant the healthiest divisions. Cover the bed with evergreen boughs, hay, or straw to protect them over the winter. Water the replanted bed once or twice a month if the soil dries out.

☐ WATER DEEPLY. Hot, dry summers can be hard on shrubs and trees, even established ones. Leaves that turn brown or drop prematurely in late summer are signs of seriously stressed plants. Water deeply by setting a sprinkler in place and letting it run for an hour, or use a root irrigator to inject water around the drip line twice a month until the ground freezes. — *M. T.* ◆

WHAT TO DO IN YOUR GARDEN IN SEPTEMBER

PLANNING

☐ **LANDSCAPING AID ONLINE.** The city of Albuquerque, in collaboration with landscape professionals David Cristiani, Judith Phillips, and George Radnovich, offers six free Xeriscape designs with accompanying plant lists on the Internet: www.cabq.gov/hot/xeriscape.html. The Xeriscape Council of New Mexico, which promotes the use of water-saving plants and techniques, has a website (www. xeriscapenm.com) that covers the principles of Xeriscape, plus has databases to consult and lists demonstration gardens to visit.

PLANTING

☐ **ANNUAL FLOWERS, HERBS.** Zones 1A–3B (Flagstaff, Taos, Santa Fe): Set out lavender, nasturtiums, oregano, and pansies. Zones 10–13 (Albuquerque, Las Vegas, Tucson, Phoenix): Set out transplants of calendula, chives, cilantro, dill, marigolds, marjoram, oregano, and parsley.

☐ **LANDSCAPE PLANTS.** Replace thirsty plants with native or desert-adapted shrubs and trees. Zones 1A–3B: Choices include butterfly bush *(Buddleja davidii),* junipers, redbud *(Cercis canadensis), Rosa rugosa,* Siberian peashrub *(Caragana arborescens),* and smoke tree *(Cotinus coggygria).* Zones 10–13: Attractive shrubs include cassia, dalea, fairy duster *(Calliandra*

californica or *C. eriophylla),* Mexican or red bird of paradise *(Caesalpinia mexicana* or *C. pulcherrima),* and sugar bush *(Rhus ovata).* Among trees, consider acacia, African sumac *(Rhus lancea),* desert willow *(Chilopsis linearis),* feather bush *(Lysiloma microphylla thornberi),* and palo verde *(Cercidium* species). For more choices, see *Plants for Dry Climates: How to Select, Grow, and Enjoy,* by Mary Rose Duffield and Warren Jones (Perseus Publishing, Cambridge, MA, 2001; $25; 800/386-5656 or www.perseuspublishing.com).

☐ **VEGETABLES.** Zones 1A–3B: Sow seeds of bok choy, carrots, kale, radishes, salad greens, spinach, Swiss chard, and turnips for fall harvest. Zones 10–13: Sow seeds for all the above, plus beets, kohlrabi, leeks, peas, and salad greens. Plant onion sets and transplants of broccoli, brussels sprouts, cabbages, and cauliflower.

MAINTENANCE

☐ **DIVIDE PERENNIALS.** Zones 1A–3B, 10: Divide overcrowded clumps of daylilies, hostas, and peonies. With a spade, loosen the soil around the clump, then lift it out of the ground. Use a sharp knife to cut the plants into approximately 1-gallon sizes. Replant the divisions immediately.

☐ **REJUVENATE ROSES.** Zones 11–13: Cut out any dead or damaged canes, and shoots emerging from the rootstock. Cut remaining canes back by one-third. Fertilize and water thoroughly to encourage fall bloom. — *Kim Nelson* ◆

Mediterranean-style gardening in the West

Gardens of the sun

Close your eyes and picture a garden somewhere near the Mediterranean Sea. Surrounding a home with thick whitewashed or ocher-colored walls in Spain or Tuscany, perhaps. Does it contain a patio or grape-covered arbor for shade, a trickling fountain, and sturdy, heat-loving plants like citrus, olive, lavender, and brilliant bougainvillea? Most likely. Is it shimmering in sunlight? Most certainly, because Mediterranean gardening is, above all, a celebration of a climate.

Only 2 percent of the globe enjoys this benign weather pattern, envied by the rest of the world, where warm, dry summers follow mild, wet winters. The dry half of the year may not suit some thirsty plants. But most people love it, because there's no humidity to make your clothes stick to you, and few insects to leave itchy bites. If you use plants that are well adapted to this weather pattern, you'll have few warm-season gardening chores.

As the gardens shown here and on the following pages prove, the Mediterranean way of gardening is winning the West. It looks right. It feels right. It suits our light, architecture, and lifestyle. It saves resources (most dry-climate plants are not heavy feeders, and they don't need a lot of water). Best of all, Mediterranean gardens are designed for pleasure. You can incorporate ideas from them into your own garden, no matter where you live.

By Sharon Cohoon • Photographs by Steven Gunther

Drifts of purple sea lavender, yellow santolina, spiky lavender blue Russian sage, and silvery lamb's ears sweep a path in Pasadena. DESIGN: Chris Rosmini Landscape Design, Los Angeles (323/258-1195)

ABOVE: Water trickles from an olive oil jar reborn as a fountain. Sweet flag grows among moist stones at the base. RIGHT: Gold Mexican feather grass, kangaroo paw, and a ferny jacaranda tree frame the entry garden of Charles and Susan Shaughnessy in Santa Monica. DESIGN: Sunshine Greenery, Los Angeles (310/473-5102)

What makes it Mediterranean?

CLIMATE, GEOGRAPHY, AND PLANTS

Mediterranean refers to the countries that rim the Mediterranean Sea—France, Greece, Italy, Morocco, Spain, Syria, and Turkey—that enjoy the best-known dry-summer climate. It also refers to the climate itself. California, central Chile, southwestern Australia, and the Cape Region of South Africa share this weather pattern with the countries of the Mediterranean Basin.

Plants that grow naturally in each of these regions thrive in all dry-summer climates, so gardeners have a surprisingly large plant palette from which to choose. The familiar herbs—lavender, rosemary, sage, santolina, and thyme—are common choices for good reason: They provide sensual pleasure as well as beauty, and they're tough as nails. California natives such as ceanothus, fremontodendron, and sagebrush, are other handsome choices. Also try blue hibiscus *(Alyogyne huegelii),* grevillea, kangaroo paw, and *Westringia fruticosa* from Australia; Cape mallow *(Anisodontea* x *hypomandarum),* Cape plumbago, kniphofia, leucospermum, and lion's tail *(Leonotis leonurus)* from South Africa; or Pride of Madeira *(Echium candicans)* and rockrose from the Mediterranean region. All have developed strategies for surviving dry summers.

What you need

■ Subtle foliage

Leaves lean toward gray green, blue green, and olive hues, with fuzzy or waxy textures.

■ Vivid colors

Forget pastels. The Mediterranean sun calls for bold-colored flowers like bougainvillea or kangaroo paw (shown).

■ Expansive hardscape

Patios, terraces, paths, and other paved surfaces predominate over lawns.

■ Shady shelter

Cast by an arbor or simply an umbrella, shade offers cool refuge on a hot summer day.

■ Herbal scents

Rosemary, lavender, sage, and
thyme give the Mediterranean
garden its aromatic appeal.

■ Cooling water

Fountains, pools, and other water
features reflect appreciation for a
scarce resource in an arid climate.

■ Artful containers

Pots and urns, planted with
flowers, herbs, or succulents,
accent paved areas.

■ Alfresco living

Generous spaces for outdoor
dining and entertaining take
advantage of the mild climate.

DECORATIVE DETAILS

To provide color and style, Mediterranean gardens have always relied on artful
accessories, not just flowering plants. In ancient Arabia, for instance, glazed
tiles were often used to add year-round color to simple evergreen plantings.
They lined fountains, covered benches, and embellished walls. Pots, of course, are
quintessentially Mediterranean. The Greeks and Romans filled them with flowers
to add color to courtyards without greatly taxing the water supply or used them
to grow lemon trees or other plants that would otherwise be too tender for their
climate. But they also used them as beautiful objects in and of themselves—a classic olive oil jar at the end of an allee, a row of bulbous pots atop a ballustrade, or a
stone urn atop a pedestal, for instance. Nymphs and satyrs and gods and god-
desses, in the form of statuary, were also essential elements in the classic Mediterranean garden.

Going Mediterranean? Here is help

■ Gardens to visit

The Adamson House in Malibu, California, a wonderful Spanish-style house from 1929, with tiled fountains, Moorish pots, and more. *7–sunset daily; tours 11–3 Wed–Sat; free. 23200 Pacific Coast Hwy., Malibu; (310) 456-8432.* The Mediterranean Conservatory at the Rio Grande Botanic Garden in Albuquerque displays Mediterranean herbs and flowers. *9–5 daily; $7. 2601 Central Ave. NW; (505) 764-6200.* The VanDusen Botanical Garden has 2½ acres of Mediterranean-rim plants. *10–6 daily; $7 Canadian. 5251 Oak St., Vancouver, British Columbia; (604) 878-9274.*

For more gardens, visit the *Sunset* website: *www.sunset.com/garden/med.html.*

■ New book

Sun-Drenched Gardens: The Mediterranean Style, by Jan Smithen, with photographs by Lucinda Lewis (Harry N. Abrams, New York, 2002; $39.95; 800/759-0190). Smithen, a well-known garden instructor in Southern California, has been preaching the Mediterranean message for at least a decade. Her passion for the style comes across in every page of this book.

■ Club

The Mediterranean Garden Society has a local branch in Northern California and another in Southern California. This international group will hold its annual general meeting October 1–3 (2002) in Pasadena. Visit *www.mediterraneangardensociety.org.* for more information. ◆

LEFT: Grasses and yarrow edge adobe pavers that provide a display platform for a gallery of potted succulents. ABOVE: *Agave parryi* reposes in a classic bowl. DESIGN: Mark Bartos, BEM Design Group (626/403-0056). RIGHT: 'Barbara Karst' bougainvillea brightens the front yard of Celso and Regina Frazao in Palo Alto. Russian sage and woolly thyme fill accent pots; foreground plants include lavender, Swan River daisy, and blue fescue. *Dymondia* grows between pavers. DESIGN: Ron Benoit Associates, Palo Alto (650/326-4268)

THOMAS J. STORY

LEFT: Spires of Excelsior mix foxglove and dainty pink columbines flank a stream in this Oregon garden. DESIGN: Lindsay Reaves, Garden Artscapes, Springfield, OR (541/744-0372 or www.gardenartscapes.com). ABOVE LEFT: Flower spikes of Excelsior mix foxglove are packed with tubular blossoms that open from bottom to top of stem. ABOVE RIGHT: 'Pam's Choice' foxglove dangles white bells with maroon throats.

Flower towers

These old-fashioned charmers give the garden vertical punch

By Steven R. Lorton and Lauren Bonar Swezey

■ Gardens, like good short stories and movie scripts, need climactic moments to give them punch. Delphiniums, foxgloves, hollyhocks, and verbascum provide the perfect accents, punctuating beds and borders with statuesque candles of bloom.

Plant these beauties at the rear of a border, where they'll make colorful backdrops for shorter plants. Cluster them in the middle of island beds so they'll anchor lower-growing plantings that sweep around them. Or, for drama, fill a bed with a small forest of towering blooms.

Fall is the time to scout catalogs and nurseries for these inspirational vertical bloomers. In mildest climates you can sow seeds of biennials now for handsome plants next summer and blooms the following year (some biennials may even bloom the first year). In cold or wet climates, wait until spring or summer to sow seed. *(Continued on page 304)*

Foxglove *(Digitalis)*

Majestic spikes of tubular flowers rise in late spring and summer; their flowers come in a wide range of colors. Of the many foxgloves available, two are hardy perennials, while the rest are biennial (see page 304). Most biennial foxgloves reseed themselves in the garden. All prefer regular water.

Biennials

D. purpurea (Sunset climate zones A2–A3, 1–24 from the *Western Garden Book)* is the most common species and includes many beautiful strains. Heights vary, depending on the climate. (In the mild-climate West, they generally grow taller than the heights described on seed packets.) Plant in partial or full shade, except in cool-summer climates, where they'll take full sun.

■ COLOR MIXES. Excelsior mix, with large spotted flowers in shades of white to dark pink, grows at least 5 feet tall. Shorter (to 3 feet tall) Giant Shirley mix bears flowers in colors from white to dark pink with crimson or chocolate spots inside the tubes; it reseeds easily. Foxy (to 3 feet tall), in cream, rose, white, and yellow, blooms the first year from seed sown in spring.

■ SINGLE COLORS. Outstanding ones are 'Apricot' and 'Apricot Faerie Queen' (both grow to 5 feet tall), with beautiful soft apricot bells. 'Pam's Choice' (3 to 4 feet tall) has elegant white bells and showy maroon throats (isolate it from other foxgloves to maintain the rich flower color on plants that sprout from seed). 'Primrose Carousel' (2½ feet tall) is the first yellow foxglove that comes true from seed (retains its color and other characteristics).

Perennials

D. x *mertonensis* is coppery pink. Plant in partial or full shade (full sun in cool-summer climates). Its flower spikes grow 3 feet tall and it is hardy in zones 1–10, 14–24.

In all but the coldest climates, put established nursery-grown biennials or perennials in the ground now, and they'll have the cool winter months to become established. Then, as the season progresses and plants grow taller, you will be amazed by your perfectly punctuated beds.

Is it biennial or perennial?

Delphiniums and some verbascum are short-lived perennials, blooming every year for three years or more. Most foxgloves are biennials, producing lush foliage the first year and a dramatic spike of flowers the second year. In a few cases, modern hybridizing has blurred the lines between annuals and biennials so that now you can grow a biennial foxglove ('Foxy') or hollyhock (Summer Carnival mix) that blooms the first year when planted from seed in spring followed by a second year of bloom.

Planting and care

Planting. Set out plants in well-drained soil amended with compost.
Fertilizing. To assure a robust flower spire, feed plants in late winter or early spring with a balanced dry fertilizer or a top dressing of well-rotted manure or compost.
Pruning. Cut the bloom stalks off delphiniums, foxgloves *(Digitalis purpurea)*, and hollyhocks *(Alcea rosea)* as soon as they fade—but well before they set mature seed. In most cases, plants will send up a new flower stalk later in the season.
Disease control. Most hollyhocks are prone to rust, a disease that produces orangy pustules on the undersides of leaves and spots on the leaf surfaces. It's most severe in coastal areas when temperatures are between 64° and 70° and moisture is present for several hours. At the first sign of rust, prune off damaged leaves and spray with sulfur mixed with horticultural oil.

(Continued on facing page)

SAXON HOLT; BELOW: THOMAS J. STORY (2)

ABOVE: Hollyhocks stand out beautifully against walls or tall fences.
CENTER: Single mix hollyhock. **BOTTOM:** Chater's Double Scarlet.

Hollyhock *(Alcea)*

These tall (5 to 9 feet) plants from the Mediterranean region have rough, roundish heart-shaped leaves and 3- to 6-inch-wide single, semidouble, or double flowers that appear in early to midsummer. They're favored for cottage gardens from Santa Fe to the Pacific Northwest (zones 1–24). Plant them where they'll get full sun and regular water.

Most hollyhocks are strains of *A. rosea* and are considered biennial or short-lived perennials. *A. ficifolia* Antwerp mix, with palm-shaped leaves, is a new rust-resistant strain.

■ **SINGLE BLOOMS.** *A. rosea* Old Barnyard mix, Country Garden mix, and Single mix are collections of old-fashioned single flowers in shades of all or some of the following colors: maroon, pink, rose, white, and yellow. *A. r. nigra* has rich chocolate maroon flowers.

■ **DOUBLE BLOOMS.** *A. rosea* Chater's Double is a perennial strain in single and mixed colors. 'Peaches 'n' Dreams' is creamy pink with tinges of raspberry. Powderpuff is a bright mix of maroon, red, white, and yellow. Summer Carnival mix blooms the first year if started in spring.

ABOVE: Candle delphinium like these English hybrids can reach 6 to 8 feet tall.
BELOW: Verbascum 'Southern Charm' bears inch-wide flowers on 2- to 4-foot-tall spikes.

Plant and seed sources

PLANTS

In mild climates in fall, most nurseries sell delphiniums, foxgloves, and verbascum. Hollyhocks may not be available until spring.

Wayside Gardens (800/845-1124 or www.waysidegardens.com).

Weiss Brothers Perennial Nursery (530/272-7657 or www.plantperennials.com). Ships only until October 29 in fall; spring shipping begins February 26.

SEEDS

Renee's Garden (888/880-7228 or www.reneesgarden.com).

Thompson & Morgan Seedsmen, Inc. (800/274-7333 or www.thompson-morgan.com).

Delphinium

Elegant spires of blue, lavender, mauve, pink, purple, red, or white, up to 8 feet tall, develop above lobed or fanlike leaves. All are perennial (though most are short lived). Provide full sun and regular water.

Varieties of candle delphinium (*D. elatum;* zones A1–A3, 1–10, 14–24) are the most dramatic of the genus. For the tallest blooms, try mixed colors of the Pacific strain or named varieties ('Blue Bird', 'Galahad', 'Summer Skies').

Large-flowered Centurion grows 4 to 5 feet tall and will bloom the first year from seed when planted in spring. It's also more reliably perennial. Blue Springs and Magic Fountains mixes are shorter (to 2½ feet tall).

Varieties of *D.* x *belladonna* (zones 1–9, 14–24) are shorter (3 to 4 feet tall) and have airier flowers. The plants are also longer lived than the tall varieties of *D. elatum.*

Verbascum

Grow these striking plants for their large leaves as well as their spiky flowers. Some species and hybrids are biennial and others are perennial. All types prefer moderate water (allow the soil to dry out somewhat between waterings) and full sun.

V. bombyciferum 'Arctic Summer' (biennial; zones 2–11, 14–24) has 1½-foot-long furry, gray green leaves. The yellow flowers form on 6-foot-tall, powdery white spikes.

V. chaixii (perennial; zones 2–11, 14–24) has 6-inch-long hairy, green leaves and 3-foot-tall spikes of pale yellow flowers with a red eye. 'Album' is white with a purple center.

V. phoeniceum hybrids (perennial; zones 1–10, 14–24) have 6-inch-long dark green leaves that are smooth on top, hairy on the bottom. Pink, red, violet, and white flowers appear on 2- to 4-foot-tall spikes. 'Violetta' has dark violet-purple flowers.

Other verbascum hybrids: 'Banana Custard' (biennial to 6 feet tall), with yellow flowers; 'Copper Rose' (perennial to 6 feet tall), with flowers in apricot, buff, rose, or tan (it blooms the first year from seed sown in late winter or early spring); and 'Southern Charm', which comes in apricot, cream, dusky pink, and lavender. (All grow in zones 3–10, 14–24.) ◆

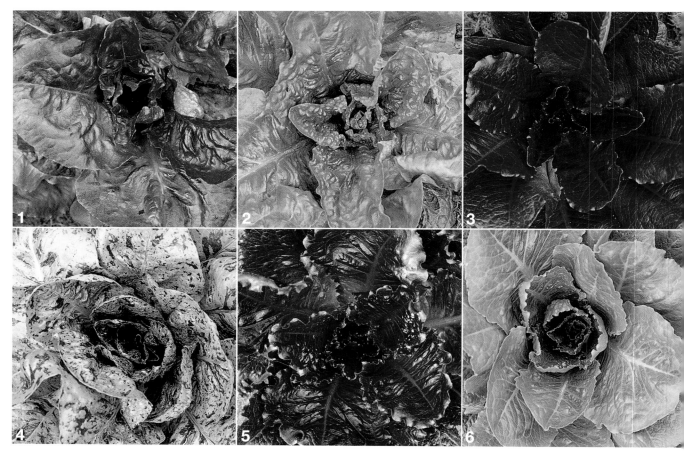

Your freshest Caesar

Romaine lettuce tastes best when you grow your own

By Lauren Bonar Swezey • Photographs by E. Spencer Toy

Determined chefs go out of their way to find the freshest, most tender heads of romaine lettuce available. Grocery shoppers, on the other hand, are often limited to big heads with tough, strong-tasting leaves.

Luckily, lettuce is one of the easiest crops to grow. Seeds germinate quickly and plants grow with little fuss. In most areas of the West, you can grow successive crops in fall and spring; in mild coastal areas, you can grow lettuce year-round. So get going and soon you'll be able to serve a salad of your homegrown romaine.

SOWING. Start seeds three to four weeks before you plan to set them out into the garden. Sow in flats or sixpacks filled with moistened potting soil or seed-starting mix. Cover seeds with ⅛ inch soil. Place flats in bright, filtered light. Keep the soil moist and maintain soil temperature between 40° and 68°. For successive crops, sow seeds every week. Plant seedlings between developing heads.

PLANTING. When seedlings are ready to go in the ground, gradually introduce them to full sun over a few days. Transplant into rich, well-composted soil. Keep the soil moist—particularly critical the first week after transplanting. Lettuce can also be grown in containers filled with potting mix.

HARVESTING. For baby lettuce, harvest leaves when 3 to 4 inches long. For a crispy head, let it reach full size.

Some greens are red: Six colorful lettuces are shown above and described below. Abbreviations after variety names refer to seed sources listed below.

1) **'Blushed Butter Cos' (S, T)**. Very tender romaine-butterhead lettuce grows 10 inches tall; 50 days from sowing to maturity.

2) **'De Morges Braun' (T)**. Grows 8 to 10 inches; 65 days. Slow to bolt (go to seed).

3) **'Rouge d'Hiver' (S)**. Heirloom grows 8 to 12 inches; 60 days.

4) **'Flashy Trout's Back' (T)**. Improved heirloom reaches 8 inches; 55 days.

5) **'Outredgeous' (T)**. One of the reddest, it reaches 10 inches; 52 days.

6) **'Remus' (C)**. Classic romaine grows 8 to 10 inches; 60 days. Resists bolting and mildew.

Seed sources: (C) The Cook's Garden; (800) 457-9703 or www.cooksgarden.com. **(S) Shepherd's Garden Seeds;** (860) 482-3638 or www.shepherdseeds.com. **(T) Territorial Seed Company;** (541) 942-9547 or www.territorialseed.com.

A spiral fence for peas

It makes growing and harvesting a snap

By Sharon Cohoon
and Lauren Bonar Swezey

Snow peas cling to fencing attached to poles.

C limbing crops like snow peas require a fence or trellis for support. The trellis doesn't have to be ruler-straight to be effective; it just needs wide mesh to weave the vines through, with a little help from you.

The fence pictured above coils into a sinuous spiral. Besides throwing a curve into the usually angular vegetable garden, it saves space and is less likely to topple in wind. In addition to snow peas, you can use it to support bush cucumbers, bush squash, some nasturtiums, and sweet peas.

We borrowed the idea from Gary Nigro, a vegetable gardener in Reno, Nevada. Nigro wanted to use leftover cattle fencing to make trellises in his vegetable garden, but he found that

keeping it from coiling was a challenge. He decided to work with that tendency rather than fight it.

We used fiberglass rebar poles, but you can substitute bamboo or wood poles.

COST: About $25

TOOLS: Hammer or mallet and wire cutters

MATERIALS

- 7 poles, each 5 feet long
- 21 feet of 3-foot-wide, 2-inch-mesh plastic-coated fencing
- 21 or more plastic-coated twist ties
- Soaker hose
- 1 packet snow pea seeds (we used 'Oregon Giant')

DIRECTIONS

1. Using the drawing at left as a guide, set out the poles at approximately 3-foot intervals. Pound each pole 1 foot into the ground to secure.

2. Using wire cutters, cut off a 21-foot-length from your fencing roll.

3. Attach fencing to the poles. Start at the center pole and secure fencing, top, middle, and bottom, using twist ties. Continue uncoiling wire and securing to remaining poles (you may need to reposition the last one).

4. Lay soaker hose. Place capped end at the spiral's center and continue around the inside to the other end.

5. Plant seeds of snow peas, or other low, vining crops, following package directions, along the outside of the fencing. ◆

Deep red 'Winston S. Churchill' aster pairs well with variegated moor grass in Carolyn Temple's Seattle garden.

NORM PLATE

Stars of the late show

Easy-to-grow asters belong in the autumn garden

By Sharon Cohoon

When most other perennials stop blooming, asters are just getting started. These hardy perennials are the backbone of the late show, says Gary Ratway, co-owner of Digging Dog Nursery in Albion, California.

"Most of the year asters are just a promise, just a nice clump of green foliage," he says. "But then, finally, late in the season, when you're craving another jolt of color, out they come with these great clouds of flowers."

Those clouds, appropriately enough, are often blue. But asters also come in a full range of reds and pinks, plus white.

And asters attract winged guests: Monarchs and other butterflies love the flowers. Bees like them too.

Autumn is the time to go nursery shopping for asters in bloom. Where winters are frost-free, you can plant any time as long as the soil isn't soggy. In cold-winter climates, get plants into the ground no later than mid-October or wait until next spring.

Best asters for the West

A. cordifolius. Violet blue flower clusters resembling baby's breath are borne on stems 4 to 6 feet tall. Great in bouquets. *Sunset* climate zones 1–10, 14–21 from the *Western Garden Book*.

A. x frikartii. One of the earliest-flowering asters, it's also one of the latest bloomers. The variety 'Mönch' bears 2½-inch-wide lavender blue flowers on a 2- to 3-foot-tall plant; 'Jungfrau' and 'Wonder of Staffa' are similar. Plant looks best when stems are staked or grown in a hoop. Zones 2B–24.

A. novae-angliae hybrids. Very upright (3 to 5 feet tall), this stout-stemmed aster has 2-inch-wide flowers and hairy leaves. 'Alma Pötschke' (salmon pink), 'Purple Dome', and 'September Ruby' are popular varieties. Zones 1–24.

A. novi-belgii hybrids. Plant form is similar to *A. novae-angliae,* but the leaves are smooth. There are scores of named varieties ranging from dwarf kinds like 'Bonny Blue' (violet flowers; 10 to 12 inches high) to tall ones like 'Winston S. Churchill' (raspberry red; to 3 feet) and 'Climax' (true blue; to 6 feet). Zones 1–24.

A. pringlei 'Monte Cassino' (also sold as *A. ericoides* 'Monte Cassino'). Sprays of small white daisies are borne on branching 3- to 5-foot-tall plants. Excellent cut flower. Zones 1–24.

ABOVE: Pink *A. novi-belgii.*
LEFT: *A.* x *frikartii* 'Mönch'.

MARK TURNER (2)

Growing tips

■ Most asters need full sun, but *A. cordifolius* tolerates light shade. They all grow luxuriously if watered regularly, but *A.* x *frikartii* and *A. pringlei* can tolerate drought. Many gardeners, especially those blessed with loamy soil, also water *A. novi-belgii* sparingly to discourage it from spreading too aggressively.

■ Taller varieties can be floppy. Often this is only a first-year problem, tending to self-correct. If it doesn't, cut plants back by half when they put out a growth surge but before setting buds. This produces sturdier stems. If you don't get to it in time, support plants with stakes or other supports.

■ At season's end, cut plants back to rosettes. To maintain productivity, dig and divide plants every three years in late fall or early spring. Discard the old centers and replant young divisions from the outside of the clump. Some gardeners divide *A. novae-angliae* and *A. novi-belgii* more ruthlessly, pulling up the whole plant because they know any tiny fragment left behind in the soil will generate another.

Sources

A. x *frikartii* and short- and medium-height *A. novae-angliae* and *A. novi-belgii* hybrids are available at many nurseries. Taller asters are harder to find; shop at specialty nurseries or try one of the following mail-order sources.

Bluestone Perennials: (800) 852-5243 or www. bluestoneperennials.com.
Canyon Creek Nursery: (530) 533-2166 or www. canyoncreeknursery.com.
Digging Dog Nursery: (707) 937-1130 or www. diggingdog.com.
Forestfarm: (541) 846-7269 or www.forestfarm.com. ◆

Spring surprises

Desert wildflowers are easy to grow if you sow them soon

By Sharon Cohoon

Desert wildflowers are almost ridiculously easy to plant. Just roughen up the soil surface, broadcast the seed, and turn on the sprinkler. Or wait for rain. "Gentle gardening," is how Amy Carlile of Southwest Gardener, a Phoenix garden shop, describes it. "Child's play," says Tera Vessels of Tera's Garden, also in Phoenix. "Just stand there and throw," she says.

Keeping your seedlings going is easy too. All that young wildflowers need is a little water and plenty of sun. Note, however, that unless your local water-use regulations allow sprinkling, you may need to postpone planting until it rains.

Forget controlling exactly what comes up, though. The same seed mix in the same soil produces different results every year. "The unpredictability is half the fun," says Vessels.

Tips for seeding

1. Make sure seed is in good contact with soil, but don't bury it. Seeds should be no more than ¼-inch deep. If seeds are too deep, the seedlings exhaust their food supply before reaching the soil surface. This is the most common mistake gardeners make, say seed growers.

2. Sow seed at the right time. Desert wildflowers germinate best when daytime temperatures are consistently around 80° and nighttime temperatures around 50° (70°/40° is okay too). When temperatures go lower, germination ceases. Depending on where you live in the Southwest, these conditions occur between September and early December.

Desert bluebells pop up around paving stones flanked by scarlet- and pink-flowered penstemons in Wally and Vivian Simons's garden in Carefree, Arizona.

Try wildflowers a few seasons and you'll understand her response. Waiting for a new surprise each spring quickly becomes addictive.

Mixes versus single colors

If you want to be sure at least some seeds germinate, use a wildflower mix. Many suppliers (see list below) formulate mixes especially for the Southwest. Wild Seed in Tempe, for example, offers a Sonoran Desert Native Wildflower Mix that includes arroyo lupine, California desert bluebells *(Phacelia campanularia)*, bladderpod, desert lupine, desert marigold *(Baileya multiradiata)*, desert senna, dyssodia, firewheel, owl's clover, penstemon, and verbena. No matter what the weather conditions, at least some of the seeds in your packet will likely germinate.

Some gardeners, however, prefer to buy packets of individual flower species and scatter them in drifts. California desert bluebells or other low growers near a pathway where they

Seed sources

Plants of the Southwest. Santa Fe; (800) 788-7333 or www.plantsofthesouthwest. com. Several Southwest mixes, plus single species.

Wildlands Restoration. Tucson; (520) 882-0969. Specialized mixes, such as Old Town Tucson, Old Town Vegas, Red Rock Country, Santa Cruz Foothills, plus many single species.

Wild Seed. Tempe, AZ; (602) 276-3536. Many specialized mixes—Catalina Foothills, Great Basin, Mojave, Sonoran—plus lots of single species.

Wildseed Farms. Fredericksburg, TX; (800) 848-0078 or www.wildseedfarms. com. Only one mix for the Southwest, but lots of single species. Color catalog.

ABOVE: Wildflowers fill a pocket beside a boulder in the Simons's garden. RIGHT: Desert marigold, red firecracker penstemon, and yellow Mexican poppy bloom in Fred and Marion Emerson's garden. DESIGN: Carrie Nimmer, Phoenix (602/254-0300).

can be appreciated, for instance. Or penstemon near rocks for a natural look, since that's where they're often seen in the wild. If you want to try this technique (often called "painting" with seed), choose wildflowers that germinate readily, such as California and Mexican poppy *(Eschscholzia)*, desert marigold, bluebells, and penstemon. Avoid more temperamental seeds, like owl's clover.

Planting

Select a site that drains well and gets at least six hours of sun a day. Rake the soil lightly—no deeper than 1 inch (the less you disturb the soil, the fewer weed seeds you bring up). If decomposed granite covers your property and you don't want rake marks, skip this step and move to the next one; the seeds will fall down in between the gravel.

To make the seed easier to distribute, mix it with native soil or sand.

Broadcast half the seed over the desired area, then sow the remainder in a direction perpendicular to the first.

After sowing, walk over the seed to make sure it is firmly in contact with the soil. Or rake *very* lightly *once*.

Water seeded area with a sprinkler set on fine spray or use a garden hose with a mist nozzle. Keep the area moist until seedlings emerge—usually 5 to 14 days later. When seedlings have grown to a few inches high, taper off irrigation. Thereafter, apply water only when young plants appear stressed.

Bird protection

Birds love both wildflower seeds and young seedlings. Put out quail blocks or birdseed to distract hungry birds.

After-bloom care

If you want your annuals to come back on their own, you'll have to let them set seed. After the foliage has begun to turn brown and most of the seeds have ripened, pull up the plants and scatter the remaining seed. If your spring wildflower crop is sparse, plan on reseeding again in fall. ◆

WHIMSICAL SCARECROWS created by Sierra foothills artist Katie O'Hara-Kelly stand guard over this pumpkin patch. For details on these playful stuffed "people," see page 316.

October

Autumn glory in Yakima

■ If you love trees, there's no better time or place to celebrate them than this month at the Yakima Area Arboretum. As night temperatures cool, deciduous trees here put on a foliage show in a range of autumnal hues.

Begun in 1967, the arboretum displays specimens of more than 900 species of trees across 46 acres, including ponds and wetlands. Stop by the Jewett Interpretive Center and pick up a brochure for a self-guiding tour. Bring a camera and a notebook to record landscape ideas you can adapt in your own garden. Most of the trees are labeled.

Be sure to stroll through the Joyful Garden. Built around a pond with enormous basalt outcroppings, this Japanese garden will be ablaze with fiery Japanese maples playing off evergreen conifers like Hinoki false cypress and Tanyosho pine (*Pinus densiflora* 'Umbraculifera').

Not all the autumn splendor here comes from leaves. Crabapples and hawthorns are studded with bright fruits and the tawny seed heads of ornamental grasses sway and rustle in the breeze.

The grounds, at 1401 Arboretum Drive, are open dawn to dusk daily. The interpretive center and gift shop are open 9 to 4 Tuesday to Saturday; free. (509) 248-7337 or www.ahtrees.org. — *Steven R. Lorton*

Potting pavilion

■ Dan and Shirley Eichenberger turned part of an uncovered patio into a well-protected potting porch that snuggles against one corner of their Portland home.

First, they created the 10- by 16-foot area by extending a roof over an eave of the house. To brighten the space underneath, they built two 8- by 2-foot tinted-glass skylights into the roof. At the entry, they installed pressure-treated cedar fence panels and a door. Inside, they put up shelves and ran a cold-water line to a faucet mounted on a custom stainless steel sink and countertop. Original pavers serve as the floor.

Shirley Eichenberger uses the open-air space to pot up azaleas, begonias, and flowering bulbs that go into her extensive gardens. Fertilizer, potting soil, garden tools, and extra containers are also stored here. — *Jim McCausland*

BOOKSHELF

Container tips from Western pros

How to create container gardens of vegetables, herbs, fruits and edible flowers.

by ROSE MARIE NICHOLS McGEE & MAGGIE STUCKEY

■ Few people know more about growing food in the Pacific Northwest than Rose Marie Nichols McGee, owner of Nichols Garden Nursery in Albany, Oregon. Now, McGee has teamed up with Portland gardener Maggie Stuckey to write the definitive work about culinary container gardening. *The Bountiful Container* (Workman Publishing, New York, 2002; $16.95; 212/254-5900) has major sections devoted to vegetables, herbs, fruits, and edible flowers. You'll find plenty of recipes, including one for rosemary pesto. Study this book during the cool months; by the time seed catalogs arrive, you'll be inspired to fill every pot you have. — *J. M.*

The advantages of fall planting

Spring isn't the only planting season in the West. There are good reasons to set out shrubs, trees, and other landscape plants in early fall, as these illustrations show.

■ Early Fall

Air is cooling; new plant loses less moisture through leaves. Soil, still warm from summer's heat, encourages root growth.

■ Winter

Rain irrigates garden. Cold air and short days slow top growth. Cold soil has lots of moisture. Roots continue to grow.

■ Early Spring

As air warms up, top growth emerges on plant. Maturing roots continue to grow, preparing the plant for hot summer days.

■ Late Spring

Plant is ready for a full surge of top growth. Larger root system supplies maximum water and nutrients.

Pumpkin patch whimsy

■ These scarecrows aren't just for birds. "They make people laugh," says creator Katie O'Hara-Kelly, whose playful stuffed "people" decorate gardens and porches throughout the northern Sierra foothill towns of Downieville, Sierra City, and her own Goodyear's Bar. Her harvest couple dressed in country duds stands guard over a pumpkin patch (below). Elsewhere, Mrs. Blossom, a lady decked out in a bright pink straw hat adorned with butterflies, seems to dance through the crops.

They're folk art, not high art, says O'Hara-Kelly. "I make them whimsical, not precious," she says.

O'Hara-Kelly made her first scarecrow for her own garden ("Living in the country, I'm always looking for new projects," she explains). Then she decided to sell them. She made 20 more scarecrows, set them in front of the house, put up a few fliers, and sold all of them in three hours.

She searches thrift stores to find the scarecrows' attire. "Clothes make the person, you know," she explains. Her latest find, a sequin-flowered shirt, will soon be transformed into a hummingbird lady in kelly green pants, a magenta hat, and a halo of glittering hummingbirds.

O'Hara-Kelly sells her life-size scarecrows for about $70 each, including a collapsible stand (530/289-3588 or www.gardenfolk.com).

— *Lauren Bonar Swezey*

Grasses in autumn glory

During summer, ornamental grasses are supporting actors in the garden, serving mainly as textural foils for their flowering companions. But later in the season, after the flowers fade, grasses assume starring roles as their foliage turns shades of gold and red and their seed heads become kinetic sculptures, swaying and swishing in the breeze.

The species and varieties listed at right thrive in full sun and are hardy to at least *Sunset* climate zone 2B. All of them are clump-forming perennials.

• **Feather reed grass** (*Calamagrostis* x *acutiflora* 'Karl Foerster'). Foliage becomes golden yellow in fall and winter. Reddish purple flower spikes age to straw-colored seed heads. 4 to 6 feet tall.

• **Fall-blooming reed grass** (*Calamagrostis brachytricha*), shown at right. Burnt orange to burgundy foliage in fall. Purple-tinged flowers fade to buff. 4 feet tall.

• **Little bluestem** (*Schizachyrium scoparium*). Bluish green foliage turns blazing burgundy red in fall. 2 to 4 feet tall. Hardy to zone 1.

These grasses are available from High Country Gardens (800/925-9387 or www.highcountrygardens.com). — *Marcia Tatroe*

A hot border in Denver

■ A fine-arts degree with a concentration in painting taught Mary Kobey how to spin the color wheel successfully. In designing this border for the front of her Denver townhouse, Kobey combined spring-blooming flowers and foliage with contrasting or complementary colors.

Rising through the blue Crown pansies and *Vinca minor* are tulips in shades of orange ('Lightning Sun' and 'Temple of Beauty') and purple ('Cum Laude'). Between the flowers, chartreuse-leafed *Spiraea japonica* 'Limemound' forms broad strokes of color for Kobey's painterly plot.

Kobey orders most of her tulips from John Scheepers (860/567-0838 or www. johnscheepers.com). She plants the pansies and tulips in October, putting down seven to nine bulbs of one variety side by side in each 10-inch-deep hole, adding bone meal and bulb food to the soil according to package directions. Then she blankets the bed with a mulch of leaves to protect the plants from erratic temperatures.

During winter, she waters at least once a month—a step she says is crucial to her border's success. The next spring, at the end of April or in early May, Kobey feeds the pansies with liquid fertilizer (15-30-15). She treats the pansies and tulips as annuals, pulling them up after they wither and replacing them with summer annuals, followed by fresh bulbs planted each autumn.

— *Colleen Smith*

THOMAS J. STORY

Happy Birthday, Gamble Garden

■ Palo Alto was just 8 years old when Edwin and Elizabeth Gamble's house was built at 1431 Waverley Street.

The formal gardens surrounding the three-story Colonial/Georgian revival house were designed by Walter A. Hoffas as a series of outdoor rooms.

They included a rose garden, cherry allée, cutting garden (visible through the gazebo in the photo above), and sundial garden.

When the city of Palo Alto took over the property in 1981, renovations of the house and garden began. Now the Elizabeth F. Gamble

Garden is a thriving community horticultural foundation offering memberships, gardening classes, and a beautiful public garden (open daily from sunrise to sunset; admission is free). *Call (650) 329-1356 or visit www.gamblegarden.org.*

— *L.B.S.*

Liquid assets in a desert garden

■ Growing up in Chicago near the shore of Lake Michigan had a profound impact on Lil Cashman, who now resides in Paradise Valley, Arizona. "I *have* to be near water," she confesses. "When we camp, I always pick the spot near the stream, even if there's only a trickle of water in it. And my gardens have always contained water, even if it was only in a birdbath." Cashman's current garden, which she shares with husband, Don, contains two water features, both designed by Phoenix landscape architect Greg Trutza of New Directions in Landscape Architecture (602/264-5202).

On a patio, a recirculating waterfall (shown above) cascades into a semicircular spa. The splashing sound masks noise from a busy nearby street. This water feature is flanked by raised planters that Cashman fills with seasonal color like pansies, petunias, and snapdragons.

Near the house a small waterfall fringed by cattail and horsetail spills into a shallow pond bisected by flagstones. The pond narrows to a stream that ends just outside her kitchen door. — *Sharon Cohoon*

Peonies for mild climates

If you've ever visited a cold-winter climate during the height of peony season, you know why most mild-climate gardeners envy the breathtaking display of 5- to 6-inch-wide single or double flowers in coral, pink, red, or white that grow there with what seems to be little effort. Although most peonies need substantial winter chill to thrive, some types—any early-season one, for example—do well where winters are mild.

Midseason doubles (such as 'Dr. Alexander Fleming', shown at right), or any single-flowered or Japanese type, are other good choices. But don't expect these plants to grow as tall as they would in colder climates; in Northern California's lower elevations, they'll reach about 2 feet tall (not 3 feet as in cold climates). Avoid all late-season peonies. Prepare the soil by mixing in organic matter (not manure) to a depth of 18 inches. Refill the hole and tamp down well. Plant peony roots no more than 1½ inches deep, and 3 to 4 feet apart. Keep the soil moist and do not fertilize the first year. Do not control any ants that appear; they may help buds open.

Some of the following varieties are available from Brent and Becky's Bulbs (804/693-3966; www.brentandbeckys-bulbs.com). Most are sold by Marde Ross & Company (707/938-9062).

Some good peonies for mild climates: 'Big Red Boomer Sooner' (red), 'Coral Charm' (coral), 'Dr. Alexander Fleming' (deep pink), 'Fairy's Petticoat' (dainty pink), 'Festiva Maxima' (white flecked with red), 'Henry Bockstoce' (dark red), 'Krinkled White' (white), 'Mons. Jules Elie' (silvery rose), and 'Mrs. F. D. Roosevelt' (shell pink). — *L. B. S.*

Good mates: "sprawlers" with brick

■ True geraniums and brick paths make fantastic partners, says La Jolla gardener Helen Dawson. When plants sprawl out onto a walkway, softening its edges, the path looks more enticing, she says.

Geraniums have just the right amount of spill. Dawson's current favorite is *G.* x *oxonianum* 'Claridge Druce', the main presence on both sides of the walkway in the photo at left. It's vigorous, with cool pink flowers, and it comes true from seed. Other favorites for lining the path include 'Russell Prichard' and 'Biokovo' geraniums, as well as alpine strawberries, diascia, nemesia, and sweet alyssum.

Brick is a good partner for sprawlers, Dawson says, because it does not get as hot as concrete or stone, so it won't fry your plants.

— S. C.

CLIPPINGS

• **Two new books.** Bay Area nursery veteran and broadcaster Bob Tanem has spent years learning about plants that grow well in Northern California. His two latest books (cowritten with Don Williamson), *Perennials for Northern California* and *Annuals for Northern California* (Lone Pine Publishing, Renton, WA, 2002; $19 each; 800/518-3541), feature hundreds of varieties particularly suited to the climate. There's plenty of practical advice accompanying each entry.

Nursery adventure

■ If you're not an Aussie, Australian plants can seem a little scary, at least upon first exposure. They don't look much like the plants that American gardeners already know, explains Jo O'Connell, owner of the Australian Native Plants Nursery in Casitas Springs. (The pinecone-shaped flowers she's holding in her arrangement— three species of *Banksia*—prove her point.) But, familiar or not, these plants all work well in Southern California gardens.

"All the plants I sell to the cut-flower growers—*Crowea, Astartea, Boronia,* Geraldton waxflower, *Kunzea, Thryptomene*—do great in home gardens," O'Connell says. "And they're nice to cut even when they're not in bloom because most have aromatic foliage." Many of these plants start blooming in winter, when not much else is in flower—another plus, she points out.

Other winter-blooming Australian shrubs to consider, suggests O'Connell, are the spotted emu bush *(Eremophila maculata), Hakea, Grevillea, Correa,* and *Banksia.* Though drought-tolerant once established, many of these shrubs are used to summer rain, so they can handle regular garden irrigation.

Open by appointment. 9040 N. Ventura Ave., Casitas Springs; (805) 649-3362 or www.australianplants.com.

— S. C.

AUSTRALIAN NATIVE PLANTS

STEVEN GUNTHER (3)

Pretty and productive

■ Some gardens are so inspiring that after you've visited them, you want to go home, rip yours out, and start over. Barbara Shelton's garden in Corona del Mar has that effect. It's not just that her garden is colorful; except for vegetables that grow in tidy raised beds, it's also remarkably low-maintenance. In fact the native and mediterranean plants are nearly self-sustaining. Her artemisia, buckwheat, ceanothus, and Cleveland sage (whose spikes of lavender blue flowers rise behind bougainvillea in the photograph above) never have to be fed or fussed over and, most years, survive entirely on natural rainfall. Even Shelton's non-natives, like Mexican sage and 'Moonshine' yarrow, are remarkably unthirsty. "Nothing here gets watered more than once a month," she says. "Even in the summer."

The most thrilling aspect of Shelton's garden, though, is how much life it supports. Finches, hummingbirds, sparrows, and dozens of other birds drop in routinely. Butterflies are frequent visitors too, as are hover flies and other beneficial insects. And Shelton has so many honeybees that you can see her perennials quivering with activity from halfway across the yard.

What makes the garden work, Shelton believes, is that most of the ornamentals in it are from the same plant community, the coastal chaparral, and evolved to be mutually supportive. "It's not just the same water requirements," she says. "It's a kind of symbiosis."

The influences that shaped Shelton's garden include her membership in the Orange County Chapter of the California Native Plant Society and visits to native-plant nurseries.

— S.C.

Nearly wild flowers

■ The soft, delicate look is hard to pull off in a desert garden, but Janet and Bill Rademacher achieved it in the front yard of their home in Litchfield Park, Arizona. And they accomplished this feat by pairing two desert-adapted perennials with rather unlovely common names: spreading fleabane *(Erigeron divergens)* and five-needle dogweed (also called golden dyssodia).

That's the white-flowered fleabane encircling the prickly pear cactus, hovering around the bases of the palo verde trees, and generally behaving like a cloud that has descended to earth. Depending on where you live, it's an annual or short-lived perennial, but it hardly matters, says Janet Rademacher, because "once you plant fleabane, you have it. It both meanders and reseeds."

Swirling through the fleabane is yellow-flowered dogweed, a Southwest native. Its habit is similar to fleabane's, but its nature is slightly less exuberant.

Both fleabane and dogweed bloom through the spring, then take a rest in summer (if given irrigation, they'll start blooming again in fall). To produce this show, the Rademachers started with only 10 1-gallon containers of *each* species. It took about two years for the plants to form the floral carpet pictured here. (The hot pink blast behind the cactus is *Penstemon triflorus.*)

After the last bloom, lop the brown seed heads off the fleabane and dogweed with a nylon string trimmer or hand shears. Pull out any fleabane that reseeds where it's not welcome. — *S.C.*

WHAT TO DO IN YOUR GARDEN IN OCTOBER

PLANTING

☐ **BULBS.** Choose from crocus, daffodil, grape hyacinth, hyacinth, scilla, tulip, and a host of minor bulbs. Plant before rains begin or the ground freezes.

☐ **COVER CROPS.** *Sunset* climate zones 4–7, 17: There's still time to sow Austrian field peas, crimson clover, and tyfon greens. They'll cover the ground and prevent erosion through winter, then enrich the soil when you plow them under next spring. Territorial Seed Company (541/942-9547 or www.territorialseed.com) sells the crops above, plus fava beans, which are both a cover and a food crop (you can cook and eat immature pods or wait to harvest mature seeds and prepare like lima beans).

☐ **GARLIC.** Separate garlic cloves from "mother" bulbs and cover each clove with 1 to 2 inches of soil in mild-winter climates, 3 to 4 inches in areas where the ground freezes. A good source is Filaree Farm (509/422-6940 or www.filareefarm.com).

☐ **GROUND COVERS, PERENNIALS.** Planted now, their roots will become established over winter, then grow and flower well when the weather warms up.

☐ **LAWNS.** Zones 4–7, 17: Install a sod lawn any time this month. To prepare the site, till the soil 6 to 8 inches deep, pick out rocks, and level the ground. Then lay the sod and water regularly until rains take over.

☐ **SHRUBS, TREES.** This is the best month for planting balled-and-burlapped or container-grown shrubs and trees. When you shop, keep an eye out for ones that have great fall color.

MAINTENANCE

☐ **ANNUALS.** Zones 1–3: Pull and compost annuals when they stop blooming or freeze. Zones 4–7, 17: Feed one last time with liquid fertilizer early in the month.

☐ **MAKE COMPOST.** As you clean out the summer garden, put everything but diseased material onto the compost pile. Turn the pile weekly and keep it moist to encourage bacterial activity. In zones 4–7, once rains begin cover the pile with a tarp to keep nutrients from washing out.

☐ **MULCH.** Spread a 2- to 3-inch layer of organic mulch such as compost or pine needles around perennial flowers, shrubs, strawberry beds, and vegetables to insulate roots from freeze damage and reduce soil erosion.

☐ **TEND FUCHSIAS.** Zones 1–3: Bring fuchsias into a protected, dark place like a basement or frost-free garage for the winter. Zones 4–7, 17: Early in the month, give plants their last feeding with liquid fertilizer. Bring them inside before frost, or mulch them for the winter.

☐ **WATER.** Keep watering until rains begin, especially in coldest climates. Drought-stressed plants are far more likely to sustain freeze damage than properly hydrated ones. ◆

WHAT TO DO IN YOUR GARDEN IN OCTOBER

PLANTING

☐ **BULB COVERS.** *Sunset* climate zones 7–9, 14–17: Cool-season annuals planted over bulbs will give a colorful show before and after bulbs pop up. Choose colors that complement the bulbs, such as blue violas with white daffodils, blue forget-me-nots with yellow tulips, salmon *Primula obconica* with purple tulips, or purple and white fairy primrose *(Primula malacoides)* with pink tulips.

☐ **GRAPES, FRUIT TREES, BERRIES.** If you plan to purchase special varieties of fruits by mail, get your orders in soon, so you get the types you want in time for dormant-season planting. Some local nurseries—Yamagami's Nursery in Cupertino (408/252-3347) and Orchard Nursery & Florist in Lafayette (925/284-4474), for instance—take a one-time special order this month.

☐ **ONIONS.** Zones 7–9, 14–17: Fall is the best time to plant onion seed for full-size bulbs in spring. Intermediate-day 'Pantry Trio' from Renee's Garden (888/880-7228 or www.reneesgarden.com) is a widely adapted mix of white, bronze, and red onions.

☐ **PERENNIALS.** Zones 7–9, 14–17: This is a good time to plant almost any hardy perennial, but it's especially important to get early bloomers such as campanula, candytuft, columbine, coral bells, delphinium, foxglove, and verbascum

Sunset
CLIMATE ZONES
☐ Mountain (1-2)
☐ Valley (7-9)
☐ Inland (14)
☐ Coastal (15-17)

into the ground so they develop plenty of roots to support a good spring flower show. For the best value, plant from sixpacks or 4-inch pots.

☐ **PLANT FOR THE BIRDS.** Zones 1, 2, 7–9, 14–17: Set out plants that produce berries, and the birds will come (as long as you don't have cats that chase them away). Some choices include barberry, beautyberry, cotoneaster, currant, elderberry, gooseberry, holly, mahonia, mountain ash, nandina, pyracantha, and strawberry tree (not all of these plants grow in every zone; check *Sunset's Western Garden Book* for specifics).

MAINTENANCE

☐ **CLEAN UP DEBRIS.** To reduce the number of sites that harbor insects and diseases over winter, pull weeds, spent annuals, and vegetables. Clean up all fallen leaves and fruit. Compost only pest-free plant debris.

☐ **DIVIDE PERENNIALS.** If blooms on perennials such as asters, bellflowers, callas, daisies, daylilies, helianthus, rudbeckia, and yarrow were smaller than normal this year and plants are weak or crowded, it's time to divide them. Dig out each clump so the rootball comes up intact. Wash or gently shake off excess soil and cut off divisions using a sharp knife, pruning shears, or shovel (for tough roots). Each division should have leaves and plenty of roots. Replant immediately.

PEST CONTROL

☐ **SNAIL CONTROL.** Cool, damp fall weather brings on a full attack of snails. To control these pesky creatures without risking the health of children and pets, use a bait containing iron phosphate, such as Sluggo (it's safe to use around edible crops). Or surround the edge of pots or raised beds with copper strips or barriers. Both are available at many nurseries or from Peaceful Valley Farm Supply (888/784-1722 or www.groworganic.com). ◆

WHAT TO DO IN YOUR GARDEN IN OCTOBER

PLANTING

☐ **BULBS.** Continue to plant spring-flowering bulbs. Choices include anemone, daffodils, Dutch iris, leucojum, ornithogalum, ranunculus, and scilla. Also look into wonderful South African bulbs such as babiana, freesia, ixia, sparaxis, and watsonia.

☐ **VEGETABLES.** Coastal, inland, and low-desert gardeners (*Sunset* climate zones 22–24, 18–21, and 13, respectively) are entering their best vegetable-growing season. Choices include beets, broccoli, brussels sprouts, cabbage, carrots, cauliflower, celery, chives, garlic, kale, kohlrabi, lettuce, onions, parsley, parsnips, peas, potatoes, radishes, spinach, Swiss chard, and turnips. Looking for something new? Try kailaan, komatsuna, misome, mitsuba, or mizuna. These and other intriguing Asian greens are available from Kitazawa Seed Company (510/595-1188 or www.kitazawaseed.com).

☐ **CHRYSANTHEMUMS.** Mums are plentiful in nurseries now and will provide color for a long period. (See "Autumn jewels," page 334, for some of the new cultivars on the market.) Choose among hundreds of varieties at the chrysanthemum specialty nursery Sunnyslope Gardens (8638 Huntington Dr., San Gabriel; 626/287-4071).

Sunset CLIMATE ZONES 1-3 7-9 11 13 14-24

☐ **SLOPE STABILIZERS.** Some of the best plants for erosion control are California natives. Their deep, dense roots are unparalleled at holding soil in place and helping to prevent mud slides. Choices include buckwheat, ceanothus, Cleveland sage, hollyleaf cherry, lemonade berry, *Ribes,* scrub oak, and toyon. Many native-plant societies host plant sales this month (check the garden calendar of your local newspaper). Or visit a native-plant specialty nursery like Las Pilitas Nursery in Escondido (760/749-5930 or www.laspilitas.com) and Santa Margarita (805/438-5992) or Tree of Life Nursery in San Juan Capistrano (949/728-0685 or www.treeoflifenursery.com).

MAINTENANCE

☐ **RECYCLE LEAVES.** Fallen leaves are humus in the making. Use them in the garden instead of throwing them out. Mow with a mulcher right where they've fallen. Or, if your mower has a bag attachment, use the chopped-up leaves as a mulch in flower beds. No mower? Put raked-up leaves in a heavy trash bag with a handful of soil and fertilizer. Moisten lightly, turn every few weeks, and by spring you'll have compost.

☐ **RESET SPRINKLERS.** Once temperatures cool, reprogram controllers for automatic watering systems. Irrigate for the same length of time as always, but increase the number of days between waterings.

☐ **CARE FOR LAWNS.** Rake out thatch buildup to improve water penetration and eliminate insect habitat, or use an aerator. Feed fescue and other cool-season turf grasses with a complete lawn fertilizer.

PEST CONTROL

☐ **PROTECT COLE CROPS.** Those little white butterflies flitting around your bok choy, cabbage, and kale are laying eggs that will turn into hungry green caterpillars. Cover your crops with row covers to keep the butterflies away. Or dust plants with *Bacillus thuringiensis* to kill young larvae. ◆

WHAT TO DO IN YOUR GARDEN IN OCTOBER

PLANTING

☐ **COMPANIONS FOR SPRING BULBS.** For a more colorful spring display, overplant spring-blooming bulbs with early-flowering perennials; the bulbs will grow up between the flowers. Good perennial choices include basket-of-gold *(Aurinia saxatilis),* common aubrieta, creeping basket-of-gold *(Alyssum montanum),* English primrose *(P. polyantha),* and wall rockcress *(Arabis caucasica).*

☐ **GARLIC.** Choose hardneck types like 'Chesnok Red'. Break bulbs into cloves; plant each clove 4 to 6 inches apart and 3 to 4 inches deep in good garden soil in a bed that receives full sun. Mulch the bed after planting. Filaree Farm (509/422 6940 or www. filareefarm.com) sells many garlic varieties, including 'Chesnok Red'.

☐ **LANDSCAPE PLANTS.** Set out hardy ground covers and container-grown trees, shrubs, and perennials no later than six weeks before the ground normally freezes in your area. From fall through winter, water the transplants often enough to keep their rootballs from drying out.

☐ **PERENNIAL TULIPS.** Most tulips are short-lived hybrids that last

Sunset
CLIMATE ZONES
☐ 1-3   ☐ 10-11

DEBRA LAMBERT

only one or two seasons. But species tulips come back for several years or longer if the bulbs are kept dry over the summer. Among the species tulips that form large colonies over time are *T. bakeri, T. batalinii, T. clusiana, T.c. chrysantha, T. greigii, T. pulchella, T. praestens,* and *T. tarda.* A good mail-order source is High Country Gardens (800/925-9387 or www. highcountrygardens.com).

MAINTENANCE

☐ **CLEAN OUT BIRDHOUSES.** Wearing rubber gloves, remove and discard nesting material from birdhouses. To help prevent the spread of avian diseases and parasites, rinse birdhouses with a solution of 1 part bleach to 10 parts water.

Allow them to dry thoroughly, then remount.

☐ **CUT BACK PERENNIALS.** After the first hard freeze, cut back perennials such as aster, campanula, daylily, phlox, and veronica, leaving 6-inch stubs above the ground.

☐ **DEAL WITH PINE NEEDLES.** In the fall, older needles on the inside of pine branches turn brown and drop off. Gardeners in fire-prone areas should rake up and discard pine needles. In other areas, needles can be left where they fall under trees to act as mulch or raked up and spread elsewhere in the garden. For a finer mulch, run needles through a chipper or shredder.

☐ **HARVEST, STORE CROPS.** Pick broccoli and brussels sprouts before a killing frost hits. Cut pumpkins and winter squash with 2-inch stems; store at 50° to 60°. Beets, carrots, potatoes, and turnips keep best at 35° to 45° in barely damp sand. Onions and shallots need cool, dry storage in mesh bags or slotted crates. Store apples and pears indoors in separate containers at 33° to 40°.

☐ **IRRIGATE.** If local water-use ordinances permit, continue to irrigate flower beds, lawns, shrubs, and trees when the soil is dry 2 to 3 inches beneath the surface.

☐ **MULCH FOR WINTER.** After a hard freeze, spread 2 to 3 inches of compost, weed-free straw, or other organic matter to protect bulbs, perennial flowers, strawberries, and vegetables. — *M. T.* ◆

Coping with drought in Colorado

Due to severe drought conditions that persist in Colorado, the Denver Water Board and some other local water utilities recently imposed a total ban on lawn watering, effective October 1 (2002).

Lawns of Kentucky bluegrass, buffalo grass, and tall fescue go dormant in winter and can survive without irrigation for many months. To protect dormant lawns in areas where watering is banned, limit foot traffic and do *not* fertilize, dethatch, or aerate the grass. For more turf management tips from Colorado State University Cooperative Extension, go to www.colostate.edu/Depts/CoopExt/4DMG/Lawns/drought1.htm

WHAT TO DO IN YOUR GARDEN IN OCTOBER

PLANTING

☐ **COOL-SEASON FLOWERS.** *Sunset* climate zones 1A–3B (Flagstaff, Taos, Santa Fe): Set out transplants of chrysanthemum, dianthus, forget-me-not, Iceland poppy, Shirley poppy, and sweet alyssum. Zones 10–13 (Albuquerque, Las Vegas, Tucson, Phoenix): For winter color, set out transplants of calendula, pansy, petunia, poppy, scabiosa, and snapdragon. For blooms in late winter and early spring, sow seeds of 'Dwarf Double Mixed' nasturtiums and 'Cuthbertson Multiflora Mixed' sweet peas from Roswell Seed Company (505/622-7701).

☐ **LANDSCAPE PLANTS.** Zones 1A–3B: Consider long-lived dwarf coralberry (*Symphoricarpos* x *chenaultii* 'Hancock') with bronze and green foliage, pink flowers, and purplish-red fruit. Or plant redtwig dogwood (*Cornus stolonifera*) to enjoy its bright red bark and clusters of white flowers. For color and fragrance, plant common or French lilac (*Syringa vulgaris*) or Asian hybrids (*S. hyacinthiflora*). Zones 10–13: All types of hardy ground covers, shrubs, trees, and vines develop strong root systems and thrive when planted this month.

☐ **SPRING-BLOOMING BULBS.** Zones 1A–3B: Plant allium, crocus, daffodil, galanthus, hyacinth, summer snowflake (*Leucojum aestivum*), and tulip. Zones 10–11: In addition to the above, plant freesia,

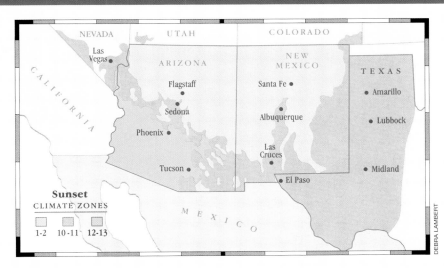

galtonia, iris, and ranunculus. Zones 12–13: Set out amaryllis, grape hyacinth, iris, oxalis, tulip, and watsonia.

☐ **VEGETABLES.** All zones: Separate garlic cloves from "mother" bulbs and cover each clove with 1 to 2 inches of soil in mild-winter climates, 3 to 4 inches in areas where ground freezes. A good garlic source is Filaree Farm (509/422-6940 or www.filareefarm.com). Zones 10–13: Sow seeds of beets, bok choy, carrots, kohlrabi, peas, radishes, salad greens, Swiss chard, and turnips. Set out transplants of broccoli, brussels sprouts, cabbage, cauliflower, and onion.

☐ **WILDFLOWERS.** Zones 10–13: Sow wildflowers in sunny areas. Lightly rake the soil and remove weeds, then scatter the seeds of single species or mixtures. Keep the soil moist until the seeds sprout, then reduce irrigation.

MAINTENANCE

☐ **CONTROL EROSION.** Drought and wildfires have left many properties vulnerable to soil erosion. To hold soil in place in zones 1A–3B, install drought-tolerant plants with dense root systems such as common snowberry (*Symphoricarpos albus*), creeping mahonia (*M. repens*), juniper, and wild lilac (*Ceanothus* species); in zones 10–13, use bull grass (*Muhlenbergia emersleyi*), juniper, *Mahonia trifoliolata*, and rosemary.

☐ **CUT BACK ON WATER.** As temperatures cool, reduce watering frequency. — *Kim Nelson* ◆

Japanese barberry

Japanese maple

Chinese witch hazel

Pieris japonica 'Variegata'

Lamb's ears

Aster

MARK TURNER

MARION BRENNER

ALLAN MANDELL (3)

color your garden for fall

Mix shrubs, trees, and perennials in rich autumn hues

■ At nurseries during early fall, plants like butter yellow maidenhair tree can have more visual impact than rows of annuals. Browse on a chilly morning and you'll find dazzling combinations on every scale to bring late-season color to your garden: witch hazel with *Camellia sasanqua; Sedum* 'Autumn Joy' beside *Rudbeckia fulgida sullivantii* 'Goldsturm' or purple fountain grass; or the pas de deux of burgundy smoke tree and *Muhlenbergia capillaris* 'Regal Mist'.

All it takes to bring fall color to a corner of your garden is a few flame-foliaged shrubs, some late-season perennials, and perhaps a small-scale deciduous tree with gold or bronze red leaves. This month is the best time to buy them: most are wearing a crown of fall leaves or flowers, so you can choose plants for the colors you want. And there's no better time to plant—cooler days, longer nights, and increasing rainfall help plants become established with little extra input from you. By spring, they'll be ready to charge into the new season with vigorous growth supported by the roots they put down during the winter. Then they'll grace your landscape with gorgeous hues for many autumns to come.

Our lists will help you get started; they highlight some of the best fall color-makers. Visit our website for a helpful chart (www.sunset.com/garden/colorchart.html). Take our suggestions to a nursery, grab a wagon, and start matching plants.

By Sharon Cohoon and Jim McCausland

SAXON HOLT (2)

Drifts of bronze *Sedum* 'Autumn Joy' and lavender Russian sage color an otherwise neutral palette of ornamental grasses in this garden corner.

ABOVE: Reddish bronze Japanese maple (*Acer palmatum* 'Atropurpureum') pairs with flaming red *Euonymus alatus* 'Compacta' for a glowing combo in the wide border. A low, deep green Bird's nest spruce (*Picea abies* 'Nidiformis') grows between them. RIGHT: A maple drops its buttery yellow leaves like snow.

start with a
tree

FOR FOLIAGE
- Chinese pistache *(Pistacia chinensis)*
- Crape myrtle *(Lagerstroemia)*
- Eastern redbud *(Cercis canadensis)*
- Japanese maple *(Acer palmatum)*
- Maidenhair tree *(Ginkgo biloba)*
- Paperbark maple *(Acer griseum)*
- Persian parrotia *(P. persica)*
- Smoke tree *(Cotinus)*

FOR FRUIT
- Flowering crabapple *(Malus)*
- Hawthorn *(Crataegus)*
- Japanese persimmon *(Diospyros kaki)*
- Mountain ash *(Sorbus)*
- Pomegranate

ABOVE: Oakleaf hydrangea, in shades of bronze to brilliant crimson, smolders beside eulalia grass *(Miscanthus sinensis)* and orange smokebush *(Cotinus).* LEFT: Silvery lamb's ears and lime green spiraea brighten brownish 'Rose Glow' Japanese barberry. BOTTOM LEFT: Sumacs *(Rhus glabra,* foreground, and *R. typhina)* show off their brilliant fall hues.

add a few
shrubs

FOR FOLIAGE
- *Enkianthus campanulatus*
- Fothergilla
- Heavenly bamboo *(Nandina domestica)*
- Oakleaf hydrangea *(H. quercifolia)*
- Winged euonymus *(E. alatus)*
- Witch hazel *(Hamamelis × intermedia)*

FOR FRUIT
- Cotoneaster
- European cranberry bush *(Viburnum opulus)*
- Pyracantha
- Toyon *(Heteromeles arbutifolia)*

FOR FLOWERS
- Camellia *(C. sasanqua)*

finish with

perennials

and

grasses

- **Florists' chrysanthemum** (*Chrysanthemum x morifolium*)
- **Gaillardia** (*G. x grandiflora*)
- **Gloriosa daisy** (*Rudbeckia hirta*)
- **Golden fleece** (*Thymophylla tenuiloba*)
- **Goldenrod** (*Solidago*)
- **Japanese anemone** (*A. japonica*)
- **Mountain sage** (*Salvia regla*)
- **Pineapple sage** (*Salvia elegans*)
- *Salvia* 'Indigo Spires'
- *Sedum* 'Autumn Joy'
- **Sneezeweed** (*Helenium*)
- **Sunflower** (*Helianthus annus*)

FOR FOLIAGE AND SEED HEADS

- **Muhly** (*Muhlenbergia*): *M. capillaris* 'Regal Mist'; *M. lindheimeri* 'Autumn Glow'
- **Sedge** (*Carex*): *C. buchananii*; *C. comans* 'Bronze'; *C. flagellifera* 'Toffee Twist' ◆

To perfect your color scheme, play with plant combinations on a nursery cart. The sunny combo pictured above includes purple Mexican bush sage, yellow *Tagetes lemmonii,* and verbena with small purple flowers— shown in 1- and 2-gallon cans. Fill in with smaller plants, like *Carex* 'Frosted Curls', from 4-inch pots. Once planted, the sage and tagetes grow rapidly, mingling together as shown at right, and bloom into late fall in mild climates.

STEVEN GUNTHER (2)

Great ideas for your garden

Conversation areas are good places for conversation pieces. Here, beside the trellis, are metal sculptures and an elaborate birdhouse.

Old objects can acquire new uses. Davis is a skilled recycler. The trick is to look for objects that can be adapted to new contexts. She discovered a pumphouse at a yard sale and turned it into a colorful garden shed. A column jutting from one of the berms near the pool's end (shown left) was a drainage "second" from a local concrete dealer.

Color can unify a landscape. One visual theme unites this space— purple. "It's a soothing color for gardens," explains Davis. One of her largest berms is covered with catmint *(Nepeta* x *faassenii),* which has soft purple flowers and also makes a seductive place for her four cats to loll.

Backyard art park

An artist turns her garden into a sculpture gallery

By Peter O. Whiteley

Photographs by Saxon Holt

A pair of sling chairs—each with its own freestanding frame—creates a relaxing oasis for swinging into a laid-back conversation. The lavender color theme unites the pool chairs, blossoms, and ball. Steel silhouettes of ravens stand near a new "ruin wall."

'W' e set it up like a city park," says artist Ginny Davis of her ever-changing backyard in Napa, California. The rectangular half-acre is divided into free-form zones: an open grassy area for groups and playing, intimate sitting areas for midday relaxing, sheltered places for enjoying a meal, and a pool for swimming laps. Davis's studio opens directly to this landscape through sliding doors. Indeed, the garden is a kind of outdoor gallery showcasing her metal and kinetic sculptures and collections of found objects. She uses the garden to show clients how works of art can blend into natural settings.

Davis and her husband, Tom, have been designing, adding to, and re-building the garden for 13 years. Now berms, rock walls, masses of plants, serpentine pathways, three arbors, a dining pavilion, and a colorful garden shed provide the backdrops for her collection.

The garden had a head start on the sculptures, which began to appear after Davis took metalworking classes at a local community college. Her pieces are usually cut from big sheets of steel with a plasma torch. She draws inspiration from everyday experiences; for example, the 3-foot-tall ravens dotting the lawn are modeled on real ones that cawed rudely at Davis when she swam laps early one morning.

DESIGN: Ginny Davis (www.metalgardenart.com) ◆

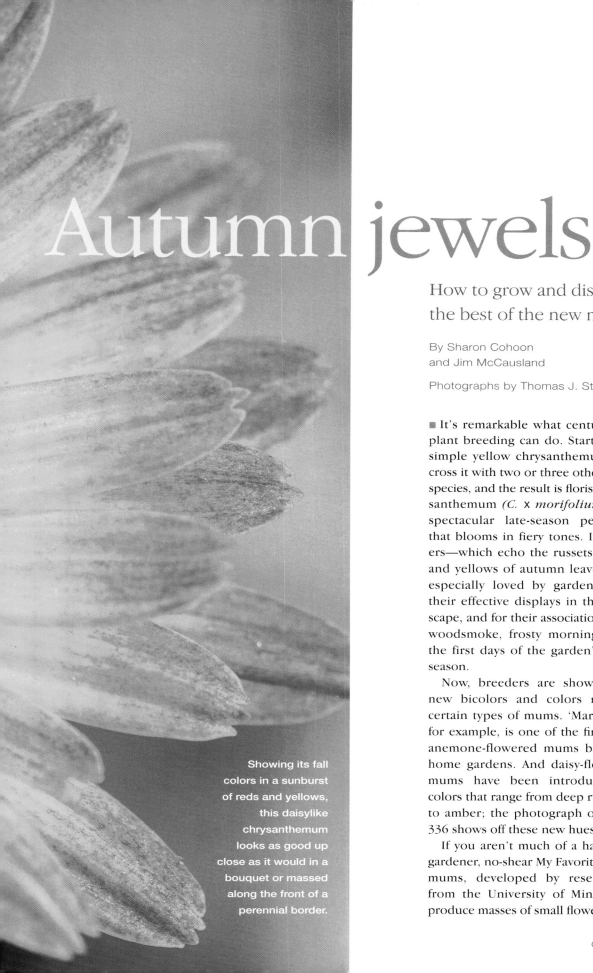

Autumn jewels

How to grow and display the best of the new mums

By Sharon Cohoon
and Jim McCausland

Photographs by Thomas J. Story

■ It's remarkable what centuries of plant breeding can do. Start with a simple yellow chrysanthemum and cross it with two or three other Asian species, and the result is florists' chrysanthemum *(C.* x *morifolium),* the spectacular late-season perennial that blooms in fiery tones. Its flowers—which echo the russets, golds, and yellows of autumn leaves—are especially loved by gardeners for their effective displays in the landscape, and for their associations with woodsmoke, frosty mornings, and the first days of the garden's quiet season.

Now, breeders are showing off new bicolors and colors new to certain types of mums. 'Mary-Jane', for example, is one of the first pink anemone-flowered mums bred for home gardens. And daisy-flowered mums have been introduced in colors that range from deep ruby red to amber; the photograph on page 336 shows off these new hues.

If you aren't much of a hands-on gardener, no-shear My Favorite series mums, developed by researchers from the University of Minnesota, produce masses of small flowers over

Showing its fall colors in a sunburst of reds and yellows, this daisylike chrysanthemum looks as good up close as it would in a bouquet or massed along the front of a perennial border.

a long season. These compact plants need cutting back only once, after fall bloom. They include Autumn Red, Yellow Quill, Twilight Pink, White, and Coral.

Beautiful as they are, florists' mums are also versatile. You can mass them in big pots or in garden beds, or combine them with shrubs or perennials. Some combinations are pictured on the facing page.

Are florists' mums just for florists?

Florists' chrysanthemums come in two types: garden mums, which are bred for the perennial border, and pot mums, which are bred for forcing as gift plants.

Unfortunately, most nursery labels don't tell you which are which. (There are hints, however: Yoder Brothers, the country's largest mum producer, gives garden mums women's names and gives pot mums the names of towns and cities.) The chart at right outlines the differences.

Garden mums take to the perennial border like a fish to water. Buy them in bloom, and plant them in full sun (light afternoon shade in hot climates). They like rich, well-drained soil and protection from dry, cold winter winds.

Pot mums, which are sold all year, ultimately take the same growing conditions. But since they must endure the stress of forced bloom and off-season transplanting, they need special handling to make the transition from hothouse to garden. Put them in a bright place indoors for no more than two weeks after you get them, watering as needed. Then move them to a protected place outdoors that gets filtered sun and no

	GARDEN MUMS	POT MUMS
▪ Leaves	smaller	larger
▪ Flowers	more, smaller	fewer, larger
▪ Height	12–16 inches	15–18 inches
▪ Natural bloom season	mid-August to mid-October	mid-October to late November

New mums offer a smorgasbord of delightful colors, shapes, and petal counts. That's 'Vicki' top left and 'Sweet Stacy' below it. Garden mums pictured at right (clockwise from top left) are 'Vanessa', 'Sweet Stacy', 'Bold Felicia', 'Donna', 'Cecilia', 'Helen', 'Stephanie', 'Olivia', and (center) 'Natasha'.

frost, for two weeks. Finally, cut the plants back by about two-thirds and transplant them into the garden.

If you live in a cold-winter climate and buy a pot mum in late summer or in fall or winter, cut it back after blooms have faded and keep it in a cool room or greenhouse until spring. Then transplant it into the garden.

Where to buy chrysanthemums

Since chrysanthemums are among the most widely sold perennials, they are easy to find in bloom almost anywhere this month. But if you want your pick of a broad range of flower and plant forms, try a specialist. Sunnyslope Gardens (8638 Huntington Dr., San Gabriel, CA; 626/287-4071) is a fine retail supplier that's been around for years.

To order by mail, check out King's Mums (209/759-3571 or www.kingsmums.com). Though they ship only from March through June, they have an open house at their facility in Clements, California (near Lodi) in October and November.

Mum care calendar

Spring, summer

WATER

Apply it often enough that the soil never dries out completely ½ inch below the surface.

FERTILIZE

In garden beds. When new growth emerges in spring, apply complete fertilizer (14-14-14 controlled-release fertilizer is a good choice). Feed again in late spring and again in mid-July. When the first flower buds show color, apply low-nitrogen plant food (like fish fertilizer).

In containers. If you're growing chrysanthemums as container plants, start with a dose of controlled-release fertilizer, then feed weekly with liquid fertilizer until buds show color.

PINCH

When new growth first reaches about 5 inches tall, pinch or shear off the top inch of foliage. Three weeks after first shearing, again cut off the top inch of new growth. For taller varieties, pinch back twice more, for a total of four times.

Pinching or shearing new growth forces the plant to branch where you cut it and to build up a strong under-carriage that supports heavier top growth later in the season. Plus, sheared plants produce more, smaller blooms, compared to un-sheared ones, so make a greater impact in the garden.

Yellow 'Donna' mingles with variegated sage and lemon thyme (top), while orange clumps of 'Olivia' line a dry creek bed (bottom) along with 'Aurea' Japanese barberry.

Late fall

CUT BACK PLANTS

Few plants respond better to the human touch than chrysanthemums. In late autumn after bloom, cut off chrysanthemums about 6 inches above the ground. This tidies them up for winter and makes it easier to spot new growth in spring. However, if you live in a climate with winters marked by regular hard freezes, you can improve your mums' winter survival by cutting off tops after new growth begins in spring.

If you're growing one of the new no-shear My Favorite se-ries mums, cut back the plant only once, after fall bloom. ◆

Hedges you can bet on

Formal or informal, evergreen or deciduous,
let a hedge work for you

By Steven R. Lorton

Closely spaced shrubs of *Solanum rantonnetii* form a seamless hedge cloaked with violet flowers. Regular pruning stimulates more bloom, keeps hedges neat.

Whether sheared for a formal look or allowed to grow naturally, a hedge is one of the hardest-working elements in the landscape.

A low hedge can frame a flower bed or mark a corridor to your front door, while a tall one can create a privacy screen or form "green walls" that divide your garden into separate rooms.

October is an excellent month to plant a hedge. Deciduous shrubs and trees and many evergreens are going into dormancy, and cool, often moist weather is ahead. Plants have the winter and spring to get established before summer heat hits.

Informal hedges require little pruning. Formal hedges need pruning at least once a growing season, in midsummer. More fastidious gardeners prune twice, in early spring and again in midsummer.

Planting tips

Dig a hole at least twice as wide as the nursery container and deep enough so the top of the rootball will be level with the surrounding soil.

Space plants so they will be slightly past the point of touching when they reach their ultimate width. A good rule of thumb: Set plants at a distance equal to two-thirds of their mature width—2-foot intervals for plants that spread to 3 feet, for example.) Mulch their root zones with 2 to 4 inches of organic matter. Irrigate regularly until they are well rooted.

How to prune a formal hedge

Boxwood, privet, and yew are classic plants for formal hedges. While it is tempting to trim these, or any other, hedges so their sides are perfectly vertical, that practice leads to ever-sparser growth lower down. Instead, shear the hedge at an angle so that the top is slightly narrower than the bottom. That way, sunlight and rain can reach the entire surface of the hedge, encouraging healthy, even growth.

Choice plants for hedges

These plants have evergreen foliage unless noted.

Framing a bed, this two-tone hedge is composed of Japanese boxwood (front left) and wall germander (*Teucrium chamaedrys*). BELOW: Hop bush provides informal screening for a yard on a busy street.

Low to midsize
(4 to 12 feet tall, unless sheared shorter)

Boxwood (*Buxus* species). English boxwood (*B. semper-virens*) has glossy oval leaves about the size of a fingertip. *Sunset* climate zones 3B–6, 15–17 from the *Western Garden Book*.

Japanese boxwood (*B. micro-phylla japonica*) has small, rounded leaves that are bright green in summer, turning bronzy in cold winters. Zones 3B–24.

Citrus. Lemon trees, when closely spaced (8 to 10 feet for standard-size plants, 3 to 4 feet for dwarfs), can be trained into hedges. Zones 8, 9, 12–24, H1, H2.

Holly (*Ilex* species). English holly (*I. aquifolium*) comes in many varieties. Most have prickly, dark green leaves; some female plants produce red berries. Zones 4–9, 14–17, H1.

Japanese holly (*I. crenata*) has glossy leaves resembling boxwood. Zones 3–9, 14–24.

Indian hawthorn (*Rhaphiolepis indica*). Glossy dark green leaves; flowers in white or shades of pink appear from late fall to late spring. Zones 8–10, 12–24, H1, H2 (worth a risk in zones 4–7).

Mexican orange (*Choisya ternata*). Apple green foliage; fragrant white flowers appear in early spring. Makes a loose, informal hedge. Zones 4–9, 14–24.

Mirror plant (*Coprosma repens* 'Pink Splendor'). Glossy green leaves with pink shading and yellow margins. Zones 14–24, H1.

Natal plum (*Carissa macrocarpa*). Glossy green leaves; red or purple fruits and fragrant white pinwheel blooms often appear together. Thorny. Zones 22–24, H2.

Privet (*Ligustrum* species). California privet (*L. ovalifolium*) has dark green leaves. Semiever-green. Zones 3B–24, H1, H2.

Japanese privet (*L. japonicum*) has oval leaves that are deep green above, pale beneath. Zones 4–24, H1, H2.

Pyracantha (species and hybrids). Glossy green leaves; orange or red berries in fall. Thorny. Zones vary.

Rosemary (*Rosmarinus officinalis*). Aromatic dark green leaves resemble conifer needles. Upright varieties like 'Tuscan Blue' are best for hedges. Zones 4–24, H1, H2.

Solanum rantonnetii. Bright green oval leaves; violet blue flowers. Needs regular pruning. Zones 12, 13, 15–24, H1.

Yew (*Taxus* x *media* 'Brownii'). Dark green, needlelike leaves. Zones 2–6, 14–17.

Tall screens
(to 20 feet or more)

Beech (*Fagus* species). Glossy dark green leaves in summer. Deciduous. Zones vary.

Canada hemlock (*Tsuga canadensis*). Green needles. Makes an outstanding clipped hedge. Zones A3, 2–7, 17.

Hawthorn (*Crataegus monogyna*). Deeply lobed, glossy dark green leaves; fragrant white flowers in spring followed by dark red fruit. Plant 5 feet apart for dense screen. Thorny. Deciduous. Zones 1–12, 14–17.

Hedge maple (*Acer campestre*). Lobed leaves are dull green above, downy beneath. *A. c.* 'Queen Elizabeth' has glossier foliage and more erect habit. Deciduous. Zones 2–9, 14–17.

Hop bush (*Dodonaea viscosa*). Willowlike green leaves; showy seed capsules in late spring or summer. *D. v.* 'Purpurea' has bronzy foliage that turns purplish in winter. Fast-growing informal hedge. Zones 7–24, H1, H2.

Leyland cypress (x *Cupres-socyparis leylandii*). Flat sprays of foliage in shades of bright green, gray green, and grayish blue, depending on variety and season. Zones 3B–24.

Mahonia **species.** Spiny-edged, glossy leaflets are medium to dark green. Use as an informal hedge. Zones vary.

Myrtle (*Myrtus communis*). Glossy bright green leaves. Zones 8–24, H1, H2.

Nerium oleander. Dark green foliage resembles olive leaves; flowers in shades of red, pink, yellow, and white appear late spring to fall. All parts are poisonous. Zones 8–16, 18–24, H1, H2.

Pacific wax myrtle (*Myrica californica*). Tooth-edged leaves are glossy dark green above, paler beneath. Zones 4–9, 14–24

Victorian box (*Pittosporum undulatum*). Wavy-edged, glossy green leaves; fragrant white flowers in spring. Zones 14 and 15 (with protection), 16, 17, 21–24, H1, H2. ◆

Pansies put on fresh faces

Gorgeous new colors and patterns will make your garden smile

By Lauren Bonar Swezey • Photographs by E. Spencer Toy

Like clothing designers, flower breeders respond to changing fashions. In recent years, pansies *(Viola* x *wittrockiana)*—the West's top-selling cool-season annual—have been the subject of intensive breeding efforts.

"There have been huge strides in pansy breeding, with a lot of focus on color," says Steve Jones of Bodger Seeds in South El Monte, California. Solid, deep-colored flowers are giving way to unusual multicolor blends and pastels. Some plants even yield differ-

ent shades of the same color, due to genetic variation.

"Breeders used to throw away pansies with 'color breaks' [patterns of color] that would show up in plant trials for solid-colored flowers," says John Nelson of Sakata Seeds in Morgan Hill, California. "Now they're using these pansies to create new multicolored flowers, such as those found in Ultima Impression."

Lately, there's also been a big emphasis on mixes—combinations of closely related but differently

Meet the new pansies (clockwise from top left): Maxim Bronze, Ultima Beacon Yellow, Ultima Baron Mahogany, Maxim Sunset, Jack-O'-Lantern (black), and Jack-O'-Lantern (orange).

colored types. They range from the soft pastels of Silhouette Supreme to a Halloweenish black-and-orange mix called Jack-O'-Lantern.

Behind the scenes, breeders have been developing pansies that are more floriferous, focusing on plants that produce a more abundant

Pick a winner

Pansies come in a wide variety of single or multiple colors with or without faces (blushes of contrasting color in the center of the bloom). Use them in borders with other cool-season annuals, in containers and window boxes, and as fillers between perennials and shrubs. We note some of our favorite colors in parentheses below.

Multiflora (sometimes called superflora). Their small flowers are about 1 to 2 inches wide. Multifloras are bred to branch more and develop more blooms per plant than typical large-flowered types. They also bloom over a long season and tend to be more cold-hardy than larger pansies. Two of the best series are Nature and Universal Plus (Citrus, Mariner, Rhapsody mixes).

Medium-flowered types. Their flowers reach 2 to 3 inches wide. Some of the best for long bloom and weather resistance are Accord/Banner ('Red Wing'; Daffodil and Passion mixes), Crystal Bowl Supreme (Pink Shades), Iona ('Frosty Lemon'), Maxim Supreme (Marina), Panola (Autumn Blaze mix, Pink Shades), Ultima (Lavender Shades; 'Scarlet & Yellow'), Ultima Beacon (Bronze, Yellow), Ultima Impression, Ultima Morpho (2002 All-America Selections winner), and Ultima Silhouette Supreme mix.

Large-flowered types. These blooms reach 3 to 5 inches wide. The newest series are more floriferous and bloom longer than older issues. Some of the best are Atlas (Jack-O'-Lantern, Meadow, and Windjammer mixes), Dynamite ('Purple Rose and White'), and Majestic Giant II.

Pretty pansies shown above are (clockwise from top left) Atlas Windjammer (purple), Maxim, Ultima Impression Rose Shades, and Atlas Windjammer (white).

show of 1- to 3-inch-wide flowers rather than fewer but larger blooms. These recent introductions also have bushier, less floppy habits and more vigorous root systems. In addition, the plants are more tolerant of heat and generally are hardy to the low 20s (if not mulched) or even 0° (when mulched or covered with snow).

Thanks to one of the most significant breeding breakthroughs, most newer pansies can continue blooming during the short days of winter.

Planting and care

Pansies are widely sold in sixpacks and 4-inch pots. You can also start them from seed, but you need to sow the seeds six to eight weeks before you plan to set out plants. In mild climates, plant in fall for winter-to-spring (or longer) bloom. In the Pacific Northwest, plant pansies by October or wait until spring. In cold-winter climates, wait until spring (or plant next August for overwintering).

Site selection. In mild climates, choose a site that gets full to partial sun or bright, filtered light. In hot, inland climates, plant in partial shade. To avoid foliage diseases, plant pansies where they'll get good air circulation.

Soil. Set out plants in well-drained soil amended with plenty of compost. If desired, mix in a controlled-release fertilizer.

Watering. Keep the soil moist but not soggy.

Pest control. Bait for snails and slugs at the first sign of damage.

Maintenance. Remove spent flowers regularly to keep blooms coming. Apply a balanced fertilizer in spring to give plants a boost. ◆

BOB WIGAND

THIS GARDEN IN VISTA, CALIFORNIA, is a sanctuary for a variety of creatures, winged and wild. For tips on creating a wildlife habitat in your own landscape, see pages 362–365.

November

Cherry red
heath and
pink heather
bloom around
a bench.

ROBIN CUSHMAN

A heavenly hillside alcove

Heath and heather wrap a bench with flowers and foliage

■ Fall-blooming heather and its close cousin, heath, form a living tapestry around this semicircular bench at the base of a hill in Oregon. Mark and Val Bloom created this contemplative nook at their home above their nursery, Bloom River Gardens, overlooking the McKenzie River Valley. "It's a restful spot to sit with a cup of tea," says Val Bloom.

Mark Bloom built the base of the 6-foot-wide bench with bricks collected from an old farmhouse chimney. Basalt rocks joined with mortar form the seat and back. The bench also functions as a retaining wall.

Around the back of the bench is *Erica vagans* 'Mrs. D. F. Maxwell', a Cornish heath whose cherry red flowers appear for six weeks starting in September. Blooming among the heath plants is *Calluna vulgaris* 'County Wicklow', a Scotch heather with double pink blossoms that open from white buds. At front right, the green foliage of *C. v.* 'St. Nick' will be covered with lavender flowers in December.

The Blooms planted the heath and heather from 1-gallon containers, spacing them 36 inches apart in soil amended with river loam and plenty of compost; they grew into a seamless quilt in three years. After flowering, the plants are lightly sheared to maintain compact growth and encourage next year's bloom. — *Mary-Kate Mackey*

Growing herbs in northern climes

■ When it comes to culinary herbs, gardeners in the West's intermountain regions face a basic challenge: how to grow them successfully where summers are short and winters are cold. Canadian writers Ernest Small and Grace Deutsch have addressed this challenge head-on in *Culinary Herbs for Short-Season Gardeners* (Mountain Press Publishing Company, Missoula, MT, 2002; $20; 800/234-5308 or www.mountain-press.com). Small and Deutsch describe more than 50 species of herbs, with extensive notes on their cultivation, harvest, culinary or medicinal uses, and health cautions (if any). Besides standards like basil and oregano (shown at left), the authors discuss less commonly grown ones, such as lovage and sweet cicely.

The 182-page paperback is illustrated with botanic drawings and sprinkled with herbal trivia, such as "The ancient Romans believed dill had fortifying properties, so they applied it liberally to food given to gladiators."

On the practical side, Small and Deutsch offer valuable advice. For example, they suggest selecting a site with southern or southeastern exposure, preferably in front of a house or garden wall, and planting in raised beds, where the soil warms up more quickly in spring than soil in ground-level beds, giving seedlings a head start. — *Dick Bushnell*

ILLUSTRATION: MOUNTAIN PRESS PUBLISHING

Waterwise tactics for the winter garden

As winter approaches, many communities in Colorado continue to experience drought conditions that have stressed plants and led to outdoor watering restrictions. Wherever you live, here's what you can do to help your plants make it through the cold, dry weather.

- **Irrigate landscape plants where allowed.** If local water-use ordinances permit, continue to deep-water your valuable trees and shrubs. Set a sprinkler under the drip line of trees and apply enough water to soak the soil 1 foot deep (use a trowel or screwdriver to check). Or use a bubbler attachment on the hose, moving it as needed.

- **Mulch with organic matter.** To help conserve soil moisture, spread a 3- to 4-inch layer of organic matter over bulb beds, around perennials, and under trees and shrubs. Shredded leaves, pine needles, hay, and straw all work well as winter mulch. Keep mulch 12 inches away from the base of trees and shrubs.

- **Mulch with snow.** In addition to insulating roots from subfreezing cold, snow helps replenish soil moisture as it melts. When snow accumulates, shovel it off driveways and sidewalks and pile it onto perennial beds, around roses, and beneath trees and shrubs. If you've already spread organic mulch, pile the snow on top.

- **Spray evergreens with antitranspirant.** Dwarf conifers and broadleaf evergreens such as holly and rhododendrons are susceptible to dehydration and windburn in winter. To protect them, spray the foliage with an antitranspirant product like Wilt-Pruf, following label instructions. — *Marcia Tatroe*

ANNE COWLEY

Encore for a shed

Potting with pizzazz

■ *Editor's note: We couldn't resist sharing this letter from a Canadian reader.*

In the June 2000 issue, you ran an article entitled "Potting with Pizzazz," which showed a wonderful potting shed [right]. When my husband, David Hartwick, asked me what I would like for my birthday, I said a garden shed like the one in your picture. He rolled his eyes and I thought that was the end of it. This summer he amazed me by building the potting shed shown in my enclosed photo [above]. — *Anne Cowley, Victoria, B.C.*

For more on Sunset's cottage-style shed, visit www.sunset.com/garden/pottingshed.html

THOMAS J. STORY (2)

Natives to the rescue

■ Three years ago, a Corona Heights neighborhood group asked landscape architect Richard Wogisch and his partner Bassam Salameh to care for a slice of public land at Levant and States Streets in San Francisco. Weeds and blackberries had been removed, but most of the plants that replaced them were not thriving because irrigation was sparse.

"I saw this as an opportunity to display gardenworthy natives," says Wogisch, a native-plant enthusiast.

Just before the rainy season of 1999, Wogisch and Salameh planted the area. On the upper slope, they used blue-eyed grass, bush anemone, California fescue, Catalina ironwood, checkerbloom, coast live oak, Pacific Coast iris, purple needle grass, and tufted hair grass. To keep these plants thriving, they installed an irrigation system.

The lower slope, which survives on winter rainfall alone, is planted with *Arctostaphylos,* Cleveland sage, *Ceanothus* 'Dark Star', flannel bush, California fuchsia, and California poppy. Wogisch and Salameh cut back seed heads in early summer and trim plants in winter.

The once-neglected area is now a beautiful tapestry of colorful native plants—and is the hit of the neighborhood.

— *Lauren Bonar Swezey*

Euphorbia and friends in Menlo Park

■ It's a dazzling combo—purplish blue Dutch iris growing in front of pillowy lime-colored *Euphorbia characias wulfenii.* And it stops passersby in their tracks when bloom peaks in spring at *Sunset's* headquarters in Menlo Park.

"The colors play off each other really well," says head gardener Rick LaFrentz. "The combination is a real showstopper."

LaFrentz planted the row of evergreen euphorbia, which grows to about 3½ feet, several years ago in a spot that gets full sun. He spaced plants 18 inches apart. Fairly drought-tolerant and easy to maintain, they provide a year-round backdrop for a changing cast of seasonal flowers.

Each fall, he plants a

mass of Dutch iris bulbs (he likes 'Blue Ribbon') about a foot in front of the euphorbia in well-tilled soil. They grow to 18 inches. He waters them at least weekly until the winter rains come.

The plants bloom together briefly in spring (the euphorbia continues blooming for another 4 to 6 weeks after the iris is finished). LaFrentz clips spent blooms from the iris but leaves the foliage to dry naturally, which helps bulbs store nutrients for the next year's show. He prunes back spent euphorbia to where new growth emerges at the base.

For summer color, he plants *Nemesia caerulea* 'Blue Bird', purple statice, and 'Profusion Orange' zinnias. — *Julie Chai*

NORM PLATE

Unmown, red fescue is an easy-care ground cover that tolerates some shade.

Waves of grass

Creeping red fescue makes a meadow in Palo Alto

■ Jenny and Toby Gottheiner may live in suburban Palo Alto, but nothing about the garden behind their house is typical of suburbia. Instead of the usual lawn surrounded by flower beds, Jenny—an avid gardener from South Africa—wanted something more natural and free-flowing. So she hired landscape architect Bob Cleaver of Lafayette to design a garden that uses traditional elements in an untraditional way.

In place of a turf lawn, Cleaver planted a meadow of native creeping red fescue *(Festuca rubra)* behind a seat wall made of stone from a quarry in Napa County (visible just behind the grass at far right in the photo). The low-maintenance grass adds contours to the flat lot, says Cleaver. In spring, naturalized yellow trumpet daffodils

pop up around the meadow's edges. In keeping with the garden's casual theme, the outdoor dining area is paved with decomposed granite.

Surrounding the meadow and patio are native Californian and Mediterranean-climate trees, shrubs, and ground covers, most of which need little water.

Richard Sullivan of Enchanting Planting, Orinda, worked with Cleaver to create a plant palette. In beds throughout the garden, they combined ceanothus, miscanthus, native coral bells, 'Apricot Queen' New Zealand flax, *Phlomis*, roses, and silver spear. *Teucrium cossonii majoricum* and *Euphorbia myrsinites* sprawl at the base of the seat wall.

"The garden is a study in color, texture, and form," says Cleaver. — *L.B.S.*

MIKEL COVEY (2)

Paradise under glass in Salt Lake City

■ In 1975, with only $1,000, Lorraine Miller opened a tiny plant shop in Salt Lake City. Plunging into a horticultural career represented a major shift for Miller, who holds a degree in history and once worked as a medical technician. But cultivating cactus to sell seemed like a good idea, since they weren't widely available in northern Utah at that time. Eventually, her investment grew into Cactus & Tropicals, a complex of nine greenhouses that contains a balmy slice of paradise at the foot of the Wasatch Mountains.

Today, visitors can find cactus ranging in price from $2 to $2,000, and in size from specimens of *Frailea* no bigger than a thumb to a 40-inch-diameter golden barrel cactus that's 100 years old. Miller also offers a variety of tropical plants, including bromeliads, bougainvillea, citrus, hibiscus, and orchids. For the less adventurous, there is a selection of low-maintenance houseplants such as ficus and pothos.

Outside the greenhouses, hardy perennials, native trees, and shrubs are displayed and sold during summer.

By mid-November, Miller and her staff plant more than 6,000 amaryllis and paper white narcissus bulbs in terra-cotta pots decorated with moss, ribbons, and small ornaments. A shop sells gifts with a garden motif, including candles, patio lights, and picture frames. In December, parents roam the outdoor lot looking for Christmas trees, both living and cut, while their children roast marshmallows.

9–7 Mon–Fri, 9–6 Sat, 11–5 Sun. 2735 South 2000 East; (801) 485-2542 or www.cactusandtropicals.com.

— *Hilary Groutage Smith*

A new garden shop sprouts in Phoenix

■ When Poppybox Gardens opened its store in Phoenix earlier this year, manager Michael Olesen says he had one goal in mind: "We wanted people to feel like they can grow anything."

The 18,000-square-foot store has an airy floor plan with tabletop and wall displays designed around specific themes. On one table, for example, you'll find potted herbs, herb seeds, and books about herbs. Other tables offer similar setups featuring ivy, orchids, glass vases, and more. Pots are organized by type and color, making it easy to match plants with the perfect container. Bird feeders, garden tools, and organic fertilizers and potting soil are also stocked.

More than half of the space is devoted to an outdoor nursery that stocks a range of annuals, perennials, ground covers, succulents, shrubs, and small trees suitable for the low desert. The store offers a lifetime money-back guarantee on all plants.

As part of the store's commitment to cultivating successful gardeners, free classes for customers are offered on Saturdays beginning at 11 on topics such as container gardening and landscaping with shrubs. Call for a schedule.

10810 N. Tatum Blvd.; (602) 569-2087. — *J.C.*

CLOCKWISE FROM TOP RIGHT: *Agave vilmoriniana, Agave filifera, Aloe ferox,* and *Euphorbia milii* 'Jerry's Choice'.

CLAIRE CURRAN

Shady secrets

Northern exposure: from deep gloom to glory

■ Cindy McNatt, garden and home design staff writer for the *Orange County Register*, relishes a gardening challenge. So when she moved into her current home in Tustin, the first planting area she tackled was the north side of her house. As gardeners who have faced this situation know, the north side of a house is especially difficult to landscape, as it's in deep gloom all winter yet can face harsh late afternoon sun in summer. Most of us settle for plant survival in these spots, but McNatt wanted glory. "I knew I couldn't rely on flowers to create interest," she says, "so I concentrated on foliage color and texture instead."

McNatt used many shades and shapes of green leaves. But she also added a strong splash of burgundy, primarily from 'Gulf Stream' heavenly bamboo *(Nandina*

domestica) in the background and fat-leafed *Iresine herbstii* (bloodleaf) in midborder. For brightness, she brought in golden Japanese sweet flag *(Acorus gramineus)*, the grass at the border's edge, as well as lime green zonal geraniums in pots. Splashes of silver—lamb's ears and bulbous oat grass—add further light. The few flowers coordinate with leaf accent colors. The burgundy flower spikes belong to two species of *Persicaria,* and the big poufs of lime green are garden hydrangea *(H. macrophylla).*

Conquering this northern exposure has been immensely satisfying, says McNatt. "Over time, the border has become richer—more layered and textured," she says. "Now it's my favorite section of the garden."

— *Sharon Cohoon*

Recycled charm in Oregon

ROBIN CUSHMAN

■ This greenhouse has an eye-pleasing appeal that belies its practicality. In spring and fall, Nancy McFadden of Eugene uses it to start cuttings. During the summer, she hangs bundles of herbs to dry in the warm air near the ceiling.

The greenhouse was designed and built by Nan and Steve Reid, Jr., a mother-and-son team whose company, the Gardener's Dream (541/937-2419), specializes in fabricating structures from salvaged components.

For McFadden's greenhouse, recycled windows were freshly caulked, reglazed if needed, then framed between remilled cedar posts. Measuring 5 by 7 feet at its base, the structure tops out at 10 feet. Fitted with a French door (recycled, of course), the greenhouse has dark green trim to complement the colors of the house.

Greenhouses made by the Gardener's Dream range in price from $1,800 to $8,000 (McFadden's cost $2,200). Models are on display at Little Red Farm Nursery in Springfield, Oregon, and Nichols Garden Nursery in Albany, Oregon.

— M. M.

Spice-up strategy for shade

When a big, shady space needs a face-lift, remove overgrown or scraggly plants so you can make a fresh start. Add shrubs and perennials whose foliage brightens or punctuates all-green plantings. Most shade-tolerant plants will grow in part shade—the sort typically cast by a house wall, a solid fence, or a high hedge.

■ **Mix in plants with variegated foliage.** They add visual texture and definition. Choices include winter daphne (*D. odora* 'Marginata'), lily-of-the-valley shrub (*Pieris japonica* 'Variegata'), and *Weigela* 'Variegata'.

■ **Brighten dark corners with lime or gold foliage.** Plants such as Japanese sweet flag (*Acorus gramineus* 'Ogon'), Hinoki false cypress (*Chamaecyparis obtusa* 'Nana Lutea'), Gold Coast juniper (*Juniperus chinensis* 'Aurea'), and some hostas give the illusion that rays of sunshine are penetrating the gloom.

■ **Add bronze or chocolate-red for punch.** Shrubs such as Japanese barberry and dwarf red-leaf plum (*Prunus x cistena*) and perennials like carpet bugle (*Ajuga reptans*) and *Heuchera micrantha* 'Palace Purple' add visual punch among all-green foliage.

■ **Weave in some blues.** They add subtle shadings beside green foliage. Choices include blue fescue (*Festuca glauca* 'Elijah Blue' or *F.g.* 'Siskiyou Blue') and many hostas. ◆

NORMAN A. PLATE

Nine steps to seeding a new lawn

1. Start with bare soil (kill weeds).
2. Add new lawn fertilizer and a 2- to 3-inch layer of compost.
3. Rotary till the soil 6 to 9 inches deep, crossing several times at right angles.
4. Level the soil by dragging a board scraper over it.
5. Use a (rented) roller to lightly firm the soil.
6. Sow grass seed with a seeder as shown.
7. Lightly rake the surface, then rake again at right angles.
8. Scatter a ⅛-inch layer of organic mulch over the seed.
9. Water often to keep the soil moist. — L. B. S.

Wild for wildflowers in Silver Lake

■ Seasonal changes tend to be pretty subtle in Southern California, unless you happen to live on Timothy Stirton's block in Silver Lake.

Walk by Stirton's house in late summer, and you probably wouldn't give his parched parkway a second glance. Stroll by in early spring, though, and you'll be totally transfixed by the explosion of color there. Lupine, poppies, phacelia, and clarkia are in glorious bloom. The annual wildflower show is a clear signal that spring has arrived, says Stirton; his neighbors love the ritual and drama of it.

Stirton sows the wildflowers in mid-fall to take advantage of winter rains. Though his soil is thin and compacted, he doesn't bother to add amendments before broadcasting seed; even so, plenty of wildflowers germinate. (He buys most of his seed from the Theodore Payne Foundation in Sun Valley: 818/768-1802 or www.theodorepayne.org.) Stirton has never fertilized the parkway, and he rarely waters it. Thinning out the phacelia to keep it from dominating the strip is his main chore; he also cuts back the poppies occasionally to encourage repeat bloom. — *S. C.*

■ If you live in southern Arizona's citrus-growing belt, you've probably seen oranges and other trees with stark white trunks. There's a good reason for painting the exposed bark of citrus. It is particularly sensitive to sunlight, and the paint reflects the ultraviolet rays that can cause sunburn and cracking. Unfortunately, white trunks stick out like sore thumbs in the landscape.

Now there's an alternative. Go Natural paint was developed by Chuck Robbins, a former citrus-grower in Mesa, Arizona. Formulated to match the natural color of citrus bark, the paint provides the same ultraviolet protection as white latex but lasts longer. You can use it to coat other thin-barked fruit trees such as peaches, and it will also protect the bark of young landscape trees. Like any latex paint, you can apply it with a brush, roller, or sprayer, and it cleans up in water.

Go Natural paint is sold in 1-quart, 1-gallon, and 5-gallon containers at many nurseries and garden centers in Arizona. *Call (480) 396-0116 for local retailers.*

— *Lance Walheim*

BACK TO BASICS

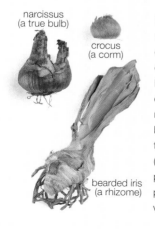

narcissus
(a true bulb)

crocus
(a corm)

bearded iris
(a rhizome)

NORMAN A. PLATE (3)

Bulb talk. Commonly grouped together as "bulbs" are many plants with underground organs that store nutrients. But the only **true bulbs** are those with stem bases composed of embryonic plants surrounded by scales— Dutch iris, hyacinth, leucojum, muscari, narcissus, Oriental lily, tulip. To divide them, separate offsets from mother bulbs. **Corms** (crocus, freesia) are swollen stem bases composed of solid tissue, not scales. To divide them, separate new corms from old. **Rhizomes** (bearded iris, Japanese iris) have thickened stems with a primary growth point at one end and additional growing points along the sides. To divide, cut into sections with visible growing points. — *L. B. S.*

WHAT TO DO IN YOUR GARDEN IN NOVEMBER

PLANTING

☐ **AMARYLLIS.** Among the most spectacular flowering plants you can grow indoors, amaryllis are sold as bulbs and as plants in bud or bloom. Give plants bright light and regular water.

☐ **CAMELLIAS.** Zones 4–7: Hiemalis and sasanqua camellias start flowering this month and continue through spring. Display these winter bloomers espaliered against a wall or place them under eaves so rain won't disturb their flowers.

☐ **FALL FOLIAGE COLOR.** Zones 4–7: November 1 is peak color time for many trees and shrubs. Shop for *Fothergilla major,* many maples, Persian parrotia, sour gum *(Nyssa sylvatica)*, sourwood *(Oxydendrum arboreum)*, weeping katsura, and winged euonymus *(E. alatus)*.

☐ **LANDSCAPE PLANTS.** Container-grown trees, shrubs, and ground covers set out now will grow much more strongly next spring and summer.

☐ **SPRING BULBS.** Bulb catalogs and nurseries offer anemones, bluebells, crocuses, daffodils, freesias, grape hyacinths, hyacinths, irises, paper white narcissus, ranunculus, and tulips. Plant as early in the month as possible.

☐ **WILDFLOWERS.** Fall-sown wildflowers always come up earlier than those sown in spring. Scatter seeds in weed-free beds. West of the Cascades, you'll see seedlings by January and get first bloom in early spring.

MAINTENANCE

☐ **BRING IN HOUSEPLANTS.** If you haven't done so already, bring houseplants indoors for the winter. First, rinse off the foliage thoroughly to reduce the chance that you'll bring in insects too.

☐ **CLEAN UP PLANTING BEDS.** Weed, till, and amend beds now so they'll be ready for planting early next spring.

☐ **COMPOST.** Toss fallen leaves and the remains of summer annuals on the compost pile.

☐ **LAST MOWING.** Pick a dry weekend to mow the grass one last time until spring.

☐ **LIFT AND STORE DAHLIAS.** Before first frost, dig up dahlia tubers, shake off the dirt, dry them in a shady spot, and put them in storage for the winter.

☐ **MAINTAIN TOOLS.** Sharpen shovels, spades, hoes, and pruners; rub down wood handles with linseed oil; and wipe metal blades with an oily cloth to protect them against rust.

☐ **OVERWINTER TENDER PLANTS.** Before a hard freeze hits, dig fuchsias and pelargoniums, pot them, and bring them into a cool, dark, frost-free place for the winter.

☐ **WEED.** Hoe or pull weeds now before they or their offspring become problems. ◆

WHAT TO DO IN YOUR GARDEN IN NOVEMBER

PLANTING

☐ BEST AUTUMN COLOR. Zones 7–9, 14–17: **Trees:** Chinese pistache, Chinese tallow, crape myrtle, dogwood, Japanese maple, liquidambar, ornamental pear, Persian parrotia, and persimmon. **Shrubs:** deciduous azaleas, euonymus, oakleaf hydrangea, smoke tree, and viburnum. **Vines:** grape, *Parthenocissus,* and wisteria.

☐ HERBS. Zones 7–9, 14–17: Plant biennial and perennial herbs now, so they get established this fall and winter and provide a good harvest in spring. Try chives; Greek oregano; marjoram; parsley; 'Blue Boy', 'Blue Spires', or 'Gorizia' rosemary; sage; and lemon or common thyme.

☐ NATIVE SHRUBS. Zones 7–9, 14–17: A few good medium to tall shrubs include *Arctostaphylos* 'Howard McMinn' (to 6 feet), bush anemone (4–6 feet), chuparosa (to 4 feet), Oregon grape (to 6 feet), Pacific wax myrtle (10–30 feet), *Rhamnus californica* 'Mound San Bruno' (4–6 feet), *Ribes speciosum* (to 8 feet), *Salvia clevelandii* (to 5 feet), and toyon (6–10 feet).

☐ A POT OF GREENS. Zones 7–9, 14–17: Chard, kale, lettuce, and mustard greens are not only good to eat, they are also handsome ornamentals. They're particularly easy to grow in pots. Try mixing gorgeous red leaf lettuces with 'Rainbow' chard, 'Red Russian' kale, and 'Red Giant' mustard.

Sunset CLIMATE ZONES
☐ Mountain (1-2)
☐ Valley (7-9)
☐ Inland (14)
☐ Coastal (15-17)

DEBRA LAMBERT

☐ SWEET PEAS. Zones 7–9, 14–17: In most areas, there's still time to start sweet peas, as long as you get them in the ground or containers right away. If the weather turns cool and wet, plants may grow very slowly or seeds might not germinate. A favorite for fragrance is 'April in Paris' from Renee's Garden (available on seed racks or from www.reneesgarden.com).

☐ WILDFLOWERS. Shop for mixtures that contain reliable species like California poppy, clarkia, lupine, and tidytips. Broadcast seeds over weed-free soil in a sunny spot. Rake the area lightly afterward to barely cover seeds with soil. If rains don't come, keep the soil consistently moist until seeds germinate.

☐ WINTER VEGETABLES. Continue to sow seeds of beets, carrots, onion, parsley, peas, and radishes. Set out broccoli, cabbage, and cauliflower seedlings.

MAINTENANCE

☐ LIFT WARM-SEASON BULBS. If your soil is heavy and wet, tubers of begonias and tuberous roots of dahlias can rot during the winter rains. To ensure that they'll survive for next season, lift them after stems die down. Cut stems to 4 inches, shake off loose soil, and allow them to dry out in the sun for several hours. Store them in trays covered with peat moss, sand, or sawdust and place in a cool, dry, dark place.

☐ WATER VEGETABLES. If rain is spotty, keep an eye on the vegetable patch; irrigate when the soil starts to dry out several inches down. The small rootballs of newly transplanted seedlings need water more often than established vegetables.

PEST CONTROL

☐ SPRAY FRUIT TREES. To control peach curl, a fungal disease that distorts the leaves and infects the fruit, spray peach trees with lime sulfur after leaves have fallen. Make sure to spray the entire tree, including the trunk, branches, and twigs. ◆

WHAT TO DO IN YOUR GARDEN IN NOVEMBER

PLANTING

☐ **COOL-SEASON ANNUALS.** Except in the mountains, there's still time to set out early-blooming annuals such as African daisy, Iceland poppy, lobelia, ornamental cabbage, snapdragon, and stock. And don't forget pansies, one of the longest-blooming annuals around. To keep them blooming, Evelyn Weidner of Weidners' Gardens in Encinitas recommends picking flowers weekly to use in small bouquets indoors. The more you pick them, the better the pansies flower, she says.

☐ **LONG-TERM COLOR.** To add color to your fall garden, shop for plumbago, Mexican sage, sasanqua camellias, *Tagetes lemmonii,* and other late-blooming shrubs. Or choose trees and shrubs with colorful fruit or berries, such as heavenly bamboo, holly, persimmon, pomegranate, pyracantha, and toyon.

☐ **WILDFLOWERS.** Broadcast seeds by hand over weed-free soil in a sunny spot. Rake the area lightly afterward to barely cover seeds with soil (or walk over soil to tamp). Wait for rain, or irrigate the seeds yourself; keep the soil consistently moist until seeds germinate. Look for mixtures that contain reliable species like California poppy, clarkia, lupine, phacelia, and tidytips *(Layia platyglossa).* Two good wildflower seed sources are the Theodore Payne Founda-

Bishop

NEVADA

CALIFORNIA

San Luis
Obispo

Bakersfield

Tehachapi

Santa
Barbara

Lancaster

Los Angeles

Palm Springs

Sunset
CLIMATE ZONES

1-3 7-9 11 13 14-24

San Diego

MEXICO

DEBRA LAMBERT

tion in Sun Valley: (818) 768-1802 or www.theodorepayne.org; and the Tree of Life Nursery in San Juan Capistrano: (949) 728-0685 or www.treeoflifenursery.com.

☐ **WINTER VEGETABLES.** Early November is a fabulous time to start cool-season crops in most areas. In zones 13 (low desert) and 14–24, sow seeds of beets, carrots, chard, onion, parsley, peas, radishes, and turnips. Set out broccoli, cabbage, and cauliflower seedlings. Coastal gardeners can also continue to plant lettuces. In the foothills and Central Valley (zones 7–9 and 14), sow seeds of peas and spinach, and plant garlic and onions.

MAINTENANCE

☐ **CONTROL WEEDS.** Pull out bluegrass, chickweed, sow thistle, and other young weeds as they emerge. If these aren't allowed to set seed, next year's weeding will be easier.

☐ **DIG DAHLIAS.** Dig up dahlias, trim off remaining foliage, brush off soil, and allow bulbs to dry out in sun. Store in peat, perlite, sand, or vermiculite in a cool, dry location until spring.

☐ **PRUNE BERRY CANES.** Old canes of blackberry, boysenberry, and loganberry should be cut back to the ground. Leave the new, smooth-barked canes to bear fruit. Wait until December or January to cut back low-chill raspberries.

☐ **TEND MUMS.** Support still-blooming plants with stakes and ties. After bloom, cut back plants, leaving 6-inch stems. Lift and divide old clumps; cut roots apart and discard woody centers.

PEST CONTROL

☐ **PROTECT CABBAGE CROPS.** Squadrons of little white butterflies—called cabbage whites—seem to descend on cabbage and other *Brassica* crops the minute you plant them. To foil them, cover the young seedlings with floating row covers right after you plant. The next best option is spraying with *Bacillus thuringiensis* to kill the young caterpillar larvae. ◆

WHAT TO DO IN YOUR GARDEN IN NOVEMBER

PLANTING

☐ COVER CROPS. After vegetables are harvested, spade several inches of manure into beds and sow seeds of hairy vetch, white Dutch clover, or winter rye. These cover crops prevent soil erosion during the winter and add nutrients when tilled into the ground the next spring. Seeds of all three are available from Gardens Alive! (812/537-8651 or www.gardensalive.com).

☐ HERBS INDOORS. In a sunny window, try oregano, rosemary, sage, sweet marjoram, and thyme. In a window with less light, try bay, chives, peppermint, and spearmint. Garden centers and some supermarkets sell herb plants in 2- or 4-inch pots; transplant these into 6-inch or larger pots filled with well-drained potting soil. Allow the soil to dry slightly between waterings.

☐ PAPER WHITE NARCISSUS. Plant bulbs in a pot filled with horticultural sand or pebbles and store in a cool room (50° to 60°) until shoots emerge, then move the pot into a bright, cool window. Bulbs started by midmonth should bloom during the holidays.

Sunset
CLIMATE ZONES
☐ 1-3   ☐ 10-11

DEBRA LAMBERT

☐ SPRING BULBS. If you haven't set out hardy bulbs yet, get them into the ground immediately. Pot up extra bulbs for forcing indoors. Put the pots in a dark, cold place (33° to 40°) for 12 weeks, then bring them into a brightly lit room to induce bloom.

MAINTENANCE

☐ PREPARE PLANTING BEDS. Before the ground freezes, till a 2- to 3-inch layer of composted manure or compost into planting beds. Leave the soil in large clumps; freezing and thawing will break them down, and the bed will be ready to plant as soon as the soil warms in spring.

☐ PROTECT PLANTS FROM DEER. To prevent deer from damaging young trees and shrubs, surround them with wire cages made from chicken wire or hardware mesh. Use stakes to hold cages in place.

☐ PROTECT YOUNG TREES FROM SUNSCALD. Trees with trunks less than 4 inches in diameter are vulnerable to sunscald, a damaging form of sunburn caused when the low winter sun shines on tender bark. Paint the trunks with white latex or protect them with a commercial tree wrap.

☐ PROVIDE AID FOR WILD BIRDS. As cold weather sets in, birds have greater difficulty finding natural food, so they seek out bird feeders. Seed-eaters such as evening grosbeaks, goldfinches, and pine siskins prefer black oil sunflower and niger thistle. Insect-eaters like flickers and nuthatches favor suet. To provide water in freezing weather, install an electric heater in your birdbath. Avian Aquatics (800/788-6478) sells a variety of birdbath heaters.

☐ RECYCLE POTTING SOIL. As you clean out containers, toss dead annuals on the compost pile but dump the soil and attached roots into a large plastic garbage can (drill a few small holes in the bottom for drainage). Leave the can outside without a lid over the winter. The roots will break down organically, and the soil will be ready to reuse next spring.

☐ STORE FROST-SENSITIVE CONTAINERS. Birdbaths, fountains, and pots made of concrete or terra-cotta are susceptible to damage from freezing weather. Remove soil and scrub out pots, then store in a dry shed or a garage. — *M. T.* ◆

WHAT TO DO IN YOUR GARDEN IN NOVEMBER

PLANTING

☐ **COOL-SEASON FLOWERS.** Zones 10–13 (Albuquerque, Las Vegas, Tucson, Phoenix): Sow seeds of nasturtium and sweet pea. Set out transplants of calendula, dianthus, pansy, petunia, snapdragon, and stock.

☐ **COOL-SEASON VEGETABLES.** Zones 10–13: Sow seeds of beets, carrots, kale, leeks, parsnips, peas, radishes, rutabagas, salad greens, spinach, and turnips. Set out transplants of broccoli, brussels sprouts, cabbage, and cauliflower.

☐ **FORCE BULBS INDOORS.** This technique works with crocus, daffodil, hyacinth, paper white narcissus, and tulip. Refrigerate bulbs for 8 to 10 weeks, then plant the chilled bulbs in containers of potting soil mixed with controlled-release fertilizer. Space bulbs so they are just touching with tips protruding from the soil; water gently. Place the containers in a cool, low-light location for one week. Then take them into a warm, well-lit room to bloom.

☐ **LANDSCAPE PLANTS.** Zones 10–13: Set out desert-adapted shrubs and trees like Baja fairy duster *(Calliandra californica)*, purple hop bush *(Dodonaea viscosa* 'Purpurea'*)*, Texas mountain laurel *(Sophora secundiflora)*, and Texas olive *(Cordia boissieri)*.

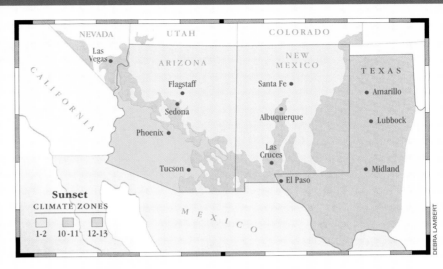

Sunset CLIMATE ZONES
1-2   10-11   12-13

DEBRA LAMBERT

☐ **SWEET POTATO.** To grow a lush houseplant, select a firm sweet potato at the grocery and a tall glass jar with an opening narrow enough to hold the tuber (avoid using toothpicks). Fill the jar with water, insert the tuber, and set in a sunny indoor location. Sprouts will develop in 2 to 4 weeks. Change the water regularly, taking care not to disturb the tender roots. In the spring, cut the shoots into separate plants and transplant them into containers of potting soil.

MAINTENANCE

☐ **ADJUST IRRIGATION SYSTEMS.** As the weather turns cooler, increase the number of days between irrigations.

☐ **CONTROL PESTS.** Blast aphids off landscape plants and vegetables with a jet of water from the hose, or spray with insecticidal soap. Watch for cabbage loopers and harlequin bugs; pick them off by hand.

☐ **HARVEST CITRUS.** Grapefruits, lemons, limes, oranges, and kumquats ripen now. This early in the season, pick only what you'll immediately use, since the longer fruit stays on the tree, the greater its sugar content will be. If you have more fruit than you can use, call a local food bank and arrange to donate your excess.

☐ **PREPARE FOR FIRST FROST.** If frost is forecast, move container plants to protected locations under trees or house eaves. Water tender landscape plants so they'll be well hydrated and better able to resist cold. — *Kim Nelson* ◆

Gate

ways

Sunset readers
open up about their
garden gates

By Sharon Cohoon

A good garden gate makes you want to sneak a peek at the landscape beyond. But a *great* garden gate goes further. It makes you want to meet the people responsible for its design. That was our conclusion after we asked readers to tell us about their one-of-a-kind garden gates, and the snapshots came pouring in. Regional character, handsome design, wit and whimsy—those things we'd expected. But we weren't prepared for the wonderful stories that came along with these gates. A few of them follow; perhaps they'll inspire you to look at gates in a fresh way as you choose one for your own garden.

CELEBRATING THE ONION ▶

Aptos, California ▪ Cristie Thomas and Scott Lindberg, who design and fabricate arbors, gates, and other landscape ornaments under the name :L:M:N:O: Arts, describe their professional style as "eclectic and graceful." So what is the couple doing with this delightfully silly fence in their own backyard? Having a good laugh, says Thomas. "We were harvesting Walla Walla onions—we've been growing them for at least a decade—and I was suddenly struck by how beautiful they were," she says. "The wispy little roots, the sensuous bulbs, the floppy tops." So, on a whim, Thomas took several onions to the studio, made templates from them, and created this fanciful steel gate. The onion tops are made from flat bar, the roots are old welding rod bent to shape, and the gate frame is solid square rod. *:L:M:N:O: Arts (831/728-3998 or www.lmnoarts.com)*

ZEN AND THE ART OF TIME MANAGEMENT

Centennial, Colorado • "Garden projects keep me off the psychiatrist's couch," says dentist Kent Sellers. With the pressure of staying on schedule all day long, Sellers craves slower-paced, contemplative tasks on his days off. Designing and building Japanese-inspired gates for his tea garden, for instance. This gate, one of three in his garden, is made of Russian olive branches and twigs from trees cut down along Interstate 25 in Denver when sound-barrier walls went in. "I'd been looking for wood with lots of joints and curves to inspire me," he says. "When I pulled over and saw these, I knew they were perfect." Sellers doesn't re-create any particular Japanese style. Instead, he lets the wood dictate the design. Because each junction is screwed in by hand, the gates are labor-intensive. Not that Sellers minds. Sometimes, time is not an issue.

A TRIBUTE TO MURIEL

Ross, California • The spirit of Muriel Waltz still haunts the land that Juliet and Ashford Wood live on. And that suits Juliet just fine. "Muriel has captured us completely," she says. From the 1940s through the '60s, Waltz was a famous fuchsia hybridizer who had a commercial nursery on the Woods' property. Juliet honors that garden. She's retained most of the plants, built a stone wall around the perimeter, and put in a gate—exactly in the spot Waltz had imagined, say Muriel's surviving friends. Muriel, we think, would have loved it. The gate is a tree of life design made from hand-forged steel and hand-tinted ceramic tiles, a trademark combination of Lake County gate designer-maker Brian Kennedy. The blooms, appropriately enough, are fuchsia buds. *The Freedom of Craft by Brian Kennedy, Lake County, California (707/928-5124 or www.thefreedomofcraft.com)*

THREE HELPFUL DESIGN TIPS

Imagining your gate

1 Tell a story
Your gate can convey something about you—that you have a good sense of humor, for example, or that you love color or onions or wood, or that you have a fondness for old materials. While a gate may be a significant artistic element in its own right, it can also echo the design and color of your house, or an element of your garden such as a leaf, vine, blossom, or branch. To find a style that appeals to you, look for inspiration in books and magazines, and check out gates around your neighborhood.

FRAMEWORK FOR A FAMILY

Olympia, Washington · The gate Walter Penwarden made for his home in South Pasadena was a backdrop in family portraits for decades. Then it disappeared from photo shoots for a long time. Now, thanks to one of Penwarden's granddaughters, Luan Laws, the gate's back. Here's what happened: Penwarden, a professional ironworker, built the gate for his family sometime in the 1920s or '30s. When the Penwardens sold their home in the '70s, daughter Laura removed the gate but found she had no place to use it at her home in Huntington Beach. So it languished in storage for decades. Later, Laura's daughter DeAnn tried it out at her home in Utah, but it didn't work there, either. Then Laura's other daughter, Luan, brought it to her garden in Olympia, where, to the family's great relief, it looks perfectly at home. Once again, it provides a backdrop for family photos.

RECYCLED MAGIC

Cambria, California · Jeanette Wolff is an artist. Windows are a recurring motif in her paintings, and window frames hang throughout her garden. She also has a junk box full of intriguing objects waiting to be incorporated into new creations. Knowing these things, relatives and friends feed her collection. And that brings us to her gate. The starting point was a tiny window that her brother Richard salvaged from a demolished barracks at Fort Ord and gave to her. "It seemed magical," says Wolff. "So small, square, and 'Hobbity.'" She sketched out a design that incorporated the window, and her husband, Peter, built the gate, using redwood from an old deck. Then, Jeanette embellished it. The faux hinges and crown are from an old kitchen table, the aged handle from her junk box, and the tiny wolf knocker, a present from a friend. Assembled in her inimitable style, say the artists' admirers, the gate cries "Wolff." ◆

Select appropriate hardware

Decide whether you want your gate to swing in, out, or both, and whether you'll need a lock. Use sturdy hinges and latches—the sturdier the better—to support the gate's weight and frequency of use. If you're not sure which hardware is most suitable to your gate's design, consult a professional gate builder or someone at your local hardware store.

Keep the gate in scale with its surroundings

If you have a small house and yard, don't choose a huge gate. Most garden gates measure about 36 inches across—wide enough for a wheelbarrow to pass through. The height will depend on how prominent you want it to be: An entry gate might be taller or shorter than the fence it intersects; a side gate could be the same height as the fence. — *Julie Chai*

In Barbara Thuro's garden, the pond is a water source for birds. Jupiter's Beard and sweet alyssum (foreground) supply nectar for butterflies.

Gardening for wildlife

Your landscape can be a sanctuary for birds, butterflies, and other lovely creatures

By Lauren Bonar Swezey and Sharon Cohoon

■ "I've seen animals do things in my backyard you don't get to see on *National Geographic*," says Barbara Thuro, whose garden in Vista, California, is a sanctuary for a variety of creatures, winged and wild. Dragonflies perform aerial acrobatics over the pond. Raccoons sleep under her deck; at night they join skunks, opossums, and other prowlers rustling in the bushes while crickets serenade them.

Up north in Pleasant Hill, California, the chirping sound of white-crowned sparrows fills the air every fall in Pamela Simonds's garden. Simonds, who lives near one of the Pacific flyways, welcomes these seasonal visitors to her garden by offering them food, water, and respite from the noise, congestion, and lawn-filled gardens that surround her small, sub-urban oasis. "I can identify the season by the kinds of birds that appear in the garden," says Simonds. "When they arrive, I hear their presence before I see them."

Thuro and Simonds are two of a growing number of Westerners who are turning their gardens into backyard wildlife habitats, then having them certified by the National Wildlife Federation. Make your garden creature-friendly enough to be certified, says Thuro, and animals will come. The longer they stay, the more accepting they'll become of your presence. Then they'll behave in your garden as they would in the wild. That, say habitat gardeners, is when the entertainment—and education—begins.

In Simonds's garden, for instance, birds feel so at home that they perform mating rituals, build nests, hatch young, and nurture fledglings.

With all this live action going on, it's no wonder that owners of habitat gardens would rather watch critter comings and goings in their gardens than on TV.

simple things you can do for your garden's wildlife

1. **Install feeders** for birds and squirrels atop tall posts, out of reach of passing cats. Place them under trees for protection from hawks and other flying predators.

2. **Buy a big rock** with a depression in its top. Place it in a sunny spot—by a perennial border, for example—then fill it with water for birds and butterflies.

JANET LOUGHREY (2)

3. **Fill a bucket** with water and leave it by the hose or spigot for an easy-to-fill sipping station. Change water frequently to keep it clean and free of mosquitoes.

4. **Tie a wad of dryer lint** with yarn and hang it from a branch to provide nest material. Or nail a can filled with loosened cotton balls to a fence.

CLAIRE CURRAN

5. **Create perches** by nailing a 2-by-4 to a vine-covered post for a nest site. Place tall, twiggy prunings or trellises near birdbaths so birds can preen and dry off.

6. **Hang up a bird-house** or several, spaced around the garden. This one, made from a hollowed birch log, is the perfect size for a chickadee brood.

BEN DAVIDSON (3)

Bird-pleasers: Oregon grape berries, trees and shrubs for cover, and *Phygelius* 'Winchester Fanfare'—a nectar source.

Elements of a habitat garden

As housing and commercial developments spread into wildlands, they encroach upon the habitats that would supply—in their natural state—all the food, water, and shelter that birds and other creatures need to live. By incorporating these resources into your garden, you can help many critters survive as their true habitats disappear.

Food. To keep wildlife in the garden, you need to offer a year-round food supply. "Diversity is the key to enticing the greatest variety of wildlife," says Judy Adler, environmental educator and owner of a backyard wildlife habitat in Walnut Creek, California.

To provide food, use native plants (which many creatures have adapted to in the wild), or blend natives with non-natives. Create a living smorgasbord that includes plants with berries, foliage, fruit, nectar, nuts, pollen, sap, and seeds, so critters can dine on what they like. Insects also provide food for birds, toads, and other creatures. (For all wildlife to thrive, it's critical that you avoid using toxic chemicals in the garden.)

"Use plants that bloom at different times of the year," says Adler. "For instance, hummingbirds are attracted to coral bells and columbine in spring, scarlet monkey flower and salvia in summer, and California

fuchsia in late summer and fall." If your garden lacks food during certain months, put up bird feeders.

"My bird feeders go up in winter and come down in spring when the insects appear," says Lisa Albert, owner of a certified habitat in Tualatin, Oregon. "I try not to rely on feeders because there are lots of cats in the neighborhood." Instead, Albert's garden offers wild visitors evergreen huckleberry, flowering red currant, Oregon grape, salal, and other food plants.

Water. It's essential for wildlife survival, so a backyard habitat must include a year-round source.

Ponds are handsome garden features, and they attract many kinds of wildlife (control mosquitoes with *Bacillus thuringiensis israelensis,* manufactured for pond use in granules or doughnut-shaped disks). The sound of water from a waterfall or fountain enhances the attraction.

Water can also be supplied on a smaller scale—in birdbaths, buckets, or water bowls. One easy way to keep them filled is to run a drip irrigation line to each source. Hose them out every other day (particularly during the warm season), then periodically scrub them with a brush. In cold-winter climates, add a heater to your birdbath to keep it from freezing.

Shelter. Birds and other wild critters need leafy or twiggy covering to protect them from predators and the elements. Dense shrubbery can provide shelter, as can brush piles, thickets of rugosa roses, or tall evergreen trees such as coast live oak, deodar cedar, or redwood. Additional cover can be made from hollow logs, stacked rocks, and woodpiles, which form perfect hiding places for lizards, quail, rabbits, and other small animals.

Nesting places. The same dense shrubbery, tall trees, and grasses that shelter passing wildlife also provide nesting places for a variety of creatures. Supplement them by hanging up bat houses, birdhouses, and orchard mason bee homes (blocks of wood drilled with holes).

Keep in mind that cats and wildlife don't mix. Bells worn around cats' necks to warn wildlife don't always work. It's best to keep cats indoors. If that's not possible, feed your cat indoors at prime bird-feeding times (early morning and early evening), and place feeders and nesting boxes where cats can't reach them.

The habitat program

stablished by the National Wildlife Federation in 1973, the Backyard Wildlife Habitat Program helps birds and other creatures who are losing their home turf to urban sprawl by encouraging the development of habitats in home gardens. To date, NWF has certified more than 33,000 habitats, ranging from small urban balconies to thousand-acre plots. Most of the gardens are residential, but school campuses and workplace landscapes also can be wildlife habitats. Whole communities can get involved too. In Alpine, California, so many residents and businesses created wildlife habitats that the NWF gave a certification to the entire community—a first for the program.

LEFT: Flowering dogwoods in Lisa Albert's Oregon garden provide nesting sites and shelter for birds. ABOVE: Sign identifies Sunset's editorial test garden in Menlo Park, California, as a certified wildlife habitat. Seed and nectar plants keep birds and butterflies happy here.

How to certify your garden

For details about backyard wildlife habitats and the certification process, order the National Wildlife Federation's booklet, *Wildlife Habitat Planning Guide for Backyards and Beyond* ($14.95, including shipping. NWF, Backyard Wildlife Habitat, 11100 Wildlife Center Dr., Reston, VA 20190; 585/461-3092). To apply for certification, request an application by mail from the NWF, or download one at www.nwf.org./backyardwildlifehabitat. To help the certification process, include the following with your application:

- **Snapshots,** which allow the naturalist-reviewers to see what's described in the application

- **Common names** of plants and animals in your garden

- **The wildlife food and water** that your garden supplies in each season ◆

Judy Adler's Walnut Creek, California, pond attracts damselflies, dragonflies, frogs, and a black phoebe. Around it, ornamental grasses mingle with blue ceanothus, yellow sulfur flower (Erigonum umbellatum), and iris.

Prevailing wind

1 Exposure to wind desiccates plants and stunts growth

2 South and west walls concentrate heat by reflecting sunlight

3 North wall is the coolest spot on the property

4 Sloping ground allows cold air to drain downhill like water

7 Overhanging eaves protect delicate flowers

6 East wall basks in gentle morning sun

5 Cold-air pockets occur in low spots

8 Shade trees and overhead structures cast filtered shade

9 Dry banks on south-facing slopes get full sun

Know your microclimates

Identifying your garden's pocket climates
can help you grow the right plants in the right place

By Jim McCausland

How can one gardener grow perfect plumerias year after year, while a close neighbor invariably fails? Or why does one vegetable plot produce tomatoes until October, while another just down the street nearly always freezes out two weeks earlier? *Sunset's* garden staff constantly fields such questions; the answers usually involve microclimates—small pockets that are seasonally colder, warmer, or windier than the rest of the garden or neighborhood.

Wherever you live in the West, your garden falls into one of the 32 *Sunset* climate zones mapped and defined in the *Western Garden Book*. But every garden also harbors a number of microclimates that make a world of difference to plants: the chill air that helps set buds on an apple tree can freeze orange blossoms.

The illustration above shows nine microclimates typically found in Western gardens. Each situation presents gardening challenges and opportunities.

Fall is a good time to start observing your own garden's microclimates and making notes about sun angle, wind direction, and daily minimum and maximum temperatures. It's also a good time to modify the microclimates where you can—by planting hedges for windbreaks or trees for shade—or to move struggling plants from an unfavorable area to a better one.

Nine common microclimates

1 Exposure to wind ▪ For this part of the garden, choose wind-resistant trees, shrubs, and perennials such as daylily, lavender, and penstemon. Or block the wind: a hedge or a windbreak of closely spaced trees planted on the windward side can create a sheltered area extending 10 to 20 times its height (a 10-foot-tall hedge will shelter 100 to 200 feet of ground behind it). If your property has a breezeway—a narrow passage between a house and a detached garage or other structure that funnels wind—you can buffer the upwind side with a hedge or line the passage with conifers or other wind-tolerant plants.

2 South and west walls ▪ Masonry and stucco walls soak up solar energy and radiate it back at night. In cool-summer areas, that extra heat can help ripen summer vegetables like tomatoes, peppers, and eggplants. In hot-summer areas, plant trees to shade these walls, or screen walls with heat-loving vines like bougainvillea.

3 North wall ▪ Since it gets little direct sun, it's ideal for shade-loving plants like ferns. In warm climates, the north side of the house is the place for temperate plants such as hydrangea and viburnum that would burn up with too much sun exposure.

4 Sloping ground ▪ As it flows downhill, cold air mixes with warm air just above so it is a bit warmer than the still air on mountaintops or in valleys. That's why sloping ground is favored for growing oranges. Grapes planted on a south- or west-facing slope pick up extra heat that helps sweeten fruit.

5 Cold-air pockets ▪ Low-lying spots allow cold air to pool. Chill air can also be blocked behind structures and landscaping elements like hedges (some typical cold-air traps are discussed at right). Frost-tender plants like citrus and plumeria that need heat don't belong in cold pockets. But such spots can be used to advantage in mild climates, where the extra chill encourages lilacs to bloom and apples, apricots, cherries, peaches, and pears to set fruit.

6 East wall ▪ Although it can get up to a half-day of sunshine, the sun is less intense here than on a west-facing wall. This makes it perfect for plants that like plenty of light but not much heat, such as azaleas and fuchsias.

7 Overhanging eaves ▪ They protect delicate flowers like camellias from shattering or turning mushy in the rain. Eaves also provide a couple of degrees of frost protection for tender plants underneath. Remember to irrigate under overhangs.

8 Shade trees and overhead structures ▪ A canopy of leaves or the latticework from an arbor casts filtered shade preferred by hosta, impatiens, and many other plants. On frosty nights, the air beneath stays a few degrees warmer than the open ground.

9 Dry banks ▪ They have fast-draining soil that's prone to erosion. Cover these banks with heat- and drought-tolerant ground covers such as *Acacia redolens,* ice plant, or trailing lantana or rosemary; Mediterranean shrubs like rockrose or santolina; or Western natives like manzanita *(Arctostaphylos),* wild lilac *(Ceanothus),* penstemon, or salvia.

TROY DOOLITTLE/TOPDOG ILLUSTRATION

Check your property for cold-air traps

Like water, cold air runs downhill and pools in certain places in the garden, particularly in low spots and behind structures and plantings. Walk around your property on a morning when the temperature is around 32° and you'll see where frost has collected in these cold pockets. Keep tender or marginally hardy plantings away from these areas, or provide plants with extra frost protection.

Ironically, a hedge installed to block wind can also trap cold air if the planting runs across the contour of a slope. You can use such cold-air pockets to your advantage by growing chill-loving plants there. However, if you don't want to trap cold air, thin the existing windbreak to open up its base. That way, the hedge will allow cold air to drain through but still break the force of the wind.

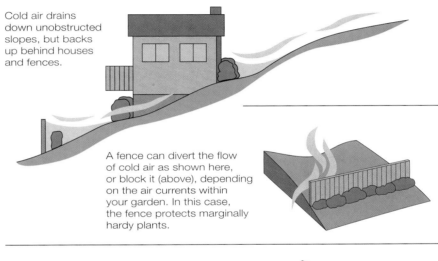

Cold air drains down unobstructed slopes, but backs up behind houses and fences.

A fence can divert the flow of cold air as shown here, or block it (above), depending on the air currents within your garden. In this case, the fence protects marginally hardy plants.

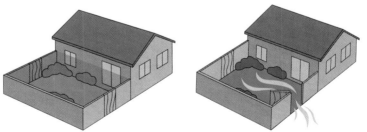

Cold air settles in an enclosed patio like water in a pool (left). One break in the walls, such as an open gate (right), allows cold air to drain out, providing plants with slightly more frost protection.

Houses, fences, and hedges can act as dams that block wind, causing cold pockets (whenever air stagnates, temperatures drop). Check winter and summer air movement in order to keep the windbreak, with all its summer advantages, from creating disasters in winter. ◆

Mexican evening primrose shows its natural tendency to wander.

Runaway beauties

These garden plants benefit from corralling

By Debra Lee Baldwin

No sooner are you thrilled that a certain plant is thriving than it pops up unexpectedly where you didn't plant it. Then, before long, it has merrily spread its way through your garden.

Some reproduce themselves easily by seed, thanks to birds and breezes. Others spread aggressively by stolons (stems that creep along the soil surface, taking root and forming new plants at intervals). Eventually stoloniferous plants can choke out or smother their neighbors. Pulling or hoeing them barely fazes the plants; any stolons left in the soil just resprout. The upside to these lovely invaders is that they make good soil binders for slopes, and they grow where nothing else will.

The nursery plants listed on the facing page have aggressive tendencies that can make them nuisances for meticulous gardeners. Encourage the seed-spreaders where you want them, and pull up unwanted ones. You can restrain stolon-types by planting them in raised beds or in soil pockets surrounded by paving. Regularly dig out any unwanted shoots that do appear.

Runaways to watch

Savvy gardeners develop strategies for using runaway beauties to advantage, letting them spread only where they want them. Some plants, however, cannot be safely controlled. In some regions, plants introduced as ornamentals have jumped the garden fence and threaten to crowd out native species or choke waterways. Scotch broom *(Cytisus scoparius)*, with pretty yellow flowers, and purple loosestrife *(Lythrum salicaria* and related species) are examples. A good source for information on invasive plants is the website for the Federal Noxious Weed Program: www.aphis.usda.gov/ppq/weeds. Native plant societies in many states also maintain lists of problem plants.

Jupiter's beard covers banks in foreground with rose pink blooms.

Seed-spreaders

Forget-me-nots *(Myosotis).* True to their name, these demure little blue flowers refuse to be forgotten, persisting for years as they self-sow. Easy to pull where you don't want them.

Johnny-jump-up *(Viola tricolor).* This petite-flowered member of the viola clan is so loved, it's easy to overlook its habit of relentless reseeding. Easy to pull or hoe.

Jupiter's beard *(Centranthus ruber).* Self-sows prolifically thanks to small, dandelion-like parachutes on the seeds. Plant it in fringe areas; cut off old flowering stems to prevent self-seeding.

Stolon-spreaders

False dragonhead, obedient plant *(Physostegia virginiana).* Pink flower spikes resemble snapdragons; it's "obedient" only in that blossoms stay in place when twisted. To keep clumps within bounds, divide them every two years in spring.

Garden asters. Hardy, small-flowered types sold simply as garden hybrids quickly lace the soil with stolons and send up new shoots everywhere. Curb them in pots or raised beds.

Indian mock strawberry *(Duchesnea indica).* A trailing ground cover with wiry (and wily) stems that root; thrives among open shrubs or small trees. Flowers are yellow and single petaled; berries are small, nearly tasteless. Can be a rampant invader. If you must grow it, confine it to big pots with saucers, and display it on a paved patio.

Matilija poppy *(Romneya coulteri).* Six-foot-tall, gray green stems produce yellow-centered white flowers that resemble fried eggs. Plant in marginal areas such as on hillsides; keep away from less vigorous plants. Withhold summer irrigation to keep growth in check.

Mexican evening primrose *(Oenothera speciosa).* Pink, poppylike flowers bloom profusely in spring and summer. Will grow downhill, following water. Grow it in raised beds, or in planting pockets surrounded by paving.

Periwinkle *(Vinca major).* This blue-flowered ground cover has trailing stems that root wherever they touch the ground (useful on banks). But it's extremely invasive in sheltered, forested areas, and is on noxious weed lists in some states. Dwarf periwinkle *(Vinca minor)* is less invasive.

Russian sage *(Perovskia).* In mild climates, these woody perennials with blue spires spread rapidly even in arid soil, sending up whiplike shoots of silvery leaves that are difficult to pull.

Sweet violet *(Viola odorata).* Heart-shaped leaves and demure purple flowers belie this ground cover's boldness; it quickly carpets land where soil is moist and trees create semishade. Easy to pull.

Sweet woodruff *(Galium odoratum).* Low ground cover with pretty green leaves and fragrant white flowers. Spreads rapidly in moist, shaded gardens; can become a pest if allowed to grow unchecked. ◆

Daylilies bear more flowers when plants are divided periodically.

4 easy steps

1. Pop the whole clump out of the ground with a shovel or spading fork.

2. Hose off the rootball, removing as much soil as possible.

3. Use a butcher's knife or pruning saw to cut the clump into quarters.

4. Pull the quarters apart and further divide them with your hands or a knife. Each division should have a sturdy root and from one to three leaf fans (more fans result in faster growth and flowering). ◆

Multiply by dividing

Perk up your perennials—and get more plants for free

By Jim McCausland

Division is the easiest way to propagate new plants from existing perennials. Most clump-forming perennials benefit from division every few years; without it, their bloom and flower size start to decline, especially near the center of the plant. Reinvigorated by division, established perennials typically produce more and larger flowers.

The list below indicates which perennials to divide in fall. For those not included, the rule of thumb is to divide spring-flowering kinds in fall and fall-flowering kinds in spring. Bearded iris and Oriental poppies are two prominent exceptions: both are best divided during summer dormancy. In areas where the ground freezes, it's risky to divide perennials any later than mid-October.

When dividing plants that develop woody growth in the middle, such as chrysanthemums and summer phlox, discard the centers and make divisions from the more vigorous outer sections of the clump.

Replant divisions immediately in prepared, amended soil and water them in well. In cold-winter climates, cover plants with 3 to 4 inches of organic mulch.

Divide in fall

- *Aster* x *frikartii*
- astilbe
- *Bergenia cordifolia*
- columbine
- coreopsis
- *Crocosmia* hybrids
- daylily
- delphinium
- *Dianthus deltoides*
- *Gaillardia* x *grandiflora*
- *Geranium* 'Johnson's Blue'
- *Geum chiloense*
- heuchera
- hosta
- *Lobelia cardinalis*
- *Lychnis coronaria*
- *Monarda didyma*
- peony
- *Scabiosa columbaria*
- Shasta daisy
- Siberian iris
- snow-in-summer
- summer phlox
- yarrow

Plans and clippings are easy to find in this binder. Tabs divide the sections by subject, and vinyl pouches hold seed packets.

Grow a garden journal

It keeps track of plant labels, seed packets, and more

By Jim McCausland

When a friend asked me how long pressure-treated posts last in my garden, I confidently answered, "Ten years." I know this because I keep a garden journal. It remembers the important things I would forget—things that help me grow plants successfully.

I assembled the journal in a large three-ring binder with front and rear pouches. Then I filled it with the following materials from a stationery store for about $60 (but you could do it for less if you shop wisely).

- Graph paper for garden plans
- Wide-ruled paper for notes
- Four vinyl pouches for labels, seed packets, drawing tools, and dried flowers
- Tabbed dividers
- Vinyl pockets to hold magazine clippings

Organizational scheme

I break my journal into the sections that follow, but you could arrange yours by month.

■ **Winter, Spring, Summer, and Fall.** In these four sections, I record what goes on from season to season. For example, when I noticed how well *Rudbeckia* 'Goldsturm' went with 'Autumn Joy', I made a note in the Fall section. When I heard the year's first frogs (which coincide with the first mosquitoes), I noted it in the Winter section.

■ **"Got to try this."** Here I've reminded myself to experiment with 'Spanish Roja' garlic, 'Yellowstone' landscape rose, and a new kind of weeder. When I clip an article, I slip it into a vinyl pocket.

■ **Landscaping notes.** Here I keep a plan of my landscape with plant names penciled in, to help me reinvent or rework landscaping ideas. After planting, I stuff the identifying labels into the vinyl pouches.

■ **Annual recaps.** When I rip out vegetables and annuals, I note winners and losers in this section.

■ **Miscellany.** Here I note things like the address of a sensational camellia mail-order supplier.

■ **Challenges and solutions.** The place to keep tabs on insects, diseases and weeds. ◆

NOBLE FIR AND EUCALYPTUS PODS create this welcoming wreath and garland. For details on making your own elegant holiday decorations using purchased evergreens, colorful berries, and fall leaves, see pages 382–387.

December

Colorful poinsettias in stores now

'Marblestar'. Clearly defined salmon and white markings on the bracts (modified leaves that look like flower petals) make this variety, pictured at right, one of the best of the "marble" types.

'Strawberries and Cream'. A reversed pink and white bicolor (dark pink on the outside and cream in the center) with unique oak leaf–shaped leaves. (Supply is limited this year.)

'Plum Pudding'. The first true purple poinsettia. Its unique color attracted attention last year, when it was first introduced in small numbers; this year 'Plum Pudding' is widely available. Display it on its own in a decorative pot, or pair it with a pink or white poinsettia.

'Winter Rose Red'. Incurved red bracts give this variety the look of an old-fashioned rose. A similar variety now comes in pink.

Poinsettias with fresh looks

Although red poinsettias are still big sellers (70 percent of the market), varieties in other colors and patterns are gaining in popularity. Soft colors such as pale coral and salmon give people more decorating options, says Laurie Scullin of premier poinsettia grower Paul Ecke Ranch in Encinitas, California. Here's a sampling. —*Lauren Bonar Swezey*

Big trees in small packages

Now you can send somebody the world's biggest tree—*Sequoiadendron giganteum*—in the mail for only $25, including shipping. The giant sequoia is just one of the trees sold as 1- to 2-foot-tall seedlings by an Oregon nursery. The nursery offers other conifers, including Colorado blue spruce, deodar cedar, Douglas fir, and coast redwood. The gift-boxed trees come in 3-inch pots with a card and planting instructions.

Most of these conifers grow to be quite large. If space is an issue, choose another favorite whose ultimate size will be more manageable. *Order from New Growth: www.newgrowth.com or (800) 605-7457. —Jim McCausland*

Narcissus carries its fragrant blooms above deodar cedar clippings.

Seasonal scents in a basket

Few greens bring the fragrances of the season indoors like fir, pine, or redwood. Such prunings are festive enough when displayed alone, but arranged around potted narcissus plants, they're elegant.

This basket, lined with black plastic, contains three pots of narcissus (each 3 inches in diameter). If you don't have conifers to fill in around them, buy prunings at a nursery or use other long-lasting evergreens such as holly or juniper.

—*Kathleen N. Brenzel*

Garden shoes

Every gardener needs waterproof shoes. Two types are available: clogs (open-heeled) and slip-ons. Shoes come in men's and women's sizes unless noted.

CLOGS

Best for quick trips outdoors, not for heavy yard work. Open heel is good for aeration, but dirt can enter here. All brands can be hosed off after removing insoles, which (except for Birkenstock's) are washable.

Pictured: Anywears Ⓐ are made from polyurethane, with ½-inch-thick cushioned insole and wide toe box. *About $42.* **Everywears Ⓑ** are more streamlined, accommodate higher arches. *Women's sizes only. About $45. Anywear Shoe Company; www.anywears. com or (888) 425-0077.*

Other choices:

• **Outdoor Clog,** from Baffin. Flexible rubber with ⅛-inch-thick insole, slip-resistant outsole. *About $20. www.baffin.com or (888) 223-3467.*
• **Premium Garden Clog,** from Sloggers. Flexible polyvinylchloride with ¼-inch-thick cushioned insole. *Women's sizes only. About $25. www.sloggers.com or (877) 750-4437.*
• **Super Birki Clog,** from Birkenstock. Polyurethane with a removable cork-and-latex insert. *About $60. www.birkenstock.com or (800) 761-1404.*

FULL-COVERAGE SLIP-ONS

These provide full support and are more useful for heavy jobs. Insulated liners provide warmth. Made of waterproof rubber with reinforced heels and toes.

Pictured: Edgewater Camp Shoe Ⓒ is foam-insulated for warmth and has air-mesh lining for breathability. *About $50. Muck Boot Company; www.landscapeusa. com or (800) 248-1981.*

Another great choice:

• **All Weather Shoe,** from Sloggers. Neoprene liner. *$40. www.sloggers. com or (877) 750-4437. —L. B. S.*

High tech for hands

These garden gloves are designed for comfort and durability

▲ **Work Glove**
Upper layer of breathable nylon mesh is paired with synthetic suede palm that has the strength of leather.

▼ **Waterproof Glove**
Extra padding at palm and fingers protects hands from blisters; inner layers provide warmth and keep out moisture.

Wintertime gardening can be tough on hands, especially in wet weather. Two new gloves, pictured here, can stand up to the most demanding of chores, such as pruning or digging up well-rooted perennials, yet fit perfectly, the way gloves should. If you're not a gardener yourself, they make great gifts for friends.

The Work Glove combines an upper layer of breathable, flexible nylon mesh with a synthetic suede palm that's as strong as leather but won't crack or peel. Extra padding protects palms from blisters, and fingers are reinforced with an additional layer of faux suede. An absorbent terry-cloth covering on the back of the thumb serves as a brow wipe. Velcro wrist closures keep the gloves snug. They're better for heavy chores than delicate tasks (like planting seeds), which require greater dexterity.

The Waterproof Glove is made of the same outer material as the Work Glove but is insulated to prevent frozen fingertips. It has three layers to keep hands warm and dry—an outer shell, a breathable waterproof middle layer, and a soft inner lining. Silicone gripper dots on the palms improve your grasp on wet tools.

Both models have the look and feel of skiing and cycling gloves; they were designed by Beverly Schor, a San Francisco–based sports apparel designer and cyclist who grew tired of frequently replacing her garden gloves. She drew upon her knowledge of cycling gloves (which stand up to heavy use and weekly washings), as well as expertise with technical fabrics, to create them. "Gardening is a venue where technical fabrics are extremely useful," she says.

The Work Glove ($18) and Waterproof Glove ($26), both from West County Gardener, are available at garden centers across the West. They come in several colors and are available for women and men in small, medium, and large. For a list of retailers, visit www.westcountygardener.com or call (415) 282-1238.

—Julie Chai

BOOKSHELF

Northwest's indispensable directory

When Stephanie Feeney passed away in 2000, some Northwest gardeners feared that the eighth edition of her privately published horticultural directory would be the last of a series dating to 1989. Fortunately, a local publisher has picked up Feeney's torch and issued the ninth edition of *The Northwest Gardeners' Resource Directory* (Sasquatch Books, Seattle, 2002; $24.95; 800/775-0817 or www.sasquatchbooks.com).

Now edited by Debra Prinzing, this 340-page paperback remains true to Feeney's vision to "compile all the wonderful resource tips and 'secret sources' that I found coming my way from generous gardening friends and mentors." Nurseries, seed sellers, arboretums, plant societies, public gardens, and gardening-related websites are all listed.

There are a few changes. Event dates have been replaced by contact information, for instance. But for the most part, the latest edition is done in a way that would probably please Feeney immensely.

— Jim McCausland

BACK TO BASICS

Keep cut trees fresh longer. Warm, dry houses are hard on cut Christmas trees. The longer they're indoors, the quicker their needles turn brittle. Slow down the process by following these guidelines.

1. Cut an inch off the bottom of the trunk, then store the tree outdoors in a bucket of water until you're ready to decorate it.

2. Spray the foliage with an antitranspirant (available at nurseries).

3. Before bringing the tree indoors, cut another inch or more off the trunk and place it in a water-filled stand; refill as needed.

—L. B. S.

WHAT TO DO IN YOUR GARDEN IN DECEMBER

PLANTING AND SHOPPING

☐ AMARYLLIS. Shop for amaryllis plants in bud or bloom so you get exactly the color and size you want, or buy the bulbs and grow them yourself. Some will flower within a few weeks, while others may take three months or more to bloom. Give them plenty of light and regular water.

☐ CAMELLIAS. Zones 4–7, 17: Winter-blooming camellias (mostly *C. sasanqua* and some *C. hiemalis*) are among a handful of flowering plants that bloom all season in the Pacific Northwest. Plant immediately, water well, and spread mulch over the roots to protect them from freezing. Camellias look great when espaliered against a wall or planted under eaves where rain can't spoil their blooms. (For more on camellias, see page 388.)

☐ TREES, SHRUBS. Zones 4–7: Plant any time the temperature is above freezing. It's a perfect time to shop for conifers, including living Christmas trees. Good candidates include alpine fir, Douglas fir, noble fir, and white fir; try to limit their indoor stay to 10 days.

MAINTENANCE

☐ CHECK STORED BULBS. Examine stored summer bulbs like begonias and gladiolus, and throw out ones that show any signs of rot. With dahlia tubers, cut out the bad spots, dust the wounds with sulfur, and store away from remaining tubers.

☐ FEED HOUSEPLANTS. Fertilize winter-blooming kinds as soon as flower buds start to swell, but wait to feed those that bloom in spring and summer.

☐ GLEAN FRAGRANT GREENS. Cut snippets of fragrant foliage to scent your house. Try pungent cedars, firs, pines, and rosemary, plus native Oregon myrtle *(Umbellularia californica)*.

☐ PROPAGATE EVERGREENS. Scrape a dime-size patch of bark off the bottom of a low branch of azalea, camellia, daphne, hydrangea, maho-

nia, or rhododendron. Dust the wound with rooting hormone and without cutting the branch off, press the scraped area into a shallow depression in the soil. Firm a little soil over the branch, leaving its tip and leaves above ground, and use a brick or rock to press it into the soil. Next fall, you can cut a new plant free from the parent and replant it elsewhere.

☐ PRUNE FOR SWAGS. When cutting evergreens for swags, follow standard pruning practices: use sharp shears, make each cut just beyond a side branch (don't leave stubs), and keep the plant's finished shape in mind as you work.

☐ SAND ICY WALKWAYS. Unlike salt, sand doesn't hurt plants when it washes onto them, so it's a good choice for concrete and asphalt paths and driveways. Don't use sand on glazed tiles or wood decks, however, since it scars. ◆

WHAT TO DO IN YOUR GARDEN IN DECEMBER

PLANTING

☐ **CYCLAMEN.** Zones 8, 9, 14–17: Cyclamen come with flowers in a wonderful array of colors, sizes, and shapes, including ones with ruffled petals. Most nurseries carry pots of blooming plants throughout winter. So flowers aren't spotted by rain, plant cyclamen in a container and set the pot under an overhang or on a covered porch. Choose a spot that gets partial shade, or morning or late-afternoon sun. Set the top of the rootball slightly higher than the surrounding soil. Zones 1–2: Grow cyclamen in a cool, bright location indoors.

☐ **LIVING CHRISTMAS TREES.** Most nurseries carry the following selection: dwarf Alberta spruce, Aleppo pine, Colorado blue spruce, giant sequoia, and Monterey pine. Before bringing the tree indoors, water the pot thoroughly and hose down the foliage. Display the tree in a cool location with a waterproof saucer beneath the pot. To hide the nursery can, cover it with corrugated metal sheeting or drape it with festive material. Check soil regularly and water enough to keep it evenly moist but not soggy.

Sunset
CLIMATE ZONES
☐ Mountain (1–2)
☐ Valley (7–9)
☐ Inland (14)
☐ Coastal (15–17)

☐ **PERENNIAL VEGETABLES.** Zones 7–9, 14–17: Set out bare-root plants of asparagus, horseradish, and rhubarb in well-tilled soil. Water well at planting time and in between rains.

☐ **ROSES.** Zones 7–9, 14–17: Roses start appearing in nurseries this month. Shop early, while selections are good. Choices may include climbers, floribundas, hybrid teas, miniatures, and shrub roses. If you can't find what you're looking for in your area, try one of the following mail-order rose nurseries. **Amity Heritage Roses** (antique as well as modern types): *www.amityheritageroses.com or (707) 768-2040.* **Regan Nursery** (many kinds): *www.regannursery.com or (510) 797-3222.* **Sequoia Nursery** (miniatures): *www.sequoianursery.biz or (559) 732-0309.*

MAINTENANCE

☐ **CUT BACK PERENNIALS.** Zones 7–9, 14–17: If catmint and other perennials are looking scraggly, you can cut them back now and fill in the empty space around them with pansies and other annuals.

☐ **WATCH FOR COLD WEATHER.** Zones 7–9, 14–17: You never know when the first freeze of the season will hit. The past few years have been fairly mild, but a cold snap can hit at any time. If cold weather is predicted, move tender container plants under eaves and cover frost-tender plants that are in the ground (insert four stakes around the plant and drape burlap or plastic over them; the stakes should be tall enough so the cover doesn't touch the leaves). If additional protection is necessary, put a lighted string of Christmas tree bulbs under the canopy. Remove the cover in the morning.

☐ **WATER.** Zones 7–9, 14–17: If late-fall and early-winter rains are light, check soil moisture periodically and water when the soil is almost dry to the touch. Also water plants growing under eaves where rain doesn't reach, and make sure plants are adequately watered if a freeze is predicted; drought-stressed plants are susceptible to damage. ◆

DEBRA LAMBERT

WHAT TO DO IN YOUR GARDEN IN DECEMBER

PLANTING

☐ **BARE-ROOT PLANTS.** Shop for bare-root roses, deciduous fruit trees, cane berries, asparagus, artichoke, and rhubarb. Plant as soon after purchase as possible. If ground is soggy from rain, plant for the time being in containers.

☐ **LIVING CHRISTMAS TREES.** If you want to keep your tree in a container and reuse it in subsequent years, select a spruce, suggests Ron Vanderhoff of Roger's Gardens in Corona del Mar. Unlike most pines, which grow several feet a year, spruce hardly grows at all in our warm climate. Or, for a very So Cal look, buy a rosemary shaped into a tree.

☐ **NATIVES.** California natives take hold most easily if planted in time to take advantage of winter rain. If you are growing natives for the first time, trouble-free choices include California fuchsia *(Zauschneria),* Cleveland and California white sage *(Salvia clevelandii and S. apiana),* lemonade berry *(Rhus integrifolia),* toyon, deer grass *(Muhlenbergia rigens),* and monkey flower *(Mimulus).*

☐ **WINTER VEGETABLES.** Plant onion sets and garlic. Set out broccoli, brussels sprouts, cabbage, and cauliflower plants. Start beets, car-

rots, chard, collards, kale, lettuces, peas, radish, spinach, and turnips from seed.

MAINTENANCE

☐ **FERTILIZE CYMBIDIUMS.** Use a bloom-promoting fertilizer, such as a 15-30-15 formula, until buds open.

☐ **PREPARE FOR RAIN.** Apply mulch 3 inches deep on all your garden beds to keep soil from compacting in the rain. Use portable concrete edgings to channel water away from low spots so it drains properly and doesn't back up. Set potted plants in a protected area, away from pounding rain and wind. Place clean plastic trash cans where they'll collect rainwater for houseplants and other container plants.

☐ **PRUNE EVERGREENS.** Conifers and broad-leafed evergreens benefit from shaping this time of year, and

you can use the clippings for holiday decorations. Good pruning candidates include cotoneaster, holly, juniper, evergreen magnolia, pyracantha, and toyon. Cut to side branches or to about ¼ inch above buds.

☐ **PRUNE RASPBERRIES.** Low-chill (ever-blooming) raspberries bear fruit on new wood. To keep plants under control, cut back all canes to within a few inches of the ground this month or next. New growth will emerge in spring.

☐ **TUNE UP TOOLS.** Use fine sandpaper or steel wool to clean and smooth the steel parts of cultivators, hoes, and shovels. Then rub with a well-oiled rag to ward off rust. Clean pruner blades with Corona CLP (cleaner, lubricant, and protectant), suggests tool specialist Bob Denman, of Denman & Company in Orange. (Break-Free CLP, available at sporting goods stores, is the same product with a different name.)

PEST CONTROL

☐ **APPLY DORMANT SPRAY.** After leaves fall, spray roses and deciduous flowering and fruit trees with dormant oil to kill overwintering insects like scale, mites, and aphids. ◆

WHAT TO DO IN YOUR GARDEN IN DECEMBER

SHOPPING

☐ LIVING CHRISTMAS TREES. Good choices include alpine fir *(Abies lasiocarpa)*, Colorado blue spruce *(Picea pungens glauca)*, Engelmann spruce *(Picea engelmannii)*, and white fir *(A. concolor)*. Keep the tree in its nursery container and try to limit its indoor stay to 10 days. Water regularly. If you don't have space to plant your tree in the garden after the holidays, consider the subtropical Norfolk Island pine *(Araucaria heterophylla)*, which can be grown as a houseplant.

MAINTENANCE

☐ CARE FOR POINSETTIAS. Poinsettias with brightly colored bracts and dark green foliage, like the one pictured on page 374, will keep their lovely hues over a long season if you treat them right. Set the poinsettia in a brightly lit, cool room with indirect sunlight, away from cold drafts and heater vents, for six hours a day. Water when the soil's surface feels dry; never let soil get soggy or let water pool up in the saucer.

☐ COAX CHRISTMAS CACTUS TO REBLOOM. So-called Christmas cactus *(Schlumbergera x buckleyi, also sold as S. bridgesii)* are actu-

Sunset
CLIMATE ZONES
☐ 1–3 ▨ 10–11

ally able to flower several times a year. Place blooming plants near a sunny window, water just enough to keep the soil evenly moist, and fertilize every 7 to 10 days. When bloom ceases, rest the plants for six to eight weeks in a cool, darker room and water very little. Then move the plants back to a sunny window, water more frequently, and within a few weeks they will bloom again.

☐ HARVEST GREENS. Prune conifers now so you can use the cut boughs for holiday garlands and wreaths. Don't leave stubs; cut just above side branches that you want to grow. Prune evenly for shape.

☐ INSULATE ROSES. After temperatures drop below freezing for a few weeks, mound soil over the plant's base; if it's a grafted rose, be sure the soil covers the bud union (the enlarged knob from which canes emerge). Once the soil surface freezes, set a cylinder of chicken wire or a tomato cage around each plant and fill with a mulch of leaves, pine boughs, or straw. Postpone pruning until spring.

☐ PROPAGATE HOUSEPLANTS. It's easy to start new plants by propagating them from existing parents. *For ivy,* snip tip cuttings from the parent plant, dip cut ends in rooting hormone, and place them in moist potting soil. *For pothos,* snip off elongated stems and immerse cut ends in water until roots form, then transplant to potting soil. *For spider plant,* snip off runners, dip cut ends in rooting hormone, and place them in potting soil.

☐ TRIM A TREE FOR WILD BIRDS. Decorate a small conifer or other evergreen tree with garlands of unsalted popcorn and cranberries and grapes strung on heavy-duty thread. Add ornaments of oranges and grapefruits sliced into wedges, dried corn on the cob, and pinecones slathered with a mix of ½ cup peanut butter and 2½ cups cornmeal or oatmeal. Tie ornaments to the tree with heavy-duty thread.

—*Marcia Tatroe*

WHAT TO DO IN YOUR GARDEN IN DECEMBER

PLANTING

☐ BARE-ROOT ROSES. Zones 12, 13: Shop nurseries and garden centers for plants with pliable roots. Before planting, soak the rootball overnight in a bucket of water. Dig a hole 1 foot deep and 2 feet wide. Form a 10-inch-tall cone of soil in the center of the hole and drape the roots over the cone. Fill the hole with remaining soil, making sure that the bud union (the swollen part from which the canes grow) is at least 2 inches above the soil surface. Tamp the soil and build a watering basin around the plant. In zones 1A–3B (Flagstaff, Taos, Santa Fe), 10, and 11, wait until spring, after hard freezes.

☐ COOL-SEASON FLOWERS. Zones 10–13: Set out transplants of alyssum, calendula, chrysanthemum, cyclamen, dianthus, Iceland poppy, Johnny-jump-up, pansy, petunia, primrose, snapdragon, stock, sweet alyssum, and sweet pea.

☐ COOL-SEASON VEGETABLES. Zones 10–13: Set out transplants of broccoli, cabbage, cauliflower, kohlrabi, lettuce, and onion seedlings. Zones 12, 13: Sow seeds of beets, bok choi, carrots, chives, collard greens, dill, fennel, green onions, lettuce, radishes, spinach, and turnips.

☐ LIVING CHRISTMAS TREES. Zones 1A–3B: Consider Colorado spruce *(Picea pungens)* or Douglas fir *(Pseudotsuga menziesii).* Zone 10 (Albuquerque): Choose from Arizona cypress *(Cupressus arizonica),* Colorado spruce, Douglas fir, or piñon *(Pinus edulis).* Zones 11–13 (Las Vegas, Tucson, Phoenix): Use Aleppo pine *(Pinus halepensis),* Afghan pine *(P. eldarica),* or Italian stone pine *(P. pinea).* Display the tree in its container indoors for no more than two weeks. Decorate with cool lights; water to keep the soil moist. After the holidays, plant outdoors in a hole as deep as the rootball and at least twice as wide.

MAINTENANCE

☐ CREATE A BOTANICAL WREATH. Gather materials from your garden and local craft shops to make a Southwest-style wreath. Use florists' wire and hot glue to attach juniper boughs, *Dalea,* or eucalyptus branches to a wreath base. Fill in with clusters of herbs (bay, oregano, sage, thyme), rosemary sprigs, tiny bouquets of lavender, and seed pods (from carob, crape myrtle, Texas ebony, or mesquite). Finish with accents such as dried chilies, devil's claws *(Proboscidea),* pomegranates, sunflowers, or yucca pods.

☐ IRRIGATE. Dormant deciduous trees need water only once a month. Irrigate established landscape plants every 10 to 14 days. Water cool-season flowers and vegetables once or twice a week. —*Kim Nelson*

DEBRA LAMBERT

HOLIDAY PROJECT

Use purchased evergreens, colorful berries, and fall leaves to bring the season home

Simple, elegant wreaths & garlands

By Jil Peters ▪ Photographs by James Carrier ▪ Styling by Philippine Scali

Each Christmas, my mother makes an elegant wreath for the front door. She uses magnolia leaves from the tree in the backyard—the same kind of leaves my cousins and I strung together to make hula skirts when we were kids. I always look forward to seeing the wreath for what it signifies: the holidays, and that we're home to celebrate with family and friends.

Sunset's wreaths and garlands also capture the spirit of this magical season. Stylish, welcoming, and understated, they can be assembled without too much fuss, with purchased evergreens as the starting point. You can use whatever greenery is available; we used noble fir for its thick, dense needles as well as lush cedar. The addition of the simplest pod, berry, or leaf can transform plain greens into enchanting decorations.

You can probably gather many of these natural embellishments right in your own neighborhood. The examples here are intended as guidelines—use your imagination and local resources to make your own memorable creations infused with a sense of place.

◀ Noble fir, magnolia leaves & chestnuts

YOU WILL NEED
- One 24-inch conifer wreath
- About 30 magnolia leaves
- About 30 chestnuts
- Glue gun

Apply dabs of hot glue to ends of magnolia leaves (**A**), then tuck leaves in between fir branches. Use the same technique with clusters of chestnuts (**B**).

▲ Noble fir & eucalyptus pods

YOU WILL NEED
- One 24-inch conifer wreath
- One garland
- Eucalyptus branches with about 300 pods
- Floral wire

Cut the eucalyptus branches with pods into 3- to 4-inch stems. Attach each stem to a sprig of fir by wrapping the two together several times with floral wire. Repeat the process, evenly distributing the clumps of pods along the garland. Use the same technique to decorate the wreath.

Ruffled miniature carnations and spiky fir needles create a striking contrast.

Maintaining wreaths and garlands

As soon as you get the greenery home, spray it with an antitranspirant, available at most nurseries. This will hold in moisture and help prevent foliage from falling from the branches.

You can expect fir and cedar wreaths and garlands that have been sprayed with antitranspirant to last for approximately two weeks inside and at least a month outside (assuming they are not in direct sunlight). For interior use, consider purchasing a spare wreath and keeping it outside in a cool, shady spot until it is needed.

◀ Noble fir & miniature carnations

YOU WILL NEED
- One 12-inch conifer wreath
- About 12 white miniature carnations
- About 12 floral water tubes
- Floral wire

Trim carnation stems to fit into tubes. Fill tubes with water, insert flowers, and tuck them into the greenery. Secure them to the wreath with floral wire.

Cedar, eucalyptus bark & dried moss ▶

YOU WILL NEED
- One garland
- Long strips of eucalyptus bark
- Dried moss
- Glue gun

To make eucalyptus ribbons, soak strips of bark in water for several hours so they become malleable (**A**). Straighten the garland so it will be easier to work with. Remove a bark strip from the water, blot it with a towel to remove excess water, and use hot glue to connect one end of the bark to the back of the garland. Wrap the bark loosely around the garland until you reach the end of the strip, then attach its end to the back of the garland with more hot glue. Start the next strip where the previous one ended and repeat the process until you reach garland's end. Rub vegetable oil onto bark to preserve its color. Hot-glue clumps of moss for additional decoration (**B**).
DESIGN: Jeffrey Adair, J Floral Art, Menlo Park, CA

▲ Noble fir & nandina berries

YOU WILL NEED
- One garland
- One 30-inch wreath
- Several bunches of nandina berries
- Floral wire

Use red berries, such as nandina, for a traditional red and green combination. Leave a few inches of stem on the berries and tuck them securely into the greenery. Distribute clumps of color evenly for a dramatic appearance. To create the pendant at the center of the garland, group several berry stems together and attach them with floral wire. ◆

'Miss Tulare',
a *C. reticulata* hybrid
with very large,
rose red
flowers and ruffled
petals, echoes the
quince behind.

Pink *C. japonica* makes a lovely accent beside an arched entry.

Champion camellias

Plant them in the right spot and they'll reward you with blooms for years

By Lauren Bonar Swezey

In late fall and winter, when many other plants are dormant, camellias unfurl exquisite blossoms of red, pink, or white to dress up the garden. These stately shrubs come in a range of sizes and growth habits, from upright, spreading ground covers to bushy 10-foot shrubs. And camellias' shiny foliage provides a beautiful evergreen backdrop for other landscape plants. Combine early-, mid-, and late-season varieties for a layered effect, and you'll get a long season of blooms—from fall to spring.

Camellias are so simple to grow, it's easy to take them for granted and plant them in ways that underplay their beauty. Too often, we see them jammed against the side of a house, or blended into a shapeless mass.

But when given room to show their shape, or when grown as accents in a border, these long-living treasures from Asia have few equals. Here are ways to use the various types in your landscape.

Keep in mind that early and mid-season bloomers tend to flower over a longer season than the late bloomers, which give a bigger show all at once.

Flowers are classified by the number of their petals and the way the petals are arranged—single, semi-double, anemone form, peony form, formal double, and rose-form double.

Sasanqua camellias

First to bloom are the sasanquas—the earliest ones start in September. By November, almost all sasanquas are in full bloom. Sasanquas come in a diverse range of growth habits, from spreading and vinelike to upright and bushy. Flowers range from 2 to 2½ inches across.

Mounding ground covers. Grow these 2- to 4-foot-tall plants with a 3-foot spread below windows, in borders, and as low, unclipped hedges.

Rose-red 'Shishi-Gashira' (double) and soft pink 'Showa-No-Sakae' (semidouble to peony)—both sold as *C. sasanqua* although they've been reclassified as *C. hiemalis*—are two of the best varieties for these uses.

Espaliers. Compact, upright sasanquas grow well against walls and trellises (prune to direct growth). Try white 'Setsugekka' (semidouble) or orange red 'Yuletide' (single).

Lacy hedges. Upright, shrubby sasanquas look attractive softening a wall. Prune to keep plants 3 to 4 feet thick. Best choices include three singles—'Cleopatra' (rose pink), 'Hana Jiman' (white edged with pink), and 'Hugh Evans' (pink)—and the semidouble 'Kanjiro' (rose red).

Japonica camellias

The early varieties start blooming in October or November, the mid-season ones in January or February, and the late-season ones in March (in colder climates, plants start blooming in winter and continue into May). Flowers are 2 to 6 inches across.

Specimen plants. Lush foliage makes *C. japonica* a striking background plant for borders. Most grow 6 to 12 feet tall. Of the dozens to choose from, the following are fanciers' favorites. Early to mid-season: 'Debutante' (light pink peony), 'Nuccio's Gem' (white formal double), 'Silver Waves' (wavy white semidouble). Midseason: 'Kramer's Supreme' (red peony). Mid- to late

C. japonica 'Lily Pons' white single to semidouble blooms.

Caring for camellias

Hardiness. Plants grow in *Sunset Western Garden Book* climate zones 4–9, 12, 14–24 (*C. reticulata* needs winter protection in zones 4–6; plant it under house eaves). The green buds are fairly frost-resistant, but open flowers can be damaged by cold, especially if the sun hits them early after a frosty night.

Sun protection. Plant *C. japonica, C. reticulata,* and their hybrids where they're shaded from hot afternoon sun. *C. sasanqua* can take full sun even in hot, dry climates when given regular water.

Soil. Plant in well-drained, slightly acid soil. If your soil drains poorly, plant in raised beds. Either way, dig a hole twice as wide as the rootball and mix equal parts soil and peat moss.

Water. Keep the soil moist but not wet. During the dry season, check it with a trowel; if dry in the top 4 to 6 inches, water slowly and deeply.

Fertilizer. Use camellia food; begin feeding plants at the first sign of new growth (water well the day before feeding).

C. reticulata hybrids—rose pink 'Pleasant Memories' and soft pink 'Lasca Beauty'—mingle with a fern.

NORM PLATE (2)

C. japonica 'Twilight'. BELOW: Espaliered 'Taylor's Perfection' (design: Michelle Comeau).

season: 'Pearl Maxwell' (pink formal double). Late: 'Elena Nobile' (red rose-form double).

Multitrunk trees. Old upright specimens of *C. japonica* are particularly suited to pruning, which you may want to do if the shrub is leggy or blocking a window. To create a multitrunk tree, identify three to five main trunks (stems) that have the best position and form, then prune off the rest of the lower trunks and branches.

Reticulatas

These types have the largest flowers of the camellia clan. When some buds are removed, the remaining flowers can reach 7 inches across.

Plants eventually grow into lanky trees 8 or more feet tall. Set them in the backs of borders and hide their gawky forms with hydrangeas, rhododendrons, and other shade-loving shrubs. Avoid heavy pruning.

Some of the best reticulatas and their hybrids, all semidoubles, are 'Butterfly Wings' (rose pink), 'Curtain Call' (deep coral rose), 'Lasca Beauty' (soft pink), and 'Tali Queen' (reddish pink).

Plants by mail

Most nurseries carry a good selection of camellias. For a larger selection, order from *Nuccio's Nurseries (626/ 794-3383)*. No shipping Dec 1–Jan 1. ◆

NORM PLATE (2); ABOVE LEFT: THOMAS J. STORY

Just a touch of red

Ⓐ *Sempervivum* Ⓑ *Sedum* Ⓒ *Aichryson* Ⓓ *Echeveria elegans*
Ⓔ *Echeveria* hybrid Ⓕ *Sedum rubrotinctum* 'Aurora'

Dish gardens

Plant one for a friend—
or treat yourself

By Ann E. Ellingson • Styling by Jil Peters

Even if you don't have a patch of ground, you can quickly create an indoor dish garden to brighten your home or give as a living gift. Small specimens of cactus and succulents are ideal for these tabletop gardens, and many plants can coexist happily in the same container.

Part of the fun in designing a miniature garden is choosing among myriad plants, pots, and textured mulches. Cactus and succulents have shallow roots and don't need deep containers. We used rectangular ceramic pots 3 inches deep, 6½ to 8 inches wide, and 9 to 11 inches long. One dish takes about 20 minutes. Cost starts at about $20.

Two cactus—*Pilosocereus* (front) and *Cleistocactus* (rear)—are paired with *Echeveria* and other succulents in a desert-style garden.

Shades of blue and purple

Ⓐ *Echeveria* Ⓑ *Sedum morganianum* Ⓒ *Echeveria*
Ⓓ *Echeveria* Ⓔ *Sedum spathulifolium* 'Cape Blanco'
Ⓕ *Echeveria* Ⓖ Purple heart (*Tradescantia pallida*)

Good choices for dish gardens

Look for specimens of the cactus and succulents listed below in 2-inch pots at garden centers and nurseries. Determine where the dish garden will be displayed, then choose plants suited to the light conditions in that location. Containers situated near windows should be placed several inches away from the glass to avoid foliage burn.

Make it yourself

MATERIALS

- Container with drainage hole
- Potting mix for cactus
- Gloves
- Assorted cactus and succulents
- Small trowel
- Mulch (decomposed granite, gravel, or coarse sand)

DIRECTIONS

1. Partially cover the hole in bottom of pot with a pottery shard to prevent soil from spilling out. Fill the container with potting mix to ½ inch below the rim.
2. Wearing gloves to protect against spines, arrange potted plants on the soil until you like the design. Place shorter or trailing plants around the perimeter of the container.

With a small trowel or your fingers, scoop out planting holes as deep as rootballs, then slip plants out of their nursery pots and set them in the holes. Gently tamp the soil around the base of each plant.
3. Spread mulch evenly over the soil surface. Water thoroughly but infrequently, letting the soil dry out between waterings. ◆

CACTUS	SUCCULENTS
Bright light	**Bright light**
• *Echinopsis*	• *Aeonium*
• Hedgehog cactus (*Echinocereus*)	• *Agave*
• *Parodia*	• *Aichryson*
• Any with a lot of wool or hair	• *Aloe*
	• *Crassula*
Low light	• *Echeveria*
• Chin cactus (*Gymnocalycium*)	• *Sedum*
• Wickerware cactus (*Rhipsalis*)	• *Sempervivum*
	Low light
• Any with a lot of skin showing	• *Haworthia*

Article Titles Index

MAGGIE MacLAREN (3)

Trio of daylily beauties: 'Judith' (top), 'Lullaby Baby' (center), and 'Leebea Orange Crush' (bottom).

General Subject Index

Plant names are followed by page numbers only when significant information on the plant is given, when a photo clearly identifies it, or when it forms part of a useful list. Less specific or passing references are not noted.

Oregano, 83, 179
Oregon grape, 364
Organic gardening, 24–27, 287
Origanum, 83
Osteospermum, 113
Outdoor living spaces, ideas for, 154–155, 173, 245, 247, 248, 278–279

Pacific Northwest, garden ideas and information for
  backyard makeover creates natural haven (Issaquah, WA), 150–151
  blazing border gives lessons in color (Boise), 136
  horticultural directory for region, 376
  lifelong gardener shares her secrets (Bellevue), 208–211
  new book for month-by-month gardening, 137
  penstemons suited to region, 206
  Queen Anne Hill rock gardens on view (Seattle), 97
  regional planning for year-round color, 30
  success secrets for fabulous rhodies (Aberdeen, WA), 142
  waterfront deck cloaked by container plants (Tacoma), 247
Pacific wax myrtle, 339
Pansy, 30, 340–341
Papaver, 205
  atlanticum, 169
  orientale, 30, 33
Papyrus, 265, 273
Parkways, planting on, 166–167, 352
Parrotia persica, 330
Parsley, 83–85, 120
Paths and walkways, ideas for, 128, 166, 272, 320
Patios, ideas for, 102, 144, 154–155, 199, 232–234, 245
Pavers, planting among, 117, 199, 245, 320
Peach, 11
Pear, 127
Peas, 269, 307
Pelargonium, 272
  angel types of, 140
  zonal, 184, 274
Pennisetum setaceum
  'Rubrum', 184
Penstemon, 33, 35, 113, 169, 202–206
  baccharifolius, 34
  clutei, 125
  x *gloxinioides,* 29
  parryi, 34, 41
  pseudospectabilis, 125
  triflorus, 322
Peony, 319, 370
Pepper, AAS-winning ornamental, 8

Perennials
  award-winning, 8
  buying tips for, 115
  for containers, 240–241
  defined, 111
  for fall color, 332
  heat-tolerant, 214–215
  longest-blooming, 113–114
  planting tips for, 112
  postseason care for, 116, 370
  supports for, 115
  unthirsty, 285
Perilla frutescens, 274
Periwinkle, 369
Perovskia, 114, 169, 215, 285
Persian parrotia, 330
Persicaria, 273, 350
Persimmon, 330
Pest control
  for birds, 184, 311
  for mosquitoes, 364
  natural, 122, 287
  for nematodes, 72
  for red imported fire ants, 177
  with summer oil, 226
  See also specific plants
Petasites japonicus, 156
Petroselinum, 83–85
Petunia, 70, 99, 272
Phlox, 48, 53
  drummondii, 49
  paniculata, 114, 215, 370
  subulata, 33
Phormium, 68
Phygelius, 114, 364
Physocarpus opulifolius, 143
Physostegia virginiana, 369
Picea, 330
Pieris japonica, 68, 328, 351
Pincushion flower, 114, 215
Pistacia chinensis, 330
Pittosporum undulatum, 339
Planting times
  in California, 28
  in Mountain zones, 32
  in Pacific Northwest, 31
  in Southwest, 35
Planting tips, 283
  for bulbs, 268
  for chrysanthemums, 336
  for clematis, 100
  for a cutting garden, 50–51
  for hedge plants, 338
  for perennials, 112
  for roses, 57
  for shrubs and trees, 315
Platycodon grandiflorus, 215
Plectranthus argentatus, 177
Plum, 127, 351
Plumeria, 226
Poinsettia, 374
Poliomintha maderensis, 34
Pomegranate, 330
Ponds, ideas for, 150–151, 171, 220, 258–265, 273, 278, 284, 288, 362
Poppies, 30, 33, 169, 183, 205, 272, 369

Portulaca, 272
Potato vine, 29
Pots
  and Mediterranean style, 70, 300
  for rooftops, 198
  sources for, 225, 236–237
  uses for broken, 104
Potting sheds, 133, 315, 345. *See also* Greenhouses
Primroses, 29, 30, 38
Privacy, designing for, 141, 155, 173, 249
Privet, 339
Projects
  construction, 184, 195, 196, 234, 265, 307
  craft, 371, 382–387
  culinary, 81, 83, 85, 123
  planting, 103, 172, 201, 213, 393
Propagation methods, 201, 370
Prosopis chilensis, 248
Pruning, 12, 117, 338
Prunus x *cistena,* 351
Purple coneflower, 33, 114, 214, 215
Puya coerulea, 212
Pyracantha, 331, 339

Rabbitbrush, 285
Raised beds, 73, 102, 118–119, 282, 321
Ramadas, 194–195
Ranunculus, 39
Ratibida columnifera, 34
Recipes. *See* Projects, culinary
Red bird of paradise, 248
Redbud, eastern, 330
Red-hot poker, 246
Rehmannia elata, 273
Renovation, garden, 90–91, 150–156, 166–167, 168–169, 173, 288
Reseeding, plants prone to, 71, 104, 176, 322, 369
Rhaphiolepis indica, 339
Rhododendron, 142, 180. *See also* Azalea
Rhus, 331
Rock gardens, 73, 97, 246, 286
Rockrose, 169
Romneya coulteri, 369
Rosemary, 85, 143, 225, 339
Roses
  AARS winner 'Love and Peace', 10
  'Altissimo', 61
  arranging, 140
  bare-root planting of, 57
  black spot–resistant yellow, 62
  'Blaze', 69
  climbing, 11, 61, 69, 218
  for color, 90–91
  fragrant antique, 54–57, 220
  glauca, 143

Roses *(cont'd)*
  'Joseph's Coat', 218
  renovated public garden for, 139
  that benefit charities, 39
Rudbeckia, 28, 211, 240
  fulgida, 113, 179
  hirta, 29, 30, 33, 332
Ruellia, 34
Russian sage, 114, 169, 214, 215, 285, 329, 369

Sage, 114, 205
  autumn, 34
  bog, 179
  culinary, 85, 163
  desert, 169
  golden, 177
  Mexican bush, 29, 34, 332
  mountain, 332
  pineapple, 332
  Russian, 114, 169, 214, 215, 285, 329, 369
  tropical, 29, 34
Salix integra 'Hakuro Nishiki', 199
Salvia, 114, 205
  coccinea, 29, 34
  confertiflora, 113
  dorrii, 169
  elegans, 332
  greggii, 34
  'Indigo Spires', 332
  leucantha, 29, 34
  officinalis, 85, 163
  regla, 332
  x *sylvestris,* 143
  transylvanica, 285
  uliginosa, 179
  viridis, 53
Santa Barbara daisy, 241
Santolina, 169
Saponaria, 125, 215
Saxifraga umbrosa, 97
Scabiosa columbaria, 29, 114, 215, 370
Scaevola aemula, 207
Schizachyrium scoparium, 316
Screening plants, 101
Scutellaria resinosa, 215
Seating, ideas for outdoor, 42, 129, 200, 219, 271–272, 282, 344
Sedge, 169, 332
Sedum, 170, 276, 286, 392, 393
  'Autumn Joy', 30, 329, 332
Seeding
  a desert meadow, 310–311
  a lawn, 351
Sempervivum, 170, 392, 393
Senecio x *hybridus,* 71
Senna nemophila, 248
Shade gardening, 180, 350
Shasta daisy, 33, 114, 370
Shiso, 274
Shrubs
  Australian, for winter color, 320